INSIGHT GUIDES

Created and Directed by Hans Höfer

CHiLe

Edited by Tony Perrottet
Updated by Christopher Sainsbury
Managing Editor: Roger Williams

Editorial Director: Brian Bell

Houghton Mifflin

APA PUBLICATIONS

ABOUT THIS BOOK

Höfer

Chile has been the focus of much international attention since its return to democratic rule and its subsequent economic upturn. Visitors have been discovering that this long strip of land in the remote south of the globe – boasting Andean mountains, glaciers, lakes and forests – is one of the most spectacular, friendly and comfortable travel destinations in the whole of Latin America. For all these reasons and more, it lends itself especially well to the approach developed by **Hans Höfer**, Insight Guides' founder who created the series in 1970 with a guide to Bali. Insight Guides pioneered the award-winning formula of excellent photojournalism and incisive writing which combine to broaden travelers' horizons. Each of the 190 books in the series encourages readers to celebrate the essence of a place rather than try to reshape it to their own expectations and is edited in accordance with Höfer's belief that, without insight into a people's character and culture, travel can narrow the mind rather than broaden it.

Insight Guide: Chile is carefully structured. The first section covers the country's history and culture in a series of lively essays. The main Places section provides a comprehensive run-down on everything worth seeing. Finally, a listings section provides all the necessary addresses and telephone numbers. Complementing the text, remakable photography sets out to communicate directly life as it is lived by the locals.

Perrottet

The book was masterminded by **Tony Perrottet,** an Australian journalist based in New York and editor of several other Insight Guides. He first visited Chile as a foreign correspondent in the 1980s and vividly remembered tales of relatives who once worked on Chile's Patagonian sheep farms. For Insight Guide: Chile he returned to explore every corner of the country, from its desert north to its remote Pacific possessions.

To produce this guide, Perrottet assembled a team of experienced journalists in Santiago, all long-term residents. **Tim Frasca**, an American-born correspondent for a British national newspaper, had worked in Chile for nearly a decade, and took on the task of introducing his adopted home's wild geography. A specialist in mining issues, Frasca also wrote the chapter on Chile's northern deserts, which he has explored many times for his work. More relaxed motives have taken him many times to the famous Lake District: Frasca's experiences from many a long, calm vacation beneath Chile's smouldering volcanoes all went into his chapter on the area.

Frasca

Sagaris

Canadian poet and journalist **Lake Sagaris** had also lived in Santiago for a decade, also working for a British national newspaper as well as for Canadian television. Her first book of poems, *Exile Home/Exilio en la Patria,* was published in Canada in 1986, followed by *Circus Love* in 1991. Her third book, *Four Seasons in a Day,* interweaves two islands: Newfoundland in Canada and Chiloé in Chile. Sagaris wrote the chapter on Chilean people, while her poetic insights enhanced the sections on Chiloé and the island's fascinating mythology. She also produced the chapters on Chile's New Song Movement, Excursions from Santiago and Wildlife.

Chilean-born writer **Patricio Lanfranco** wrote about the city of his

Lanfranco

birth, Valparaíso. Twice expelled from university for political reasons during Chile's military rule, he dedicated himself to music, an art form that often carried political messages during the dictatorship. Having traveled for several years in the south, Lanfranco was also well qualified to write the chapter on Chile's Mapuche Indians.

The history of Chile was assigned to British journalist **Imogen Mark**, since 1984 the Chilean correspondent for the *Economist*, *Daily Telegraph* and *Latin American Newsletters*. Her wide range of writing experience went into chapters as diverse as Chile's wines, the Aisén district and a survey of issues facing Chile today.

Mark

Coad

Another British journalist, **Malcolm Coad**, wrote the key chapter on Santiago, the bustling capital where most visitors to Chile start their journeys. A correspondent for British and American papers, Coad is also an expert on Latin American cinema.

Australian radio correspondent **Rebecca Gorman** provided a lively view on Chilean rodeos and an exhaustive guide to Chile's cuisine. Fellow Australian **Lesley Thelander** spent several months exploring Chile from end to end to compile the Travel Tips.

Assigned the sections on adventure travel and Chile's central valley was **Helen Hughes**. Originally from Oklahoma, she grew up in Europe and North Africa before settling down in Chile. Well known as a photographer, she has also traveled around the country both as a journalist and member of Ancient Forests International, an ecology foundation dedicated to the creation of private reserves for native forests.

Hughes

The bulk of images were contributed by a photographer familiar to readers of Insight Guides' South American titles: Argentine-born **Eduardo Gil**. He studied sociology and worked as a commercial pilot before dedicating himself to photography, and his exhibitions have appeared in galleries across Latin America, Europe and New York.

Gil

Specialist photography from the Juan Fernández islands and Paine National Park was undertaken by Swiss-German **Daniel Bruhin**. He spent three months in the spectacular Paine, waiting for perfect conditions to shoot the unique images which appear in this guide.

Bruhin

Steven Rubin, a photographer for *Newsweek* and New York's *Village Voice*, contributed some key images from his two-year stay in Santiago.

American-born **Thomas Daskam** is renowned in Chile and overseas for both his oil paintings and spectacular wildlife photography, examples of which appear here along with his work on Tierra del Fuego and Magallanes. Also represented is the work of Belgian-born photographer **Jacques Halber**.

Finally, special thanks should go to **Victor Engelbreit** of Chile's *Ladeco* airlines for the invaluable help in transporting Apa's international team, and to **Dr Paul William Garber Schick**, who helped to correct and update the book for the previous edition. **Christopher Sainsbury**, a freelance photojournalist, has brought the book up to date for the current edition. He traveled the world, visiting 45 countries, while working as a staff photographer for the Operation Drake and Operation Raleigh expeditions, and now lives in Chile for much of the year.

CONTENTS

Preceding pages: shingles on Paraguay church; Lake Llanquihue.

CONTENTS

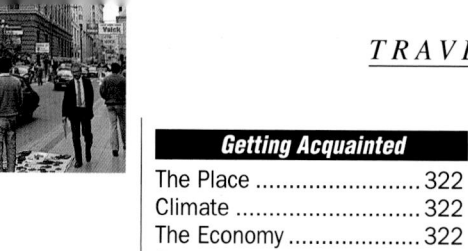

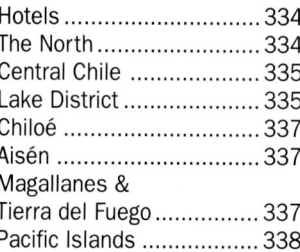

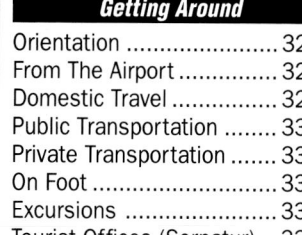

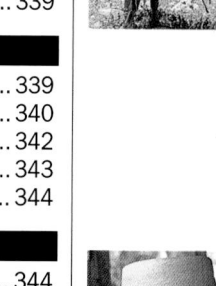

BIENVENIDOS

The Nobel Prize-winning Chilean poet Pablo Neruda affectionately referred to his homeland as "the thin country." Certainly, Chile's unique geography is what many people first learn about this South American republic: squeezed between the Andes and the Pacific, never more than 180 km (110 miles) wide, this spaghetti-like strip of land extends over 4,300 km (2,700 miles) of coastline. Within its borders are the world's driest desert, lush expanses of forest and a spectacular array of glaciers and fiords. And, stretched directly along the Pacific "ring of fire", Chile also has some 2,085 volcanoes of which 55 are active. In some parts of the country, earth tremors are an almost weekly occurrence.

This wild geography hasn't stopped Chile from becoming one of the continent's most developed nations. In fact, you will soon tire of hearing it described as "the Latin American country that works." Travelers are often surprised by the efficiency of Chile's banking system, its transport and services – but behind the affluent surface are social and economic imbalances waiting to be redressed.

Chileans are predominantly *mestizos* – the descendants of mainly Spanish immigrants and native Amerindians – although there are pockets of pure-blooded Mapuche Indians and considerable numbers from German, Swiss and even former Yugoslav immigrant communities that had, until recently, maintained their separate identities. Indeed, the feeling of Chile's cities and the manners of Chileans remain strongly European. They are an urbane and elaborately courteous people, who will go ten blocks out of their way to show a stranger directions. Among Latin Americans, Chileans are renowned for an unusual creative flair: Chilean folk musicians, poets, painters and theatre groups are followed in every country on the continent. And their reputation for legalizing (new laws are hawked in the streets of Santiago alongside chocolates and newspapers) and business acumen has earned Chileans a somewhat facetious label as the "English of South America."

But it was recent political events in Chile that pushed this hitherto obscure country into the world's eye: first, in 1970, when Chile democratically elected a socialist government; then, in 1973, when it suffered a bloody military coup. For the next 16 years of dictatorial rule under Augusto Pinochet, Chile's freedom become an international *cause célèbre*. But since March 1990, when democracy was reinstated, more acceptable governments and economic stability have given the country a renewed vibrancy.

The traditional hospitality of Chileans, noted by travelers from the 18th century onward, is even more evident today. After years of dictatorship, Chileans have welcomed the influx of foreigners as a sign of support for their democracy. And with Chile's economy one of South America's most robust, a new confidence and optimism adds to the already invigorating Andean atmosphere.

Preceding pages: statue of the Virgin, Carro San Cristobal, Santiago; Grey Glacier, Torres del Paine National Park; Valley of the Moon, Atacama; Mapuche farmers near Chol-Chol in the Lake District; Castro, Chiloé Island. Left, a southern farmer.

NO
FUMAR

EARTH, FIRE AND ICE

Chile must be a top candidate for the world's strangest geographical layout. With a land mass smaller than any other South American republic except Ecuador, its 4,300-km (2,700-mile) coastline makes Chile seem enormous. Though it is never more than 180 km (110 miles) wide, a trip from Arica in the North to the port of Punta Arenas in the far south covers the same distance as New York to Los Angeles or Paris to Teheran. In places Chile is so narrow that the Andean peaks of its eastern border can be seen from the Pacific beaches.

Yet the PanAmerican Highway running down the country's spine connects every imaginable climactic zone: it crosses vast expanses of total desert, an agricultural valley the size of California's, and a province of mountain lakes and volcanoes; hops the continent's second largest island and winds for hundreds of kilometers past a scarcely inhabited archipelago; detours around a glacier field, and re-enters Chile at the tip of the continent to connect with the sheep farms of Chilean Patagonia.

Despite this substantial expanse, Chile is seperated from the rest of the world. Its northern desert, the Atacama, is drier than any other spot on earth. The Andes, which form the 4,000-km (2,500-mile) frontier with Argentina, rise in sharp grades on the Chilean side, from sea level to as high as 7,000 meters (23,000 ft) in little more than 100 km (60 miles). To the south, Chile leads to nothing but the polar ice. To the west, it faces the broadest ocean in the world; its south-sea possession, Easter Island, is the most isolated bit of land on earth, a thousand kilometers distance from any other South Pacific island group. "Such a country should be called an Island," wrote a Chilean geographer, Benjamín Subercaseaux, "even though its borders do not strictly fit the definition."

Perhaps it is this geographical isolation that causes Chileans to reflect so obsessively on themselves, to examine their national

Preceding pages: Mapuche farmers near Chol-Chol in the Lake district; dawn display at El Tatio geysers near San Pedro de Atacama. **Left,** the Atacama desert, driest on earth.

character and their prized idiosyncrasies, to lay claim to myriad faults and virtues.

From the driest desert to lush valleys: The extreme north of Chile, the Norte Grande (Great North), annexed from vanquished Peru and Bolivia after the 19th-century War of the Pacific, does not at first glance seem worth the trouble. The brown, barren hillsides and parched Atacama desert include places where no rain has ever been recorded.

Beneath this unendearing landscape, however, lie ample mineral deposits, such as nitrate, a key ingredient in fertilizer and at one time the basis of Chile's national income. Silver, copper and gold are also present in commercial quantities. Aside from highland indigenous communities, oases that predate the Spanish colonists, mining centers, and tiny crossroads scattered around the desert, the Great North's inhabitants are concentrated in the few large ports, economically dependent on commerce and military installations and living on imports of everything from building materials to water.

The Great North ends where the vegetation begins. In the semi-arid Norte Chico (Little North) irrigation has extended Chile's agricultural heartland north to the dusty valley town of Copiapó. Here the many mountain rivers maintain a year-round flow, fed by both seasonal rains and Andean snows. Despite the blistering sun, there is considerable humidity and minimal temperature changes, making the region excellent for irrigated farming. Tropical fruit, especially papaya and *chirimoya* (custard apples) for which La Serena is especially known, are commercially grown. Ideal atmospheric conditions for astronomical work have led to the construction of important observatories in the hills near La Serena.

Just at the country's mid-point is Santiago, the capital, set next to the steep Andean foothills and ringed with a lovely but unfortunate set of smaller hills that trap the increasingly polluted air as the city's population edges toward five million. In this central valley and along the coast, rains come sporadically from May to October while the intervening summer months of January to March are uniformly cloudless and hot. The central region has an abundant agriculture with ample rivers fed by melting Andean

Left, Osorno volcano, in the lush Lake district.

snows which cut across Chile at regular intervals. The famous wine grapes and other fruit such as peaches, nectarines, apples, pears, kiwis and cherries flourish under their intense, dry heat.

Towards the chilly South: Further south in the Lake District, year-round precipitation keeps the landscape green but limits farming to the growing of more traditional grains and the pasturing of animals. An active volcano belt provides picturesque landscapes (most of Chile's 55 active volcanoes are in the area), but also can disrupt the lives of villagers with dangerous clouds of toxic particles. Twelve great lakes, including the continent's fourth-largest, Lake Llanquihue, dot the area both in the valley and higher up on the Andean slopes.

Where the lakes end, the Central Valley becomes submerged in the sea, and the coastal mountain range becomes a 1,000-island archipelago headed by Grand Chiloé Island. The Chilotes' surviving folklore as well as the island's unique clapboard structures are known throughout the country. Rainfall of over 4,000 mm annually are registered in some of these islands, giving Chile both precipitation extremes.

On the mainland, the Austral Highway begins at this point: an unpaved road through one of the most virgin zones on the continent. Foreign trout fishermen fly to the provincial capital of Coyhaique to fish in untouched streams and lakes nearby. The road reaches San Rafael Lake and the sunny mini-climate around Chile Chico and finally ends at the town of Cochrane where the only landmass is covered by impassable glaciers.

The furthest tip of Chile is accessible only by boat, plane, or via a long detour through Argentina. Punta Arenas, with 70,000 inhabitants, is the southernmost city of its size in the world. It is an oil production center and a military encampment. Temperatures rarely rise above 10°C in this gusty port blanketed by almost constant cloud. Further south are only Tierra del Fuego, the 'land of fire' at the tip of South America, (where Chile nearly went to war with Argentina in the late 1970s until the Vatican sponsored negotiations that led to a treaty) and Antarctica, a large part of which Chile claims.

Left, icebergs floating in Grey Lake, Paine National Park.

Chile was never a top priority for South America's explorers and empire builders.

The Incas only made their way down from present-day Peru in the mid-15th century, when Tupac Yupanqui defeated the northern tribes and established Inca rule as far as to present-day Santiago.

The native Atacameño and Diaghuita cultures which had thrived in the northern deserts for centuries, were fairly organized societies compared with the Araucanians further south. Both of the northern groups were farmers. They grew beans, maize, potatoes and coca, using irrigation techniques which suggest they had a central authority strong enough to impose rules on their small societies. They kept llamas, wove cloth and baskets, made pots and decorated them, and traded with each other and with the peoples in Peru. The Atacameños mummified their dead in preparation for some kind of afterlife; the Diaghuitas took their wives to the grave with them. Little more is known about their civilizations, though their numbers were estimated at about 80,000.

Fierce tribes of the South: But beyond present day Santiago, the Incas ran into serious opposition. From the river Aconcagua down to Chiloé lived the Araucanian Indians, around one million of them. There were three main groups, all using the same language, but they had significant cultural differences.

The Picunches ("men of the north"), lived in the fertile Central Valley between the Aconcagua and the Bío Bío. They grew most of the same crops as the Diaguitas and Atacameños but with much less effort in their temperate climate and well-watered soil. The Picunches lived in small peaceful self-sufficient family groups, and were no match for the Incas when they arrived.

It was the quarrelsome Mapuches, ("men of the land") and the Huilliches, ("men of the

South"), and, to a lesser extent, the nomadic hunters and gatherers, the Pehuenches, Puelches and Tehuelches, whom the Incas called "the rebel peoples" and gave up trying to tame. The Mapuches lived precariously, farming temporary clearings in the dense forests, moving on once the land was exhausted, in the area between the Itata and Toltén rivers. The Huilliches lived in the same way between the Toltén and the island of Chiloé. Both groups were full of fighters, obeying a single leader only in wartime. The

Incas gave up on these wild nomads, who did not recognize a central authority or understand any form of tribute. The new rulers set their frontier at the river Cachapoal, and left the rest of the Araucanos to themselves.

The Incas interfered little with the customs and practices of the natives, as long as they paid tribute, in gold, and provided labor for local work. Inca rule lasted less than 40 years. An internal power struggle developed, and the garrisons were withdrawn from Chile back to Cuzco. The Incas' quarrel ended with their defeat at the hands of the Spanish *conquistador*, Francisco Pizarro, and the end of their empire.

Their lasting contribution in Chile was "the trail of the Incas," a series of paths which went as far south as Talca. There were three routes, one along the coast, one through the desert, and one over the *altiplano* (high plane) and along the Andes. They were used by the Spanish explorers later, in their comings and goings to their base in Peru.

The Spaniards arrive: The first European to see Chile was the Portuguese explorer, Hernando de Magallanes, who sailed through the straits which took his name on 1 November 1520. He only glanced at the new territory as he sailed up its coast.

Next to arrive was Pizarro's comrade-in-

Peru, Almagro tried to take on Francisco Pizarro for control of the Andes. He lost the civil war that followed and paid for the uprising with his life.

The reward for one of Pizarro's backers was Chile. Pedro de Valdivia set off to subdue the southern territory. He could take for himself and his followers any land he found. But Almagro's unfruitful trip had discouraged other fortune-seekers and Valdivia had a hard time finding recruits. Eventually he set off with only a dozen others, and his faithful mistress, Inés de Suárez.

As he had hoped, though, other bands of marauder-explorers joined him on the way. There were 150 in the motley band when

arms, Diego de Almagro, who made his way over the Cordillera from Cuzco in 1536 with a couple of hundred men and high hopes of treasure. They reached Copiapó, where the Indians received them peacefully enough, then traveled on to the valley of the Aconcagua and scouted about in vain for the fabulous gold mines the Incas had told of.

A solitary captain and 80 men were sent down to the Magellan Straits, but they returned, having got no further than the river Itata, with terrifying tales of ferocious natives. Spirits sank, and Almagro's men resisted his proposal to stay and colonize the new territory. Once back, empty-handed, in

they reached the river Mapocho in the fertile Central Valley, and decided to make their first settlement. This was Santiago, founded by Valdivia on 12 February 1541.

Pressganged into service by the newcomers, the local Mapuche Indians waited for a few months and then rebelled. On 11 September a local chief, Michimalongo, attacked the new settlement, while Valdivia and most of his men were away. Inés de Suárez, in a chainmail jacket, fought alongside the men in a day-long battle. At the end of it, they stood, triumphant, on the burned-out site, but all of their belongings – food, seeds, even their clothes – were destroyed.

Establishing the settlement: Despite living in hunger and scarcity, Valdivia fell in love with the new land, and wrote enthusiastically to the king: "This land is such that life here cannot be equalled. It has only four months of winter...and the summer is so temperate and has such delicious breezes that men can walk all day in the sun and not suffer for it. It is abundant in grass, and can support any kind of cattle or livestock and plants that you can imagine; there is plenty of very beautiful wood for building houses, great quantities of wood for fuel for heating and working the rich mines. Wherever you might dream of finding them, there is soil to sow, materials for building and water and

least they died baptized as Christians.

Valdivia pushed south towards the Magellan Straits, to secure them for Spain. He also needed more land for his men, and more Indians to work it. More troops had come from Peru, and though there were constant skirmishes with the Mapuches around Santiago, he wanted to continue the conquest.

In 1550 he founded Concepción, and a year later, Imperial, Valdívia, Villarríca and Angol. In each, Valdivia left 50 or 60 men to building the "city" with the help of the subdued Indians. But his troops were stretched thin. At the end of 1553 he left Concepción with only 50 men. The fort at Tucapel when they reached it, on Christmas

grass for the animals, so that it seems as if God had created everything so that it would be at hand."

Gradually the central valley Mapuches were subdued. Valdivia handed out parcels of land to his followers, along with tribes of Indians in groups known as *encomiendas*. They were souls to be saved, and convenient bodies to labor in the fields, and pan for gold. If they died in the harsh conditions of Spanish service, the invaders reasoned, at

Day, was a smoking ruin. As they surveyed the wreckage, the Indians attacked. Valdivia and his men fought back, but by dusk most of them were dead. Valdivia was tied to a tree by his conquerors, legend has it, and forced to swallow molten gold.

The victor was Lautaro, who had worked for the Spaniards before going off to fight them. He was the first Mapuche to realise that the Spaniard and his horse, a creature unknown to the native Chileans, were two separate animals. Lautaro advanced on Santiago, but he was knifed by a traitor on the night before the attack. Morale fell, and smallpox soon decimated his men. Santiago

Left, Inés de Suaréz defends Spanish battlements. **Above**, Fortress of Quitor, last Inca stronghold in Chile.

was saved.

But with Valdivia's death, three rivals fought to succeed him as governor, until in 1557 Peru sent a new governor, García Hurtado de Mendoza. Mendoza re-established Spanish rule in the area around Concepción, restored the city and quelled the rebellious Mapuches. Two new cities, Osorno and Cañete were founded. His period as governor, up to 1561, marks the end of the period of conquest.

But the war with the Araucanos was far from over, and the Spaniards, fighting as a part-time citizens' army, were ill-equipped to win it. At the end of the century, another governor, Martín García Oñez de Loyola,

lost his life in a major Indian uprising. The settlements south of the Bío Bío were wiped out, and the northern bank of the river became the frontier of the Spaniards' territory. The colony by then numbered about 5,000 Europeans.

Frontier life: War with the Indians was a background noise for the whole of the next century, and most of the one that followed. There were periodic uprisings and massacres, and the governor of the territory was based permanently down on the frontier in Concepción.

By this time the colonizers had recognized that there were no rivers of gold or fabled silver cities in Chile, and that wealth needed to be tilled from the land or dug from the mines. Indians, or mixed race *mestizos* were put to work. Soon the new territory was exporting wheat, copper, leather and wine.

But the Spanish authorities sent out from Madrid could not impose law and order. A sinister and unscrupulous figure, Doña Catalina de los Rios known as *la Quintrala*, reflected the worst aspects of the colony in the 16th century. A lady from what was high society, she is credited with poisoning her father, cutting off the ear of one of her lovers, arranging a tryst with another and then having him murdered while she watched. Lower beings such as servants and slaves were killed or mutilated according to her whims.

Many members of the Church set no better example for their congregations. Chroniclers recorded open fights between members of the Augustan and the Franciscan orders. The clergy had to be banned by the bishop from going into public gambling houses, or even from having packs of cards in their own homes. Gambling was a passion, and the main entertainment for men. For society women, and for some men too, the passion was clothes, the richer, more embroidered with gold thread or pearls, the better.

By the end of the 17th century Chile was beginning to be more civilized. The influence of the French Bourbons, now the rulers of Spain, brought French culture and manners to the distant colony. Governor Cano de Aponte arrived in his new domain in 1720 with "twenty-three boxes of furniture and dishes, a clavicord, four violins, a harp and various Andalusian tambourines, as well as fifteen mules loaded with fine clothes." The Jesuits brought over craftsmen – architects, engineers, pharmacists, weavers, painters and sculptors. They also collected the best library in the colony – 20,000 volumes by the mid-18th century.

Stirrings of revolt: The Spanish monarchs tried to keep their colonies free of foreign influences. They banned the entry of books printed outside Spain and prohibited printing presses within the colonies. But colonials still traveled to Spain, France and England, picking up subversive books, and new ideas.

The French Revolution and the revolt of the English colonies in North America in the late-18th century set conflicting examples.

The excesses of the French rebels could be held up as an awful warning. But the sober, enterprising Americans were rather an encouragement to their southern neighbors.

As it turned out, it was events in France – the ambitions of Napoleon – and their repercussions in Spain which were to lead directly to independence for the Spanish colonies. French invasion of Spain led to the abdication in 1808 of the king. Napoleon installed his brother, José Bonaparte. The Spaniards were outraged. In each city the leading citizens set up a *junta* to govern in the name of the deposed king. Soon, the local bodies delegated power to a central *junta* in Seville.

According to the Spanish governor in the

done. In Chile the governor called a *cabildo abierto*, a formal meeting of the leading citizens. They gathered on 18 September 1810 and chose a junta, which swore undying loyalty to the Spanish king.

Their first act was to see to the defence of their new nation. An infantry battalion was formed, along with two cavalry squadrons and more artillery. Envoys were sent to buy arms in England and Argentina. The junta also decreed free trade with all nations, hoping to boost the state's income from customs duties.

Finally, it convoked a national congress, which was to be representative and also to guarantee that there were no abuses of

American colonies, the *junta* in Seville represented authority while the true king was absent. But many colonials felt they shared the same status as the Spanish cities, and had the right to elect their own authority, subject only to the king.

In Chile that was what they did. The inept Spanish governor was persuaded to resign in favor of a native Chilean, Don Mateo de Toro Zambrano. The next step was to form a ruling *junta*, as the Argentines had already

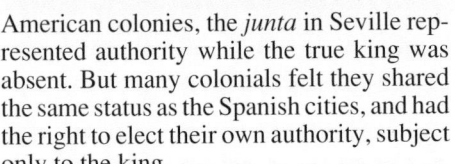

Left, colonial painting, church of Parinacota. **Above**, Conquistador Pedro de Valdivia. **Right**, 18th century Spanish fashion.

power – two radical new notions that had infiltrated from Europe and the United States. The voters were people who "by their fortune, work, talent or qualities enjoy consideration in the parts where they reside, being older than 25 years." They elected deputies who "for their patriotic virtues, talents, and acknowledged prudence may have merited the esteem of their fellow citizens."

Conservatives and Liberals: The selection of the deputies went ahead in early 1811. The first National Congress gathered, on 4 July 1811, and, once again, its members swore their loyalty to the Spanish king. A majority of its members were conservative landowners, who wanted only a minimum of reforms.

But an energetic elite wanted radical change. The first to make a bid for the leadership of the nation were the Carreras. Three brothers – José Miguel, Juan José and Luis – and one sister, Javiera, came from a wealthy Santiago family. But their ideas were extreme for the day, and their methods direct. On 4 September that year Juan José and José Miguel stormed the Congress at the head of a mob and presented a list of "the people's demands."

It was a *coup d'etat*. A cowed Congress agreed to sack some of its most conservative members and set up an executive junta.

After that, the reforms came faster, but still not fast enough for the Carreras. José Miguel forced Congress to set up a new junta, with himself at the head, and then dissolved the Congress, in December that same year.

The Carreras had their sights set on Chile's independence, but they were a minority. One of their first acts was to acquire a printing press and put a radical priest, Fray Camilo Henríquez, in charge. He began publishing revolutionary ideas about popular sovereignty in a weekly paper, *La Aurora de Chile*.

In 1812 the government promulgated a new constitution. Formally it still recognized the Spanish king. But it proposed that the king in turn should recognize Chile's constitution and sovereignty. The new constitution also established the rights of the individual, and set limits on the powers of the government, which from now on was to be elected by the people. That was a drastic change from being ruled by a supreme monarch.

Most of Carrera's compatriots, especially among the aristocracy, were not ready for such revolutionary gestures, and did not like either the man or his ideas. But before they could get together to do anything about him, the Spaniards took a hand.

The wars begin: On 26 March 1813, Spain invaded the Chilean Central Valley, using officers from Peru and 2,000 men recruited among Royalists in Valdivia and Chiloé. They took Talcahuano and Concepción, and started to move north. Carrera took command of the army and organized the defence of the capital, together with the another military leader, Bernardo O'Higgins.

O'Higgins was another product of the ruling elite. He was the illegitimate son of a former governor, Ambrosio O'Higgins, an Irishman who had emigrated via Spain and Peru to Chile, where he became one of the most effective governors. An *affaire* with a lady of Chillán, Doña Isabel Riquelme, produced Bernardo, whom his father sent to be educated in Lima and then in England.

Back in Chile he was elected a deputy to the Congress. He then distinguished himself as a military leader, and took over command of the army in 1813 from the more impetuous José Miguel Carrera. But by the end of the year the war was going badly. An English officer, James Hillyar, arrived with the approval of the viceroy of Peru to negotiate a truce. Both sides were exhausted.

In March 1814 the treaty of Lircay was signed. But the Carrera brothers and their troops rebelled and took the government again. O'Higgins set off to overthrow the new regime, but before he and the Carreras clashed came the news that a new Royalist army had disembarked at Talcahuano. Divided and unprepared, the Patriots met them at Rancagua on 1 October, and were soundly beaten. O'Higgins and the Carreras all fled together to Argentina.

Under the Royalist thumb: Ironically, it was the Spanish reconquest which finally convinced the Chileans that independence was their only option. The Spaniards tried to turn the clock back to 1810. Every reform the Patriot governments had made, from allowing free trade and free schools, ending slavery and forming a national library, were all annulled.

There was direct persecution of the Patriots . Many were sent into internal exile – one group was banished to a cave on Juan Fernández Islands. Another group in the public prison in Santiago were shot. The rest of the citizenry had to prove their loyalty to the crown; Patriot public servants lost their jobs, others, their property. Heavy fines were exacted from all wealthy citizens. Chileans were not allowed to travel without permission, or carry arms. Public festivals were banned, a very unpopular move, and the gaming houses were closed.

Meanwhile, the remains of the Patriot army, led by O'Higgins, had joined forces with the Argentine José de San Martín and

Right, footsoldier in Chile's revolutionary army.

spent the next two years in Mendoza preparing to invade. A spy network kept the Patriots in touch with sympathizers in Chile. Its leader was Manuel Rodríguez, a young lawyer who helped form guerrilla bands to harass the Spaniards. Rodríguez became a national folk hero; the tales of his clever disguises and narrow escapes from the Spaniards passed into legend.

On one occasion he took refuge in a Franciscan monastery and, disguised in a monk's robes, showed his pursuers around the convent to prove he was not there. Another time he dressed as a beggar and politely helped the Spanish governor to alight from his carriage. Even if they were not all true, the

from Peru, and took Talca. The Patriots soon recovered and inflicted a final defeat on the Spaniards at Maipo on 5 April 1818. That settled Chile's future. But O'Higgins continued to fight for the independence of the rest of South America, not least because Chile would never be secure while the Royalists held Peru. A navy was formed, under the command of a Scotsman, Lord Thomas Alexander Cochrane, with ships begged and borrowed from all parts and mostly foreign officers and sailors. In 1819 the new force patrolled the coasts of Peru, disrupting the enemy's supplies. At the end of the year the navy took Valdivia, one of the few remaining Royalist strongholds in Chile.

stories helped to keep people's spirits up.

By 1817 O'Higgins and San Martín were ready, and their "army of the Andes," 3,600 men strong, crossed the Cordillera. On 12 February they met the Royalist troops at Chacabuco and won. They entered Santiago in triumph, welcomed now by the great mass of Chileans, for whom Spanish rule was well and truly odious.

The first job was to set up a new government. O'Higgins was named *director supremo*. On 1 January 1818 the new regime declared the independence of Chile. But there was still fighting to be done. The Royalists counter-attacked with a new force

On 20 August 1820 the army of the Andes, now mainly composed of Chileans but led by the Argentine San Martín, set off for Peru. With the fall of Lima and the final defeat of the Spanish, Chile's independence was assured.

Writing the Constitution: Once independence was secure, the Chileans had to work out how to replace two and a half centuries' rule by an absolute monarch with a republic. They tried out five constitutional formulas, and went through 11 changes of government in the following 13 years.

Most of the experiments and changes were made quite peacefully. In 1823 O'Higgins ran into determined opposition from the land-owning aristocracy. He was forced to resign and went back to Peru, where he lived the rest of his days dreaming of return. He died in 1842, but his body was only brought back to Chile in 1869.

The other revolutionaries fared worse. Two of the Carrera brothers were shot by the Argentines in 1818; then José Miguel was shot, too, in Mendoza three years later. A secret society, known as the *Logia Lautarina* formed originally by O'Higgins and San Martín in Buenos Aires in 1815, was said to have given the orders for their executions. Only Javiera escaped, to Uruguay. She returned to Chile after O'Higgin's downfall.

Manuel Rodríguez, who had been closer to the Carreras than to O'Higgins, was a problem for the new government. He was a headstrong, popular leader. O'Higgins tried to send him into gilded exile in the United States as a diplomat. Rodríquez refused, and ended up first in prison and then, in 1818, shot – "while trying to escape," said the official report.

But most of the decade was taken up with the struggle between Conservative land-owners and the Church against the Chilean Liberals, who were strong in the towns, and among the intellectual elite. The Liberals hung onto the government until 1829, when they lost control of Santiago and the administration.

Finally, in 1833, the conservatives were able to impose an authoritarian model of government that lasted until the next century. On paper, the president was all-powerful, Congress was a sideshow. Congress sat for only four months, the president could veto any law for a year, and had personal representatives in each province. The president could also veto electors, which gave him enormous influence over the election of Congressmen and his successor.

Eminence gris: The real leader of the Conservative movement, though he never ran for president and preferred to rule from behind the throne, was Diego Portales, best-known until then as a businessman.

The secret of Portales's success was that he brought back authoritarian government, which people were used to. Writing to a friend he explained: "The Republican system is the one we must adopt, but do you know how I understand it for countries like this? A strong, centralizing government whose men are true models of virtue and patriotism, and thus will strengthen the citizenry in the path of order and virtue. When morality has been established, then comes a true liberal government, free and full of ideals, in which all citizens can take part." He was for democracy, in other words, but not yet.

While the Congress was writing the new constitution, Portales was busy imposing the authority of the central government. He

himself was minister for the interior, foreign affairs, the army and the navy. He purged the army of its rebel leaders, and exiled some to Lima. The military academy was reorganized; officers were to return to the professional, non-political status they held before Independence. To encourage this, Portales reinstated a system of local militias, directly loyal to the government.

A successful campaign stamped out banditry in the countryside. Economic and financial reforms cut the size of the army and the civil service and brought in better bookkeeping and fiscal controls. Such was Portales's influence in these years that in

Left, revolutionary leader Bernardo O'Higgins who led Chile to independence. **Right**, members of the clergy in the early 19th century.

1833 the British consul wrote home that "Every measure of the government originates with him (Portales) and no state body dares carry out any order without his express approval..."

The model lasted, with a few changes, for nearly a century. But Portales's longest-lasting contribution was his model of austerity and of incorruptibility in public service which has distinguished Chile, compared with some of its neighbors, to the present day. But Portales made too many enemies and he was gunned down by political opponents in July 1838.

Stability and prosperity: For the next 50 years there was a more or less peaceful

succession, and eight presidents were elected, constitutionally if not democratically. José Manuel Balmaceda was the only one to be overthrown before the end of his term, in 1891.

The rest of Chile – nearly one and a half million people in the middle of the century, over three million by the end of it – got on with the business of making a living. A lucky few made money.

Most successful were the foreigners, mostly Englishmen, French and North Americans. They had skills, from accounting and banking to mining and farming, which the new colony lacked, and often got

monopoly positions on the strength of them. Foreign settlers, especially Germans, were encouraged to come and develop farming in the South. But the real money was in overseas trade, and in copper and silver mining.

In shipping, the British were dominant. In 1825, 90 British ships called at Valparaíso, compared with 70 US vessels. But 15 years later the number of British ships had nearly doubled, while the US ships had dropped. By 1875 Britain took 70 percent of Chile's exports and sold it 40 percent of its imports.

A lot of the growth came from copper exports. In 1826 Chile shipped out 60 tons; by 1831 that was up to 2,000 tons, and by 1835 it was 12,700. By 1860 it represented 55 percent of all Chile's exports. But copper sales taught Chile about the dangers as well as the benefits of joining the world economy. The industrial revolution in Britain had boosted demand for copper in the 1830s. Then later industrial slumps in Europe in the 1850s and in the 1870s, hit hard. The daily price of copper on the London Metal Exchange became a national obsession from then on.

Another problem that Chile faced first in this period was the cost of being so far from its markets. In the 1840s Chile found a profitable new market for its wheat and flour in California, at the height of the gold rush. Its exports leapt more than 70-fold in three years. But by 1854 the North American farmers were back on top, and Chile's sales slumped. When the gold rush started in Australia a little later, Chilean farmers could not compete in price with their Californian rivals. For the rest of the century there was a steady flow of migrants from the countryside and its everless viable mini-farms, to the towns and the mining centers of the North.

Transport was a problem internally. The first railway line was planned in 1845, from Copiapó to the little port of Caldera. An energetic American, William Wheelwright, organized the finances from the private sector and by 1851 the first 81 kilometers were inaugurated. Another line from Valparaíso to Santiago was finished in 1863. A telegraph line linked the main port and the capital in 1852; by 1876 there were 48 national lines, and one each to Argentina and Peru. And in 1853 Chile introduced postage stamps, introduced in Britain only 13 years before.

THE MAN WHO WOULD BE KING

Orelie-Antoine de Tounens lived the first 33 years of his life as a mediocre lawyer somewhere in provincial France. Then, in 1859, he packed his bags and sailed to the remotest corners of southern Chile, where he would gain an eternal place in the annals of failed dreams: for a brief but glorious time, Tounens became king of the Aravcanian (Mapuche) and Patagonian Indians.

The inspiration for this singular plan appears to have been a popular epic work by the sixteenth-century Spanish poet Alonso deErcilla praising the virtues of the Araucanian Indians, as yet unconquered by either the Spanish *conquistadores* or the 40-year-old Republic of Chile:

> *Robust and beardless,*
> *Bodies rippling and muscular,*
> *Hard limbs, nerves of steel*
> *Agile, brazen, cheerful,*
> *Spirited, valiant, daring,*
> *Toughened by work, patient*
> *of mortal cold, hunger and heat.*

Tounens reasoned that these exemplars of Rousseau's 'Noble Savage' fantasy would elect him the king of their nation. Landing after an arduous sea voyage in the middle of Chile's north Atacama desert, the Frenchman exchanged letters with the Mapuche *cacique* (chieftan) Manil and, encouraged by the positive response, headed south of the Bío Bío river in the Chilean Lake District. With him were a translator and two other Frenchmen – one already appointed Minister for Foreign Affairs, the other Secretary of State for Justice in Tounen's future kingdom.

By a bizarre stroke of fortune, *cacique* Manil had recently died, muttering that a bearded white stranger would lead his people to freedom. The new *cacique*, Quilapan, welcomed Tounens – who promptly prepared a document that would establish constitutional monarchy. Before long, the Patagonian Indians on the other side of the Andes (now Argentina) had also agreed to accept the Frenchman as their king.

Drunk on power, Tounens left his new Indian lands for the Chilean port of Valparaíso, where he drew up a constitution for 'La Nouvelle France.' He was soon humiliated to learn that neither the Chilean government nor his French compatriots back home would recognize his rule.

Nine months later, he returned to his kingdom with a servant called Rosales – the man who would play Judas to Tounens' messiah. This time the foreign king was bent on war. As the Tricolor flag whipped in the Patagonian wind, the Frenchman announced that he would organize an Indian army to enforce the frontier with Chile. According to an account by the historian Armando Braun Menéndez, the cry went out "Long kive the Unity of the Tribes! Under a Single Chief! Under a single flag!" And Tounens planned to gather no less than 30,000 warriors for his campaign.

Traveling whiskey-vendors sent news back to the Chilean authorities, and this time the Frenchman was taken more seriously. The servant Rosales lured Tounens into a trap: Army officers jumped the king and dragged him off to a cockroach-infested jail in the nearby town of Los Angeles. After several weeks of dysentery and bad food, Tounens agreed to leave Chile.

The king was deported to France, but returned to South America no less than three times to reassert his authority. Each time he was intercepted by the Argentine or Chilean police and sent back to his family. In 1878, he died in the obscure French village of Tourtoirac where he had been working as a streetlamp lighter.

But this was not the end of the kingdom of Aravcania and Patagonia. Since the Tounens family had left no successor, a French champagne salesman, impressed by the history, decided to assume the vacant throne as *Achille ler.*

To this day his descendents maintain a court-in-exile in Paris. And the tale of the original king has continued to grip the imaginations of South Americans – most recently with a 1987 Argentine film *The Film of the King.*

Left, marketown on Chile's southern frontier in the 1860s. Above, the Frenchman Orelie-Antoine de Tounens, who declared himself king of Araucania.

Currency problems: Getting a banking system organized was a major task. There was a physical shortage of coins and paper money – the first bank notes began to circulate in 1839 – and in the mining sector the owner-entrepreneurs started to use their own trade bills as a form of exchange, and to coin lead tokens to pay their workforce. Their logical next step was to set up a bank. By 1850 there were 60 operating, including the Banco de Chile. The government regulated their currency issues, but did not produce its own.

Already by the 1840s contemporary chroniclers were noting the effects of a period of stability and prosperity. Wealth was conspicuously displayed. There were fine

the 19th century the northern desert area close to the Peruvian and Bolivian borders had attracted little attention. But from the 1850s onwards its deposits of natural fertilizers – guano and nitrate – were discovered. Guano became a main source of income for the Peruvian government, and Chile and Bolivia disputed deposits along the coast from Coquimbo northwards.

By 1874 Peru and Chile had agreed to a formula for both to exploit the guano. But the Chileans had a stronger presence – the workforce was mostly Chilean. In 1878 new disputes broke out, this time over nitrate deposits. In 1879 Chile occupied Antofagasta, which was Bolivian territory.

new houses in Santiago – the Palacio Cousiño, for one. There were two theaters, a school of painting, and several literary magazines, not just in Santiago, but in La Serena, Copiapó and Valparaíso, too.

In 1843 the University of Chile was founded for research and debate. The Instituto Nacional was the only higher education center, but there were schools for music and art. In 1860 primary education was made free and a state responsibility. At this date only 17 percent of the population was literate, but 60 years later the figure had risen to a creditable 50 percent.

War with the neighbors: In the first half of

When it discovered that Peru and Bolivia had a secret defence pact, it declared war on both its neighbors.

The ensuing War of the Pacific gave Chile a future source of wealth, nitrate, and its best-loved national hero, Captain Arturo Prat Chacón. His statue graces even the smallest village and the day of his heroic death, 21 May, is a national holiday.

The story of his death is in the best naval tradition of heroic defeats: Prat's ship, the *Esmeralda,* was trapped in the bay of Iquique by the two biggest battleships of the Peruvian fleet, the *Huascar* and the *Independencia.* Prat refused to surrender and his ship resisted the enemy fire for two hours, until the *Huascar* rammed it. Sword in hand, Prat leapt into the *Huascar*, with only a handful of men, and was cut down.

The Peruvian commander, Admiral Grau, was gentlemen enough to send back the Chilean's sword and a letter he had written to his wife. It earned him equally generous treatment when the Chileans fought and captured the *Huascar* later that year, and so gained control of the seas.

The Chilean army marched north through Tarapacá province and then into the Peruvian capital, Lima. Peru had to sue for peace; the treaty of Ancon, signed in 1893, gave Chile Tarapacá and the towns of Arica and

whose wealth it had won in the war, financed the Chilean state for the next 40-odd years. But the man who made most money was not a Chilean but an Englishman, John Thomas North. During the war of the Pacific, he bought up title deeds cheap to some of the best nitrate deposits. Then, back in England, he raised money on the stock market to work the mines. "Chile saltpetre" caught the British public's imagination. The shares sold like hot cakes and North became a famous figure. "He's a typical charlatan," wrote one of his competitors, "but shrewd. He's the most important man in England at the moment, with the possible exception of (prime minister) Gladstone."

Tacna for 10 years. Bolivia ceded Antofagasta in 1894, and lost its only exit to the sea. Since then, successive Bolivian governments have pressed the Chileans to give them even just a strip of coast to build their own port. Peru finally resigned its claim to Arica in exchange for Tarapacá in 1927. But Peruvian army officers still swear an oath to recover Arica.

Nitrate boom: Taxes from the new nitrate mines (or "offices" as they were called),

Left, Araucanian Indian graveyard, c. 1890. **Above**, Valparaíso became one of the world's busiest ports in the 1880s.

But the bubble burst by the beginning of the 1890s. There was overproduction, and the price fell. Early in the next century, a cheaper substitute had been invented. Attempts to cut production failed, the price went on falling, the industry declined, until by the 1930s only a handful of offices were still producing. Once-bustling camps and villages such as Humberstone still stand today, deserted but amazingly preserved by the dry desert air, ghost witnesses to the past.

Civil war: The power struggle between president and Congress had been muted during the 1860 and 1870s by a succession of mild-mannered presidents, and some minor reforms. But the key issue remained – the president's power to elect the Congress he wanted. Congress was not much more than a debating society, although it could block effective government. Presidents played off party faction against each other to buy support. By the end of the century the factions, now more like organized parties, were becoming ever more difficult to pacify with crumbs of power.

Under President José Manuel Balmaceda, the issue came to a head. Balmaceda faced a factious Congress, made some politically-inept appointments, and reacted to criticism by trying to assert his presidential powers. He finally lost his majority in Congress.

new middle class was organizing in the Radical party formed in 1888. A strong force within it were the freemasons, whose lodges were political debating centers.

A new working class was forming too. Industry had grown up in the early and mid-century in specific centers – everything from biscuit and pasta factories in Valparaíso that supplied passing ships, to beer plants started by German settlers in the South. The new railways needed workshops, and the growing towns needed textiles, shoes, soap, furniture. Business boomed, as did the numbers of urban artisans.

It was getting steadily harder to scratch a living in the countryside, so peasants were

When he tried to rule without it, and refused to convoke a special session to approve the military budget, the navy rebelled. Congress and the rebels organized an army and defeated government troops. Balmaceda committed suicide.

New actors: The civil war had tilted the balance of power in favor of the Congress and against the presidents, who were reduced to refereeing the fights for cabinet posts among the parties.

But by this time there were new actors on the political scene. The railways had made travel easier, the towns were growing, and with them a new cultural and social life. A

drawn to the nitrate mines of the North. Once there, they were often stuck, earning low wages and paid in tokens that could only be exchanged for goods in the company store. Primary schools, a police force and adequate courts were practically non-existent. Alcohol was easier to come by than water in the mining camps of the pampa.

The miners were a ready audience for anyone suggesting ways they could improve their lot – from forming mutual aid societies, forerunners of trade unions, to taking up the banners of anarchism and socialism. One such preacher of revolution was a former printworker, Luis Emilio Recabarren, who was twice elected to parliament, but never allowed to take his seat – his ideas were too dangerous, said the authorities.

His politics were Marxist – he traveled on one occasion to Russia and was photographed sitting in a Congress with Lenin and Trotsky. His Socialist Workers Party, founded in 1912, later became the basis of the Communist Party – though Recabarren's role was downgraded for years by the new leaders because his political ideas were deemed unsound, anarchistic and too "social democratic."

Recabarren got an audience among the miners for his political message by publishing newspapers which carried news – obitu-

María in Iquique in 1907. The strike leaders and a mass of about 4,500 miners and their wives and children were in the school, and another 1,500 in tents and dispersed in the Plaza Manuel Montt. An eye witness gave this account of when the army arrived:

"On the central balcony…stood 30 or so men in the prime of life, quite calm, beneath a great Chilean flag, and surrounded by the flags of other nations. They were the strike committee…All eyes were fixed on them just as all the guns were directed at them. Standing, they received the shots. As though struck by lightning they fell, and the great flag fluttered down over their bodies."

Most thought that would be the end of the

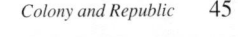

aries in particular – from other regions of the country. It helped the immigrants isolated in the pampa to keep in touch with their homes. Desperate and determined to improve their lives, the miners organized, and struck and marched again and again to demand better pay and conditions. The result was often a massacre, as the mineowners invariably called in the army.

Desert slaughter: One of the worst such incidents took place in the school of Santa

Left and above, mine workers in the northern desert became the backbone of Chile's union movement.

incident. But, said the witness, "There was a moment of silence as the machineguns were lowered to aim at the school yard and the hall, occupied by a compact mass of people who spilled over into the main square… There was a sound like thunder as they fired. Then the gunfire ceased and the foot soldiers went into the school by the side doors, firing, as men and women fled in all directions."

The army general later reported that there had been 140 victims. The eyewitness quoted talked to doctors and others involved, and estimated the figure at 195 dead, and 390 wounded. Others reported many more.

But party and union organization went

ahead. As the nitrate industry declined during the 1920s and 1930s, many of the mineworkers went back to the countryside or to the towns, with radical new ideas and organizing experience.

There was a general sense of unrest and discontent, which even filtered through parts of the ruling class. By 1910 one sector of the governing Liberal party was ready to agree that "social legislation" was needed to give minimum protection to working people.

But the state was in a financial hole. Revenues from nitrate taxes were falling as sales slowed, though copper exports were growing steadily. Agriculture was stagnant – the great landowners lived in style in town or in

finally, from a predictable quarter – the army. But first there was a brief national love affair with the charismatic figure of Arturo Alessandri.

Alessandri, the son of an Italian immigrant, was a genuine *caudillo* or strong man. He promised only timid social reforms, but the man was a populist, who went out and pressed the flesh, wept frequently, and spoke of his own ambitions for his country as "the vibrations of a passionate, sincere soul."

The voters loved it, and with a little help from the usual party machinery, Alessandri was elected. But he had no more power than his predecessors over Congress. He looked for allies in the barracks. The young officers

Europe, and left the business of running the farms to overseers. Import figures for 1907 illustrate the ruling class's priorities: 3.7 million pesos were spent on bringing in agricultural and industrial machinery; 6.8 million pesos went to the real necessities – French champagne, jewels, silk and the latest perfume from Paris.

It was money the country could ill afford. The state had a substantial debt with foreign banks. Tax revenues did not even cover running costs. There was a sense of malaise, and there began to be talk of the need for "an iron hand in the government."

Populists and officers: The iron hand came,

in the army had their own reasons for dissatisfaction – the commanding officers were less qualified than their juniors, incompetent, and clinging grimly to their posts. Already-low wages were being eaten away by inflation. They staged a coup in 1928, finally making Alessandri president with strong powers.

The coup marked the end of the long line of traditional ruling class governments. The old right had no answer to a widespread view that the international capitalist system was on its last legs, and that the future lay in some form of socialism. National socialism, qua Hitler or Mussolini was one way forward;

communism, qua the Soviet Union, was another.

A very mild local variant of national socialism came first, in 1927 with the election of a military *caudillo*, Colonel Carlos Ibáñez del Campo. His models were Mussolini and Spain's José Primo de Rivera, and he was a fierce critic of the traditional political structures, especially the parties, some of whose leaders he "invited" to leave the country. But he was even more fiercely anti-communist, and had communists and union leaders arrested and deported. It was a return to authoritarianism such as Chile had not seen since the years of Diego Portales.

But Ibáñez and the military sent the country off in a new direction: The state began to be used as an active agent to develop the economy. Besides setting up institutions such as the airline LANChile and the daily paper *La Nación*, Ibáñez's government bequeathed the idea that the state should take a central role, and not just leave it to the private sector. It was to be a central aspect of economic policy for the next half century.

It was a bad time to be increasing state expenditure, however. With the crash of Wall Street in 1929 and the world recession that followed, the Chilean economy went into a crisis. Nitrate sales had long been declining, and now too the expanding copper industry was hit as the Great Depression hit its markets. There was widespread unemployment and even wider social unrest. The government set up an emergency employment programme, and printed money to pay for it. Inflation rose, and so did the protests.

Ibáñez was forced to resign. He left for exile in July 1931, but his elected successor was promptly overthrown by a military-civilian junta. In June 1932 a "Socialist Republic" was installed by Colonel Marmaduque Grove, but he lasted only 10 days as defence minister, before being packed off to exile on Easter Island. Elections held in October brought back Arturo Alessandri. Alessandri duly purged the army, clamped down on strikes, the unions and the opposition press. A semblance of order was restored to the country.

It was only a holding operation though. In the next elections, in 1938, the reformists were back. The next variant was a mild social democrat programme from a Radical president, Pedro Aguirre Cerda. At first he had the support of the Socialist and Communist parties, but disputes later broke the alliance. Aguirre Cerda's elected successor, another Radical quickly outlawed the Communists.

The Radicals boosted the state sector of the economy substantially and usefully, with a steel industry and a nationwide electrification programme. But where government intervention had a bad effect was in the countryside. Strict price controls on farm produce meant the landowners had little incentive to invest and produce more. Public

opinion was beginning to feel that farming would simply never take off under ruling class ownership and that the only hope was to take away the land and give it to those who could produce.

The other conflict which began to loom was the ownership of the copper mines. The main deposits had always been owned and worked by US corporations. During World War II, and later in the Korean war, the US government bought copper from them at a special low price. That meant a substantial loss of tax revenues for the Chilean state. Control of such a major source of national wealth was bound to become an issue.

Left, Santiago shopping mall at the turn of the century. **Right**, outside the Correo Central, Santiago, c. 1900.

The caudillo returns: By the end of the 1940s party infighting and petty corruption had once more paved the way for a "strong man." Back in 1952, came Carlos Ibañez as elected president, demanding "a fundamental change of direction" and brandishing a symbolic broom, with which he would sweep away politicking and corruption. He had the useful support of a redoubtable figure, María de la Cruz and her Feminine Party of Chile – women got the vote, finally, in 1949 and promptly reinforced the conservative forces.

Ibañez had the personal charisma to get himself elected, but no organized support. He tried to get the constitution reformed to give the president more powers, failed, and sat out the rest of his term in political impotence. Arturo Alessandri's son, Jorge, succeeded the old general in 1958, elected almost solely on the strength of his father's name. He was the last president of the right to be elected in Chile.

The centre and the left were now grouped in two definable camps. In one, the Socialist and the Communist parties, full-blooded Marxist-Leninists who talked of armed struggle and overthrowing "the bourgeois state" but were actually engeged in building up their electoral strength to win it by peaceful means.

Their rival, proposing very similar reforms in, for example, land ownership or nationalization of the copper mines, was the Christian Democrat party. It had originated in the 1930s from a group of young Catholics from within the Conservative party, initially with vaguely fascist leanings, who called themselves the Falange Nacional. By the end of the 1950s their ideas had been modified to Christian socialism and they were growing fast in the middle and working classes. They had strong links to the Catholic Church and a comparably strong anti-communist message. Their slogan was "Revolution in freedom." Between the programmes of the two camps there was not a vast difference.

In the early 1960s when the influence of the Cuban revolution was sweeping through Latin America, the Christian Democrats throughout the region looked like the best answer to the Marxist threat. The Chilean party was the first of its kind in the region to get into government, in 1964, with a good deal of US financial support. The following year they won a solid majority in Congress, which made their Eduardo Frei the first president in Chilean history to have at least theoretical control of both the executive and the legislature.

Unfortunately success went to their collective head, and they boasted that they would govern for the next 30 years, like their Italian counterparts. But the Frei government made two powerful enemies: the old landowning class, which bitterly opposed his government's attempt at land re-

form; and the military, who felt underpaid and unappreciated. An army general, Roberto Viaux, staged an uprising in 1969 to protest against their conditions.

The old right, which for lack of any alternative had helped vote Frei into office, withdrew to reform itself into a new party, the Nationals. The tensions within Frei's own party led to a split in 1969, and his leftwingers, who felt the reforms had not gone far enough, went off to join the Marxists.

The Allende years: In 1970 a leftwing coalition known as Popular Unity put forward as their candidate (his fourth attempt) a middle-class doctor turned Socialist senator, Salva-

Left, Santiago's busy Paseo Ahumada in the 1930s. **Right,** Chilean poet Gabriela Mistral receives the Nobel Prize in 1945.

dor Allende. This time he won, by a paper-thin margin (36.3 percent of the votes). One of the first electoral promises he honored was to give every poor child in Chile a pair of shoes, and to start a programme of free milk distribution in the schools.

But the new government faced a formidable array of enemies. In the United States, Secretary of State Henry Kissinger said forthrightly that he did not see why the United States should stand idly by "and let a country go communist due to the irresponsibility of its own people." President Richard Nixon's government pumped in around US$8 million in covert financing over the next three years to help, for example, to keep

against food and other shortages. A year later, the shortages were worse and the queues much longer when the truckowners went on strike. Many of them were owner-drivers who opposed a government proposal to create a state transport system.

Doctors, shopkeepers and busowners joined in, and industrialists staged lockouts. Workers in dozens of small factories reacted by taking over their workplaces. Neighborhood committees set up their own retail networks, bringing goods direct from the factories. By this time the opposition – the *momios* or mummies as the left had dubbed them – had thoroughly convinced itself that Allende was out to instal a full-blooded

the anti-Allende publishing group, *El Mercurio*, going.

At home the government had some early successes. For example, it got all-party support in Congress, in 1971, to nationalize the copper mines. But when Allende decided not to pay compensation to the US owners, that sparked an official US boycott of aid and credits for Chile (except for military aid) . The US government also tried to ban its copper from world markets.

The political tension grew. When Fidel Castro of Cuba visited in November 1971, upper and middle class women held the first "march of the empty pots" to demonstrate

Marxist state. The far-left of Allende's own Socialist party encouraged this impression; ironically the Communist party was a moderating force in the unruly coalition, committed to a "peaceful road to socialism."

In March 1973, despite the growing chaos, the government won an increased majority (44 percent) in the parliamentary elections. The opposition decided that it could not wait until the next presidential elections, scheduled for 1976. In August Congress declared that the government was unconstitutional. Days later, on the morning of 11 September, the tanks rolled into the streets of Santiago, the military took the radio stations and announced a curfew, and called on President Allende to resign.

Besieged in the presidential palace of La Moneda with only a handful of advisers, he refused. Photographs from the palace show him in a helmet and armed with a machine-gun given him by Fidel Castro and the popular image remains of Allende fighting to the end before being cut down by the Army's bullets. In his final broadcast message to the nation, he ordered his supporters not to try to resist, yet he himself refused an offer of a safe conduct to the airport and exile. Allende's doctor testified that he died by his own hand, alone, in the ruins of the palace which the airforce had bombed, but Pinochet tells the story in his subsequent memoirs, in which he portrays himself in a central role).

Though he was a late participator, General Pinochet soon gained a taste for power. What was to have been a rotating presidency of the ruling four-man junta of service chiefs, and a short-term military interregnum, soon became a permanent army-led government, which was to last for nearly 17 years.

At least 1,000 people were killed in the 1973 coup around Chile. Soon all political parties and the labor movement had been banned, their leaders either shot, imprisoned or driven into exile. A secret police force run by a close crony of Pinochet's rounded up

the truth of his end may never be known

Pinochet's regime: Ironically, Allende reportedly worried as the coup started about the fate of his loyal commander, General Augusto Pinochet. That gentleman had been kept out of the plot by the rest of the conspirators until a day or so before, when he was let into the secret and told to choose which side he was on. (That, naturally, is not the way

Far left, Socialist president Dr. Salvador Allende. **Left**, General Augusto Pinochet, who took power in 1973 after a bloody military coup. **Above**, bombing of La Moneda in Santiago during the 1973 coup.

malcontents and kept an eye on dissenters within the armed forces, and the judiciary was cowed into submission.

The new ruler's political ideas were limited to a primitive anti-communism, but a clique of right-wing conservative Catholic thinkers supplied the policies. Their politics meshed conveniently with the teachings of an equally doctrinaire school of economists, trained in the University of Chicago under the economist Milton Friedman. Criticism from abroad for the government's ill-treatment of its opponents was brushed aside as Communist-inspired propaganda.

Pinochet's advisers got on with a drastic

reform of the economy using military might to enforce its will. The state apparatus was sold off in chunks, and the role of the state reduced. Unemployment and tough new labor laws kept the workforce docile.

Despite serious economic problems in the mid 1970s, by the end of the decade inflation was falling. There was a brief consumer boom, and the regime pushed through a new constitution, approved, without public debate, in a national plebiscite in 1980. (Voters were asked to vote "yes" for Pinochet by marking a box with the Chilean flag; "no" by marking under a black rectangle). The new constitution was tailor-made to allow Pinochet to stay in power until 1997, provided he

won majority support in another plebiscite scheduled for 1988. But the general's plans went awry.

Dictator's downfall: The debt crisis in 1982 and the international recession of 1983–84 sent copper prices tumbling. Chile's economy slumped, (GDP fell by nearly 14 percent in 1983), and the regime faced a period of more intense and widespread political protest than it had ever experienced.

The political parties, still illegal but by now more or less functioning, led the protest movement, which took the form of sporadic one-day strikes. But Pinochet introduced measures that would buy his support from

truckowners, taxi-drivers and farmers. From mid-1984 onwards the opposition was divided along the old lines – left versus centre – and the protest movement lost its way. The parties eventually accepted that winning the 1988 plebiscite was the only way of getting rid of Pinochet, and the military.

Only the Communists cherished the idea of a more radical solution. In August 1986 the army found several large arms caches in the north, and a month later the Manuel Rodríguez Patriotic Front very nearly killed Pinochet in an ambush.

By early 1988 the other opposition parties finally united to campaign for a "No" vote against Pinochet in the plebiscite. The general was hoping that the relatively robust Chilean economy would win him a "Yes" vote, and left his army uniform in the barracks to campaign in suit and tie.

But, on October 5, a 54 percent majority did vote "No." Pinochet and the army finally admitted defeat. That meant general elections, and in December 1989 a Christian Democrat, Patricio Aylwin, the candidate of a 17-party opposition coalition known as the Concertation for Democracy, won the presidency with 55 percent of the votes. In Congress, Aylwin and his supporters won control of the lower house, but in the senate the presence of nine non-elected senators named by the outgoing regime gave control to the right-wing opposition parties. In such a peaceful handover of power some compromise was inevitable.

The government took office on March 11, 1990, but Pinochet did not relinquish all power. He kept cronies in eight seats in the Senate and stayed on as head of the army, ensuring no revenge was taken on either himself or those who might have perpetrated injustices during his dictatorship when some 2,000 people "disappeared". Bit by bit, however, confidence and democracy returned, helped by what some saw as an "economic miracle", which made debt and hyper-inflation seem like two more bad dreams from the past. Events came full circle at the end of 1993 when the centre-left Democratic Coalition's Eduardo Frei, son of the 1960s president, was elected as Aylwin's successor.

Above left, campaigning for a "no" vote in the 1988 plebiscite. **Right**, Patricio Aylwin inaugurated as president in March, 1990.

Back in the 1930s, legend has it, a group of British journalists competed to write the most boring news headline they could imagine. The winning title was: "Small earthquake in Chile: not many injured."

That more or less summed up what the rest of the world knew or cared about Chile for decades, if not centuries. But by the early 1960s the world began to observe the long thin strip at the end of the world with more interest. From then on Chile was a test lab for a series of experiments. First, under President Eduardo Frei (1964–70), Chile tried a non-communist "revolution" with the blessing of the United States that was meant to be an alternative to the Cuban model for the rest of the sub-continent. Then in the early 1970s, with President Salvador Allende, came Latin America's first democratically-elected Marxist government. It was meant to be a "peaceful road to socialism," but ended in a bloody military coup.

And finally, for a decade and a half, Chile was ruled by a military dictatorship, committed to crushing even the most limited aspirations for social reform. Its recipe was pure free market policies and the "trickle down effect" – the theory that wealth created by the private sector would gradually, naturally, flow down and benefit the workers.

A Thatcherite's dream: These policies were imposed by force, by an army government in a country without a Congress and with very restricted labor organizations – ideal, if abnormal, conditions for such an experiment. The "scientists" were a group of economists most of whom had studied at the University of Chicago, at the feet of Milton Friedman, the guru of free market economics. They were dubbed "the Chicago boys," a nickname which stuck.

They made some bad mistakes, even in their own terms. In the late 1970s the finance ministry fixed Chile's exchange rate for more than two years, and took all the controls off bank lending. Dozens of companies took out large loans from the local banks who themselves had borrowed dollars from international sources. When the government finally had to devalue the peso, there was a near-fatal bank crash. The state had to bail out most of the private banks and take over the running of the two biggest.

But by the late 1980s Chile could show nicely-balanced books and an orderly, flourishing economy with a growing export sector and a lot of interest from foreign investors. It had a model that other countries in the region were being actively encouraged to copy, not least by their bankers.

A leading "Chicago boy," Joaquin Lavín, wrote a book about the changes he saw in Chile, and called it *The Silent Revolution*. It was a paean of praise for the economic model, and it became the bible of many businessmen and right-wing politicians. Lavín wrote enthusiastically, for example, about the new fruit export business, which had grown up during the military government; and he picked out the northern region of Copiapó as a prime case of workers making good money in a new, modern industry.

It was an area where the military government was sure that it would win a majority of votes in 1988 when it held a national plebiscite to vote President Pinochet another eight years in power. But here and throughout the rest of Chile the majority of voters apparently felt that "the economy may be doing fine but I'm doing badly." More than 70 percent of the electorate told opinion pollsters before the poll that they would vote "no" against General Pinochet, in protest at "the economic situation and poverty."

And in Copiapó, the mayor told a national newspaper, after the vote: "I was sure we (the government) were going to win here with 58 percent of the votes, but now I realise people don't sell themselves for a plate of lentils. It's not enough to give them houses, they have to feel they are participating."

Divided land: The other side of Lavín's Chile was described by Eugenio Tironi, a left-wing sociologist. In answer to Lavín's *Silent Revolution*, Tironi called his book *The Silence of the Revolution: the other side of modernization*, and he wrote about the social effects of the economic policies. He described the phenomenon of "two Chiles" – "a society in which two groups co-exist practically without touching each other; a modernizing tendency for an elite which is more and more integrated into the international world; and a tendency to ever-increasing impoverishment of a majority, which relies increasingly on state help to survive."

Tironi singled out four groups in Chile whom he thinks suffered most from the "Chicago" policies. First, the lowest income groups, who lived in makeshift, overcrowded homes on the outskirts of the capital, Santiago, and scratched a living collecting waste paper and cardboard for recycling, for example, or selling goods illegally on the streets. The military government made great play of the improvement in the infant mortality rate, says Tironi. But there was a dramatic increase in the many diseases which are ployed. The third group which lost out under the military, thinks Tironi, was the workers, who lost any incentive to organize collectively to defend themselves in the marketplace because of the restrictions placed on trade unions.

And, lastly, the middle class, a large sector in Chilean society, had mixed fortunes, argues Tironi. Some professionals, those in the private sector, became part of the Chilean elite. Tironi gives as an example the former status of the teacher, once a respected figure in his community, who were turned into poorly-paid over-worked drudges with scant resources for his or her own or his pupils' cultural enrichment.

created by poverty, such as mange and other parasitic infections, like typhoid, hepatitis and impetigo.

A second group who suffered were the young people. They were "the left-overs", the "too-many-of-them," as one local rock group sang of themselves and their generation. For most of the decade young people were the biggest single group of unem-

Preceding pages: worker at Chuquicamata copper mine (Northern Deserts); rich Chileans relax after a polo game in Santiago; children playing in the Coal Town of Lota (Central Valley). <u>Above</u>, the Santiago stock exchange.

Lavín, on the other hand, saw what he calls the "teacher-businessman." Educating young people is a job for businessmen, too, he says. The need to provide alternatives for those who do not go on to the traditional universities has helped transform many educators into entrepreneurs who have set up private educational establishments.

Lavín's is a different world from the one Tironi sees, but both continue in some measure to prevail even though the economy has turned around. The economic mircale of President Aylwin has brought stability and put enough money in the treasury for his successor to pursue a modern liberal economic policy, increasing spending on social policies and healthcare, and diminshing the gap between rich and poor.

Meanwhile, Lavín's Chile, or at least his Santiago, is what most foreign visitors see: clean, well-kept streets, well-watered parks and gardens, well-stocked new shopping malls, modern banks with automatic cash machines, good telecommunications.

Lavín is proud of the fact that Chile was the first country in the region to link in to a worldwide electronic network, called Swift, for instantaneous bank transfers. As a result, it was easier to deposit money in London, Paris or Singapore than to transfer funds from Valparaíso (Chile's main port) to San-

retort that the figure was "only" perhaps 4 million.

Once the election was won, and the new government in place, one of its tasks was to try to reduce the gap between the very rich and the very poor, and restore the standard of living of the impoverished middle classes – but this without upsetting Chile's healthy balance of payments and its fiscal finances.

The new government accepted that the main lines of the "Chicago boys" macroeconomic policies were correct. Even the Socialist party said that "the market has the main role in assigning resources" and that a mixed economy with "all forms of property" is the best way to get sustained growth. One

tiago." Chile's horizons remain high. It has continued Pinochet's export-led led growth policies, looking to Japan as its biggest trading partner in the Pacific Rim. It is also anxious to become involved in any future enlargement of the North American Free Trade Agreement.

Growing poverty: Back home, for the mass of Chileans who did not have bank accounts in Chile, let alone Switzerland, life got worse before it got better. During the 1989 election campaign, Aylwin's supporters claimed there were 5 million poor people in Chile, earning less than enough to cover their basic needs. The military's advisers were left to

of its members became economy minister, part of whose job was to draw new foreign investors. Twenty years earlier, those investors were regarded with deep suspicion by Allende's Socialist government.

What the government did was to raise corporate and income tax, with the grudging assent of the right-wing political parties, in order to be able to improve the health and education services. These were consistently neglected and squeezed of resources by the Chicago boys, for whom all state-run enterprises were anathema.

Aylwin's government also had to battle some fairly timid labor reforms through

Congress to help improve wages and conditions, and give the unions more strength to defend their members. These were much more controversial than the tax rises. The business community insisted that low wages for miners, farm laborers, forestry and industrial workers were crucial if Chile was to keep its exports competitive in its distant world markets. Without stronger unions, though, the labor leaders pointed out, the workforce had no defence against routine abuses such as permanently renewable short-term contracts, which give the worker no protection and no right to social benefits.

But one big change between Chile before and after the military regime, which has

The far left has shrunk and poses no threat to the government. Nor, fortunately, is there any threat of another military coup. The navy, airforce and the police were glad to go back to barracks and get on with their professional tasks. But some sectors of the army around General Pinochet still felt that they had, and have, a mission to defend the country and the constitution. Pinochet held on to his post as army commander (officially until 1997), and talks of continuing to serve his country "at the cannon's mouth."

One reason why he stayed on, apart from his self-appointed mission to defend the country from the threat of communism, is that he and his senior comrades-in-arms are

helped to keep labor demands moderate, is the weakness of the left-wing parties.

Socialists in Chile, as in the rest of the world, were going through a time of crisis. The Chilean Socialist party, part of the coalition government, is committed to only moderate gradual social reforms, and even goes along with the mainstream plans for privitization and much else in the neo-liberal economic model. The once-powerful Communist party is a shadow of its former self.

Left, dining in a plush restaurant, Viña del Mar. **Above**, washing up in an impoverished Santiago *poblacíon.*

afraid of investigations and perhaps eventual trials for the human rights abuses committed during their years in power.

President Aylwin appointed a commission to gather evidence and write an official history of the killings, torture and disappearance of some 2,000 of General Pinochet's political opponents, and to recommend ways of compensating the victims.

The post-Pinochet governments may not be able to bring the offenders to trial, but their success in economic growth and social stability have gone a long way to heal the deep wounds inflicted in those dark dictatorship years.

LOS CHILENOS

A country full of hope
where no one believes in the future
A country full of memories
where no one believes in the past

A country that lives on ghosts
but doesn't believe in legends
A country that lives on miracles
but doesn't believe in a promise...

A country where everyone knows
each other
but no one says hello...

A country where lots happen
but many say there's no proof...

A country where people are born,
live and kill.

—Payo Grondona, Chilean songwriter

Chileans are among the most contradictory, intriguing and attractive of Latin America's peoples, particularly for visitors from the Northern Hemisphere. Perhaps there's a tendency for the Anglo Saxon and the Latin to complement each other, when combined with enough of a common language to make communication truly fruitful.

Whatever the reason, for centuries lonely travelers have made brief visits to Chile that have stretched into lifetimes and family lines which have left their mark on its people.

Politically sophisticated, obsessed with legal correctness and profoundly influenced by Roman Catholic morality, for most of their history Chileans have been cut off from the world by high mountains, dry deserts in the north, the Pacific Ocean on the west and Antarctica and the Straits of Magellan in the South. Nevertheless, they've participated with great distinction in the world's cultural development, built one of America's most developed economies and experimented with Latin America's first elected socialist government – abruptly destroyed when the military seized power in 1973.

Left, a *huaso*, or Chilean cowboy. **Right**, musician in Chiloé.

When one lives in Chile, one quickly realizes that, in spite of the huge distances from north to south, it is a small country as far as the people are concerned. The same surnames crop up over and over again in Chilean history and even today, a person's surname can help or hinder a career.

Powerful families: Chilean politics is rife with influential families wielding power publicly or behind the scenes, generation after generation. Even the new congress which was elected in December 1989 after

15 years of military rule was full of brothers, sisters, sons and daughters of past and present leaders.

And even though a population of 4 million people ranks Santiago among the world's larger cities, it's common to bump into friends and acquaintances during a stroll through downtown, even if you haven't been in Chile very long. Perhaps this is because the downtown area is quite small and only a small percentage of the population uses it.

The small town atmosphere in Chile has given it small-town vices: in Chile, gossip has been elevated to a high art – and Chilean men, in particular, excel at it.

Years of censorship and self-censorship sharpened Chileans' ability to gossip – and their dependence on it – and for years it was common for taxi drivers and others to pass increasingly incredible stories on from mouth to ear, like the old children's game of broken telephone. The habit now appears ingrained and political rumors can still fly from one end of Santiago to another.

But, naturally, gossiping is never so animated as when it is about the country's national sport, *fútbol* (soccer). World Cup years provide the most grist for the scandal mill: in 1990, Chile's national team walked out in the middle of the qualifying game against Brazil after the goal-keeper, "El Con-

have largely become extinct in other parts of the world, are still of considerable importance in Chile. While *La Epoca*, a democratic upstart born to challenge the military regime in 1988, quietly relegates its pictures of "the beautiful people" to the second last page of the paper, *El Mercurio*, the *grande dame* of the Chilean media, keeps them prominently displayed right after the editorials on page three. (International news manages a brief splash on the cover before being banished to interminable small print and columns on page 16).

An indifferent elite: It may be intriguing to glance through the social pages and meditate on the values of a 20th-century society which

dor" Rojas collapsed with a gash on his face. Chileans believed that a Brazilian fan had hit Rojas with a *bengala* (a kind of firework) – until Rojas himself confessed that the wound was self-inflicted, to stop the game just as it was obvious Chile were going to lose!

Newspapers and apparently respectable media often have sections which virtually amount to gossip. They're entertaining to read but are not always the most reliable source of information. Titbits about what ministers do between meetings, indiscreet photos of snoring senators and lots of local color help to sweeten the often bitter news.

More strikingly, the Social pages, which

still believes that bloodlines, titles and famous surnames somehow place one class of people closer to God's chosen than others. But the endless harping on surnames, private schools and living in the right *barrio* (neighborhood) reveal a rigidly structured class society which takes much of the hierarchy and dogma from Catholicism with too little interest in the messages of mercy and charity that go with it.

The way in which a distinguished economist, Alvaro Bardón, tried to justify the military government's reactionary economic policies in 1982 speaks volumes: "The wealthy don't value the fact that [more] people have televisions, radios, because they've always had them. And they're bothered by the fact that the trash are catching up... If this goes on, in ten years they'll have cars and for some people that's extraordinary, because just imagine, there won't be any differences, the trash will look just like people. That's what bothers some."

It was this privileged upper class which felt most threatened by the reforms promised by the Popular Unity's experiment with socialism in the early 1970s and reacted with the violence that finally culminated in the 1973 military coup. For them, democracy was acceptable only so long as it did not upset the unequal social order. This set of

served in folk music and poetry, as well as stories told from generation to generation (*see the chapter on The New Song Movement, page 77*). Many remember with pride how their parents and grandparents staged land occupations to win a small patch of land for themselves.

La Victoria is one of the oldest *poblaciones* in Latin America. Every November it celebrates its anniversary, with the help of musicians, artists and actors from all over Chile. During the military regime, La Victoria became famous for its fierce resistance to police and military invasions. Many of its young people were arrested, tortured, banished and killed.

wealthy families dines in the fine restaurants of Santiago's plush *barrio*, Providencia, have holiday houses in Viña del Mar for the summer and spend winter in the expensive ski resorts of the Andes.

The *pobladores*: At the other end of the social scale are the estimated five million Chileans who live in poverty, crammed into the Santiago shanty towns (*poblaciones*).

Nevertheless, the *pobladores* as they're called, are an extraordinary group of people, with strong traditions of oral history pre-

Among the victims was a popular priest, André Jarlan, killed by a police bullet while reading his Bible in a second floor bedroom one September evening. Jarlan's fellow priest, Pierre Dubois, was later expelled from Chile for his stubborn defense of his congregation, returning after the elected government assumed power in March 1990.

Pobladores or, in the countryside, *campesinos,* are responsible for the small shrines, referred to simply as *animitas* (little spirits), scattered along highways and streets, fragrant with flowers and, after dark, glowing with candles. Many Chileans believe that the spirits of those who die violently, whether in

Left, passion in a Santiago park. **Above**, Chilean flags for sale.

a car accident or at the hands of a murderer, continue to roam the areas where they were killed and that they can intercede for the living.

These spirits are said to perform miracles and the haunts of some of the better known *animitas* (like one in Santiago's O'Higgins Park) have become genuine shrines, full of plaques thanking the holy spirit for the *favor concedido* and bedecked with the crutches, dolls and other relics of desperation left behind after the spirit worked its wonders.

On the highway is another kind of popular shrine – hundreds of license plates nailed to rocks marking dangerous corners and cliffs where previous travelers met with disaster.

panies were once the main foreign – and controlling – interest in the wealthy nitrate mines of northern Chile, and Chileans' taste for *onces* (elevenses, afternoon tea) and their admiration (abstract at best) for foreign punctuality may well be linked to this connection. Chileans with some English blood will tell you they're English, and will identify with Queen Elizabeth as if she were their sister.

Chilean middle and upper class women have a peculiar mix of feminist and traditional values. Half of Chilean dentists are women and a high percentage of doctors and other professionals are women. At the same time, middle class women enjoy considerable help in their homes, and hire *empleadas*

Foreign inspirations: Chile has an unusually large middle class as far as Latin American countries go. About 40 percent of Santiago's population is considered middle class and perhaps the one characteristic common to almost all middle class Chileans is their *arribismo* – a social climbing mentality, which has made them extraordinarily open to ideas from abroad (particularly Europe and the United States) and extraordinarily closed to anything Chilean, unless its value has been proven abroad.

A great deal of the Chilean's *arribismo* is summed up in their proud belief that they are the "English of Latin America". British com-

(housekeepers and cleaning staff) and *nanas* (nannies). But professional women still spend a lot of time on their homes and children and will tell you that the family is all that really matters in their lives.

One of the nice things about the majority of Chileans is the high value they place on poetry, music, theater, and culture in general. They see no contradiction in an up and coming young doctor being a talented actor or a sharp young journalist also having a successful and prosperous career as a singer. On the other hand, they love their beauty queens and, in the past, beauty contests have been a common stepping stone for careers as models, actresses, TV emcees and news-readers.

Racial mix: Chileans are primarily *mestizo*, the product of unions between the country's original peoples, (especially the Mapuche who still exercise a strong influence in the south), and the Spanish *conquistadores*.

Their exaggerated admiration for patriotic symbols like the Spanish *conquistadores* and the great guerilla fighters of the Mapuche provides the source of one of the Chileans' most striking contradictions. They idolize both the conquerors and the natives who resisted them as part of their past, but in the present, the Spanish tradition is more dominant.

Reduced to small patches of land, generally of poor quality, the Mapuche suffer from many of the ills of native people throughout the Americas. Those who haven't emigrated to the cities usually live in large extended families, cultivating wheat, corn and potatoes along with different garden vegetables.

Others combine farming with traditional handicrafts, the woven ponchos, handmade ceramic pots, wood carvings and baskets which make a significant contribution to many family economies (*see the chapter on Mapuches, page 210*).

From the first Spanish settlements on, Chileans have seen themselves as "a people with a future." As one recent writer wryly put

In the wealthy areas of Santiago and luxury vacation spots in southern Chile, shopping centers and resorts all display names of native origin, but native people themselves mostly live in poverty, whether it be in traditional rural communities or packed into urban slums.

There are still many Aymará and other native communities high up in the northern Andes or on the border with Bolivia, while about half a million Mapuche continue to live around the southern city of Temuco.

Left, enjoying some local wine in a family picnic.
Above, teenage girls in Santiago.

it: "We're a people with a future. Father Ovalle said this in the year 1600 and it's been repeated by different people on different subjects at regular intervals ever since."

That future has long been intimately tied to the attempts of successive governments to defend the country's borders by settling the wild and virtually uninhabitable regions of the north and the extreme south. The first settlers tended to stay in the central valley region, due to the agreeable climate, the excellent agricultural conditions and to the Mapuches' 300-year resistance to Spanish attempts to invade their territory, whose border was clearly defined by the Bío Bío River.

Chile's national government continues to encourage hardy settlers to establish themselves in the southern canal region, where boats are often the only form of transportation and communication.

A mixed bag of surnames – which includes a national hero called Bernardo O'Higgins, many ending with the Slavic 'ic' (Livacic, Eterovic, etc.) and an armed forces endowed with the names Matthei, Stange, etc. – bear testimony to the variety of settlers who followed the Spanish to Chile and eventually formed small foreign enclaves within the larger population.

Other ethnic groups include the Germans, the Yugoslavs (north and south) and, more recently, the Spanish (exiled during the Civil grants had built homes along Lake Llanquihue, Osorno, Río Bueno, La Unión and as far as Valdivia. By 1900, 30,000 German colonists had cleared the native forests, planted crops and created small towns, many with schools.

Today, German surnames are still common as is the language, and the area is famous for delicious sausages, cakes and pastries. When camping out, it's common to run into small farmhouses with signs offering *küchen* to passers-by.

The family unit: In keeping with the prevailing Catholic morality, Chileans set a high value on the traditional family, or at least, they claim they do. However, middle and

recently, the Spanish (exiled during the Civil War), the Arabs, the Italians, and the Jews.

The German "colony" has played an important although sometimes ambivalent role in Chilean society. In the 18th century Ambrosio O'Higgins decided that the solution to Chile's perennial problem of colonizing the lush but harsh territory in the Lake District was to import people from Europe. This idea was not implemented until the 19th century, when a presidential advisor, Vicente Pérez Rosales, began the task of recruiting Germans. In 1853, they founded the city of Puerto Montt on the shores of the Gulf of Reloncaví. By 1860, more than 3,000 immi-

upper class women usually hire servants to take care of the children and working class women often have to sacrifice their family in order to take care of someone else's – for money.

Most Chileans tend to marry when they're young and, since divorce is illegal, marriages are "annulled" – an institutionalized piece of hypocrisy which demonstrates Chileans' overweening respect for legality and a profound understanding of its convenience in certain circumtances.

While abortion is not legal, or even talked about, many middle and upper class women have had one. And although birth control is morally prohibited by the Roman Catholic Church, average family size has dropped in Chile. You'll probably notice that while adult Chilean friends often come from families of six to twelve children, their own nucleus only includes one or two.

Chileans like to think they're very attached to their families and certainly families play a major role in Chileans' weekly rituals of visits, telephone calls, meals, etc. However, much of what goes on within the family is strictly formal, with real feelings, thoughts, plans and noses often put of out of joint by these largely ceremonial responsibilities. You will almost inevitably engage in many conversations with Chileans you meet

is less obvious than that of other Latin American males. However, while subtle, it remains pervasive. For generations it was customary for men to have two families – one with their wives and one with their mistresses – and even today many young Chilean men get their first sexual experience in a whore house and they continue to consider multiple relationships *de rigueur*.

Quiet streets and city outskirts are full of demure buildings (some without so much as a sign to identify them) dedicated to renting beds, by the hour or the night, to couples desperate for a little sexual recreation. For those with less purchasing power, young people in particular, parks are usually full of

about the unnatural *gringo* family where everyone leaves home as soon as possible, in contrast with the loving ties that bind all Chileans together.

Baby lovers: They do, however, genuinely enjoy children and many Chilean women and men are wonderful with babies. If you have one, let them dandle and flirt and generally enjoy – while you go off and relax for a while. Your child is in expert, loving hands.

In general, the *machismo* of Chilean men

couples spooning and otherwise enjoying themselves in the moonlight.

Chilean men can be incredibly cruel to foreign women (*gringas*) who they tend to see as easy sexual targets with lots of money, a real asset to their social standing. They may pick them up and drop them at will, without an explanation.

Strictures against women's participation in public life were common under the military, but not very effective, judging from the high profile of Mrs Pinochet, Miss Pinochet and other women in public office. The subsequent democratic government, whose victory at the polls was due largely to women's

Left, light refreshment in the Andes. **Above**, Mapuche woman. **Right**, dressing as a Mapuche *cacique* or chieftain.

support in the ballot box (and on the streets during the military regime), had not a single woman minister, a minimal number of women in Congress, and little participation in top posts of government administration.

There is a tendency for women's rights to be a trendy but superficial issue among Chilean women, although there is growing dissatisfaction and a sense that the new government has shortchanged them.

Lasting traditions: Scratch any Chilean, no matter how urban or sophisticated he or she may appear, and you'll find someone more superstitious and sentimental for the country's folklore. September is the best month for observing Chilean's folk traditions:

president on down, strutting their stuff and flirting formally or sexily, as men, women and children stomp the floor in the traditional one-two rhythm, twirl their handkerchiefs and generally go after each other in what is supposed to be a stylised imitation of mating chickens.

You'll also see *cumbias*, *corridas*, rock and jive, since cultural influences from more northerly countries arrived in full force during the 1980s.

Each of Chile's various regions has its own version of the *cueca* and there's also a kind of class division, between the *cueca patronal* (boss or landowners' *cueca*), characterized by the women's elegant dresses and

they're in full bloom, as Chileans dust off ponchos and handkerchiefs and get ready to celebrate their Independence Day celebrations on September 18th.

For the military, it's time for a major parade; for kids, the traditional pasttime is kite flying; for adults, it's lots of *chicha* (raw apple or grape wine) and *empanadas*; and for just about everybody it's at least one visit to the *fondas*, palm-roofed shelters which suddenly crowd empty lots, turning them into improvised dancehalls.

The *cueca* is Chile's official national dance and September is also the best time to catch a glimpse of everyone from the national

men's short, colorful ponchos and shiny black boots with ostentatious silver spurs, and the *cueca campesina*, whose performers are much more simply dressed and barefoot. The dance's formal gestures and rather strict stereotyping between the aggresive, strutting male and the shy, fluttery female have changed over the years and young people's versions of the dance often challenge more traditional versions.

Chile's folk traditions are more than skin deep. They include a wide variety of folk music which varies from Andean music of the altiplano prevalent in the north, to that of misty Chiloé toward the south, and various ethnic song and dances, particularly yugoslavian, around Punta Arenas.

Payadores are grassroots poets and musicians, who engage each other in witty, passionate poetic duels whenever they meet. This may be during a barbecue lost in the heights of the Andes mountains or in a smoky cafe in some city center.

Folk traditions include stories about each region's original inhabitants, be they human, ghostly, godly, mythical or immortal. Superstitions are intricate and easy to infringe upon, even in urban areas, and popular beliefs have blended with grassroots medical knowledge to create different kinds of faith healers. *Mal de ojo* (evil eye) is still consid-

pare. If you want to be more precise you can always specify whether you're talking about Chilean or *gringo* time.

You may sometimes feel that your Chilean friends are not being completely honest with you, as they lay on the excuses about why they weren't (or won't be) at a social gathering you had carefully planned. This isn't so much a problem of honesty, although there often are a few untruths among the painstakingly detailed explanations, but rather a generally held value that it's far better to lie to someone than tell him/her straight out why you can't meet a commitment.

They're also very lax about social appointments. If you plan something weeks ahead,

ered a common cause of stomach and other health problems and the person most equipped to cure it is still the *curandera*, whose knowledge of herbal – and magical – medicine works more frequently than sceptics might care to believe.

Chileans are more punctual than many of their fellow Latin Americans, but lateness is still the rule. This should be understood within the Latin framework where arriving early for anything is downright rude – that wouldn't give the hosts enough time to pre-

always be sure to confirm at (almost) the last minute, otherwise things may not work out the way you planned. Beware, however, about one area where lateness does not work: doctors and others who make their living through professional appointments tend to be extremely punctual and get very irritated if you apply the general laxity to their date with you. They may, however, then proceed to receive you very late.

In fact, consistency (they call it *consecuencia*), is definitely not among Chileans' many virtues.

Gathering over red meat: One of the most cherished social events is the *asado*. Don't

Left, bringing in the coal, Lota. **Above**, Chile remains a strongly traditional Catholic country.

confuse an *asado* with a barbecue, even though that's usually the way the word is translated. An *asado* is a huge steak or roast cooked over hot coals, not to be compared with the rather squalid (at least to Chileans' eyes) hamburgers and hot dogs that you would expect to find at many a North American barbecue. This ceremony more often than not occurs either in someone's backyard or in a park. While the men compare recipes and generally worry prodigiously about how the meat is shaping up, the women prepare huge tomato, potato and other salads. All drink abundant quantities of red wine and finish with sweet desserts or fruit that's in season (or both).

Chileans generally like foreigners and treat them well, but foreigners here remain foreigners all their lives. Unlike other New World countries, where the population is primarily immigrants from around the world, it often takes several generations for a family of foreign origin to become truly accepted as Chileans.

Perhaps the best source of behind-the-polite-smile information about Chileans are Chilean writers. Chile may be a small country by many standards, but when it comes to literature it's a giant. Two Nobel prize-winning poets, Gabriela Mistral (1945) and Pablo Neruda (1970) have plumbed Chileans' con-

traditions and their aspirations through their work, which is widely available in English translation.

Chilean novelists have participated in the "boom" in Latin American literature. José Donoso, Jorge Edwards and, more recently, Ariel Dorfman, Isabel Allende, Poli Délano and Antonio Skármeta, have explored Chilean events and psychology in books with universal appeal, enhanced in many cases by prolonged experience abroad. Allende's books are all available in English (*The House of the Spirits, Eva Luna* and *Of Love and Shadows*) as is work by other Chilean writers, either through inclusion in anthologies or translation of full books.

Meanwhile, Chilean theater is famous in Latin America and anyone who has a fair grasp of Spanish should try to catch a show in Santiago.

An obsession with earthquakes: Any essay on Chileans must discuss that infallible social institution: the earthquake. Popular wisdom has it that every (democratic) government in Chile gets welcomed into office by an earthquake – an act of God conspicuously absent after the 1973 military coup.

Whatever the verdict on that view, earthquakes are a major social event in Chile and are central to Chileans' mentality. While you might expect people who have built their country on a major fault in the earth's crust to be expert in seismic emergencies, earthquake-inspired panic reactions are common to all classes. Most foreigners make a mental note of the architecturally sound advice to shelter in a doorway or corner (as those are the strongest parts of buildings), should an earthquake occur. But falling trees, flying cars and snapped electrical wiring have not dampened Chileans' enthusiasm for racing out into the street at the first sign of a quake and, should tremors persist, they often move dining table, chairs and beds out and sleep there as well. After the 1985 quake, Chileans in the affected areas even defied the curfew and camped out on the streets for days.

If, while in Chile, you do happen to get caught in an earthquake – or a power failure, a wild party or an *asado* – at least you'll be in good company. The Chileans you're with are bound to keep you entertained.

Far left, young girls on the Juan Fernández islands. **Right**, Santiago's kids on the block.

*Because the poor don't have
anywhere to turn their eyes,
they turn them to the skies
with infinite hope
of finding what their worldly brother
has stolen from them, palomitay:
life is such a surprise, zambitay!*

-Violeta Parra.

You'll see her face among the wares of sidewalk vendors, in colorful posters, artful black and white etchings, perhaps even painted on stones or printed on postcards. She's usually holding a guitar. Her upturned face, moonlike, seems to emanate rather than simply reflect light. Sometimes you sense a halo around that face with its sensual lips and the long, hooked nose. Sometimes the artists themselves have put it in.

Her name is/was Violeta Parra, and also like the moon, a closeup of that strange face reveals deep pits and scars — from a childhood bout of smallpox and the grinding poverty of a lifetime trying to rescue the best of Chilean culture and win for it the recognition it deserves.

Violeta Parra, or simply, Violeta, is usually called the "mother" of Chile's New Song Movement, a powerful cultural movement that swept the country during the late 1960s and early 1970s, survived the 1973 military coup and mannaged to voice, here and abroad, the suffering and eventually the humor and strength which enabled Chileans to survive that period and work unceasingly for a return to the country's traditional democratic rule.

A tragic star: Parra's song *Gracias a la Vida* (Thanks to Life) became popular in the United States when Joan Baez recorded it on an album with the same name, a celebration of her own Spanish-American roots. Another North American singer, Holly Near, recorded her version about a decade later, emphasizing the contradictory notes of pain which are not as obvious in Baez's version.

Left, buskers in the southern Lake District. Right, Chilean artists sell portraits of Violeta Parra on every corner.

Parra's *Thanks to Life* was written shortly before she killed herself in 1967, due, according to popular legend, to financial problems and the failure of yet another passionate but fated love affair.

Her music and poetry flow from the most intimate springs of Chileans' psyche. To her mother's inheritance of traditional folk songs she added years of research, traveling Chile collecting the music of the country's different regions. She eventually began to write her own music and, as she picked her

way slowly and laboriously through the mysteries of becoming a professional, her work became increasingly modern, even as it continued to express the lives of those extraordinary creatures usually summed up by the term "ordinary people."

Following a common Chilean pattern, Violeta received little recognition from her own country until after her death, although during her lifetime she toured the world, not only as a musician but also with expositions of Chilean needlework, clay and paintings, including one presented in the Louvre.

Her unconventional lifestyle and music were not well-accepted by critics who ruled the airwaves and decided the success of Chilean popular singers in the 1950s and 1960s when she was at her height. But time accomplished the miracle which Violeta's life alone could not. In the years since her death her music has been played by rock groups, New Song groups, pop singers, classical pianists, orchestras and choirs – making songs like *Thanks to Life* carry on:

What you can do with a feeling,
wisdom alone cannot do,
nor the clearest of procedures,
nor the broadest of thoughts;
the moment changes all,
a condescending magician,

Music and revoluton: When Violeta returned to Chile for the last time in 1965, she discovered a changed country. A description by Patricio Manns, another renowned Chilean songwriter, captures a feel of this period in his book, *Violeta Parra*:

The class struggle is expressed acutely and dramatically; Eduardo Frei's 'revolution in liberty' sews the wind; the killings of workers cause consternation throughout the country; the unions split and confront each other, traditional leftwing parties hesitate with a sword to their chests, the successes of the Cuban Revolution put dynamite in the people's consciences, students are once again leaping over puddles. The last ivory

sweetly distancing us
from rancour and violence;
only love with its science
makes us this innocent again.

But Violeta was more than a troubadour tracing the often painful roads along which love leads us. She also turned her eye and her talent for rhyme and rhythm to lives of those around her. Undoubtedly this combination — this ability to love and suffer not only romantically, but also literally with her fellow human beings — which fused into the potent mixture which illuminated the music of Latin America in the decades to follow.

towers are over... Either you head down to the arena or you die in the stands: there's no other alternative.

Chilean musicians, tired of the foreign music common in the media, began to search their own roots for an authentically Chilean and eventually Latin American music. They found it in much of the folk music collected by Violeta Parra and others like her and they began to create modern lyrics to accompany the traditional rhythms, instruments and musical forms of their continent.

They rediscovered instruments like the *quena*, a plaintive Andean flute; the *zampoña*, an Andean flute, similar to the Pan flute, whose notes echo hollowly like the wind in the reeds from which it's made; the *charango*, a small stringed instrument made with an armadillo hide and played by strumming so rapidly you can hardly see the musician's hand; the *bombo*, the huge, majestic-sounding Andean drum. And they integrated the Peruvian *caja*, literally a wooden box, played by a musician sitting on it and pounding away at the box between her or his legs; the Colombian *tiple*, a kind of 12-string guitar; the *cuatro*, a four-stringed instrument similar to the ukulele; and other percussion instruments.

One of the more surprising elements of the new music was its ability to unite folkloric

A center for the new song: In 1965, two of Violeta's children, Isabel and Angel, opened a *peña* in downtown Santiago. They brought with them their knowledge of the traditional songs of Venezuela, the political songs of Daniel Viglietti (of Uruguay) and the traditional music of Atahualpa Yupanki (Argentina). It quickly became a center for musicians and young people enthralled by the new music, which became known as La Nueva Canción Chilena (Chilean New Song).

There, Angel Parra thrust a guitar into the hands of Victor Jara, who at the time was a talented young theater director and actor,

elements and themes (including protest) with classical and even traditional religious forms like Cantatas, Oratorios and Masses. The result was a cultural movement that overflowed the political boundaries, in many ways inspired it, producing works of long duration like Violeta's *Canto a la Semilla* (Song to the Seed), Angel Parra's *Oratorio para of Pueblo* (Oratory for the People), Patricio Manns' *El Sueño Americano* (The American Dream) and the *Cantata Popular Santa Maria de Iquique*, written by Luis

Left, dancing the *cueca*, Chile's national dance. **Above**, instruments for sale.

and he performed folksongs and his own compositions for the first time. Jara's songs, which sprang from an intimate connection with his own background as a poor peasant, were often intimate portraits of the aged, the poor, the hardworking, the hungry, as in his song, *The Lasso*.

His hands although so old
were strong in their plaiting
they were rough and they were tender
working the animal hide.
The plaited lasso, like a snake,
curled around the walnut tree,
and in every ship the imprint

of his life and bread.
How much time is contained in his hands,
and in his patient gaze?
Nobody has said 'That's enough,
no need to work any more!'

Two years after the *peña* opened, Violeta returned to Chile and, after singing, teaching and participating fully with the nucleus of singers which had formed there, she opened *La Carpa de la Reina* (The Tent of La Reina), an old circus tent which she turned into a nightspot, where she played, sang, waited on tables and prepared the food for her customers. Similar *peñas* sprang up on university campuses and René Largo Farías formed the *peña Chile Rie y Canta* (Chile laughs and Sings), which he recreated in 1984 when he returned to Chile from exile. In 1969, the Catholic University sponsored the First Festival of Chilean New Song, won by Victor Jara, with his *Prayer to a worker*.

It was in a *peña* in Valparaíso in 1966 that Victor Jara ran into Eduardo and Julio Carrasco and their friend Julio Numhauser and they invited him to direct their new group, Quilapayún. According to Jara's wife, Joan Turner, the first thing Jara had to teach them "was to work seriously, because one of their main characteristics was a tendency to giggle and turn everything into a joke." Huddled in a cold hall, heated only by a small paraffin stove, he applied not only his musical knowledge but also his theatrical experience, to teach the group to create an entire ambience in harmony with their song. After the 1973 military coup, Quilapayún became known worldwide, for their dramatic appearance on stage in long black beards and flowing ponchos, and their impassioned condemnation of the military regime which forced them to live in exile.

Doing the rounds of the *peñas* Jara also met the group Inti Illimani, which had developed in the Technical University *peña*. Although the band's five members were studying everything but music (several were budding engineers), they spent their summers in the countryside researching folk instruments and music and it was Inti Illimani, perhaps more than any other group of the period, who popularized the Andean instruments named above.

World attention: The musical revolution inside Chile soon overflowed its borders and Chilean artists were invited to different countries to sing and share their experiences. Jara himself was in England, working with the Royal Shakespeare Company, when he wrote what has become perhaps his most famous song, *Te Recuerdo Amanda* (I Remember You Amanda).

Amanda is the name of both his mother and his youngest daughter, although the song is also a tribute to the great hope for political and social change that swept Latin America during the 1960s, and which his music did much to keep alive, even after his death during the military coup. You can still hear a variety of renditions of this song in Chile, by young singers who perform on the streets and rattling buses, by professional musical groups who acknowledge their roots in New Song, and by the classical pianist Roberto Bravo. Patricio Aylwin, who became Chile's first democratically-elected president to assume power from the military, inaugurated his government with an event organized in the National Soccer Stadium. Bravo's rendition of Amanda, opened the ceremonies.

I remember you, Amanda
when the streets were wet,
running to the factory
where Manuel worked.
With your wide smile,
the rain in your hair,
nothing else mattered,
you were going to meet him.

The siren is sounding,
time to go back to work
And as you walk
you light up everything,
those five minutes
have made you flower.

And he took to the mountains to fight.
He had never hurt a fly
and in five minutes
it was all wiped out.
The siren is sounding,
time to go back to work.
Many will not go back. . .
one of them Manuel.

In the years which followed, Chilean musical groups like Inti Illimani and Quilapayún, along with the soloists named above and countless others, threw their energy behind the forces for social change which crystallized in the Popular Unity government, led by a member of Chile's Socialist Party, Dr. Salvador Allende, who was elected President of Chile in 1970. For these musicians, their music became a powerful political and educational tool, to inform the Chilean people and win them over to Allende's program for a better Chile. They were blacklisted, boycotted and railed against by their opponents, but they persisted, creating their own festivals and meeting places when traditional public spaces were closed to them.

As the movement grew, so did the musi-

guards. His death there has become a legend, and, according to accounts collected by his wife Joan Turner, there is truth to the story that after being beaten and tortured, a mocking guard ordered him to sing if he could, and he responded with *Venceremos* (We will Win), the hymn of the Popular Unity government overthrown by the military. His hands were broken and he was fired upon until he died.

A silent network of conspirators — peasants, bureaucrats, workers in the Santiago morgue — recognized his body and saved it from the mass graves where so many Chileans ended anonymously. Turner was able to recover his body and give him a hasty burial

cians, and the Chilean New Song Movement had an impact throughout Latin America, inspiring similar movements in most other countries.

After the coup: At the time of the 1973 military coup, many of the New Song Movement's most eminent musicians were abroad, touring and attending a series of festivals in Europe.

Victor Jara was not. He was arrested at the Technical University, along with thousands of students and professors, taken to the Chile Stadium, and tortured, starved and abused by

Above, Chilean group Inti-Illimani at a concert.

in Santiago's General Cemetery. There, in a simple niche, lies Victor Jara, his stone forever covered with red carnations and other flowers, cared for by loving, nameless hands throughout the years of military rule.

Under the new military government, 'culture' became reduced to folklore carefully trimmed of any social commentary or criticism, and the elitist (due to price, dress codes, etc. unachievable by the majority of Chileans) music, dance and theater housed in Santiago's municipal theater.

There was no room for the music of the New Song Movement, which did not respect the frilly mantel of New Speak imposed by the regime. Shortly after the coup the new authorities advised New Song musicians that folk instruments like the *quena* and the *charango* were prohibited. Blacklists began to operate on Chilean television, in major theaters and festivals, and many of those musicians not automatically exiled after the coup, found they were forced to move abroad in order to survive economically. Others, like the group Illapu, left for a European tour in 1981, only to discover they had been banned from returning to Chile.

The spirit of protest: But Chileans love their music and they found ways to rescue it and keep it alive. A group of conservatory musicians formed the "Andean Baroque" group

University of Chile students, staff and faculty banded together to form first the AFU, the University Folklore Association, and later the ACU, the University Cultural Association, which staged artistic and literary competitions, along with major theater and music festivals attended by as many as 7000 people at a time.

Ricardo García, a popular disk jockey who before the coup popularized many of the New Song Movement's prime figures, founded the Alerce recording company in 1977, producing long play recordings of new groups as they formed and disbanded in the difficult times after the coup. Isolated radio programs, like *Nuestro Canto* on the Arch-

which began to play Bach and other classical composers using folk instruments, including many of those banned after the coup. They played primarily in churches. Although they played only instrumental music, their music was a powerful declaration of life beyond the death decreed by the regime. In the same vein, the New Song band Ortiga presented its *Cantata de Cain y Abel*, which became known as the Human Rights Cantata. The familiar biblical story of Cain's killing of his brother Abel became a thinly-veiled metaphor for Chileans' lack of concern for their "brothers'" lives threatened by the military regime's human rights violations.

bishop of Santiago's Radio Chilena, and the *Peña Doña Javiera Carrera*, also gave new artists a chance to perform and meet a small and usually nervous audience.

An underground audience: Tapes by exiled musicians and popular New Song singers from other countries were smuggled into the country and thousands of illegal copies were sold by sidewalk vendors. Although contact was reduced, new musicians growing up in Chile were not completely cut off from their musical predecessors, in spite of the distances created by exile and repression. People associated with the music industry coined the term *Canto Nuevo*, which in

English translates to New Song, to indicate that a new movement was sprouting on the destroyed stumps of the old. The duo Schwenke y Nilo, the bands Illapu, Aquelarre, Santiago del Nuevo Extremo and Ortiga, and later Amauta, Napalé and Huara, along with soloists like Eduardo Peralta, Osvaldo Torres, Capri, Isabel Aldunate and Christina González, openly acknowledged their ties to the old movement by singing its songs. At the same time, their own lyrics were often metaphorical codes, designed to communicate without confronting the new authorities head on.

Concert organizers often had to submit lists of songs, musicians and even full lyrics to get permission to hold their events. Often that permission was not granted, or was withheld at the last moment, making music a perilous undertaking at best.

Many were forced into economic exile and have not returned: Ortiga to Germany, Capri to Sweden, Osvaldo Torres to France, Cristina González to Spain. Musicians were threatened and there were mass arrests of bands with their entire audience, but under and over and around it all, the music still played on.

As resistance to the military regime became increasingly public, Canto Nuevo musicians began to play to larger audiences. They also began to tour Europe, North America, Latin America.

This strengthened contact with exiled musicians and opened their horizons to music being played abroad, with similar content and goals to that of New Song. Chile's musicians brought new knowledge of and respect for jazz, the blues, and the complex joys of improvisation when they returned and their music began to explore the infinite variations of "fusion". Electronic instruments became increasingly popular. Following the example of the exiled group Los Jaivas, musicians within Chile began to plug in their folk instruments, using special electronic effects as well as non-traditional forms of playing.

Into a new era: You can still hear many of the bands and soloists forged in the crucible of the military regime: Isabel Aldunate, Congreso, Huara and, on occasion, Napalé, Amauta or Cristina (when she's in Chile).

Left, musicians perform at a political rally.

The exiled soloists and bands — Illapu, Inti Illimani, Quilapayún, Isabel and Angel Parra — have returned for concert tours or to live and their presence is felt more than ever.

New bands which became extremely popular during the last years of the regime are thriving under the new freedoms of Chile's current transition to democracy: the old-new Congreso, revived and revitalized after the coup, perhaps the band which has most successfully combined traditional folkloric elements with the excitement of electronic instruments and amplification; Fulano, with its spectacular main voice, Arlette Jequier; Dekiruza, full of sarcasm toward the old authorities and a certain healthy scepticism of the new, all packaged in a hard rock message heavily scored with Latin American percussion and sounds; Isabel Aldunate, with a new, less romantic, more hardbitten image, still hardnosed when it comes to human rights.

René Largo Farías has recreated his radio program and his peña, Chile Ríe y Canta, is a good place to go to hear more traditional singers, "popular" (ie of the people) singers you don't necessarily find on the radio, and protest music La Casona de San Isidro is another similar cafe. Ex-exiles Charo Cofré and Hugo Arévalo have created their Candela, a place to spend a pleasant evening snacking on homemade Chilean munchies and listening to anecdotes and music.

For musicians traveling in Chile who would like to get together and talk and jam with their Chilean counterparts, the Casa de los Músicos (Musicians' House) is a good place to start. Run by singer-songwriters Ismael Durán, Patricio Lanfranco and Juan Valladares, it's a center for meeting, talking, arguing and playing, complete with a small studio, cafeteria, amplification, transport and other services for musicians.

The Alerce recording company's current list is still the best place to find recordings by the groups and soloists mentioned here, although many have also produced independent recordings of remarkable quality, usually available wherever they were produced. Chile's main record stores have generally good selections of groups which are still active. For older recordings it's best to try the original recording company. If that doesn't work and if Alerce does not have an album, they may know where to find it.

"The only way to find truly Chilean food is to travel in Chile. You'll find beautiful dishes in each town, but they'll be completely different. On the ocean you might find seaweed dishes, but up in the mountains it may be rabbit. If you're lucky you can find out in each village who is the best cook in town, and that won't be the fancy, rich woman. The cook will come up with beautiful empanadas, or she will have created a fantastic dish from something grown locally."

These words of advice from the President

the traditional foods of the Mapuche Indians.

For example corn-based *pastel de choclo* and the bean soup *porotos granados* are both very Chilean. Louis Bernard admits that Chile has few unique dishes, but he says, "The people have done a marvelous job of improvising and improving on the culinary delights introduced into the country."

Because of the length of the country, "typical" food will change every couple of hundred kilometers, just as the climate and local crops change.

of the Chilean Gastronomical Society, Luis Bernard, capture the essence of Chilean cuisine, that can, superficially, appear to be boring and even unhealthy. A little investigation reveals a broad and interesting fare that includes excellent seafood, tender beef, always fresh fruit and vegetables and a rich array of pastries and desserts.

Making use of local resources: While tradition is hard to trace because of the mix of European influences, there are several dishes that are definitely Chilean, taking their origins not from immigrants, but from the particular characteristics of the region, from the most plentiful ingredients and from

The popular *empanada* – pastry packets filled with mince, egg and olives or cheese – have a definite Spanish origin. They're found in other parts of Latin America, but the onion-filled versions *El Pequen* is typically Chilean, first eaten by the poor who couldn't afford meat, and later embraced by others entranced by the flavor.

But before we launch into wonders of the Chilean kitchen, there are several things to be wary of. The health-conscious westerner will find Chileans' liberal use of salt and sugar quite disturbing. Even some vegetarian restaurants will thoughtfully flavor-up your carrot and orange juice with a dollop of sugar. The phrases "*sin sal*" and "*sin azúcar*" (without salt and sugar) should be slipped into your gastronomic vocabulary and practised to fluency before feasting begins.

The other more serious warning relates to lettuce and strawberries, the crops believed to be most affected by water contamination in the Santiago market garden region. Both, (and indeed all vegetables), should be washed thoroughly and disinfected before eating. Small bottles of vegetable disinfectant can be bought in the supermarkets in the fruit section.

Chileans love their food and they love it fresh. Breadshops bake at least three times a day and it takes a strong will-power indeed to

flour based unbaked bread). At Christmas and Easter the *pan de pascua* is eaten like a fruit cake. It's a round loaf made from dried fruits and eggs.

A wealth of produce: Chilean fruit is world renowned. Stalls everywhere are laden with the pick of the season: Chilean-grown plums, peaches, apricots, melons of all types, apples, oranges, strawberries and blackberries. Even kiwi fruits are now grown here, and of course the famous Chilean grape is everywhere, sweet and luscious.

Chile is the Southern Hemisphere's main table-grape exporter. Its other fruit exports include apples, pears, nectarines, plums, lemons and peaches. There's a similar abun-

get the bread parcel home without disturbing the warm, fluffy interior. Supermarkets usually have their own bakeries as well, and it would be rare to find a spot in Chile's far-flung wilds where fresh bread is not available. This bread is the regular white, brown or multi-grain version, in various bun-shapes and loaves, but there are more traditional varieties like *chapale* (boiled bread made from potatoes and flour), *milcao* (also made with potatoes), and *sopaipa* (a fruit and

Far left, sumptuous and varied salad spread. **Left**, chef displays his latest creation. **Above**, chicken on a spit, *a la braso*.

dance of fresh vegetables (*verduras*). The tomato is possibly the most popular vegetable. Ripened on the plant, it retains a uniquely rich, sweet flavor.

The availability of the tomato means it turns up everywhere and constitutes the most common salad, *ensalada chilena*. Sliced onions are washed several times and strained, then mixed with chopped and peeled tomatoes. Plenty of salt is added with an oil and vinegar dressing. Fresh coriander (*cilantro*) is also thrown in to create a cheap and refreshing light meal or accompaniment.

Nearly as common as the tomato is the avocado pear (*palta*), which turns up in nearly all your salads, on most hamburgers and in pulp on hotdogs (*completos*).

Potatoes, beans, lentils and corn are the main vegetable crops. The beans or *porotos* are popularly eaten as a rich warm soup known as *porotos granados*. It's made from haricot beans, pumpkin, peppers, onion and sweet corn, and served often with a beefsteak (*bifstek*) on top. The word *porotos* is believed to originate from the Quechua language of Andean Indians.

Winter fare: The other soup that helps Chileans through their biting winters is the *cazuela*. Nineteenth-century traveler Edward Revel Smith described the *cazuela* as "the best dish that can be had in Chile, and

and very early on represented a staple for the native Mapuches and Spanish settlers.

Humitas are made using the same principal as stuffed vine or cabbage leaves. Cooked or mashed corn is steamed in little parcels, and eaten, without wrapping, accompanied by *ensalada chilena*.

Pastel de choclo, with a base of meat or chicken and a mashed corn layer on the top, is much like a cottage pie, with corn replacing the potato. It is often sweetened with raisins in the meat mixture, and typical of the Chilean sweet-tooth, sugar is sometimes sprinkled over the roasted corn lid.

A passion for seafood: The cold Antarctic waters that are carried up the Chilean coast

one which, I believe, can be had nowhere else." It starts with a meat (*carne*), chicken (*pollo*), or seafood (*pescado* or *mariscos*) broth in which potato, pumpkin, corn and peppers are cooked. The dish arrives at your table as a steaming soup, a sea for large vegetable islands, under which a bed of rice is discovered. It's usually cheap and is simply very hearty.

As for corn, its little yellow cobblets are used in many Chilean dishes, but are most famous in the form of *humitas* and *pastel de choclo*. (*Choclo* is the Mapuche Indian word for corn). As a durable crop, corn is grown all year in one or another of the Chilean regions,

by the famous Humbolt Current, produce seafood of impeccable flavor. *Mariscos* or shellfish are consumed with a passion. Tan-colored shellfish known as *machas* (razor clams) are eaten either raw, or lightly baked with a sprinkling of Parmesan cheese. *Machas* can also, if you're lucky, be found in *empanadas*. Other *mariscos* include the usual prawns (*camarones grandes* or *gambas*), shrimp (*camarones*), oysters (*ostras*), sea urchins (*erizos*), mussels (*mejillones*), clams (*almejas*), squid (*calamares*) octopus (*pulpo*) and of course the famous king crab (*centolla*). The other name that could be used on the menu for crab is *jaiva* .

With more than 4,000 kms (2,500 miles) of coast it is not surprising that Chile is one of the world's largest fish producers. Much of its five-million-ton annual catch is used as export fish oil and fish meal, but with greater awareness that indiscriminate broad net fishing threatens the renewable resource, more attention is being paid to selectively harvesting table fish.

The conger eel (*congrio*), Spanish hake, (*cojinoa*), swordfish (*albacora*), seabass (*corvina*) and sole (*leguado*), make up the rich selection of fish from Chilean waters. The conger constitutes another very Chilean dish, the *caldillo de congrio,* a soup served with a piece of conger, onions and potato.

numbers means for the time being it is illegal to sell them – although some of the more unscrupulous fishermen will still offer it to you on the beach.

Fresh water trout (*trucha*) and salmon (*salmón*) represent a fantastic mix of taste and economy, especially in the south where the farming of both is growing. Very appealing for the angler, the south is home to a great variety of rivers, streams and lakes, all cold, clean and fast flowing. The trout caught in these waterways is plump, sweet and quite delicious.

There are quite a few wonderful places to eat your seafood. In Santiago the large markets next to the Mapocho river, have cheap

A good way to try a bit of everything is to order a *parrillada de mariscos*. This very sociable dish will arrive at your table on a charcoal brazier, sporting a mixture of grilled seafood. Be wary however of ordering a mixed plate of shellfish. In some Santiago restaurants it can turn out to be very expensive, and several of the more obscure *mariscos* that turn up on your plate need a rather strong stomach to throw back.

Abalone (known in Chile as *loco*) is delicious, but a dangerous depletion of their

restaurants amongst rows of fish and vegetable stalls. The little fishing villages, dotted up and down the coast, outside of the city always have small homely restaurants leaning next to the boat sheds. The fish and *mariscos* come straight from the boat onto your plate, or you can simply pick up a handful of oysters and lemons and slide down onto the sand to watch the fishermen repair their nets.

Chilean meats: In the same way that the barbeque dominates summer dining in Australia, the *asado* is the most popular way of eating meat in Chile. A typical *asado* starts late afternoon and drifts on into the night,

Left, seafood is one of Chile's greatest treats.
Above, local speciality, the *humitas*.

becoming awash with great Chilean wine.

While not considered as fine as Argentinian meat, the Chilean beast produces very credible steaks served up in restaurants known as *parilladas* . The *parilladas* cook every type of meat over a charcoal grill – anything from a steak, to a sausage or chop.

In some of the *campesino* (farming) areas, you can find great cheap *parilladas* , usually with a big fire in the middle of a rustic, heavy wooden tabled room, complete with a guitar-playing *huaso* (traditional Chilean horseman). This is a good place to try a *prieta,* a typical Chilean sausage filled with the unappetizing ingredients of cabbage and blood but allegedly very tasty. If you simply order a *parrillada*, you'll get a mixed grill comprising of a bit of every part of the beast, including intestines, a sausage or two and some chicken.

Lesser quality meat is used in hamburgers. A *churasco* burger uses several slices of very thin boiled or fried meat. Pork (*lomito*) is used commonly in sandwiches, cut and cooked the same way. The hamburger and the *completo* (hotdog) dominate the fast food market, along with roasted chicken (*pollo a brasa*). The center of Santiago has so many take-aways of this nature that it's sometimes difficult to find anything with any nutritional reputation. But perservere by walking down some of the minor city center streets where the typical *cazuela* and *empanada* restaurants are found.

The ubiquitous chicken: Chickens enjoy a long life in very few Latin American countries. In Chile, *pollo* doesn't really play an influential role in traditional concoctions. Nevertheless, the chicken, like everything else, has been integrated and Chileanised, so alongside your e*mpanadas*, you can find any number of variations on chicken and rice (*pollo y arroz*).

What is well worth catching however, and usually found in the country, is *pollo al cognac*. Well-cooked tender chicken quarters are served from a large earthen-ware bowl accompanied by *champiñones*. Both are sauced by a smooth Cognac soup and create a surprisingly gourmet meal in what is usually a rather rustic atmosphere.

One dish which covers all categories of food is the *curanto*. Taken from the Polynesians, the people of the southern Chilean islands dig a huge hole in which baked stones are piled. Vegetable leaves act as a base for layers of fish, beef, pork and vegetables. A huge pile of sand is dumped on the top, and the rich mixture beneath is left to steam. The *curranto* usually acts as the center of a party or festival.

Growing vegetarianism: In the leafy suburb of Providencia (Orego Luco 054), U.S.-born Nicole Mintz has trained her own chefs in some very original vegetarian dishes and fresh juice combinations, for her restaurant El Huerto (meaning orchard or kitchen garden). Most other non-vegetarian restaurants will provide you with a plate of tomato, avocado, green beans and rice, or perhaps a lentil or bean soup.

Multi-cultural desserts (*postres*): For anyone with a sweet tooth, Chile represents a chance for abandonment. The European influence has left a rich legacy of mousses, tortes, cakes and pastries. The German *küchen* has been adapted using Chilean fruits, and the huge array of ice-cream flavors smack of Italian *gelato* supremacy.

What is very Chilean is the obsession with *manjar* (condensed milk boiled till it's a thick sweet gooey caramel). While you can find it under numerous names in other Latin American countries, the Chileans have managed to find the most ways to sneak it into the diet. It is so furiously consumed that one finds large jars of it dwarfing staples like milk and butter in supermarket fridges.

Hence one can eat *manjar* by itself, spread it thickly on toast, find it separating layers of filo pastry, as the base for a torte, curling out of puff pastry scrolls, in ice cream form or in the national dessert known as *panqueque celestino*. But the best way to get hooked on the sticky stuff, is to buy a *churro,* a sweet donut-like pastry moulded into a cylinder, into which warm *manjar* is poured. The result is a very rich slice of decadence. Any respectable stomach will only be able to accommodate one.

A day of dining: Breakfast is *desayuno*. In most residencials this will simply be fresh buns with jam and butter (*mermelada* and *mantequilla*) with coffee or tea.

Coffee is the preferred hot drink in Chile but it will come to you as Nescafe unless you ask for *cafe express. Cafe con leche* (with milk) is served as milk coffee, so if you just want a little milk mixed in, you need to specifically ask for *un poco de leche. A cafe cortado* is the closest thing to having a dash of milk. *Cortado* means 'cut', so the coffee is half water with coffee and half milk. A *cortado* is always served with sugar, so you'll need to ask for *sin azúcar* if you prefer plain coffee. Lovers of tea in a pot will simply have to suffer since Chileans can only manage bags.

A fuller breakfast can be ordered anywhere that serves *desayuno*. Eggs and toast (*huevos con tostadas*) should be no problem. Fried eggs are *huevos fritos*, scrambled are *revueltos,* poached are *pasados*, hard-boiled are *huevos duros* and soft-boiled are *a la copa.*

Be prepared for the pleasant task of taking coffee, or a soft drink, is usually part of the deal.

A most civilized ritual performed throughout Chile between 5 and 7 p.m. is known as *once* (meaning 11 in Spanish). These hours are reserved not for cocktails, but for tea, coffee, sandwiches and cakes. Since dinner is never eaten until 10ish it acts as a hold-you-over snack. It also serves as a kind of British high-tea. Indeed the most common explanation for once stems from the British custom of "elevenses" for 11-o'clock morning tea. Folklore has it. however, that *once* refers to the time when the man of the house would sneak off for a quiet 5 p.m. drink known as *aguardiente,* the local

a long leisurely lunch (*almuerzo*), considered the biggest meal of the day. It is usually served after 1.30 p.m. and runs through till arpound 4 p.m. Set lunches (*comidas corridas* or *colaciones*) are usually very good value, and let you test out something typical without actually knowing what to order. They'll simply bring you an *entré*, something like tomatoes, cooked beans and cheese, before a main meal of perhaps *porotos granados* or *pollo y arroz* , then a little *postre*, usually ice cream and fruit. Tea and

Above, exotic local fruits, the *chirimoya* and *nisperos*.

firewater whose name contains 11 letters.

Like most Latin American countries dinner (*cena*) isn't served until after 8.30 p.m. and usually lingers late. If you are not a coffee drinker after dinner, try an *aguita* or *yerba* a fresh herb tea found everywhere.

The final word on Chilean food should perhaps come from El Sr Luis Bernard again, who cannot stress quite heavily enough the need to travel in order to catch the real Chilean flavor. "You'll find the best food if you travel in little towns where the fishermen are, or in the mountains, eating in little homely restaurants. They may look like very poor restaurants but the food is terrific."

Chileans have been making fine wines for more than a century, and probably boasting about them for almost as long.

Their great selling-point, as every Chilean schoolboy knows, is that the best wine is produced from vines which can trace their ancestry straight back to cuttings brought over in the middle of the last century from France by some enlightened Chilean vineyard owners.

Before that, the Spanish *conquistadores* had grown vines, legend has it, by planting

dustries in France, Italy and Germany.

The European growers only saved their vines by eventually grafting onto tougher, beetle-resistant American stock. But while the European vineyards were being replanted, several out-of-work French enologists went to Chile, together with their vines, to give technical advice on planting and wine-making.

The phylloxera blight never reached Chile, cut off as it is from the rest of the world by natural barriers – the Pacific Ocean, the

the pips of the raisins they had brought with them from Spain. This was the origin of what is known as "país", or "native" wine, the equivalent of California's "mission" wine. This variety still accounts for three-quarters of Chile's present-day production – about 400 million litres a year.

French roots: A couple of centuries on, a wealthy landowner Don Silvester Ochagavía, decided to improve the quality of his vines and went to France. He brought back cuttings not long before a plague of the dreaded phylloxera beetle began to chew away at the roots of the parent stock in Europe, and nearly destroyed the wine in-

Atacama desert and the high mountains of the Andes. So the Chilean vineyards boast that their vines grow naturally, ungrafted, from original stock. Wine buffs argue about the difference this makes, or doesn't make, to the wine's taste. But it certainly makes a difference to the economics of the industry, because ungrafted vines can go on producing for three or four times longer than the grafted stock that now dominate in Europe.

Señor Ochagavía brought cuttings of Cabernet Sauvignon vines, which is now the most common type used for red wine (*vino tinto*). It is usually produced as a 100 percent unblended wine, though it is sometimes blended with Merlot grapes, or occasionally with Malbec.

The white wine comes from Chardonnay grapes and from Cabernet Sauvignon Blanc. The Chardonnay varieties are more popular. Señor Ochagavia brought his cuttings of Sauvignon Blanc vines from Bordeaux rather than the Loire Valley, and the flavor, according to the experts, is softer and less pungent than the Loire valley variety. Some of the vineyards also produce a Riesling, which is not very distinguished.

Export boom: Already by the last century Chilean growers had the best wine vines and an excellent place to grow them – the long Central Valley, with its ideal, temperate cli-

wine has been dropping steadily. At the beginning of the 1970s, the average Chilean quaffed 50 litres a year. But over the past 20 years drinking habits have been changing. Beer and fizzy drinks have become far more popular, and wine consumption is now half its 1970 level, a mere 29 litres a head.

The future looked bleak for all the producers, big and small. But some of the bigger enterprises decided to test their reputations and try to sell in a big way to the outside world. That meant changing the heavy, full-bodied wines, with the strong tannin taste that the Chileans are used to, and going for the lighter and fruitier unblended wines (varietals) which are now in vogue in the

mate for all kinds of fruit, with hot sunny days and cool nights, and the right type of soil. But there is more to wine-making than growing the grapes, and only in the last four or five years have the big vineyards really begun to make consistent top quality wines that they can sell successfully to Europe and the United States.

Most of the vineyards were, and still are, rather small family businesses, with a shrinking market. Local consumption of

Left, wines maturing in the cellars of Concha y Toro vineyards. **Above**, Chilean wines are gaining an international reputation for quality.

United States and in Europe. And that meant investing in new equipment. For example, red wine has traditionally been matured in big, old wooden casks of raulí, the native redwood, which masks the taste of fruit and gives the wine an earthy flavor. The vineyards which have decided to go for export markets have had to import very expensive small casks, made from French oak, each one costing US$500 and lasting for only three or four years before they have to be replaced. They have had to put in new bottling equipment. Before, many of the wineries bottled from the casks only as and when they had a big order. So there was never any way of knowing whether one bottle from the same vineyard would taste like the last one you bought, even if it was the same vintage.

The investment for making good white wine is even larger, since white wine needs more careful handling. The grapes have to be picked in the cool hours of the morning, not in the heat of a summer afternoon. They have to be picked when they are not too ripe or else the wine lacks acidity, at least for non-Chilean tastes.

The big vineyards have been putting in new computerized pneumatic grape presses, which don't crush the pips, and stainless steel tanks, in which the temperature of the fermenting juice can be rigidly

picking starts. The Spanish-owned enterprise of Miguel Torres, which has land and a winery down near Curicó, holds a festival for the *vendimía* with a local beauty queen and other festivities around mid-March.

Public visits to most of the vineyards in the off-season are usually limited to the bottling plant, the original cellars – some of them, like those of the Santa Rita winery, near Paine, built by the Spaniards in the 18th century – and the grounds of the winery. This kind of tour takes only about an hour in all. So you might plan a visit as one part of a day out in the countryside around Santiago, but don't expect to see and be told in detail how a winery works.

controlled. The quality of Chile's white wines has improved considerably, as the world's specialized wine magazines have been noting approvingly in the last year. The big wineries have also invested in the equipment for selling wine in 1-litre and half-litre tetrapaks (aluminium-lined "bricks"), which are very handy for picnics. This is what you mostly get in the carafe when you order a house wine in a restaurant.

Visiting vineyards: Many of Chile's vineyards are close to Santiago, and some of them are open to the public. The *vendímia*, or harvest, is from early March until mid-April – the further south the vineyard, the later the

Concha y Toro, for example, which is far and away the biggest single wine producer, and the biggest exporter, has its plant out in the direction of the Cajón del Maipu, about an hour's drive from Santiago. It might be included in a weekend trip to the mountains.

Viña Undurraga is near Melipilla, about an hour's drive on the road towards San Antonio, and could be combined with a visit to the old seaside resorts of Algarrobo or Las Cruces, or the rather run-down port of San Antonio.

Much closer at hand, on the outskirts of Santiago, is the small winery of Cousiño Macul, also one of the oldest and most prestigious. The land has been growing grapes since vines were planted by its first owner, Juan Jufré, one of the *conquistadores* who came with Pedro de Valdivia. It has been in the Cousiño Macul family since 1856, and the person most responsible for the development of the winery was the stepdaughter of the first Cousiño, Doña Isidora Goyenechea, who had the cellars built and brought over an enologist especially from Bordeaux to produce quality wine.

The vineyard is sited in the foothills of the Andes, a quiet haven of trees and vineyards only 15 minutes from the city centre. It, too, can be visited, though it offers no organized tours to the grounds.

Informal tours: At Viña Concha y Toro and Viña Undurraga visitors can turn up on any weekday, preferably around midday, and be shown around. Both will offer you a rather cursory complimentary glass of their wine, but the guides are not wine experts. There is no chance to sample, and no special advantage in buying there.

Wine buffs might find more enlightenment closer to the city center. The Restaurant Enoteca on Santiago's pleasant wooded

<u>Left</u>, grounds of the Cousiño Macul vineyards, only 15 minutes from Santiago. <u>Above</u>, picking the season's grapes.

Cerro San Cristóbal offers visitors the chance to sample a huge range of Chilean wines at about half a dollar a glass. The restaurant is open from 10.30 a.m. to 10 p.m. and boasts a wine museum, meaning, largely, a display of Chilean wine bottles and labels, past and present, and some ancient wine-making equipment.

If you go casually there is no expert on hand to comment or recommend wines. But if you want to take sampling more seriously you can ring the administrator and, with three or four days notice, arrange for a private tasting session, complete with enologist to advise you.

If you want to take some Chilean wine home, try browsing in one of the big supermarkets, such as the Jumbo, the Almac or the Unimarc chains, in upmarket parts of Santiago like Providencia, Las Condes or Avenida Kennedy. They offer a large selection of wine at good prices, and the chance to look at the labels and decide at leisure.

The bigger producer-exporters are: Concha y Toro, and its subsidiary, Santa Emiliana; Santa Rita, which also owns Viña Carmen; San Pedro; and Santa Carolina. Small boutique-like vineyards are Canepa, Cousiño Macul, Miguel Torres and Errazuriz Panquehue, and Los Vascos which is now owned by Chateau Lafite of France, and produces under the Lafite label for export only.

Potent Pisco: The wine-making areas are mostly in the Central Valley to the south of Santiago. North of Santiago, most of the vines are for growing table grapes, with the exception of the pisco grapes, which are a pink Moscatel-like variety which is distilled to make the spirit of the same name.

The Valle del Elqui, close to the pretty northern town of La Serena, and birthplace of one of Chile's two Nobel-winning poets, Gabriela Mistral, is the most famous area for pisco. There are three or four main brands which are nationally distributed, but if you visit the valley or La Serena it is worth tasting and shopping around for small local brands, which have the most remarkable taste and smell of ripe grapes.

In Southern Chile you may find variants on the standard *aguardiente* in which celery or cherries have been left to steep in the liquor. The celery version is called *apiado*, the cherry drink, *guindado*.

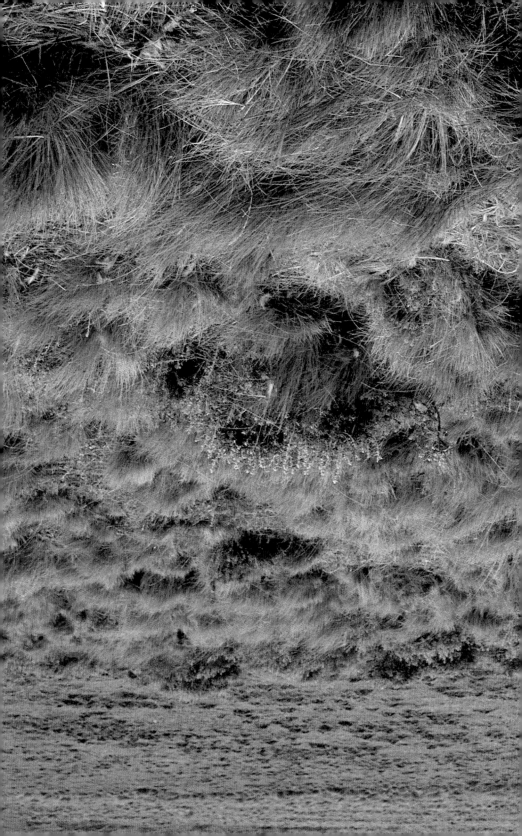

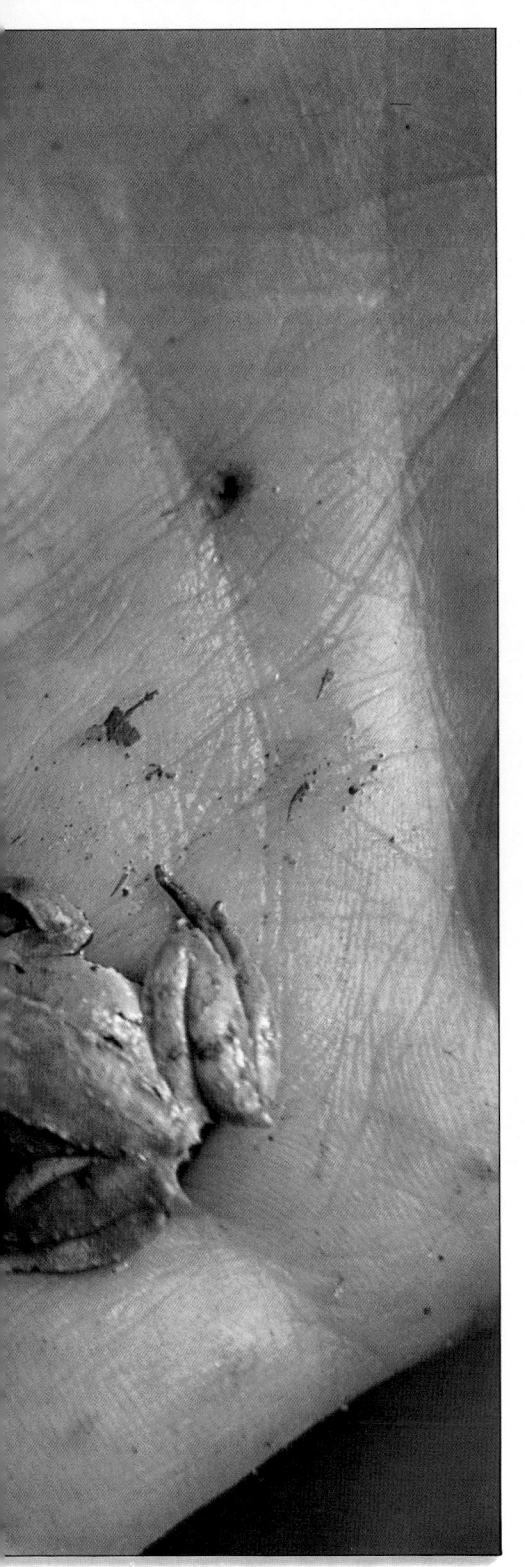

CHILE IN THE WILD

With the world's driest desert in the north and the continent of Antarctica in the south, it's not surprising that Chile's climate is divided into extremely different zones and that within that, the wildlife varies tremendously. Add to this the country's huge extension of ocean (the 320km/200-mile territorial limit is almost twice the width of Chile at its widest point) on the west and the towering Andes on the east, and you have a world of differences packed into one long strand of a country.

Perhaps one of the most pleasant surprises about Chilean wildlife, however, is that there are few dangers for the intrepid camper or hiker. There are no bears in the mountains, no poisonous snakes and only two kinds of poisonous spider (the corn spider or *araña del trigo*, with its characteristic red splash on a black body, and the brown corner spider, *araña rincon*), which you're unlikely to run into. Way up in the mountains there are different species of wildcats and pumas, but they usually avoid people.

One of the ironies of Chilean wildlife is that, while Chileans are generally proud of the numerous species unique to their country, many of these are in danger of extinction, including the world's smallest deer, the *pudú*, and the *huemul*, the large, royal-looking deer which appears on the Chilean coat of arms. On Chile's island territories (Easter Island and particularly the Juan Fernández Islands, sometimes called the Southern Galapagos) are species which, due to isolation, have formed their own unique gene pools.

Animals of the desert north: The soils of Chile's northernmost First Region are dry and the climate is harsh, but along the coast there is a wealth of seals and all kinds of birds: seagulls, pelicans and *jotes* (vultures). High up in the Andes, disguised among the low shrubs and rocks, is the occasional herd of *huemules*, hard to find but protected (at least in theory) by national parks.

There are also herds of the animals most closely identified with (and arguably best

Preceding pages, finding a nandú nest in Magallanes. **Left**, tiny Darwin's frogs thrive in southern streams.

adapted to) the extreme conditions of the altiplano: llamas, vicuñas, guanacos and alpacas. All relatives of the camel, these four species are hard to tell apart, although the llama and the alpaca are longhaired (and valued for their wool).

The French naturalist, Claude Gay, described guanacos as: "animals with gentle, timid and very curious personalities, staring at great length at anything that attracts their attention. They're very sociable and live in herds of many females with one male... They're hunted for their edible flesh and because exceptionally strong lassos can be made from the skin of their neck… Their only form of defense is spitting at people

dean mountain ranges, can be found the occasional hollow covered with the only sparse grasses capable of resisting the extreme saltiness of the soil.

Climbing slightly into the mountains, around 2,200 meters (7,200 ft) above sea level, cacti appear, accompanied by birds, some insects and lizards, the main lifeform capable of surviving in the area. Further up into the Altiplano (over 4,500 meters/14,800 ft) live *vizcachas* (a Chilean rodent, which is relatively easy to see as it functions during the day), vicuñas, alpacas, llamas and guanacos, birds like those of the First Region, and one of the world's last reserves of wild chinchilla. According to Chile's Committee

who try to come near them: at the slightest provocation they lay their ears back and fling saliva mixed with other matter which doesn't cause the least damage."

Mountain cats, wild ducks, flamingos, *nandús* (ostrich-like birds), owls, eagles and condors also add life to the dry northern landscape, 3,000 or 4,000 meters (9,800/13,000 ft) above sea level.

In the Second Region is the Atacama desert, dry and hostile to all forms of life. Only along the coast is there an abundance of wildlife, mostly in the form of birds: pelicans, petrels, penguins and other species. In the broad plains formed between the Coastal and An-

for Defence of Flora and Fauna (CODEFF), these chinchillas are particularly important because most existing animals have been born and bred in captivity, with the resulting damage to gene pools which results from excessive in-breeding. These last, wild chinchilla are key to the renewal of breeding animals and have been studied by professors at the University of Chile. The chinchilla is an endangered species: at the turn of the century, an average of 350,000 chinchilla skins were exported per year.

Claude Gay described the chinchilla as "one of Chile's most beautiful animals" and said they were easily tamed. Because they live in extensive caves dug under the surface and come out only at night, their eyes are extremely sensitive to the light.

Towards the moister Little North: By the Third Region both the climate and the landscape soften considerably and from Chañaral southward there is enough humidity to permit the growth of a large variety of cactus, many of which are valued abroad. However, over the years ruthless hunting has reduced the herds of guanacos and the number of *vizcachas* and chinchillas as well. Colourful beetles of all kinds are particularly noteworthy throughout this region.

By the Fourth and Fifth regions the climate, while still dry, is considerably more

huge dunes have formed and begun to creep steadily into formerly fertile areas, turning them into semi deserts which may be virtually impossible to recover.

Thorns, shrubs and small trees, along with wild flowers like the Cordilleran violet and camomile, give way to the forests of Fray Jorge and Talinay, full of trees more commonly found further south (particularly cinnamon and the *olivillo*).

A wealth of insects hum amongst the vegetation, including dragon flies, butterflies and beetles, which in turn sustain a sizeable population of lizards and non-poisonous snakes. Wild donkeys live in the Andean foothills.

generous toward both plants and animals and many people, both Chileans and visitors, believe these regions have one of the most pleasant climates in the world. The average temperature for the area is around 14°C (57°F) all year round and mists blown off the ocean condense on the coastal mountains and ensure enough moisture to support a wide variety of flowers, trees and other vegetation necessary to maintain animal life. However, the landscape pays dearly for those years when the moisture is not sufficient:

Left, Andean condors. **Above**, flamingoes in flight, Magallanes.

Further up into the mountains the wildlife is similar to the first three regions, with a larger population of wild birds and mice, along with the animals mentioned above. Many of these species have adapted to the brief desert springs by speeding their own metamorphosis and growth periods.

In the Fifth Region, sea swallows and cormorants join the bird species more common further north, and further inland there are thrush, turtledoves and partridges along with the other species named above. Animals include the skunk and a small marsupial weasel. Wasps, scorpions (their sting is painful but not dangerous), *tábanos* (horseflies), and both black and large hairy spiders form part of the insect population, while frogs and toads join the lizard and snake community.

Lizards and snakes: Reptiles are perhaps the one kind of creature common throughout the country except Magallanes: there are 76 different species of lizards and six species of snakes scattered through Chile's different landscapes and climates. Many reptiles are unqiue to Chile. The history of their development has been extremely difficult to trace, because of the lack of fossil evidence, but fossils in South America generally indicate lizards go back about 70 million years.

Chilean lizards live in the desert, on the coast, in tropical forests, in the heights of the

One of the best introductions to Chile's lizards and snakes is a display in the Santiago zoo, on San Cristóbal Hill. It is possible to have a close look at some of Chile's more elusive lizards, frogs, toads and snakes. Niri Vilcun can be reached at Bellavista 0380, Santiago, Phone 776520, Telex 340436.

Animals of the center and south: From the early days of the Spanish conquest, Chile's fertile central valley region, where Santiago is located, became the main area of settlement and agriculture. As a result, the main animals of the area are people and about the only wildlife you'll find is in the zoo.

While the Santiago zoo has its limitations, it does have a fairly extensive selection of

Andes and, on Patagonian and southern steppes. Some reproduce by laying eggs, while others give birth to live young.

Sizes range from 10 cm/4 in (from nosetip to tail) up to half a meter/20 in long, as is the case with the Chilean iguana. Different species prefer rocks, trees, shrubs or the earth itself for their homes and they play a key role in the ecology, living on flies, crickets, locusts and other insects and thus controlling the insect population. Birds and several of Chile's snakes in turn live on the lizards. None are dangerous: they prefer to get away if approached by humans and will only bite when there is no alternative.

Chile's wild animals, many of which are extremely difficult to spot in their natural habitats. Both the *colo colo* cat and the *guiña* (two kinds of small wild cats which live in Chile) are on display, as are small herds of vicuña, guanaco, llama and alpaca. There is also a family of *pudú*, reddish deer the size of dogs, which live mostly in the south and on the island of Chiloé and are in danger of extinction.

The zoo also has a large sample of Chile's wild birds, including the extraordinary black-necked swan, flamingos and other less exotic species. Also present are the Chilean condor, eagles and other birds of prey common to the region. The *coipo*, a sort of Chilean beaver, hard to see in the wild because it usually only comes out at night, is also on display, along with other examples of Chile's wild animals.

As you travel further south down the country the landscape changes and with it the different animals which inhabit it. In the lush forests which cover a large part of the southern region, are rabbits, hares, *coipo* and mice, wildcats and other small animals. Many of the animals which formerly populated the coast have, however, been decimated by indiscriminate hunting, particularly the different species of seals which once thrived in that area.

which is an inch or more in length with long claws. Praying mantis, colorful "stink bugs" of a bright metallic blue and different kinds of butterflies also thrive under the trees although they, like all species, have been affected by the wholesale cutting and burning of Chile's native forests and have not adapted well to foreign species like the lodgepole pine, which have been used for reforestation in some regions.

Longtailed snakes (which look similar to North American garter snakes) and shorttailed snakes feed on mice, toads and small birds. They're about 8 cm (3 in) long at birth and grow to 2 meters (7 ft), although one meter (3 ft) is more common. They are not

Birds with names like *huairavo, piquero, pollito de mar, pinguera, chucao, run-run* and *becacinas* populate the forests and the ever-present lizards are joined by four-eyed toads, the cowboy toad and different kinds of frogs. One of the more unusual is Darwin's frog which gives birth to eggs which are then swallowed and tended by the male, who, upon their maturation "gives birth" through the mouth to the young tadpoles.

Among the insects, one fascinating beetle is the *madre de la culebra* (snake's mother),

poisonous and if you feel so inclined, you can pick them up and handle them.

Solitary hunters: Up in the mountains, the "colonists" who eke out a living by growing kitchen gardens and raising sheep, goats, chickens, turkeys and cattle, run into pumas, which they call lions, on a regular basis, particularly in the winter.

The puma don't usually attack people, unless injured and cornered, and they feed primarily on hares, vizcachas and mice, attacking domestic animals only occasionally. Despite this, considerable hunting has seriously reduced their numbers. A solitary animal, the puma reaches maturity at two or

<u>Left</u>, a graceful guanaco, a relative of the camel.
<u>Above</u>, the Chilean fox (*culpeo*).

three years, and usually has two kittens per litter. Pumas are found throughout Chile and, indeed, are one of the few animal species to be found throughout the Americas, from Canada right down to the Strait of Magellan.

Condors inhabit the high peaks of the *cordillera* and Chile's mountain forests also provide homes for wild ducks, mountain partridges and tricahue parrots. Mountain cats (*felis colo colo*), which are peculiar to Chile are an altogether unnerving sight – their physical appearance is exactly that of the marmalade house cat, but they live in the wild, surviving on partridge, hare, rabbit, mice and birds.

Traveling further south, the climate becomes increasingly damp and rainy and the species change somewhat as a result. However, the considerable deforestation of the area has severely cut back on what would otherwise be a numerous population of wild animals. There are still some foxes, *pudús*, wildcats and pumas, but they tend to concentrate as far from human inhabitants as they can get, and are hard to see.

The *pudú*, a tiny deer which is unique to Chile, lives in thickets in dense forest areas between Chillán and Chiloé and is almost impossible to sight in the wilds.

Darwin's or the chilote fox is Chile's smallest, rarest fox and because of the destruction

In the Seventh Region, between Vichuquén Lake and the coastal village of Llico, is the Santuario de la Naturaleza de la Laguna de Torca. There is nothing like topping the rise and looking down on the lagoon, covered with the graceful black-necked swans whose scientific name is *cygnus melancorphus*. They feed on aquatic plants and lay their eggs on floating nests. Upon hatching, the white offspring climb on to their parents' backs.

Along the coast are colonies of penguins and swamp cormorants and in the interior after dark, small bats zoom like swallows through the night.

of its natural habitat is in danger of extinction. It has, however, been sighted recently in both Chiloé and in the forests north of Osorno.

One of the world's largest beetles is also found in the Tenth Region: the stag beetle grows as long as 9 cm (4 in) and lives in the oak and coigüe forests of this region. The male, unlike the female, has long jaws.

Dolphins begin to appear along the coast, where whales were once hunted virtually into extinction. Woodpeckers and humming birds are common in the forests, particularly near the wild fuchsia (bleeding hearts).

In the Eleventh Region, high up in the

most isolated area of the Andes, are small herds of *huemules*, which are officially protected since they are virtually extinct. However, a documentary by a Chilean television network revealed that even in areas set apart as national parks, illegal human settlements where cattle are raised are competing with the endangered deer. A television documentary, which is re-aired at regular intervals, called *Al sur del mundo* provides excellent footage of a trip made to one of the few sites where *huemules* can still be found.

In Chile's southernmost region, sea lions can be sighted along with populations of one and two haired seal and dolphins. Beavers (introduced from abroad), muskrat and *coipo* are also common, along with petrels, albatross, cormorants and other sea birds. In the steppes or *pampas* of Tierra del Fuego, there are foxes, guanacos, pumas and skunks, along with hares and other small rodents.

An island dedicated solely to the Parque Nacional de Pinguinos (National Penguin Park) and another dedicated to Los Cisnes (Park of Swans) provide effective sanctuary to a wide variety of Chile's southernmost species. Among them are a variety of seals (Ross, Weddell, Crab), sea lions and elephant seals.

The foundation for the Antarctic's delicate foodchain is krill, a name for several species of small shrimp about 5 cm (2 in) long, which thrive in about 20 million of the 36 million square km (8 million of the 14 million square miles) of the Antarctic Ocean, coming to within half a kilometer of the shores of the frozen continent itself. Their biomass is estimated at about 200 million tons. A blue whale consumes about 40,000 kilos (88,000 lb) of krill each day.

The lifecycle of the krill begins between January and July with the external fertilization of the eggs which then begin a slow steady drop through the depths, because they are heavier than water.

By the fifth or sixth day they've reached between 500 and 1500 meters (1,640/4,920 ft), at which point small larva begin an ascension which lasts until January of the next year. By then they're about 2 cm (0.8 in) long and have returned to the surface, where they may live as long as three years.

Most of the area's species live on krill and are peculiar to the region. For example 80 percent of the mollusc found in the region occur only there. Under the icy waters are starfish, sea urchins, sponges, jelly fish and other species which have adapted specially to the extreme temperatures and harsh conditions. An estimated 25 species of octopus and squid can be found in the subantarctic and Antarctic Ocean, along with five fish families.

Living on the edge between ice and water are nine species of penguins, the largest of which is appropriately called the Emperor Penguin and grows as large as 1.2 meters (4 ft), with a weight of almost 4 kilos (8.8 lb).

These penguins live in colonies with as many as 5,000 members and are characterized by a yellowish orange patch on both sides of their chests.

Blue whales, 20 to 30 meters long (66–98 ft) and weighing more than 100 tons, along with orcas and dolphins live on the krill which is plentiful in the icy waters between Chile and the Antarctic.

An estimated 10,000 are all that's left of the more than 200,000 which existed in 1800. Merciless exploitation in the 18th and 19th centuries turned them into endangered species. About 380,000 whales, belonging to 28 species, are found in the Antarctic.

<u>Left</u>, the Chilean southern-ringed kingfisher. <u>Right</u>, giant red-headed woodpecker.

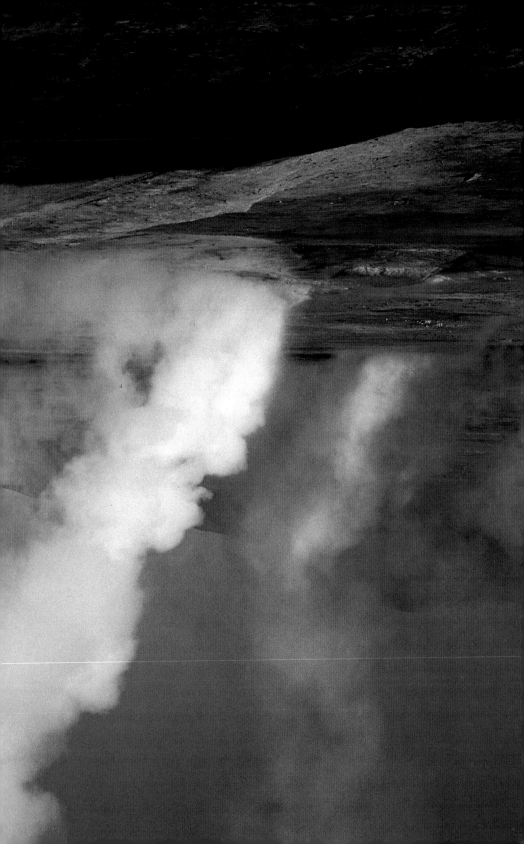

With over one third of the nation's population living in the capital Santiago, it is not hard to find somewhere in Chile to get away from it all. But Chile offers more than remote and pristine spots. Its dramatic, untamed landscape make it a land of adventure.

The options are as varied as Chile's many geographical zones: the desert north offers vast empty plains that can only be crossed in four wheel drives; the heart of the Andes must be reached either on foot or by horseback; there are volcanoes to be climbed and rivers to be rafted; while the glacier-riddled islands of the southern Archipelago can often only be visited on organised boat trips.

The season for adventure tourism is summer: November to March. This is when the weather stablizes, save on the Andean high plane on the northeastern border when the Bolivian "winter" threatens electric storms. But do not expect rain in the desert, not even in the foothills. Some places see rain every 30 to 50 years in the Atacama. From there to Santiago, rain rarely falls between October and March. The area from Puerto Montt to Coyhaique, the wettest region of the country, is best left for January or February. Much of the transportation to the more difficult to reach areas is drastically reduced or even suspended in the winter months – either because of the state of the roads and seas; or because the flow of people traveling on public transport decreases. And further south can be freezing even at the height of summer.

Northern jeep excursions: The Chilean Norte Grande offers a wide selection of geological phenomena and archaeological sites – both from ancient tribes of native peoples as well as the more recent remains of turn of the century nitrate mining ghost towns. However, vast distances between places and roads that are often barely distinguishable tracks makes traveling difficult. While some prefer to rent a car and do their own driving, some of the spots of interest are so hidden and the many unmarked splinters of the main roads

are so confusing that renting an excursion or hiring a local driver of a four-wheel drive vehicle is by far the best way to see the area.

The main rule of thumb in the desert is to never leave the road unless you know where you are going. Locals insist that that includes just pulling off unpaved roads, as it can take hours of pushing and shoving in the blazing sun to free an automobile bogged down in the sand. It is also important always to take a large supply of fresh water along. Even up in the mountains where it is possible to find

streams, the water is often so high in mineral content that it is brackishly saline and generally undrinkable.

The desert can be quite cold after the sun goes down, especially if there is a wind. In fact, it will be freezing should you arrive early in the morning to see the geysers go off in El Tatio or wildlife in the Chungara Lake. Of course, sun glasses, a hat and sun block are all necessary equipment for day time use. Also bring eyedrops to counteract the ever-present dust and glare.

In Arica, Iquique, and Antofagasta on the coast, and Calama or San Pedro in the interior, it is possible to hire drivers for shorter

Preceding pages: dawn display at El Tatio geysers near San Pedro de Atacama. **Left, reaching the Torres (towers) del Paine. Right,** an exuberant moment in the Andes.

day trips into the many places of interest near them. The excursions are generally for groups of six to ten people depending on the size of the vehicle, usually a jeep or a small van. Smaller groups are also possible, but as the price is divided among fewer people, it may run a little higher. Check local travel agencies or hotels to make arrangements.

In Antofagasta, an agency called Atacama Desert Expeditions (Washington 2562, office 313; phone number: 228 141) offer any number of trips. And in Santiago, Explorandes (Matias Cousiño 150, office 524; tel: 698 9517) offer an excursion that will take the traveler on a 10-day tour of most of the northern highlights, from Arica to An-

and prepare. Trips are generally between 4-day and 10-day outings and include five to 15 trekkers. Arrangements often depend on demand, however, and if you have enough people together with you to make up a group it is possible to design your own, unique excursion.

A warm jacket is a must for the drop in temperature after the sun goes down. And while it is up, a wide-brimmed hat and sun glasses are absolute necessities. Sun block, some sort of lip balm, and a light weight, long-sleeved shirt are also a guarantee against the scorching rays of the sun and dry air of the altitudes. Aside from this, all you need is a sleeping bag.

tofagasta. They provide food and tents in the more remote areas, although on most nights lodgings are in villages.

Trekking on horseback in the Central Andes:
There are two groups which organize excursions into the Andes on horseback near Santiago: the Astorga family who offer trips departing from different points in the Cajón del Maipo (in Santiago, contact El Huerto Restaurant; Orrego Luco 054; Tel: 233 2690) and Santiago Garcia who usually uses Farellones as his point of departure (in Santiago, Candelaria Goyenachea 4750; Tel: 218 2216). Both offer guides, the animals, and pack mules for the provisions they supply

Exploring the many nooks and crannies of the high Andes from the back of a horse is not as difficult as many would believe. Not surprisingly, it is quite a bit less work than carrying a pack on your back up 3,500 meters (11,500 ft) or more. And particular riding skills are not required either, as, given the terrain, most of the trip is a walking tour.

The guides for these trips are *arrieros*, men who run cattle herds over the Andes or take them up to pasture after the spring snow melt. Many have learned the trails from their fathers and grandfathers before them. Their tales around the campfires as the barbecue beef sizzles on the spit are worth learning

Spanish to understand, and there is usually also a musician to liven up the evenings.

The Andes reach their highest point in the hemisphere on Mount Aconcagua just north of Santiago. The trails nearby wind diagonally up steep huge hills topped by barren rock whose colors often betray their mineral content: green for copper, white for gypsum or lime, red for clay. The vegetation is sparse, trees are rarer and smaller the higher you ascend – finally reaching green summer pastures full of wild flowers and bushes. Ice from higher up has melted into streams, providing deliciously clean drinking water.

Some excursions include visits to lagoons that are not marked on road maps, such as

River in the country (when in truth the Baker River through the ice fields south of Cochrane wins this distinction), is known internationally as a "world-class" river for white water rafting or kayaking. As it winds around the Lonquimay volcano, which erupted as recently as 1987, through virgin forests and canyons, the Bío Bío's alternating rapids and calms make it the favorite of many given to these sports. On the international scale of 1 to 6, its rapids are rated grade 5 in difficulty and it is not to be attempted by anyone but expert kayakers with guides.

People who wish to float the rapids on a raft must know how to swim, while other skills will be taught by the guides of each raft

Laguna Negra and the twin lakes del Yesillo, where blocks of snow float. The wild geese *piuquenes* make their nests in the lake that bears their name.

The atmosphere is so dry and clear it seems you could see to the end of the world if only the snow-capped peaks were not blocking your vision. And there is always the majestic silence of the Cordillera, humbling to experience.

White water rafting: The mighty Bío Bío River, held by many to be the most copious

Left, a horseback trek in the Maipu River Canyon.
Above, fording a mountain river.

prior to departure. Generally, the most important rule is to follow orders from the guide for he must distribute the passengers' weight within the craft to avoid capsizing.

While there are a few North American agenices that organize excursions down the Bío Bío, there are two local agencies that also offer trips of 10 days or less: the more experienced Expediciones Altué (the Geopub, Encomenderos 83, Santiago; tel: 232 1103) and the newer Expediciones Grado 10 (Las Urbinas 56. Tel: 562-2344130; fax 562-2344138).

Excursions include all necessary gear for the rafting itself: rafts, tents, life jackets and helmets, as well as overland transportation of sleeping gear, provisions and packs where possible. Swim attire or a wet suit like those used in windsurfing are best for being on the river, with warmer clothing for night time. Sleeping bags must be provided by the traveler. Hiking trips into the surrounding forests are included, usually to recover energy following days which cross some of the more difficult rapids.

High in the Andes, the walls of the river canyons can be so steep and the waters so rough as to make the trip down it extremely dangerous. On the other hand, once the river reaches more level ground the extension of the calms can make paddling a tiresome

Mapuche Indians tell of how they were forced to move from the area because of the extensive volcanic activity. The age of the forests – not more than 250 years old – in the valleys between Freire and the mountains confirm the folk memory. More recently in 1971, the town of Coñaripe was buried below such a slide of mud, ash, lava and tree trunks; while the last time a lava flow reached the banks of Lake Villarrica was 1908).

If you care to take on one of these roaring giants, different agencies in Pucón organize hiking tours to the very crater of the Villarrica Volcano. Walking up the conical mountain, you walk through one of the centers of the Pacific Ring of Fire, surrounded by volcanic

chore. But shorter excursions on other rivers not quite as wild as the Bío Bío, but every bit as exciting, can be easily arranged. Day trips float down portions of the Maipo and the Trancura rivers and can be organised in resort towns like Pucón.

Climbing a volcano: The volcanoes Llaima and the Villarrica are the most active in Chile, with a record of 10 eruptions each during the 19th century (Llaima erupted as recently as 1994). A strong eruption in them or the nearby peaks of Quetrupillán, Lanin, or Mocho-Choshuenco can cause a chain reaction in the area. (Most recently this happed in the mid-17th century, when the

peaks. Here and there are emerald and sapphire lakes. Sometimes you hear some of the dark, hidden underground groans of Mother Earth, and feel a few tremors and shakes. To stare down the 100-meter (330-ft) drop into the crater of hellishly boiling molten lava is a sight few will forget. Here the subterranean noises reach a roar and the stench of sulphur can be almost overpowering.

The agencies, both Altúe and Expediciones Grado 10, will take hikers to the bottom of the trail near Pucón. They supply guides as well as the cramp-ons and ice axes necessary for the ascent over the ice to the top of the Villarrica at 2,840 meters (9,320 ft). Sturdy, warm hiking boots and jackets are also supplied by the agencies, necessary protection against the cold winds of the summit. The ascent of the western face now takes about four hours thanks to a ski-lift cutting the distance down, and the descent two hours. The climb is strenuous, but anyone in reasonable health and physically fit should be able to make it.

It is also possible to ascend other volcanoes such as Osorno, near Lake Llanquihue. The ascent, however, is quite a bit more difficult and involves climbing and gear like the use of ropes.

For the more advanced climber, a good source of information and guides is the Quellón, in southern Chiloé to Puerto Chacabuco, near Coyhaique, or from Puerto Montt through the wind-swept Golfo de Penas to Puerto Natales, (Navimag, Santiago: 696 3211; Puerto Montt: 253 318; Puerto Chacabuco: 351 1111; Punta Arenas: 222 593).

In many cases, small short-distance vessels are rather lacking in safety measures and have a tendency to over-crowd during the peak season, sometimes with tragic results. The calmest part of the day for navigation tends to be early morning and sunset. On these journeys, it is a good idea to take your own life jacket and water, and a sleeping bag to put over the bare mattresses or reclining chairs on the freighters. Other necessary

Federacion de Andinismo, Almirante Simpson 77, Santiago, whose members often organize expeditions for both amateurs and professionals.

Sea travel through the southern channels: There are a number of boats that visit the archipelagos of southern Chile. The most luxurious are the boats of Enceros Maritimos Skorpios (Santiago; tel: 231 1030; fax: 232 2269). Other regularly scheduled freighters make a rather spartan voyage between

<u>Left</u>, view from Villarica volcano. <u>Above</u>, inside Villarica volcano, one of several still-active cones that can be climbed.

items include woolen pants, socks and a heavy woolen sweater as wool will retain heat even when wet. Sneakers or canvas shoes will let the wearer swim in an emergency, while rubber boots are best for going ashore. Since stops are often made in pristine, uninhabited environments, the clear land tends to be marshy or at water's edge. On a walk through the damp, virgin forests, pants can pick up enough moisture – even on dry days – to soak them without waterproof protection. But it is worth the preparation to enjoy this untouched corner of the world. Here birds who have no fear (or knowledge) of man will often hop on to your shoes, to pull at shoe laces, mistaking them for hefty worms.

Camping in the sodden south: For those who wish to camp on the banks of the fiords, beware of the large differences between low and high tide in the area. Grass-covered islands in the rivers common at the inland extreme of fiords can gradually disappear at high tide, particularly closer to the full moon. More than one camper in the fiord Cahuelmo has had to keep warm in the thermal tubs carved into the hillside after he and all his gear were soaked at 2 a.m., when the full moon's tide came in. Short yellow wild flowers with bunches of tiny concave petals mark the highest tide level.

excursions into the surrounding areas of both insular and continental Chiloé.

Agentur in Santiago (Huerfanos 757, office 601; tel: 337 118) offer voyages disembarking from Puerto Montt that tour the area from there via the small hamlets of Chiloé, through the Guaiteca Archipelago, to return through inland fiords to Puyuhuapi and Puerto Cisne before continuing to the great San Rafael glacier.

An amazing wall of ice 200 meters (660 ft) high and several kilometers long breaks, crashing like thunder, into the Laguna San Rafael. The melting icebergs become top heavy and roll to expose the most incredible translucent shades of lavender powder blue

When camping in dense forest, it is worth bringing a *machete* to clear the site. Here ferns and the gigantic leaves of the *nalca* vie with the native bamboo *quila* and towering trees for ground space. Hanging flowering vines twist up thick trunks bearded by thousands of varieties of multicolored lichens. Where the dense forest canopy allows sufficient light, one finds the berry bushes of the native blue *calafates* and red *murtillas*. Along the many streams that crash down in raging waterfalls, one comes across boulders carpeted in green mosses.

Pehuén Expediciones in Castro (Thompson 229; tel: 65-63 2484, fax: 65-63 5254) offer

or emerald green like jewels floating on the water.

On one of their vessels, the *Río Cisne*, passengers can take along their automobiles and alternate between sea and land travel along the Carretera Austral. A van is provided, at extra charge, for those without their own vehicle. Passengers are lodged on board in berths with two to six bunk beds and shared baths or in settlements along the way. Meals are included on board or as picnics on land and the bar is always open. Reservations must be made well in advance.

For those who want to do more than view breath-taking scenery, the Odisea agency in

Santiago (Hotel Crown Plaza, Avda. Bernardo O'Higgins 108, local 120; tel: 396 775 or 330 883) arrange canoeing, rafting and fishing expeditions in Aisén. Four to eight pound trout are a rule rather than an exception. Some say the trout fishing is so abundant you have to keep the smaller fish from jumping into your boat with a stick – which may or may not be another fisherman's tale.

Hiking through the Torres Del Paine: Explorandes (see above for their address in Santiago, or in Punta Arenas, tel: 226 890) offers excursions in the most beautiful national park in the country, the Torres del Paine – created in 1959 and declared a Biosphere Reserve by UNESCO in 1978 – with transportation between Puerto Natales and the trails,

sky's fluffy white belly. Here the visitor will not only see some of the most incredible Chilean landscapes, but will experience everything that comes under the title "weather" from cloudless skies to thunderstorms, often in a lapse of only 24 hours.

Warm woollen clothing, plus a waterproof windbreaker and overalls are necessary. Boots should be sturdy and hopefully not new enough to cause blisters. A water bottle, sunglasses, sun block and a compass are also recommended.

While there are log cabin refuges along the trails, they are little more than a roof overhead and the distances between them are sometimes a good day's hike of as many as

tation between Puerto Natales and the trails, as well as guides, pack horses, camping gear and provisions. Their two-week excursion includes places of interest in the zone as well as a hiking tour of the park.

The park itself is centered around the amazing "towers", some of the youngest geological formations on the continent, and "horns" of rock sculpted by glaciers that point heavenward like so many daggers ripping at the

Left, starting a hike in the Torres del Paine National Park. **Above**, camping out in Aisén. **Right**, a ship makes its way through southern channels.

seven to eight hours. For those wishing to hike alone, a tent is a necessary precaution, as weather conditions can slow the hiker down and force him to camp between refuges or rivers can swell and make it necessary to postpone a crossing. Provisions for the extent of the hike must be back-packed, as must a camp stove with fuel. And please pack out your own garbage, the only sign along some of the trails that one is not the first explorer to set foot in this unblemished, primeval territory.

● *For more information on the Torres del Paine National Park, see the Magallanes chapter, page 282.*

Chileans marked the changeover of government from 16 years of military dictatorship to democracy in March 1990, with a huge celebration in Santiago's National Stadium. The night held a strange mix of emotions from relief to excitement and mourning.

In the middle of the ceremony, as all the different sections of Chilean culture performed dances and routines in the center of the stadium, two men on horseback suddenly appeared at one end of the field, galloped their steeds through the colorful pageant and skidded to a halt, the horses flinging their backlegs forward almost to a sitting position. A stunned crowd watched the riders wheel their mounts about and, holding large Chilean flags aloft, gallop back out the stadium gates. The spectacle prompted wild applause, reflecting the pride and warmth Chileans feel for their traditional cowboy or horseman, the *huaso*, and his stocky mount.

The Chilean 'cowboy': The term *huaso* is used to describe many countrymen in South America. It is believed to come from the Indian word for 'shoulder' or 'haunch'. The Mapuches had never seen horses before the Spanish conquests, and believed that the rider was attached to the horse between shoulder and haunch. (Soon, however, the Chilean Indians had learned how to ride bareback and became much finer horsemen than the Spaniards).

Today *huasos* are known as strong, proud and honest men of the country, who are excellent horsemen. The *huaso*'s partner, the stocky Chilean horse, carries the same traits. Known as the *corralero*, the Chilean horse is the inseparable companion of the *huaso*. The working pair still dominates in the movement of stock in the Chilean countryside. It is common to see a *huaso* and his son ambling along behind a mob of cattle, wearing patterned ponchos and broad rimmed hats atop their small thick-set horses.

The pair also constitute one of Chile's national sports — the Rodeo. Most rodeos are held between September and May. The most famous is the Chilean Championship, held at the end of March in Rancagua. (For further information on dates and places call the Rodeo Federation in Santiago: Tel: 384 639). Unlike Australian and American rodeos, there is no roping or riding of wild beasts, although the animal still gets knocked about somewhat.

In a semi-circular corral, a pair of riders and their mounts attempt to chase and manoeuvre a beast to a padded section of wall. Here it must be stopped and held by direct

horse-to-beast body contact. The curved nature of the corral means the horse must learn to gallop sideways, an extremely difficult task. Points are scored only when the beast is stopped on the padding. The two *huasos* must work in close fast coordination, one chasing the beast, the other hemming it close to the wall.

The exercise invariably produces spectacular shows of horsemanship, with horses spinning about on their back legs, skidding and changing direction, rearing and galloping as they track the beast about the ring.

A strict code of behaviour and dress: The riders earn good points (*puntos buenos*) or

Left, *huaso* shows off his riding spurs. **Right**, a quick game between rides.

bad points (*puntos malos*) depending on where they hit the beast, the brutality used (the rougher, the more bad points) and their appearance.

The tally for appearance begins with the hat — a broad and flat rimmed *sombrero* made either of tightly woven straw (in summer) or felt (in winter). Such is the importance of the flat rim that the *huaso* can have his hat ironed beside the ring before competing. The *huaso* also wears a starched white buttoned up shirt under a brown short jacket. Thrown over one shoulder is the brightly-colored Poncho de Huaso. These special ponchos are often striped, and are usually passed down through the generations if they

of progeny. These horses were used mainly in war, and by elite servicemen for equestrian exercises. Such was the value of this small resource that at times it was said to be worth more than the life of a human.

When peace finally becalmed Chile after the wars of Independence, the horse gradually took on a more domestic role. By this stage Spanish settlers and Indian women had intermarried to produce the fine-featured, dark skinned characteristics typical of the *huaso*. The man and his horse now began competing in the first rodeos, designed as a sport that mimicked military manouevres done in the field, and set the agenda to become national symbols. Early Chilean

survive the inevitable spills in the rodeo. Black and brown pinstriped trousers are worn almost with the air of an English banker, but the calves are sheathed in finely platted black leather leggings decorated with long leather tassles. The boots are cuban-heeled and sport large spoked spurs, ensuring a melodic jangle when he walks.

Beneath the riding huaso is a horse small in stature but immensely powerful. The first Spanish settlers brought some fine horses from Europe and by 1545 had established something of a breeding program, with 50 breeding mares on a stud ranch in Santiago. Within the century there was an abundance

landowner Gomez de Vidauvre said approvingly of the Chilean horse: "he has a small skull, strong thick neck, is agile with great resistance, is docile and obedient and is very apt for equestrian sports."

Stiff test of skill: The famous agility is put to the test before the actual rodeo begins. The competitors as individuals (rather than pairs) line up before the judges.

In turn they perform a series of exercises. First the competitors walk on a loose rein to show the placid nature of the animal. Any beast that breaks into a trot loses points. This calm is then broken by an instruction to gallop from a standing position to the other side of the corral, skid to a halt by thrusting the back legs forward and under, spinning about on those same back legs, and galloping back to the other side when the about face is executed again.

This pattern can continue for three or four passes, until the rider is sure the power, speed and responsiveness of his mount has been proved. The hyped-up horse is then asked to stand perfectly still without even shifting a hoof, while the rider dismounts and walks several paces away. The rider must stand and wait, then return to his horse and mount again. While all this is going on, the horse must remain perfectly motionless or it loses points.

The horses can then rest and feed, but the winning *huaso* has no such relaxation ahead; he is in for a long night of dancing and feasting. Somewhere beside the rodeo ring is usually an open hall with a bar at one end, a band on stage at the other, and long wooden tables in between. A hearty meal of beef and beans is knocked back with a little red, and then out come the handkerchiefs for the *cueca*, Chile's national dance. The *cueca* is an intergral part of the rodeo and a *huaso* is not roundly accomplished if his boots don't do a coordinated stomp.

To begin the *cueca* (pronounced like 'quaker'), the man first advances towards his partner in a courting fashion. She, keeping

This last exercise always silences the crowd: breaths are held as the horses twitch with impatience, then a huge collective sigh expires with each successful manoeuvre.

At the end of the rodeo, when a final pair of *huasos* have outlasted the others, the prize giving takes place. These days kitchen appliances and other household goodies are given out as trophies, but in keeping with tradition a colorful new poncho is still usually given to the winner of the first exercise routines.

her distance, sets up the pattern of pursuer and pursued. Folklore says the dance is inspired by a rooster stalking a hen. As the courting continues, both hold handerchiefs aloft and flick them about as they step in a smooth, shuffling manner.

The dance must be accompanied by festive music and a crowd of clapping onlookers, spurring the man on in his hot pursuit. The routine produces such a high-spirited and infectious response that Chileans believe that even the devil himself can't help but uncrumple his scarf and take eye for a young señorita.

Left, outmanouevering a beast during the rodeo. **Above**, a wild chase.

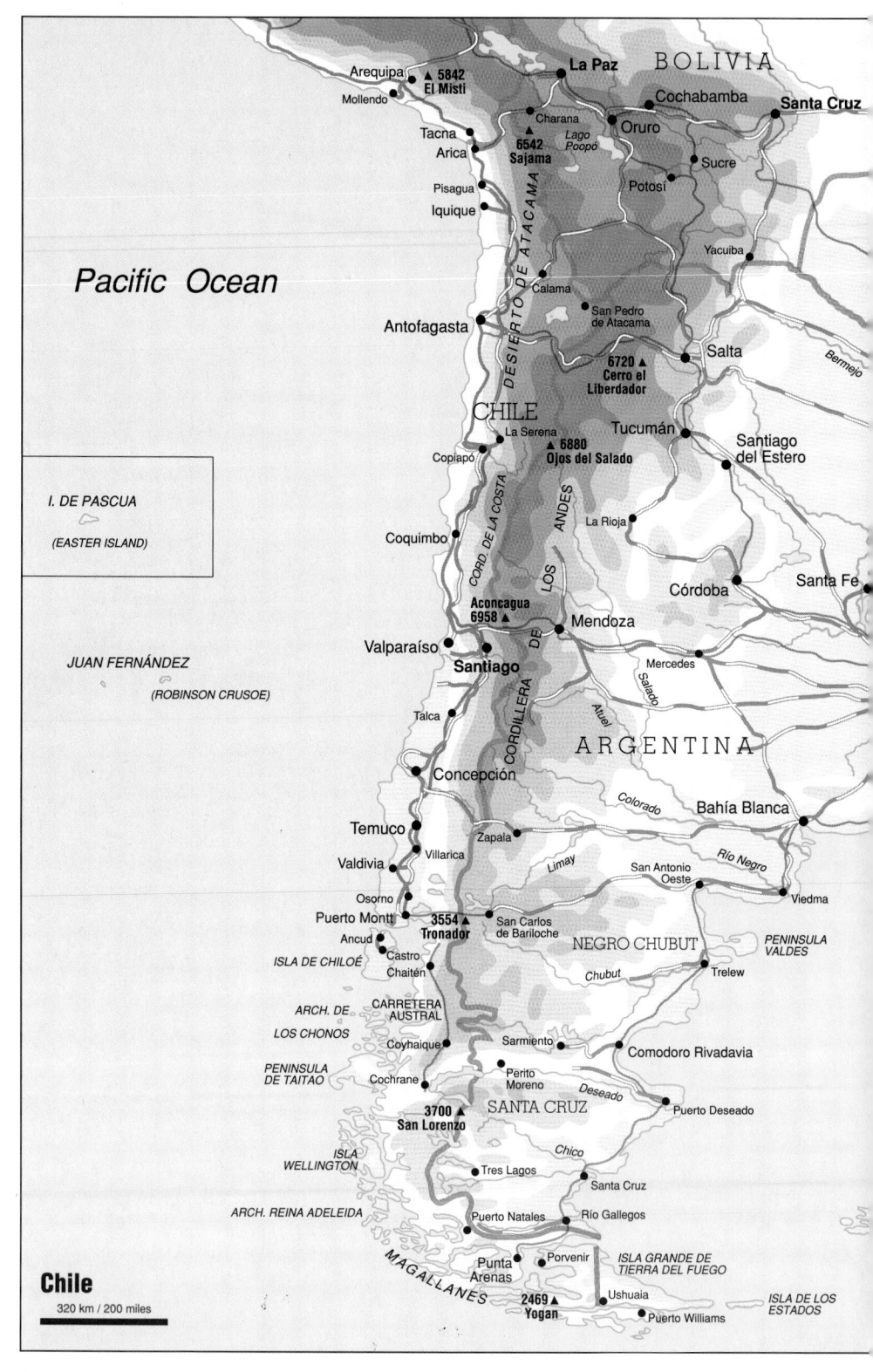

Pacific Ocean

BOLIVIA

Arequipa
▲ 5842
El Misti
Mollendo
La Paz
Cochabamba
Santa Cruz
Charana
Oruro
Lago Poopó
▲ 6542
Sajama
Cochabamba
Tacna
Arica
Potosí
Sucre
Pisagua
Iquique
Yacuiba

DESIERTO DE ATACAMA

Calama
San Pedro de Atacama
Antofagasta
6720 ▲
Cerro el
Liberdador
Salta
Bermejo

CHILE
La Serena
Tucumán
Santiago
del Estero
Copiapó
▲ 6880
Ojos del Salado

CORD. DE LA COSTA

La Rioja

Coquimbo
Córdoba
Santa Fe

ANDES

LOS

DE

Aconcagua
6958 ▲
Mendoza
Valparaíso
Santiago
Mercedes
Salado

CORDILLERA

Atuel

Talca
ARGENTINA
Concepción
Colorado
Bahía Blanca

Temuco
Zapala
Valdivia
Villarica
Limay
San Antonio
Oeste
Río Negro
Viedma
Osorno
Puerto Montt
3554 ▲
Tronador
San Carlos
de Bariloche
NEGRO
CHUBUT
PENINSULA
VALDES
Ancud
ISLA DE CHILOÉ
Castro
Chaitén
Chubut
Trelew

CARRETERA
AUSTRAL

ARCH. DE
LOS CHONOS
Coyhaique
Sarmiento
Comodoro Rivadavia
PENINSULA
DE TAITAO
Cochrane
Perito
Moreno
Deseado
Puerto Deseado
3700 ▲
San Lorenzo
SANTA CRUZ
ISLA
WELLINGTON
Chico
Tres Lagos
Santa Cruz
ARCH. REINA ADELEIDA
Puerto Natales
Río Gallegos

MAGALLANES
Punta
Arenas
Porvenir
ISLA GRANDE DE
TIERRA DEL FUEGO
2469 ▲
Yogan
Ushuaia
ISLA DE LOS
ESTADOS
Puerto Williams

I. DE PASCUA

(EASTER ISLAND)

JUAN FERNÁNDEZ

(ROBINSON CRUSOE)

Chile

320 km / 200 miles

Despite its bizarre topography, Chile is one of the easiest countries in South America to travel around. Domestic flights connect the country's major cities; modern passenger buses run to almost every minor town (and depart punctually every time); regular train services operate in many areas; and even in the remote far south, passenger boats can make the more unusual connections.

Almost all travellers flying into Chile arrive in the bustling capital of Santiago. At the country's mid-way point, Santiago is the logical base for exploring – many visitors leave their luggage in one of the capital's hotels and make excursions into the far-flung provinces.

Only three hours drive away is the capital's colorful port city, Valparaíso, stretching across a mountain-ringed bay, while the neighbouring Viña del Mar is Chile's most popular beach resort. Irregular flights from Santiago also reach the Juan Fernández Islands, famous as the temporary home of the Scottish sailor upon whom 'Robinson Crusoe' was based.

The countryside north of Santiago becomes progressively drier as it stretches towards the hauntingly beautiful Atacama desert, bordering on Bolivia and Peru. Many travellers fly directly to Calama, the support town for the spectacular Chuquicamata copper mine, then head for the oasis village of San Pedro de Atacama. Around here are ancient Indian ruins, thermal baths, salt flats and dramatic fields of geysers. The city of Iquique boasts relics of its days as a mining capital, while nitrate ghost towns are scattered in its hinterland.

The road south of Santiago runs through the lush Central Valley where most of Chile's many vineyards are found. Then, beyond the Bío Bío River, lies Chile's most famous attraction, the Lake District. A spectacular region of rivers, volcanoes, forests and (naturally) lakes, it deserves a place on every itinerary. Tens of thousands of visitors make the journey here every year to loll at resort towns like Pucón and explore the many winding roads to remote mountain villages.

The fishing port of Puerto Montt marks the end of the Lake District. Beyond this point, the landscape becomes wilder and travel more unpredictable although many opt for a luxurious cruise through the southern islands. Aisén is the vast province of woods and glaciers only recently opened up by a new highway, the Carretera Austral. Then come the vast sheep plains of Magallanes, with as their backdrop the Paine National Park – considered to be the most dramatic mountain region in South America and home to Chile's most awe-inspiring glaciers. Finally, at the southernmost tip of the country, is the windswept island of Tierra del Fuego.

And most travellers at least consider including a visit to the legendary Easter Island on their itineraries. Almost lost in the vast Pacific, this mysterious speck of land covered with ancient statues has provoked archaeological debate for centuries and still retains its unique Polynesian atmosphere.

Preceding pages, Santiago from the Cerro San Cristóbal.

SANTIAGO

When Chilean children draw or paint, in the background there is almost always a stylized line of snow-capped mountains. In Santiago, it is easy to see why. Rising immediately alongside the city, the Andes are a constant backdrop and companion, engraving themselves on the minds and subconscious of Santiaguinos from birth. For the visitor, they not only impress with their beauty (above all when bathed in rose-coloured light for some 20 minutes each evening at sunset), but also serve a very practical purpose: it is hard to lose your bearings in Santiago.

So long, that is, that the smog does not muddy your vision. Air pollution is a growing problem in the city, worsened by its almost windless location between the Andes and nearby hills, and making one wish fervently that the Spanish *conquistador* Pedro de Valdivia had been forewarned about the internal combustion engine before siting Santiago here in 1541. But this is the only real drawback to a gently attractive city, unpretentious but hospitable, whose people, though less effusive than others in Latin America, are friendly and always ready to welcome foreigners, and which is endowed with an ideal Mediterranean, or Californian, climate.

Santiago is also one of the most manageable capitals in Latin America for the first-time visitor. It is a big city, but has an almost provincial atmosphere. Standing in the compact few blocks and narrow streets of its center you'd never realize you were at the heart of a conurbation of more than 4 million people. The city's sprawling extension and relative lack of high buildings all give it a feeling of spaciousness, despite the mountains; only in the drab and fume-ridden center is there much of the sense of pressure and density characteristic of most cities of this size. The rest is residential suburbs: leafy avenues and sophisticated shopping malls in the plush

Left, hanging out in Parque Forestal.

barrio alto , and vast swathes of well tended middle-class neighborhoods and poor *poblaciones* – labyrinthine networks of tiny adobe and wooden dwellings which seldom quite merit the term shanty-towns, and which hit the headlines in the 1980s as the cutting edge of the protest movement against General Pinochet's military regime.

Economic extremes: Chile's contrasts between sophistication and underdevelopment are readily to be seen in Santiago. Banks, telecommunications and other manifestations of service technology are the most up-to-date in Latin America; but everywhere the poor scratch a living by minding cars or selling sticking plasters or grubby candies. The two-line metro is slick and clean – light years from the rickety and smog-belching buses clogging the streets above. In the *barrio alto* the brash children of the wealthy model their lifestyles on California and Miami, and in the drab but bustling center, aggressive yuppies, the legacy of General Pinochet's extreme free-market economic

policies, weave their way past lines of impoverished street pedlars hawking Taiwanese trinkets.

Most visitors are struck by the European feel of Santiago, and middle and upper-class residents look to Europe for their cultural models; recent economic and technological advances have increased their sense of international links. Other Latin Americans, indeed, can be heard to complain about this euro-centrism, and it can be distressing to hear just how readily many local descendents of European immigrants will talk of their superiority to the rest of the continent and deny that they live in what is still a largely *mestizo* nation. At the same time, centuries of geographical isolation have left them with a lingering quizzicality, even innocence, in the presence of foreigners, and Santiaginos are always keen to know just what you think of their country.

Getting around the city is easy. A brief glance at a map – there's an excellent A to Z in the back of the Santiago phone book, apart from those you can

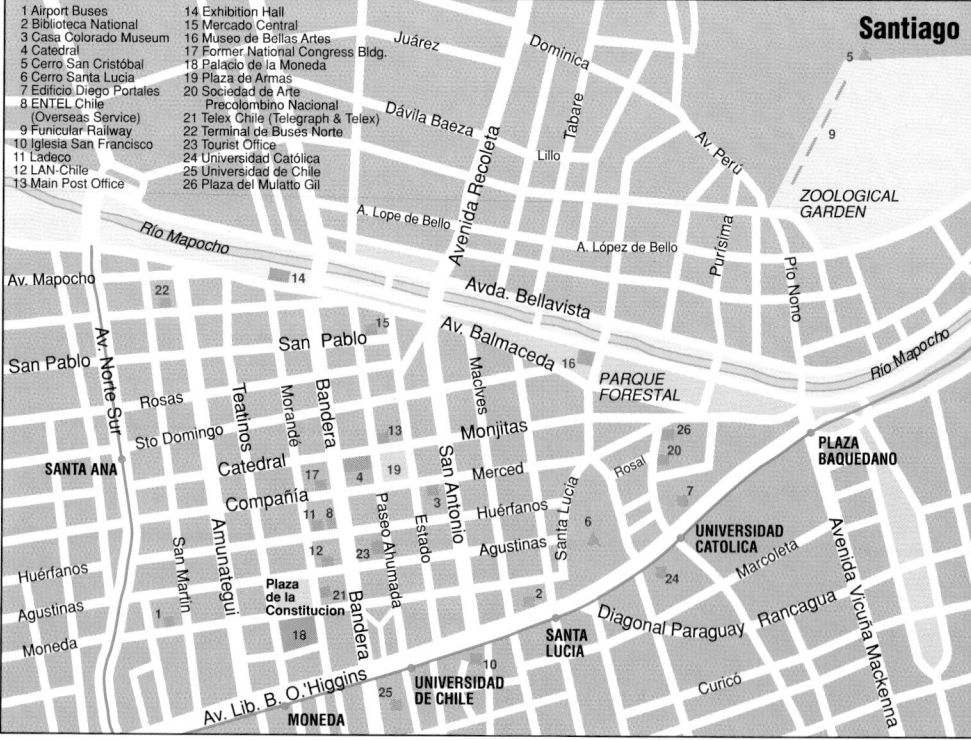

1 Airport Buses
2 Biblioteca National
3 Casa Colorado Museum
4 Catedral
5 Cerro San Cristóbal
6 Cerro Santa Lucia
7 Edificio Diego Portales
8 ENTEL Chile
   (Overseas Service)
9 Funicular Railway
10 Iglesia San Francisco
11 Ladeco
12 LAN-Chile
13 Main Post Office
14 Exhibition Hall
15 Mercado Central
16 Museo de Bellas Artes
17 Former National Congress Bldg.
18 Palacio de la Moneda
19 Plaza de Armas
20 Sociedad de Arte
   Precolombino Nacional
21 Telex Chile (Telegraph & Telex)
22 Terminal de Buses Norte
23 Tourist Office
24 Universidad Católica
25 Universidad de Chile
26 Plaza del Mulatto Gil

Santiago

pick up at bookshops and kiosks – will reveal just how straightforward the city is. You're almost bound to enter the city along the **Alameda Libertador Bernardo O'Higgins**. This broad avenue, named after the Chilean-Irish independence hero and father of the republic, has been the city's main thoroughfare since a fork of the Mapocho River was filled in before independence to create it. It is known universally simply as "the Alameda" (a word of Arab origin meaning an avenue with trees and spaces for recreation).

The first main point of reference is the imposing wrought-iron of the **Estación Central**, the city's only remaining functioning railway station. Surrounded by the hue-and-cry of one of the city's most popular and active commercial sectors, the station is Santiago's 20th-century gateway to and from the south, and worth a look.

Heart of Santiago: The ugly concrete telecommunications tower run by the company Entel announces the beginning of the **city-center** proper. A block

afterwards, the Alameda broadens, and the low form of the presidential palace, **La Moneda**, rises to the left. La Moneda, so called because it was originally designed by the Italian architect Joaquin Toesca as the country's mint, was built between 1788 and 1805. Between 1846 and 1958, Chile's presidents lived there, sharing the premises with the mint until 1929. Squat by comparison with the high ministerial buildings around it (Toesca designed it low to resist earthquakes), and covered by a nondescript facade of grey-beige concrete, many consider La Moneda one of the finest examples of colonial public buildings in the sub-continent.

But its tragic international fame came with the military coup lead by General Pinochet on 11 September 1973, when much of its interior was destroyed by rocketing from Air Force Hawker Hunters and its image, smoke and flame belching from its northern side, leapt onto the world's front pages and TV screens. It was here that the deposed president, the socialist Dr Salvador

Old and new in the Plaza de Armas.

Allende, committed suicide after the onslaught rather than give up his mandate. The newly restored palace was reinaugurated in 1981 as the seat of government.

In the **Plaza de la Libertad**, in front of the palace, is a statue of Arturo Alessandri, the liberal populist who dominated Chilean politics in the first half of this century. Ironically, he was also deposed by a military coup on an 11 September; but, this coup, in 1924, was left-wing and shortlived, and he returned to power a few months later.

Across the Alameda is the **Plaza Bernardo O'Higgins**, more generally known as the Plaza Bulnes (after the 19th-century General and President, Manuel Bulnes, whose statue is in the centre of the Alameda). This square is dominated by the **Altar de la Patria**, a structure erected by General Pinochet to house a marble urn containing the remains of O'Higgins. The Altar is topped by an equestrian statue of the Liberator and a permanently lit "flame of liberty", meant by Pinochet to celebrate national values and his coup. Unfortunately, the monument blocks an impressive view from the palace down the Avenida Bulnes, now converted into an attractive pedestrian walkway. In the centre of the Alameda to the west is another statue, this time of O'Higgins's partner in the Chilean campaign and later liberator of Peru, José de San Martín.

The Plaza O'Higgins is flanked to the east by the Defense Ministry and Headquarters of the Carabinero police. From the latter, every other day at 10 a.m., a green-uniformed and jackbooted detail of the Carabinero palace guard, a special unit whose members are selected for their height, marches to La Moneda in an impressive, Prussian-like, changing-of-the guard ceremony.

Home of tradition: Continuing along the Alameda, past the **Banco de Estado** on the left (when finished in 1945, supposedly the largest building in Latin America), is the **Club de la Unión,** Latin America's oldest and plushest gentleman's club, membership of which

Left, the modern business center. **Below**, the busy pedestrian mall of **Huérfanos**.

is still a much-prized goal for Chile's male conservative elite. The building, inaugurated in 1925, is lavishly decorated inside in Louis XIV and XV, gothic and other European styles. All the Club's tableware was specially imported all the way from France, Spain and England, and it has one of the best collections of Chilean art in the country. Also, to this day the building still bears the marks on its facade of gunfire during demonstrations which in 1931 overthrew the authoritarian regime of General Carlos Ibañez.

Opposite, on the southern side of the Alameda is the yellow-washed central campus building of the **University of Chile**. The building, begun in 1863, was designed by Lucien Henault, one of the contracted French architects who founded the neo-classical style which dominated Chilean public architecture of the time and hence much of the profile of Santiago's city centre. On the pavement outside is a statue of the University's founder, the Venezuelan exile, Andrés Bello, one of the continent's

great intellectual figures of the 19th century.

Back on the north side of the Alameda, beyond Calle Bandera, is the **Paseo Ahumada**, a busy, fountain-bedecked pedestrian walkway which bisects the city-centre from north to south. This is the natural entry to the center, to which we'll return shortly. Meanwhile, on the other side of the Alameda again, is one of Santiago's most emblematic landmarks: the red-washed colonial church of **San Francisco**. Pedro de Valdivia built the first chapel here, at the southernmost edge of his settlement, in thanks to the Virgin Mary for protection during the trek into Chile. A later church was destroyed in the 1593 earthquake, and the present building was finished in 1618, apart from the distinctive tower, which was added in 1860. Inside, on the altar, is the small and much venerated Italian-made image of the "Virgen del Socorro" which Valdivia himself brought with him firmly attached to his saddle. This Virgin was declared the Patron of Santiago by the *conquistado-*

Below, a summer dip in the German fountain. Right, "immortal phrases" for sale.

res after she supposedly saved them during the first major Indian attack in the Mapocho valley by appearing and throwing dirt into the attacker's eyes. Note the original Mudejar-influenced wooden roof inside the church, and in the museum in the adjacent Franciscan monastery, the fine collection of Chilean and Peruvian colonial art. A facsimile is also to be seen in the museum of the Nobel Prize medal given to the Chilean poet Gabriela Mistral (who died a lay member of the Franciscan order).

Behind the square outside the Church is the quaint **Barrio Londres–Paris**, two short cobbled streets named after these European capitals, whose houses, designed as a whole by a group of architects in the 1920s, jumble together imitations of styles ranging from neo-classical to moorish and gothic.

Next of note is the **Biblioteca Nacional**, occupying the main part of a block on the northern side of the Alameda. The imposing building, in late 19th-century French style, opened in 1924 and contains one of Latin America's largest national libraries and archives. Frequent free concerts are also held here.

Following the Biblioteca is one of Santiago's most curious and historically significant sites, the **Cerro Santa Lucia**. It was here, on what was then a rocky outcrop known by the Indians as Huelén (Pain), that Pedro de Valdivia and his 150 men first encamped, and Valdivia decided to found the city. He also renamed the hill after the saint of the date on which he reached it, 14 December 1540. In 1872, the great historian and intendente of Santiago, Benjamín Vicuña Mackenna, began to transform the hill into the baroque maze of pathways, gardens, fountains and squares which it now is (Vicuña Mackenna is commemorated by a statue in the square named after him just west of the Cerro itself).

Don't be startled by the cannon which is fired from the Cerro to mark every noon, ringing round the city-centre. Together with the **Parque Forestal** by the Mapocho, the Cerro is one of the city's best-loved places for lovers and strollers. If the climb intimidates you, a lift has recently been installed on the west side, on Calle Santa Lucia.

At the foot of the Cerro, on the Alameda, is a fine mural in homage to Gabriela Mistral, representing the poet herself and the main themes of her work. A few yards further on, a smooth, nine-ton rock is set in the skirt of the hill, engraved with an extract of a letter sent by Pedro de Valdivia to Emperor Charles V in 1545 extolling Chile's climatic virtues.

The Cerro marks the end of the city-centre as such, and the beginning of the last stretch of the Alameda. At this point – particularly if you are interested in shopping for handicrafts – it is worth taking a detour down Avenida Portugal, just past the Catholic University, on the southern side of the Alameda. Some six blocks down, at Portugal 351, is the beautifully restored cloister of the **Sagrado Corazón de Jesús school** (built in the 1850s, but in colonial style). As well as being a delight in itself, this is the headquarters of Cema-Chile, a **Elegant dining.**

128

charitable organization run by the wife of the army commander-in-chief, which has a wide range of handicrafts on sale from all over Chile.

Back on the northern side of the Alameda is the vast and, to many, hideous **Diego Portales building**, built in record speed and constructivist style in 1972. It was originally baptized after Gabriela Mistral, but General Pinochet's government made it the headquarters of the military junta. Now it is the Defense Ministry. Across the road, past a group of tower apartment blocks, is the Carabineros' Church, the small neo-gothic **Iglesia de San Francisco de Borjo**, and in front of it a monument to members of the force that were killed in the line of duty. Immediately afterwards comes the modern red bulk of the Crowne Plaza Holiday Inn hotel, which is opposite one of the city's best art cinemas, the Normandie.

Yards further on, the Alameda ends at the primary junction with Avenida Vicuña Mackenna and the Plaza Italia, centered on the equestrian statue of General Manuel Baquedano, commander of the Chilean army during the 19th-century War of the Pacific with Peru and Bolivia. This marks the end of central Santiago and the beginning of Providencia and the *barrio alto*. It is therefore a good point to retrace our steps and return to the Paseo Ahumada (by metro, three stops to Universided de Chile).

Shopping crowds: If the Alameda is the center's main thoroughfare for motor traffic, Ahumada is for pedestrians. Everyone – shoppers, businessmen and street vendors – seems to converge there. Business gossip is exchanged in cafes like the Haiti, where customers stand and mini-skirted young women serve them *expresos* and *cortados* (black and white coffee) with glasses of mineral water. Crowds press past the Paseo's many and varied shops, banks, department stores and well-stocked newspaper kiosks.

To the left of Ahumada is the *barrio civico,* a few blocks built in the 1930s around La Moneda in rigorously utili-

Outdoor cafe at the Plaza de Mulatto Gil.

tarian style and densely polluted by the throng of horn-hooting buses crawling along Calle Bandera, beside the Club de la Unión. Included are the **Intendencia** (corner of Moneda and Morandé), **Stock Exchange** (Calle La Bolsa, just behind the Club de la Unión), **Banco de Estado**, **Central Bank** and most ministries. Behind La Moneda is the **Plaza de la Constitución**, remodelled by General Pinochet (who built underneath it a complex network of meeting rooms, offices, emergency war – room and television studio for making broadcasts to the nation, all known popularly as *"el bunker"* – you can see entrances on three sides of the square). On the west side of the Plaza is the luxury **Hotel Carrera**, from whose upper storeys the film later shown around the world of the bombing of the La Moneda during the 1973 coup was taken.

Uptown from Ahumada, three blocks along Calle Agustinas, and past the 17th century **Church of San Agustín** (site of an interesting wooden crucifix above the altar carved in Peru in 1613), is the **Municipal Theatre**. Designed and restored by French architects – its original plans were approved by Charles Garnier, the architect of the Paris Opera – the Theatre opened in 1857. Housing the city's Symphony Orchestra and Ballet and Opera Companies, all of them considered amongst the finest in the continent, the Theatre has played host to artists from Sarah Bernhardt to Placido Domingo, who appeared there in March 1990. Opposite the Theatre is perhaps the finest example in the city of the influence of late 19th-century French style on Chile's own architects: a house built by the millionaire wine-producing family of French origin, the Subercaseaux, and now occupied by the Air Force officers' club and a bank.

Ahumada ends in the **Plaza de Armas**, the city's historic center. Originally traced out by Pedro de Valdivia in 1541, it takes its name from the weapons held in the fort built in the square to shelter the first settlers at night. Then, the Plaza was used for all public activities from troop parades and religious

Santiago's town hall fronted by a statue of Pedro de Valdivia.

processions to hangings. In the 1830s the present gardens were built, stocked with native trees and centered on an enigmatic white marble monument celebrating the liberation of America – though local people call it "the lizard statue", after the shape of its fountain vents. The origins of this somewhat incongruous work, which was sculpted by a Genoese artist who never visited Latin America and hence freely mixes European mythology and supposed Latin American figures, are obscure: it was not commissioned by Chile, but was apparently abandoned in the port of Valparaíso by agents of either the Ecuadorian or Peruvian governments, one of which ordered it, then lost interest when it arrived.

Street life: The Plaza is always a hive of activity. Shoe-shiners, instant portrait painters, blind singers and pentecostal preachers ply their wares. Sweet and peanut vendors sell from their traditional *barquitos*, or "little boats", mounted on bicycle wheels, and photographers attract your custom with ancient, brightly decorated tripod cameras. On Sunday mornings and Thursday afternoons, police and other bands play on the band-stand on the southern side of the garden.

The **Cathedral**, on the west side of the Plaza, is the fifth on the site. Its predecessors were destroyed by earthquakes in 1552, 1647 and 1730 – while the first was burned down in an Indian attack shortly after Pedro de Valdivia built it. Work on the present building began in 1747, but the final design was by Joaquin Toesca, who was brought from Italy for this task, moving on later to La Moneda – though the twin towers were not added until 1899 by another Italian, Ignacio Cremonesi. The Cathedral's internal decoration bears the somewhat heavy imprint of the Bavarian Jesuits who created much of it, although some of their work, and important local handicraft adornments, were destroyed by clumsy restoration carried out by Cremonesi. Those buried in the Cathedral include the four Carrera brothers, partners and rivals with O'Higgins in

the country's liberation from Spain, and Diego Portales, considered by many as the founder of Chile's 19th-century conservative state. Beside the Catheral, and reached through a door on its left side, is its **Museum of Sacred Art**, also worth a visit.

After the Conquest, the land along the northern face of the Plaza was owned by Pedro de Valdivia, who lived in a house on the site now occupied by the pink-toned **Correo Central** (Central Post Office). In 1541, however (and once again on 11 September, a date which appears to have an almost cabalistic significance for Chile), the house was burned down in an Indian attack; later Valdivia sold the land to the Royal Treasury in order to finance further expeditions south. Two centuries later, the Correo site saw the city's first, and reputedly magnificent, theatre, which was then turned over to the post office. The first stamps, printed in England, were sold here in 1857 (a plaque with a facsimile can be seen on the outer wall on Calle Puente) and the present building was finished in 1902.

Next door is the **Palacio de la Real Audiencia**, now the **National Historical Museum**, inaugurated in 1808 to house the seasons at which the Spanish crown's representatives heard local reports and dispense justice. This purpose was shortlived, however, and two years later, the building was used for the swearing-in of the first revolutionary government junta. The first Congress met here and the palace was the seat of government until President Bulnes moved to La Moneda in 1846. The National Historical Museum, which contains some 12,000 pieces from pre-history until the 1930s, moved there in 1980 and, just like most Chilean museums, is well worth a visit.

The last building along the Plaza's northern edge is the **Town Hall** (Municipalidad). Formerly the Palacio Consistorial, it was designed by Toesca for the colonial *cabildo* and opened in 1790. The facade was replaced last century by the present neo-classical design, and restored again after damage in the 1985 earthquake. High on the facade,

and in the wrought-ironwork above the entrance, can be seen the red lion coat of arms granted the city by the Spanish Crown after the first *cabildo* met. In front is a bronze equestrian statue of Pedro de Valdivia donated by Chile's Spanish community in 1986 and showing the conqueror holding the act of foundation of Santiago.

Two other museums skirt the Plaza de Armas, and should be visited. On Calle Merced, at the south-east corner of the square, is the striking red-washed **Casa Colorada**. Built in 1769, this is the best preserved colonial house in the city. It was the residence of the President of the first revolutionary junta, Mateo de Toro y Zambrano, and, for a time, of Lord Thomas Cochrane, the maverick Scottish admiral hired by O'Higgins to command naval operations against Spain. Now it is the **Museo de Santiago**, dedicated to the history of the capital. Two blocks westwards is the excellent **Pre-Columbian Museum**, housed in what used to be the colonial Customs House (Bandera 361 – access through an ar-

Santiago's efficient Metro.

132

cade built through the building on the corner). Watch out for specially mounted exhibitions here, as well as the permanent collection.

Immediately opposite the Pre-Columbian Museum are the Law Courts, and across Calle Compañía the neoclassical grandeur of what was the pre-1973 Congress Building (now the Foreign Ministry). Previously, this was the site of the headquarters of the Jesuits (hence the name of the street, after the Compañía de Jesus), until they were expelled from the country in 1766, and later of a church which in 1863 burned down, at the cost of 2000 lives. This disaster, one of the worst of its kind in the continent, lead to the formation of the city's first fire bridge, whose headquarters is nearby at Calle Puente 978; the bell in its fine tower still tolls every time a fireman, who are all voluntary in Chile, is killed. Also close by is the curious **Palacio La Alhambra** (Compañía 1340), begun in the 1860s and later transformed into a miniature copy of the famous Moorish palace of the same name in Granada, Spain – complete with mock-Arab furniture made to order in Paris.

Markets and parks: Back in the Plaza de Armas, and if you're feeling hungry and like sea-food, you can do no better than walk north along Calle Puente (the continuation of the Paseo Ahumada) to the **Mercado Central**. This, together with **La Feria**, on the other side of the Mapocho, is the city's central market. Bustling with the character of all such markets around the world, this elegant structure (look at it inside as well as out) was designed in Chile, but built in England; it was inaugurated in 1872 by Vicuña Mackenna as the site of a National Exhibition to mark the thrusting and confident economy of the time. It is full of cheap eating places, and above all *marisquerías* serving cheap and abundant portions of Chile's remarkable sea-food, considered by many the best in the world. (Be warned, however, that Chile's coast is extremely polluted in places and illness from these delicacies cannot be discounted.)

Here too is the fine, white-fronted shell of what used to be Santiago's second railway station, the **Estación Mapocho**. Opened in 1912, and designed by another of Chile's leading French architects, Emile Jecquier, this was the terminus for trains from the coast, until the line was discontinued in the mid-1980s. Now the building is used as an exhibition and sports centre. Its ornate facade looks across the Plaza Capitán Prat, with its green-tinged monument to the Navy and its principal hero, down the long vista of the **Parque Forestal**.

The Parque, which is generally referred to by Chileans as their Bois de Boulogne, was laid out by the French landscaper Georges Dubois at the turn of the century. The idea was to make use of the wasteland left over after the canalization of the Mapocho in its now characteristic stone course (whose walls, incidentally, make an irrestible canvas for political slogan-writers and muralists). Looking at the generally thin flow of the Mapocho (a name which in Mapuche means, "river which loses it-

The huge, wrought-iron central market.

self in the land", in reference to its partially subterranean course west of Santiago), it is hard to believe that it is capable of swelling suddenly with torrents of melting snow or rain from the Andes and plunging much of the city under water. Even now it still floods, a problem which in the past caused several disasters and was dealt with first by wide stone embankments, or *tajamares* (built by Toesca), then the present channel. Work to strengthen the course is still being carried out further downstream.

Planted with varieties of native and imported trees, the Parque contains several small squares and monuments to figures such as Columbus, Bach, the god Pan and the seminal Nicaraguan modernist poet, Rubén Dario (opposite Merced 230), who wrote his most important work, "Azul", while exiled in Chile in the 1890s. A block from the Mercado Central, in a square off Calle Esmeralda to the right, is another fine colonial house, the **Posada del Corregidor**, one-time bar and centre of

Santiago's bohemia and now a museum; the house never in fact belonged to a Corregidor, despite the whim of a later owner who placed the coat of arms of one of the city's best-known such officials, Luis Manuel de Zañartu, on the wall.

Halfway along the Parque, close to the northern tip of the Cerro Santa Lucia, is the **Museo de Bellas Artes**, the country's principal art gallery – designed by Jéquier as an approximate copy of the Petit Palais in Paris, and containing both permanent displays of contemporary and past Chilean art and visiting exhibitions. Further along still is the extraordinary **Palacio Bruna**, another turn-of-the-century mansion designed in part by one of Chile's leading poets, Pedro Prado, who studied architecture without ever graduating, and which is now the US Consulate.

A little before reaching the Palacio, a few steps backtracking along Calle Merced leads to Calle José Victorino Lastárria and the pleasant bookshop, gallery and cafe of the **Plaza Mulato**

Left, masks for sale. **Below**, testing the pressure.

Gil. Nearby just behind the Edificio Diego Portales, is the **Bíografo** art cinema and cafe-restaurant, a favourite haunt of artists and leftwing politicians. The Parque ends with the extravagantly symbolic Fuente Alemana, a monument presented by the country's German community in 1910 for the first centenary of Independence – whose fountains serve as an impromptu bathing pool and even laundry for schoolchildren and the poor in hot weather. Note too the strange art-deco house, complete with mythological beast, at Merced 84.

Artists' quarter: We are now back at the **Plaza Italia**, and shadowed on the left by the looming shape of the **Cerro San Cristóbal** (or St. Christopher, named as such by the Spanish because of the landmark it offered to travellers). Between the Cerro and the Mapocho is the closest Santiago gets to a bohemian *barrio*, **Bellavista**. To reach the Cerro, cross the river by the **Pio Nono bridge** and proceed past the 1930s pile of the University of Chile's Law School up Calle Pio Nono. At the far end is the entrance to the **Parque Metropolitano**, as the Cerro's attractions are called. You can tour the Cerro completely by private car, motorized carriage or by foot. But more a picturesque route is to ascend by the 60 year-old funicular (following in the footsteps of Pope John Paul II, who rose to bless the city during this visit in 1987 in a special bullet-proof wagon).

Perched halfway up is the **Zoo** and at the top are lookout points and the **statue of the Virgin Mary** (note the tree from the Basque town of Guernica, planted in front of the nearby chapel by Chile's Basque community). The 14-metre (46-ft) high Virgin, dating from 1908, is the centre of peregrinations and other religious ceremonies. From here you can take a ten-minute ride in the Swiss cable car, opened in 1980, along the length of the Cerro and linked hills to the end of the Avenida Pedro de Valdivia, in Providencia, with an optional stop on the way. Other attractions in the Parque, which is a favourite place to picnic, jog and cycle, include

Street artist.

two open-air swimming pools, cafes, restaurants, Chilean and Japanese gardens, and a wine-sampling centre and exhibition (Enoteca). Both at the foot of the funicular and at the end of the cable-car you can buy tickets for part or all of the round route.

Bellavista is a mixed residential and artistic neighborhood with lots of charm and interest. Its main streets, apart from Pio Nono, are Purísima, running parallel, and Antonia López de Bello, cutting across laterally. A great variety of restaurants are scattered through the *barrio* (notably on Purisima and by the ugly white-arched Puente del Arzobispo bridge, across from Salvador metro stop). Many have jazz and other music; for specifically Chilean music, try the cosy La Candela (on Purisima; it's not a restaurant, but *empanadas* and mulled wine are served) for folk and the Cafe del Cerro (Ernesto Pinto Lagarrigue 192) for all sorts, though it starts late. There are several theaters, and at night considerable street life with musicians and handicrafts sold from the pavement. The

less interesting Calle Bellavista itself has a string of more tourist-oriented shops specializing in Chile's national stone, lapiz lazuli.

Bellavista is skirted along the Mapocho by the Avenida Santa Maria, the fast route uptown to the wealthy neighbourhoods of **Las Condes, Vitacura** and **Lo Curro** (the latter has the huge and unmistakable modernistic presidential residence built by General Pinochet, but never occupied after the scandal it produced; now it is the Army's country club). Along the way, Santa María crosses under the Americo Vespuccio ring-road, which from here provides a rapid freeway connection round the north of the city to Merino Benítez airport – a useful way of avoiding the city-centre for trips between the airport and the upper *barrio alto*.

On the other side of the river from Bellavista, the Avenida Providencial runs uptown from the Plaza Italia. Several squares in fact cluster around the point at which the Alameda becomes Providencia, with monuments not just to General Baquedano, but also to President Balmaceda (an unmistakable obelisk), the Cuban independence leader José Martí, and the guerrilla hero of Chile's Independence war, Manuel Rodríguez. Between Providencia and the river is the long Parque Balmaceda, with its native trees, children's amusements and the underground **Museo Tajamares**, detailing Santiago's struggle with the Mapocho (chunks of Toesca's original dykes included). By Salvador metro is the long metal monument to Chilean aviation, erected in 1980. Buildings of interest include the convent of the Canadian order, the Sisters of Providence (Casa Matríz de las Hermanas de la Providencia, Providencia 509) and the yellow colonial-style **Iglesia del Carmen de Providencia** (Providencia 1001, actually built in 1892 by a local landowner out of gratitude for the result of the civil war of the previous year).

Providencia continues on through the plush shopping and residential area with the same name, where you can find many of Santiago's finest restaurants.

Left, a romantic interlude. **Right,** a shoeshine in the Plaza de Armas.

SANTIAGO
EXCURSIONS

On an average day the jagged peaks of the Andes hang like a backdrop over the eastern end of Santiago, always just out of reach, or so they seem. But in fact, within a day you can travel, by car or bus, far up into the mountains beside the winding course of the **Maipo River**. This rushing torrent sweeps the loose earth of the mountains downstream toward the rich, agricultural plains of Chile's central valley region, pouring itself finally into the Pacific, four km south of San Antonio.

The **Cajón del Maipo**, as it's called in Spanish, is a popular weekend day trip for the people of Santiago, tired as they often are of the relentless pressure of deadlines and the crush of people on the streets, and anxious for a few hours of fresh air and relaxation. For the sedentary it offers an easy but visually seductive drive towards the mountains' heart; and for the more active, depending on the season, there's plenty of opportunities to swim (in pools), ride horses, pinic, hike, camp or cabin overnight. The river is too rough for regular canoeing or kayaking, but agencies like Expediciones Altué offer raft rides from October to March, for five to seven people at a time. (You must be over 12 and know how to swim.)

There's also a surprising variety of wonderful country restaurants to crown your trip, offering everything from traditional Chilean foods to espresso coffee and *küchens* which would be a credit to any German pastry chef.

The canyon's economic base depends largely on tourism, which explains the varied services it offers, but since it's oriented primarily toward Chileans, prices tend to be reasonable and the Chilean flavor of the area remains distinct.

Home cooking by the roadside: Driving up the the winding highway, especially on weekends, you'll see white flags and small tables by the roadside, piled with round breads of more than a foot in diameter or jars containing intriguing liquids. The white flags mean someone is selling something they've prepared in their kitchen: bread cooked in ashes, often in the traditional ovens of baked mud; jams made with local walnuts, almonds and berries; fresh honey; the ubiquitous *empanadas*, as common in Chile as the hamburger is in the United States. The sight of the sellers' bread with *chicharrones* (dried pork) evokes nostalgic enthusiasm from most Chileans, especially those who've spent part of their childhood in the country.

Toward the summer's end (February), you may be lucky enough to have a prickly pear, or *tuna,* fall at your feet, during a relaxing trip to the area. This unappealing-looking, strangely exotic fruit can be scooped up carefully, to avoid the prickles, peeled it on the spot, and yield a mouthful of melon-like flesh, full of inedible pips small enough to swallow. The prickly pear, which the American-English poet T.S. Eliot associated with the world's whimpering end, is as common as apples in Chile, where it droops like large, green tear-

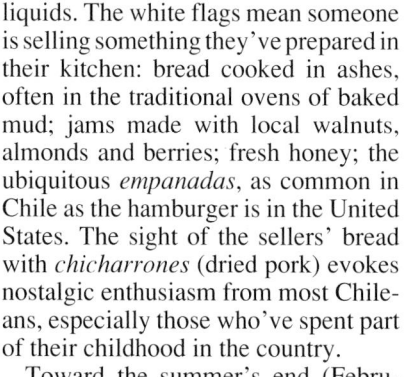

receding
ages,
nding the
elds near
antiago.
eft, loading
p in the
ountains
eyond San
osé del
laipu. Right,
ud baths
ear the
rgentine
order.

drops on cactus arms. Because of the pips, *tuna* are particularly popular crushed and blended into refreshing juices, where the pips can be filtered out.

Exploring the lower Andes: Strung out along the highway are stopping points offering spectacular views of the canyon itself, small towns and villages, campgrounds, parks and an obelisk marking the site where, in 1986, the Manuel Rodríguez Patriotic Front staged a daring ambush of the military president General Augusto Pinochet's cavalcade, which almost put an end to the general's dictatorial rule.

If you're a racing enthusiast, plan your first stop at the canyon's mouth in **Las Vizcachas**, where a private club houses Santiago's only drive-in movie theater and a race course used by both cars and motorcycles. Unfortunately, the rest of the facilities, including a large pool and pleasant picnic area, are not open to the public. But, the further you drive, the better the canyon gets.

At the roadside as you pass through

La Obra you can stop and see craftspeople working with the pale pink stone that characterizes the area and is popular for terraces and other building projects. A few kilometers further is the Sales Room of the Cuevas del Maipo, where you can visit a central valley vineyard, taste and buy wine.

Just past La Obra is **Las Vertientes**, a small town with a gorgeous swimming pool surrounded by grass and flowers where you can spend an enjoyable day swimming, lying in the sun and munching on sandwiches or anything which doesn't require a fire to prepare. If you prefer a barbecue along with your poolside lounging, you're better off stopping at one of the picnic areas whose entries line the highway.

Silver boomtowns and ski resorts: San José del Maipo, about 25 km from Santiago is the canyon's main town, founded in 1791 after silver deposits were discovered in the surrounding area. Buildings are of the adobe and straw common to this region. It's a pleasant place to stretch your legs, en-

New rotive temple of Maipu, framed by ruins of the old one.

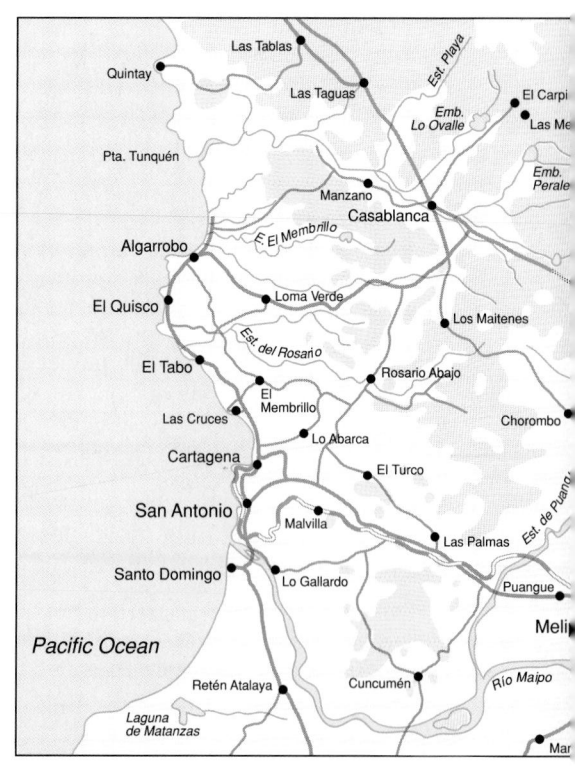

joy the fresh air and absorb some of the tranquillity of a traditional Andean town.

On the outskirts of San José, a narrow gravel road sheers off from the main highway and begins the climb to **Lagunillas**, a ski resort perched on a mountain peak, overlooking an immence bowl formed by part of the Cordillera. You have to have good nerves and a head for heights to make the trip, but it's well worth it, especially during the ski season.

If you prefer to continue along the canyon, you'll pass through the towns of **El Toyo** and **El Melocotón**, before reaching **San Alfonso**. The village sits in a generous hollow carved through the Andes by the river itself. The people who live here are a curious mixture of old country-dwellers and new agers who've come attracted by the spectacular natural setting, the peace, and the proximity to Santiago. **La Cascada de las Animas** (Waterfall of Souls), a camping and picnic ground, captures this peculiar mix. It includes a wonderful round swimming pool and hand-made cabins built with local materials, and belongs to a family which once owned most of the land the town now sits on. The sons and daughters of the original *latifundista* have formed a hippy-style community based on New Age ideals and great sensitivity to the natural environment. The result is that the park and campgrounds are maintained extraordinarily well and the trail rides organized by family members (over weekends and for week-long periods usually) provide an excellent opportunity to penetrate some of the secrets of the Andes.

For the less adventurous or those with less time, the Posada Los Ciervos offers excellent meals in a garden lined with lush, well-kept plants and, if the weather's cold, the Posada has a cosy dining room with the purple abundance of a bougainvillea to be seen through a window. A quick walk along the main road past the Posada will take you to a kiosk which serves and sells exquisite *küchen* (German pastries) made with

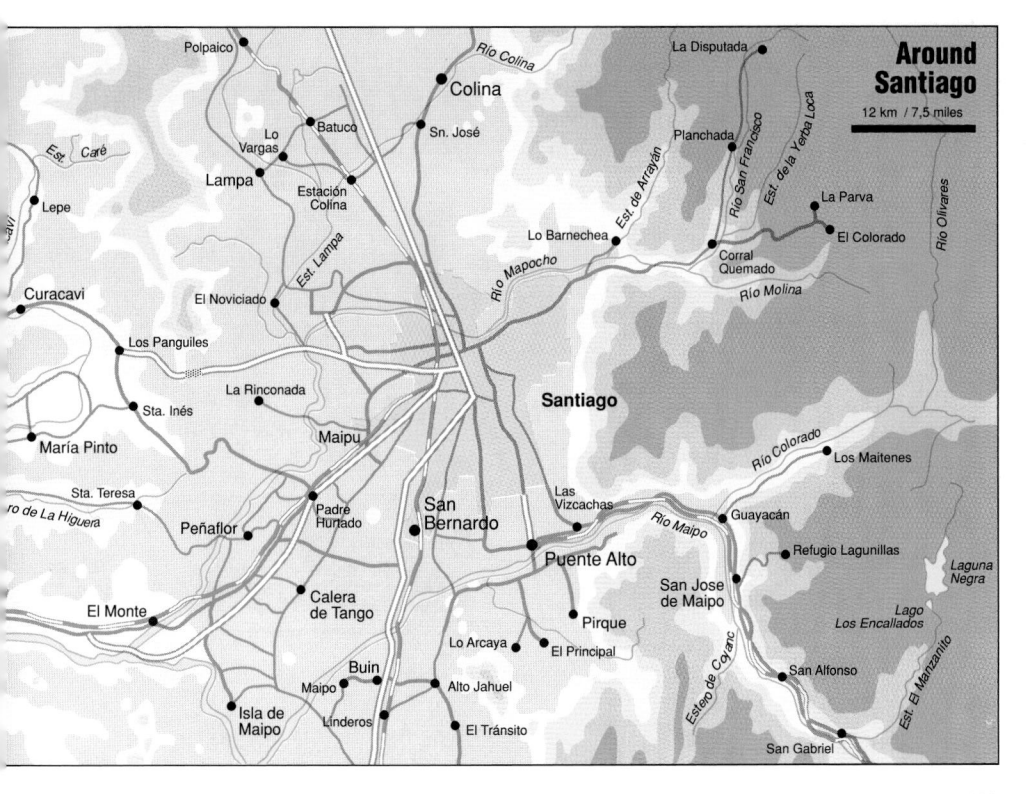

the nuts and fruit of the area.

San Alfonso is a good stopping and turning point for a leisurely day. However, it's also possible to start early in the morning from Santiago and head straight up the canyon 70 km (the last 14 on a gravel road may be difficult in the winter) to **Lo Valdés**, passing the hot springs of **Baños Morales** and continuing up past a checkpoint (this is very near the Chile-Argentine border) to the **Refugio Alemán**, a comfortable inn with a good restaurant and a spectacular view of snowy peaks and a deep natural pool, surrounded by fossils from the period when the Andes were under the sea. Eleven km further on are the Termas de Colina, hot springs open to the public from October, where the water reaches temperatures as high as 60 degrees celsius. The drive is through a spectacular moonscape, completely different from the rest of the canyon, and the baths themselves are arranged in smooth, natural pools on terraces carved into the mountainside. At the source, hot water steams out of natural caves into the hottest bath, which in turn jets into pools further and further down. The further from the source, the more bearable the temperature. In the second pool, you can rest your elbows on the edge and gaze down the valley at the mountains' extraordinary shades of grey, green and subtle pinks, as your body floats in a warm, sulphurous bath.

On the Argentine frontier: Another alternative is to turn left at **San Gabriel** (before El Volcán) and follow the **Yeso River** up to the Yeso dam high up in the Andean cliffs. You'll have to stop at a control on the way and leave your identification and camera with the military, because this is a pass to Argentina. The round trip from Santiago is 170 km, 65 of it on a dirt road, so it's a good idea to carry a picnic lunch, even if you expect to eat at a roadside restaurant.

To return it's possible to retrace your steps as far as El Toyo and then cross the Maipo River and follow the other side of the canyon back down to the Las Vertientes bridge. Here you can cross and retrace your path to Santiago, or

Enjoying a beer.

carry on through **Pirque**, a picturesque country town with a public sales and tasting room of one of Chile's most wellknown vineyards, run by the Conchay Toro company. You can tour the huge vats where wines are stored and matured and peer through the gloom and dust into the "devil's locker room" where one of the company's top wines, *El Casillero del Diablo,* is aged. If you're lucky, one of the staff will invite you to taste the wines, which you can also purchase.

The original country estate and mansion of the Concha y Toro family can be seen from the road, surrounded by the smaller cottages of the vineyards' workers. The main house, which appears on some of the labels, was built c. 1875, around the same time the French landscape designer Gustavo Renner was designing the surrounding park.

Ideally a car gives the most flexibility for traveling up and down the canyon, allowing plenty of time for visiting anything which catches your fancy. However, buses run regularly from Santiago up the canyon, some of their routes ending in San José, Pirque, Puente Alto (on the way to Pirque) or further up the canyon.

A village of potters: It is a simple matter to catch a bus from Santiago that will drop you off at the crossroads to **Pomaire**, a town where clay pottery is the unique, sustaining activity for almost the entire population. The road to the town stretches between an avenue of trees and green fields and is about a half hour's walk from the highway. In 1985, an earthquake razed the original adobe homes and they have mostly been replaced by simple wood shacks and sheds. The reddish clay once common in the town is now virtually exhausted and the raw material for practical potters and clay artists is now usually imported from the surrounding area, but the magic of this small village, built around a one-way loop of road, remains potent.

Designs are primarily traditional, including *miniaturas*, small figures inspired by country stories and religious

Preparing the day's catch on the coast.

beliefs; decorative work; and, perhaps the most beautiful of it, the varied offerings of useful clay pots of all shapes and sizes, ideal for many Spanish and Chilean dishes, a shapely, sensual parade of vessels with names like *pailas, fuentes, tenazas, tinajas, maceteros*, all considerably more enticing than the one English word that sums them up: pot.

You can easily spend an enjoyable day wandering up and down Pomaire's one street, trying in vain to resist the temptation of taking at least a *chanchito* (a peculiarly Chilean pig pot) or an old worn out clay shoe, back to your homeland to hold plants or trinkets or whatever special keepsakes you find.

Tucked in between the pottery are small plant stores and greenhouses, along with several restaurants, offering an excellent selection of Chilean-style meals, which range from the ubiquitous *empanadas* to the town's speciality, different pork dishes.

Down to the Pacific: If you're traveling by bus, the round trip to and from Pomaire is probably enough for a good, full day. If you're using a car, you have the option of carrying on to **Isla Negra** on the coast. (This is an odd sort of itinerary which we invented one day when we were accompanying a poet who wanted to get a good sense of Chile outside Santiago. It is wonderfully relaxing and refreshing, particularly if you don't mind driving back to Santiago after dark.)

Returning to highway 78 you continue along until just before San Antonio where you turn north to head toward the popular seaside resorts of **Cartagena**, **Las Cruces** and **El Tabo**. All are lovely places with long sandy beaches, particularly agreeable in the spring or fall, when the sun is a little more merciful and it's pleasant to stroll along the beach, watching the Pacific roaring into shore. But Isla Negra, a little further up the coast from all three, is special. It is unclear whether it's special because Pablo Neruda, Chile's great poet, chose to live there, or whether he chose to live there because it is so special. Neruda's favorite house

The beach front at San Antonio.

overlooks a particularly rough stretch of Isla Negra's beach, where the waves crash against humped rocks rising suddenly out of the white sand like prehistoric beasts or children's castles.

The fence surrounding Neruda's house provides a unique insight into Neruda's influence, which is very much alive among Chileans, particularly the young, and the very difficult times which the country is only beginning to leave behind. Lovers young and old, readers, writers, the lonely and the well-accompanied have all made special pilgrimages to this spot and left their testimony scrawled or carved or scribbled across the picket fence that surrounds the property. (See Feature: "Memories of Neruda", p. 162).

You can easily lose an hour or two yourself, hunched on the humped rocks, gazing out over the restless, changing landscape that cast its spray through much of Neruda's work. Or you can walk along the beach, searching for mussels, starfish, clams and barnacles on the damp, bared rocks.

From here it's a quick trip back down the coast to **San Antonio**, a working port with the grime of hard labor in evidence and fishing boats moored in the harbor. There are several good restaurants in San Antonio, but the *picadas*, as the Chileans say, are right on the docks themselves: small, cramped boxlike buildings where the fishing people themselves like to eat. Here you'll get huge platefulls of your favorite *marisco* (shellfish) or fish dish, with a fresh Chilean salad, rice or french fries, at very reasonable prices. The drive back to Santiago takes about an hour and a half, all on highway 78.

Winter skiing: There are five ski centres near Santiago: Lagunillas (see Maipo Canyon), Portillo (on the route to Argentina) and Farellones, La Parva and Valle Nevado, located in the same area about 50 km from Santiago.

The road to **Farellones** winds narrow and steep through the Cordillera, following most of the Mapocho River canyon deep into the Andes. It's an excellent day trip whatever the season,

he skiing
elds of
arellones.

but chains are required in the winter (they're available for rental where the road begins), due to the icy conditions. Careful driving is a must in any season. Access to the road is controlled by Chilean police and you can head up until 1 p.m., but it's good to start early in the morning. Cars can only begin the return descent after 3 p.m. Warm clothes are a must, whatever the temperature in Santiago when you leave. Snow usually begins in June and lasts until September, making the area popular with ski enthusiasts from the Northern Hemisphere, who can keep in shape skiing during their summer holidays.

Farellones is best known as a ski resort and provides excellent conditions, with rentals and classes available in the town itself. It has four well-equipped slopes which go as high as 3,333 meters above sea level and are suitable for skiers of variable experience. Group and private classes are available. Even if you're not a skier, it's worth the trip. The view from the road as you climb higher and higher, pure

sky, the clear air, and the chance to enjoy the Andes from the inside out all make the drive worthwhile. On the way, you'll have a birds' eye view of **El Arrayán**, a small town perched on the edge of Santiago, with the kind of houses architects design for themselves. You'll also see **La Ermita**, with its characteristic chapel and nearby the hydro-electric station that supplies one of Chile's main mines, La Disputada.

Near Farellones is the small town of **La Parva**, at 2,816 meters above sea level, with a spectacular view down the valley toward Santiago. La Parva usually enjoys snowy conditions until well into October and you can ski as high as 3,630 meters.

Also near Farellones is **Valle Nevado**, a modern ski center opened in 1988. The turnoff, two km before Farellones, takes you 10 km into the mountains' heart. There are two luxury hotels and a luxury apartment building, providing services as varied as video movies, a discotheque, a French restaurant, a gymnasium, a pool room, sauna, whirlpool bath and a snackbar. Stores sell ski equipment and clothing as well as rent the necessary equipment and there is a daycare center and medical center equipped for any emergency. The highest point you can ski is 3,670 meters above sea level.

In terms of equipment, accommodation and transportation, skiing in Chile is an expensive activity, practised by an elite. The prices of equipment rentals, accommodation, food and other sundries tend to be similar to those of any developed country.

For more information on horse back riding in San Alfonso, or to reserve a cabin in La Cascada de las Animas, phone El Huerto, a Santiago restaurant, 231 9889. For more information on access to Farellones, La Parva and Valle Nevado, you can phone 220 9501 in Santiago. For more information on accommodation in ski resorts, you must contact individual resorts.

Expediciones Altué at phone 211 9638 or 228 4355 offer rides in rubber rafts down the Rio Maipo from October to March.

Left, ready for action at the Valle Nevada. Right, soaking up the sun at a Pacific resort.

VALPARAÍSO AND VIÑA DEL MAR

Valparaíso and Viña del Mar may sit side by side on Chile's Pacific coast, but when it comes to urban character, they remain worlds apart.

One of the first Chilean cities founded by the Spanish, Valparaíso has been Santiago's thriving port for centuries. It is spread along some spectacularly steep hills, with stairways and streets winding up towards splendid ageing buildings. Many of the finest were built in the last century by the British, when Valparaíso was virtually run from the city of London. But down below, the streets are chaotic, full of pollution and dirt – the residue of the recent implacable economic policies.

Viña, on the other hand, is a tourist city of steel, glass and neon. It exists for the summer months, when hundreds of thousands of Chileans flock to its fine beaches. Always the reserve of the wealthy, it is a pleasant enough place to relax – but Valparaíso holds the attractions of its wild and varied history.

Traveling overland from Santiago you enter Valparaíso by highway 68, which then becomes Argentina Avenue. On Wednesdays and Saturdays, this central walkway becomes a city fair with all kinds of vegetables and fruit, fresh fish and shellfish, dry goods, spices and delicious homemade cookies. On Sundays, it becomes a Chilean flea market or *feria persa*, where you can find antiques, old magazines and odd collector's items.

Upon reaching Pedro Montt Avenue, a former horse race track, it's hard to avoid the new **Congress Building**. Its size and cost has made it controversial. For some, this is the symbol of the new Chilean democracy. For others, it represents the insolence of wealth and power in the midst of poverty.

Exploring the city: The best way to see Valparaíso is on foot and, to build up the

Preceding pages: the beach at Viña Del Mar. **Left**, twilight at Valparaíso harbor.

necessary strength, the **Vitamin Service Cafe** – with good espresso coffee, fresh fruit juices and delicious sandwiches on Pedro Montt Avenue, by **Victory Square** – is a good place to start.

Across from the cafe, at one side of the **Cathedral**, is the house where Augusto Pinochet, who headed Chile's military government for 16 years, spent his youth. It is hard to imagine that, in the 1930s, Pinochet and his friends used to stroll through the Plaza, admiring the girls and dreaming of the first Pontiac which had just arrived in Chile. Nothing suggested the prominent role that Pinochet would play in Chilean history. He was the son of a clerk and a mediocre student at the old Sacred Hearts School.

Apart from this curiosity, Victory Square (the Plaza de la Victoria) boasts a lovely **Neptune Fountain** – a war trophy which was stolen from the Peruvians in 1879.

Sauntering along Condell Street, you'll be tempted to imagine what these attractive old buildings with their carved doorways were like at the turn of the century. You can almost make out the delicate young girls of wealthy Santiago families avoiding summer heatwaves here by the Pacific Ocean's cool waters, organizing sophisticated evening gatherings in their summer mansions as a rest from activities in the sun.

Further along this narrow, curving street you reach Esmeralda, at the end of which is the **Turri Clock**, Valparaíso's equivalent of Big Ben, located at the intersection of Cochrane and Prat.

Prat is the city's financial heart and here the English influences are so obvious it's hard to believe you're in a Latin American city. At the street's end you'll find **Sotomayor Square**, surrounded by buildings housing the central lawcourts, naval headquarters, the post office, the train station and a part of the port that's open to visitors. It is its position by the sea that has shaped the city's history since its foundation four and a half centuries ago.

Beginnings: Valparaíso was the first city the Spanish founded when they reached Chile. In 1535, Diego de Al-

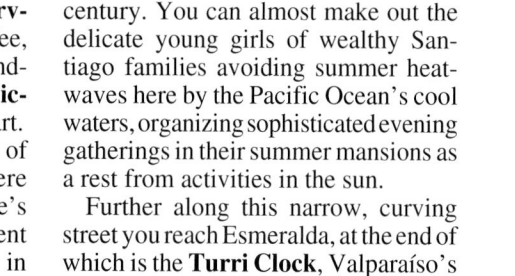

Valparaíso's busy port.

154

magro, the Spaniards' "Advanceman," organized an expedition that traveled south from Cuzco in Peru, hoping to discover an empire similar to the Incan which he'd discovered earlier along with Francisco Pizarro. In despair after traveling for months through wild and hostile territory, Almagro sent his lieutenant Ivan de Saavedra to meet with Spanish ships anchored on the coast.

Finally from a coastal mountain peak, don Juan saw the sea. He observed the Quintil Valley, surrounded by hills full of fragrant Boldo and Maiten – native trees – ravines and springs pouring into the bright, peaceful bay, at that time inhabited by the Chango Indians who lived on fish. This exuberant view flooded Juan de Saavedra with nostalgia for his distant homeland and he named the bay at this feet after his hometown in Spain: Valparaíso.

Extraordinary events would unfold in the port in the centuries that followed. Pedro de Valdivia, the founder of Santiago and Governor of Chile, would find himself here, in 1547, isolated, impoverished by wars and discouraged by the lack of news and support from the crown. With characteristic (and very Chilean) ingenuity, he called on colonists wishing to return to the more developed Northern colonies to load their fortunes (built through the exploitation of gold reserves using native slaves) and themselves onto his ships.

About 20 families prepared themselves and boarded. On the last night before setting out, under the pretext of a final goodbye banquet in the port, Valdivia set them all ashore where they cheerfully set to consuming wine and meats in huge quantities. But as the feasting reached its height, don Pedro weighed anchor and set out with the gold, leaving a beach full of furious victims. In this way, Chile inaugurated its first progressive tax system, its loyal citizens contributing 80,000 *dorados* to their governor.

Valparaíso went on to become the main port for the growing city of Santiago. This made it a tempting target for pirates and corsairs, mostly of English

Dragging a boat to sea.

or Dutch origin – the port had to build strong fortifications to repel the attacks which continued through most of the 16th and 17th centuries. The building of defensive towers and forts not only discouraged potential attackers but also acted as a strong stimulus to the trade and warehousing of merchandise which entered and left the country. Soon the English stopped raiding and became the largest trading partner of the newly-independent Chile, buying up large parts of Valparaíso.

The absence of a dock until the end of the 18th century meant that merchandise was disembarked manually. A 1799 report said: "It's pitiful to watch (the porters) in chest-deep water of such extraordinary coldness, according to most opinions, that few ports could compare." It continued: "Take a look around this town and you'll not find more than a few pitiful widows and few men of more than 50, this disgraceful practice being the prime cause of their early deaths."

Revolutions, uprising and riots: Occasionally laid waste by earthquakes and tidal waves, Valparaíso also became notorious for political disturbances. Two of the city's governors died tragically within 20 years of each other. The first was the powerful "kingmaker" Diego Portales, who was shot to death on his way to Quillota in 1837, during a brief military uprising. The other was an army general, killed on September 18 1859, during a civil uprising at the doors of the La Matriz Church, during a religious ceremony giving thanks for Chile's Independence.

Then, in 1851, General José Maria de la Cruz, supported by liberal elements influenced by mid-century European thinking, headed one of Chile's great rebellions against the first civilian government of the newly-founded republic. A bloody battle left more than 2,000 dead and 1,500 injured in Loncomilla, 300 km (180 miles) south of Santiago.

More recent events also involve Valparaíso as their "theater of war." At sunset on Monday September 10, 1973, the Chilean navy set out to sea for its

Left, turn-of-the-century buildings climb Valaparaíso's hills. Right, steep stairways.

annual Unitas exercises with the US fleet. However, at dawn the next day, the presence of the fleet back in the bay marked the beginnings of the coup which led to the imposition of a military government in Chile for 16 years. Naval foot soldiers flooded the port within an hour, but the *porteños* began armed resistance in the hills for several days. Several university and government buildings still show signs of the battles.

Walks and vistas: By the turn of this century, the old port had begun to assume its present look. Builders battled the sea for a few extra meters of earth to build the *costanera* (coast road), the railway line and Brasil Avenue. European-style buildings marked the skyline and the old street of trade became the financial and banking center for all the maritime and port activity.

The growing population began to spill out of the city's basic plan and the incredible feat of building in the hills themselves began. Each individual builder found his or her own techniques for fighting gravity and resisting earth-quakes, creating a unique city of winding streets, stairways, walks and lookout points which began to string together the different hills, each one separated by the abrupt ravines which characterize the area.

To conquer the hilltops the elevators and the *funiculares* (cable cars) of all shapes and sizes were born. They are still the main form of transport to reach up into the city's hills. You have to experience a Valparaíso elevator – appearances aside, they've proven to be a secure means for traveling up the hills, at the same time as they give a spectacular view of the Bay itself. There are several worth making a point of using.

Walking along the city's western edge, you can follow Marina Avenue to **Las Torpederas Beach**, and from there reach the southernmost point of the Bay. This is one of the most pleasant walks in Valparaíso, with a marine breeze and the chance to admire the buildings around the **Playa Ancha Hill**. At the Avenue's end, you'll find one of the elevators up the hill, which is one of the city's largest in both size and population. The residents proudly call this the "People's Independent Republic of Playa Ancha." Among other things, you'll find here Valparaíso's naval school, the hospital and cemetery, as well as the education, medicine and biology faculties of the University of Valparaíso. Their towers still bear the holes made by bullets during the 1973 military coup.

A walk around Playa Ancha is also a reminder of the port's better days of fine but unostentatious buildings which populated the hill, little by little. Walking down the 21 de Mayo Paseo gives the city's best view of the Bay and the whole port area. In the distance you can see Viña del Mar.

On a sunny day, a half-hour trip in a rowboat round the bay is well worth the effort. You can imagine how the sailors feel when they finally arrive in port after a long trip. It's particularly pleasant on a warm summer's night. On New Year's Eve, you can also enjoy Valparaíso's unique fireworks show on the water: all the ships anchored in the harbor sound their horns together to welcome the new year, producing some stunning harmonies.

In the **Caleta El Membrillo** you'll find a restaurant run by the Fishermen's Co-operative, which offers a variety of dishes common to the area: fantastic shellfish and fish which, eaten with good wines, give the sensation of a perfect world. Seagulls, pelicans and cormorants enjoy momentary possession of the fishing boats, while local women patiently prepare the nets for the next day's work.

Energy and squalor: Exploring the old and dirty neighborhood of the port ground, **Customs Square**, is to find yourself face to face with Valparaíso's colorful past. Taverns like the **Yaco, Black and White** and **La Nave** are full of the memories from the days when they attracted corsairs, businessmen, sailors, prostitutes, Nobel prizewinners (Pablo Neruda) and all kinds of lesser known personalities.

At night, although the area overflows with gaiety – especially on weekends – it's a good idea to go in a group or, better still, accompanied by a friend from the port.

Concepción Hill is also a climb back into the past. This was the residential sector preferred by the English at the turn of the century, and it still boasts attractive buildings, broad avenues and unique views of the sea. To get there, you must find the stairway which starts on Esmeralda Street, beside the old building which first housed *El Mercurio*, a Valparaíso newspaper founded in 1827 and now generally considered the dean of the Chilean press.

Another different hill, poorer in money, richer in ingenuity, is **Bellavista**. You can reach this by the elevator on Monina Street, above Victoria Square. Its thousands of narrow streets, with their flowered balconies, make an unbelievable architectural spectacle.

The hills are safe places for visitors: their people are warm and supportive, and their children – ever curious – have plenty of smiles to give away. Don't be afraid of getting lost, as the sea is al-

Left, memories of the British. Right, sweeping views of the city.

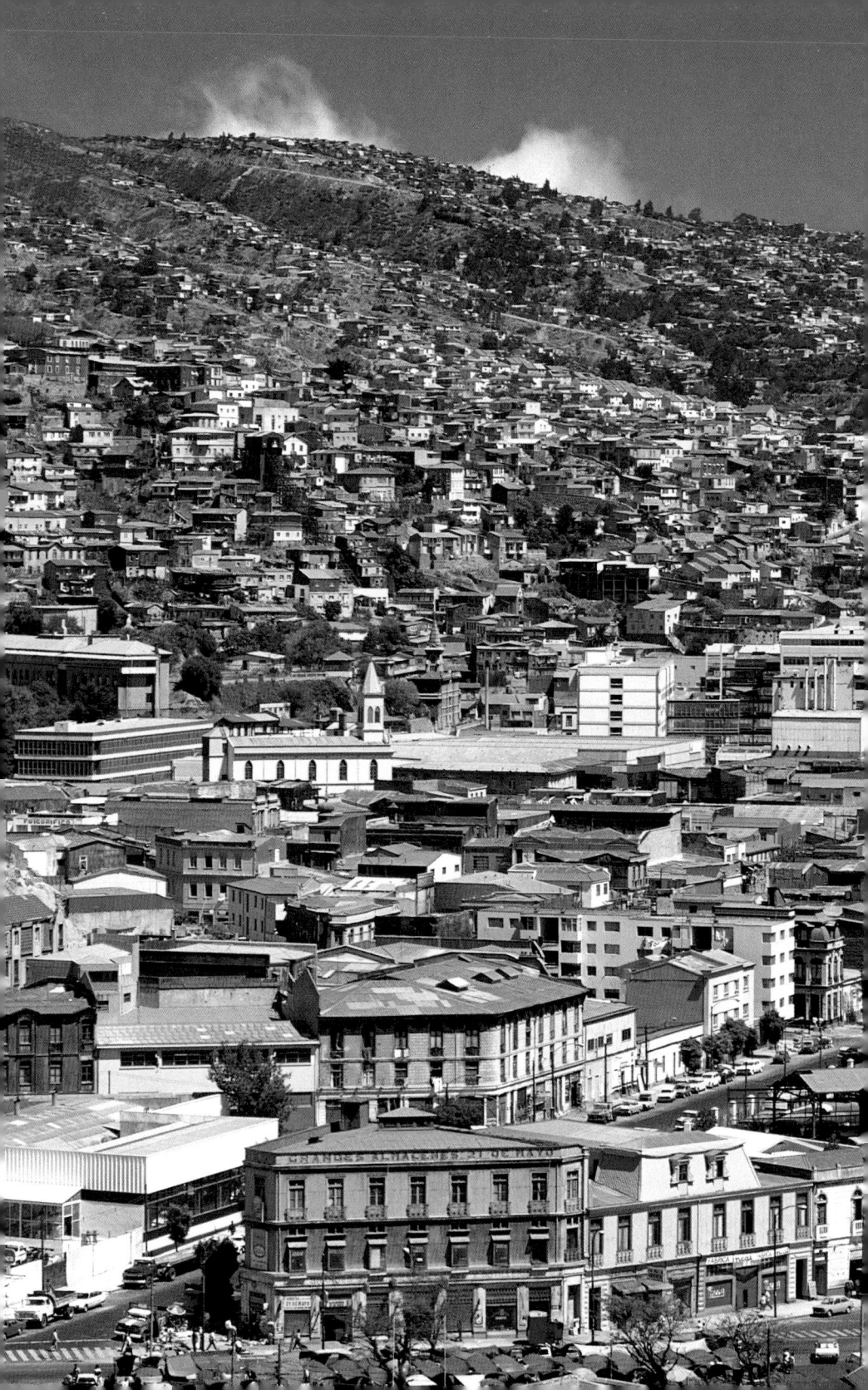

ways there as the ultimate landmark. Walking downward will inevitably bring you back to some familiar city street, present on the map.

As a curiosity, it's appropriate to visit the **Polanco Hill**, on the eastern side of Argentina Avenue, where a vertical elevator (at the end of a long, narrow but well-lit tunnel) rises up through the hill and into the sky. This is another of the ingenious architectural inventions in the city.

From there, you can walk toward the **Baron's Hill**, so-called because a European Baron once built his castle there, and then on to **Cerro Alegre**, literally "happy hill." This hill is virtuously protected by the imposing Castle of Don Federico Santa Maria, today used as a university which bears his name.

With Valparaíso as your base, you can head out on agreeable daytrips by car to the interior cities. **Quilpue, Limache, Quillota** and **San Felipe** are all small towns whose buildings recall the days of the Spanish colonies. Plazas and squares full of palm trees, peaceful landscapes, the quiet pace of their inhabitants and a climate especially kind to the elderly make these towns particularly agreeable for resting and meditating on the madness of large cities.

It's also possible to visit the seaside resort of **Quintay**, 35 km (22 miles) from the port on the road to Santiago. It's an ideal place to spend a nice day, away from the crowds on the beaches of Viña. It has a friendly inn to eat and spend the night if you prefer.

The glittering resort: As with most things, Valparaíso has its counterpart. Extraordinarily developed as a tourist attraction, **Viña del Mar** is a luxury city. It offers grand, elegant hotels, casinos, restaurants which specialize in refined, international cooking, charming beaches, great avenues of palms, boutiques, tourist-oriented stores and most of the pleasures that money can buy.

Viña was born round the bend from the port, specifically to serve as its seaside resort. In spite of the development of several industries (textiles, min-

The casino by night, Viña del Mar.

ing and metal), its major source of income is still tourism.

If Valparaíso is the city where Augusto Pinochet grew up, Viña is the city which sheltered the remains of Salvador Allende, the Chilean president who died amid the relentless bombing of the Airforce's Hawker Hunters, during the 1973 military coup. His tomb in the Santa Ines Cemetery remained unmarked until 1989; but it was always covered with fresh flowers placed by admirers. On September 4 1990, exactly 20 years to the day after he was elected president of Chile, Dr Allende's remains were finally moved to his permanent resting place, in a mausoleum in Santiago's general cemetery.

The city has been reluctantly making way for the buildings of more recent decades. Fall is the best time to see it on foot, as summer tourists have abandoned the city and only its inhabitants remain. Peru Avenue is the perfect place to stroll along the shore, enjoying the sunset and the golden colors of the huge banana trees' leaves.

If you're seeing the city by car, on a clear day the coastal road which heads northward is lovely. One by one the resorts of **Las Salinas, Reñaca, Cocha, Higuerillas** and **Concon** appear, surrounded by natural rocky outcrops and reefs where you can see sea lions, pelicans, cormorants and, with a bit of luck, a penguin that has lost its way looking for the island across from **Cachagua**, a small town 60 km (37 miles) north of Viña del Mar. Concon, at the mouth of the Aconcagua River, has very good restaurants with traditional seafood *empanadas* (the Chilean equivalent of a Cornish pasty) and tasty fish dishes and sauces.

On your way back to Santiago, climbing Aguasanta hill, you pass through a residential neighborhood with a clear view of Valparaíso. If you do this in the dark, you can enjoy a view from the crest of the hill of the marvelous firmament of lights both Valparaíso and Viña offer. By night the two very different cities can barely be distinguished, blending together in a clandestine love affair.

Below, lounging in the afternoon sun. Right, summer vacation at Viña.

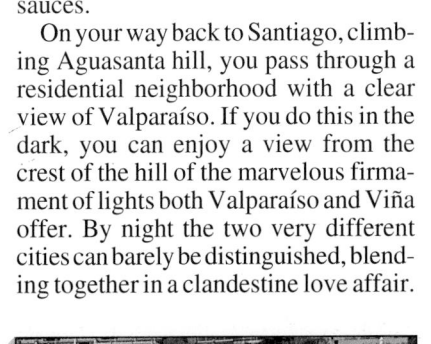

MEMORIES OF NERUDA

The winding street ends in a modest blue bungalow, with a rough stone face that sets it apart from its showier neighbors. But where the inside should begin there's a leafy patio of ladders and stairs climbing upward to rooms of glass, scattered among gardens, terraces, mosaics and a secret passage.

This is the Chascona (meaning, "Woman with Tousled Hair") on San Cristóbal Hill in Santiago. Wrested from the military regime, the Chascona and three similar houses are the fruit of the same restless spirit which

Pablo Neruda was an avid collector of books, shells, paintings, wines - and houses. By the time he died he had four: la Chascona, Isla Negra (on the coast south of Valparaíso) and La Sebastiana (in Valparaíso) and la Quinta Michoacan (in Santiago), which Delia del Carril used until her death in 1989.

Friends called Neruda a spontaneous architect: his houses just grew. On the Pacific Coast he created Isla Negra, furnishing it with treasures collected on endless rambles along beaches and through the second-

united a poet's extravagant imagination with his people's hunger for social justice and produced one of this century's great poets. Pablo Neruda, the Chilean poet who won the Nobel prize in 1971 and died shortly after the military seized power in September 1973, is still very much alive in Chile.

Poet and collector: Neruda and Mathilde Urrutia were married by the moon on the island of Capri, long before they were legally joined. In 1953, they returned to Santiago where they built the Chascona, while he was still married to his second wife, the painter Delia del Carril. Neruda named the new house for his lover's rebellious hair.

hand stores of the world.

"In Isla Negra everything flowers," Neruda wrote in *Passions and Impressions* (New York 1984). "Tiny yellow flowers linger all winter, turning blue and later burgundy in spring. The sea flowers all year round. Its rose is white. Its petals are salt stars."

In her memoirs, unavailable as yet in English, Mathilde Urrutia describes her attempts to catalog the contents of the house in Isla Negra. Her inventory takes us into the labyrinth of Neruda's mind, furnished by private and public histories, illuminated by poems. Each sculpture, beam, rock, has its own story: of travels and discovery, of bargains and gifts.

Neruda's thirst for life and his love for poetry were tempered by his sensitivity to the poverty around him. He joined the Communist Party in 1943 and was elected to the Senate. Alive, he dedicated his work to the day-to-day struggles of Chileans. In death, he left his wealth to them.

"Neruda didn't collect things in order to hoard them, but rather to share them," said Juan Agustin Figueroa, the lawyer who heads the Neruda Foundation, Neruda's legal heir. "He always imagined that his things would become the heritage of the people of Chile."

A target for repression: Upon the deaths of Neruda, Delia del Carril and Mathilde Urrutia, the four houses were to go to the Communist Party, for use as cultural centers. But after the 1973 coup, the military banned all parties and confiscated their goods. Military patrols repeatedly sacked La Chascona and the Sebastiana. They blocked an irrigation channel to make it race through the Chascona, gutting the house and smashing a fragile medley of stained glass windows, porcelain swains, bottles and shells.

The disastrous condition of the house didn't stop Mathilde from holding Neruda's wake there and his funeral became the first march against the regime.

From then until her death in 1985, she and a small group of lawyers, writers and artists waged silent war against the military's bureaucracy.

"We acted with considerable firmness and a lot of discretion," Juan Agustin Figueroa said. A loyal friend of Mathilde's, his services as a lawyer helped her through many crises.

Mathilde spent her last years in La Chascona, repairing the house and organizing Neruda's library, papers and a growing collection of editions of his books. After her death, the foundation published her memoirs and made the Chascona its headquarters. Neruda's library of rare and priceless books, his manuscripts, collections of original paintings and what personal belongings could be saved, are there.

The military confiscated the house in Isla Negra, but Mathilde never gave up possession. After a lengthy struggle, in which the navy almost took permanent control of the house, the government recognized the foundation and made its existence retroactive to Urrutia's death. Last year naval authorities granted the foundation a five-year concession over the property.

Today, visitors can tour the Chascona and researchers have access to the archives. The foundation sponsors a year-long poetry workshop and a quarterly newsletter on Neruda's life and work. Its Neruda Prize, awarded in November on the anniversary of Neruda's Nobel, was until recently the only

major literary award in Chile not subject to the regime's censorship.

The Isla Negra house has been turned into a permanent museum by Chile's newly elected democratic government. Two-hour tours can be arranged through the Neruda Foundation in Santiago (Tel: 778741), or it can be visited independently (open 11 a.m.-1 p.m., 3 p.m.-5 p.m. weekdays, 11 a.m.-5 p.m. weekends).

It is now hoped that Mathilde Urrutia and Pablo Neruda can be moved from their temporary niche in Santiago's General Cemetery, to their final home in Isla Negra, above the flowering sea.

Left, Neruda's house at Isla Negra. **Right**, Pablo Neruda, Chile's controversial Nobel Prize winner.

THE JUAN FERNÁNDEZ ISLANDS

Most people have never heard of an 18th-century Scottish seadog named Alexander Selkirk or the **Juan Fernández Archipelago**, 650 km off the Chilean mainland. Yet they are part of our popular mythology. Just think of being marooned on a 'desert isle' and you probably see a man dressed in goat skins, his flintlock at the ready, scanning the horizon for passing ships. His island — unlike the barren, windswept rocks where most mariners were washed up — has plentiful wood, crystal waters, abundant food and no wild beasts.

The scene is from *Robinson Crusoe*, of course. But although Daniel Defoe set his classic novel in the Caribbean, he based it directly on Alexander Selkirk's real-life adventures on Chile's tiny Pacific possession.

The foul-tempered young Scotsman spent four years and four months on the largest of the three deserted Juan Fernández islands. Finally rescued by a group of English privateers, Selkirk was clad in goatskins and could barely speak, croaking rather than talking. He had made himself two wooden huts with interiors lined by fur and was incredibly fit from chasing wild animals around the rocky shores. The marooned sailor became a minor celebrity on his return home and — with the more debauched side of his character being carefully tidied up — inspired one of the most enduring classics in the English language.

The inhabitants of the Juan Fernández islands today certainly aren't shy about this claim to fame. Air tickets from Santiago have a colorful drawing of the marooned sailor splashed across them. Selkirk's island was renamed **Isla Robinson Crusoe** in the mid-1970s (while another, which the Scotsman never visited, was renamed **Alexander Selkirk**). Every hotel and street name in the islands' only township refer to the shipwrecked hero, and a disproportionate number of males

on the archipelago have the Christian name of "Robinson."

These unsubtle grabs at attention might suggest that the islands are something of a tourist trap. Nothing could be further from the truth. Thanks to some spectacular transport difficulties, the archipelago is one of the least visited places in Chile. And while there are several fascinating excursions relating to Selkirk's adventures on the islands, the most lasting pleasures lie elsewhere; the archipelago is a unique wilderness area, declared a Biosphere Reserve by UNESCO in 1978; while its people maintain a 19th-century serenity and striking indifference to the lures of the outside world.

The 'real-life Crusoe': While Daniel Defoe's fictional hero was shipwrecked in a tropical storm (and so, in his more meditiative moments, saw the Hand of God at work), the real-life mariner Alexander Selkirk could only blame himself for his predicament: Selkirk actually asked to be let off his ship in the middle of nowhere.

Preceding pages, the view from Selkirk's lookout. **Left**, enormous lobsters provide the islanders' incomes. **Right**, a yacht pulls into harbor.

As sailing master of the *Cinque Ports*, a privateering vessel making a circumnavigation of the globe in 1704, the quarrelsome Selkirk found himself constantly at odds with the captain. Feelings finally came to a head over some poor repairs which had been made to a leak in the hull: Selkirk snapped that, if the boat was to go down, it would be without him. The captain agreed to land the Scotsman at the nearest island with a few supplies.

Selkirk stubbornly held to his demand until the very last moment. Sitting on the shore of Mas Á Tierra (as the island was then known), watching his former shipmates row back to their ship, the enormity of his decision struck him. Marooning was considered by pirates to be the ultimate punishment, far worse then walking the plank. A slow death by starvation or dehydration was the usual result. Most were put ashore with only their sea chest and a pistol with one ball; tales abounded of sea parties finding a lone skeleton with a shattered skull and a rusting pistol clenched in one hand.

Selkirk is said to have plunged into the ocean and chased after the departing rowboat, screaming madly that he had changed his mind. "Well I have not changed mine!" spat the captain. "Stay where you are and may you starve!"

Goats, rats and feral cats: This indecorous scene was the beginning of four years and four months of isolation for Selkirk.

Most of his time was been spent reading the Bible. A journalist who interviewed the Scotsman in a London tavern after his return to England noted that he believed himself "a better Christian while in this solitude than ever he was before, or than, he was afraid, he should ever be again."

Yet, in the beginning, Selkirk hardly took his fate philosophically. For several weeks after the marooning, he apparently wandered the coast, wailing and staring at the empty horizon. He simply could not believe that his shipmates would leave him to rot there on the shore. It took him 18 months to accept his fate, tear himself away from

Left, the fictional Robinson Crusoe. **Right**, plaque for Alexander Selkirk, the real-life castaway who inspired Defoe's classic.

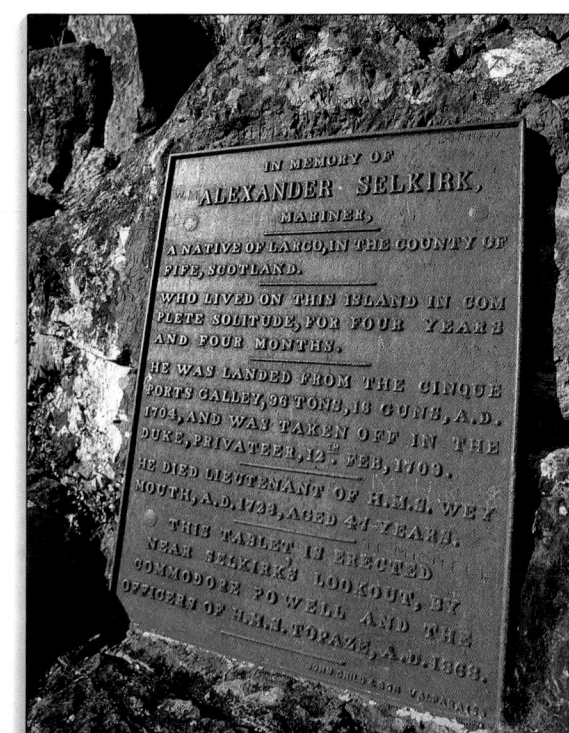

the shoreline and explore the rest of his island prison. At least Selkirk was not starved for animal company. Every night he heard the "monsters of the deep" whose cries were "too terrible to be made for human ears" – which, it turned out, were sealions that had come up to shore. Overcoming his fear, he learned how to climb behind these ponderous beasts and crack their skulls with a single blow of his hatchet.

Domestic animals had been introduced during an ill-fated attempt by the Spaniards to colonise the island following its discovery by the navigator Juan Fernández in 1570. Wild goats became the Scotman's staple food: after his ammunition ran out, he chased them on foot with a knife and became an impressive athlete. He even chased goats for sport, marking their ears as a record. But this diversion had its dangers: On one occasion Selkirk grabbed a goat just as it was leaping off a precipice. He was able to use the beast's body to cushion his fall, but was knocked unconscious for at least a full day. After this debacle,

ea lions on
ne lookout.

he decided to raise goats in a compound.

Wild rats were a less amusing animal group, invading Selkirk's hut by night to nibble his feet and tear his clothes. The Scotsman tamed feral kittens and laid them around his bed as a defence. Apparently he also taught some of his cats and kids to dance. "Thus best we picture him," intones the modern poet Walter de la Mare, "praying aloud, singing and dancing with his kids and cats in the flames and the smoke of his allspice wood, and the whole world's moon taunting and enchanting him in her seasons."

Return to civilization: Charming as these bestial balls must have been, Selkirk did not waver in his attempts to escape the island. Every day he climbed to a lookout to survey the horizon. On two occasions ships actually pulled into the bay and Selkirk thought himself saved – only to discover that they were Spanish barks that would have taken him as slave to the mines of Peru. (On the second visit, Spanish sailors even fired on the maroon and chased him into

the bushes, but were no match for Selkirk's superhuman speed. The Scotsman hid up a tree until the danger had passed.)

Finally, after 52 months of isolation, Selkirk spotted the English *Duke* and *Duchess* lowering anchor on the island with 50 scurvy-ridden sailors. Brought on board, the goat-skin clad Selkirk cut an extraordinary figure, but disbelievers were soon silenced when William Dampier came forward to recognize the maroon and confirm his story.

Despite romantic reports to the contrary, Selkirk appears to have had few qualms about returning to his old life of privateering and debauchery. Appointed a mate on the voyage, he took part in the pillage of various Spanish ports before returning with the profits to celebrity in London and his home town of Lower Largo in Fife, Scotland. He was no doubt gratified to learn that the captain and crew of the *Cinque Ports*, after dumping him at Juan Fernández, had spent the last four years in a festering Lima jail — having been captured

by the Spanish when the vessel foundered, just as Selkirk had predicted.

Drinking and whoring soon took its toll on Selkirk, sapping his unnatural fitness. He even became sentimental for his island prison, noting to one journalist that "I am worth eight hundred pounds, but shall never be so happy as when I was not worth a farthing." The Scotsman may have gone a little batty: he reportedly dug a cave in his parents' backyard to hide in, ran away to London with a milkmaid, dumped her, then signed on for another privateering expedition. He caught a fever in the tropics and died on board in 1723, at the age of 47. Selkirk never knew that his marooning on Juan Fernández – extended by Defoe to 28 years and with a Man Friday thrown in – would become a legend.

A remote destination: Getting to the Juan Fernández Islands today can seem as complicated as it was for Alexander Selkirk to get off them nearly 300 years ago. Unless you travel on a pre-arranged tour, flights to the islands from Santiago are irregular, to say the least.

Left, barbeque on a fishing boat. Right, island girl.

Winter rains flood the dirt runway and limits air traffic to the months of October through April. Two companies fly twin-engine Cessnas to the islands at those times, although getting a seat and confirmed departure date requires luck and dedication.

The flight leaves Santiago's Tabalaba airport early in the morning, leaving the capital behind in a bed of smog. Three hours later, the tiny green specks of Juan Fernández appear, looking as tall as they are wide. For years it was considered impossible to built an airstrip on this rugged terrain, but in the 1970s something looking like a giant ski-jump was blasted through a far corner of the largest island.

From the runway, a jeep half made of scrap metal heads down a 45 degree angled road to the sea, followed by a two-hour journey in an open fishing boat to town. On a fine day, the water is clear and blue, with schools of fish zigzagging below and the obese Juan Fernández seals sunning themselves by the shore. The boatmen often smoke succulent lumps of fresh cod caught on the journey over and share them around with bread and water.

Lobster village: The township of **San Juan Bautista**, where almost all of the archipelago's 4,500 inhabitants live, is located roughly where Selkirk spent his enforced leisure time. Set beneath forest-covered fists of stone with their peaks always lost in grey mist, it has only a few, unpaved streets, a bar, soccer field and one small cemetery with ship's anchors above many of the graves. There are five automobiles in Bautista, and only one of those works: the only noise is the never-ending howl of the wind.

Along the shore are tiny fishermen's huts, looking like the changing rooms at turn-of-the-century beach resorts. This is a lobster town and relatively wealthy by Chilean standards, although prices of goods imported from the mainland are also high. Despite the soporific calm, Bautista is crowded with monuments to war. Eighteenth-century Spanish cannons are set into the footpath –

Farewells on the jetty.

dug up from excavations above the town – along with a series of green pillboxes built to defend the island against Peruvian warships during the War of the Pacific last century.

Most curiously, along the path running north from the town is the spot where some famous gun shells can be seen embedded in the cliff side. They were fired by the British warships Glasgow and Kent at the German cruiser *Dresden* when it tried to retire here for repairs in 1915. (The captain blew up the ship rather than surrender).

In Selkirk's footsteps: The classic hike from town follows Selkirk's path to **El Mirador** – the lookout used by the marooned sailor every day to scan the horizon on both sides of the island. Start early, at about 8 a.m., to arrive before the mists roll in. The path runs through crops of introduced eucalyptuses into higher forests of indigenous trees. It also passes the remains of an old Spanish fort, as well as a turnoff to a rock with carvings on it from 1866 – sailor's graffiti showing a ship and giant fish.

The trail becomes a corridor through rainforest before revealing a knifeshaped peak. In the saddle of the mountain is the only place to see both sides of the island: the lush green Juan Bautista side to the west, contrasting starkly with the dry brown swirls and jagged peaks on the northern side of the mountain. A plaque was erected here by a British warship in the 19th century commemorating Selkirk's ordeal. It has more recently been joined by a small memorial from one of the mariner's descendents from Largo in Scotland.

On the return journey, call in at the **Caves of the Patriots**, where 300 pro-Spanish soldiers fled in 1814 after Chile's declaration of Independence. Unlike Selkirk, they couldn't stand the wind and rain in their huge but damp caves, so gave themselves up. Back on shore, a number of other caves vie for the title of Selkirk's home – although for most of the time the mariner lived in his own hand-made huts.

Conservation drive: Within the town is Conaf, the island's national park service financed mostly by European funds.

The center operates to protect the unique flora and fauna of the area that put the island on the UNESCO World Heritage list. The plant life is unusually varied on the island, with 101 endemic varieties including a range of enormous ferns – many of which look like they belong in Dr Seuss books. Of the unique animals, the red hummingbird is most famous for its needle-fine black beak and silken feather coverage.

Conaf spends most of its time trying to eradicate threats introduced by Man: everything from mulberry bushes to the wild goats and feral cats descended from Selkirk's days. Rabbits were a problem but have been controlled by the simple solution of paying a trapper to catch and sell 150 a day (the islanders thought this a more humane solution than using the poison Myxomatosis). Biologists here regularly turn up new finds: most recently, a fern called *dendroseries macranta* that had not been sighted since 1907 was found in a remote corner of the island.

But one of the real pleasures of any visit is just taking a seat by the wharf and watching the world go by, sipping on a beer and chatting with the islanders. Everyone will eventually mention that Juan Fernández is a paradise. And, although the archipelago doesn't boast the swaying palms or golden sands of other South Pacific islands, it does have plenty of other elements to make it a contender: beautiful scenery, good weather, plenty of food, no crime, no poverty, no racial tensions, no bad weather, no pollution. And this is no remote group of people being dragged into the 20th century, with a delicate society about to buckle under the strain. Everyone is descended from Chilean or European immigrants, and have grown up within Western culture – albiet a detached, 19thcentury version. The islanders take what they want from the 20th century – medicine, music, radios or TV soap operas – and leave the rest.

Perhaps that's why the half-familiar world of Juan Fernández is so beguiling: one admires the islanders' good sense, but, already being a part of the outside world, can never share it.

Unique fauna of the islands.

THE NORTH

"*All the deserts in the world are like [the Chilean North]. Inhospitable lands, not fit for life, end up stubbornly populated by tenacious seekers of some hidden riches. Then the riches lose their meaning; others lay hands on them, or death creeps so near that their possession loses its savor. A man should flee; instead, he remains. He no longer knows how to go back, nor desires to. Outside, there is a netherworld that pulls him in like a silent whirlwind. The provisional becomes permanent without losing its provisional character. The women become exhausted by the land's infertility and yearn for their humid gardens in the South. Many return. The men stay 'to send home money.' In fact they stay because the desert, like the sea, is something that attracts them more than life; something like the sterile love they feel for their own being.*"

— Benjamin Subercaseaux,
Chile's geographer-poet

If Chile's voluptuous South is "the country," lush, alluring, and suggestive of rejuvenation and rest, the desert North evokes exile and hardship. It is a place for prophets to wander or a young man to seek his fortune, but hardly a fit world, from the eyes of city dwellers, to carry on a life. The North is utilitarian; it has the twin roles of providing much of the country's wealth, while also being used frequently as a dumping ground for the politically inconvenient.

Much of the North was annexed by Chile late in the game; in the 1884, Chile defeated a confederation of Peru and Bolivia in the War of the Pacific to take control over the flourishing nitrate mines. This "white gold" of the North, a key ingredient in the making of fertilizer, provided fabulous wealth for several decades while copper and silver mining already flourished in the provinces closer to the capital. Later, the world's largest copper mine was developed at Chuquicamata, part of the captured spoils.

The distances from the northern wastes to Santiago and the few transport options available encouraged the idea of a journey north as a sort of banishment – whether it was self-imposed exile in the pursuit of spiritual or material gain, or literally an attempt by others to get the unlucky subject out of the way. The main male character in Isabel Allende's hugely popular novel, *The House of the Spirits*, published in 1985 and made into a film, makes his way north early in life to slog out a miserable living in the nitrate mines, accumulate capital, and return to lay a now-credible claim for the hand of his chosen fiancé. But he never goes near the North again for the rest of the book.

Bustling cities: Northerners naturally resent this skewered view of them. Unlike his southern cousin who receives the urban visitor with shy admiration and enormous instinctual hospitality, the Northerner must be convinced that the newcomer is worthy of his confidence or even his notice. In an ambience of harsh labor and brutal weather, where food and even water often must be brought in from great distances – and paid for with cash – there is less room for easy solidarity and joint muddling through. The cities of the North bustle; those of the South doze. The welcoming gifts and deference that greet the immigrant in the South are here considered just so much backwater simple-mindedness. While the small farmer or semi-serf of the South survived generation after generation in a state of amiable negotiation with the elements, the typical Northerner was a lone prospector or transient mine operator at constant war with them.

Southern peasants could be expected not only to adopt the servile dodge and shuffle demanded by their hectoring landowner-bosses but also to accept the logic of their servitude. But the Northern mineworker labored under the clear duress of class war. The Southerner was servile; the Northerner, oppressed.

For the North is the birthplace of the Chilean left, one of the largest and most firmly entrenched in all of Latin America. Away from the moderating influ-

Preceding pages, the **Salar de Atacama,** an **enormous dry salt lake. Left,** colonial **church at San Pedro de Atacama.**

ences of intermediate social forces such as small landowners, professionals and shopkeepers and the ideological grip of "leading families," the Northern laborer was face to face with the company. Mining firms sprang up not on fertile, inhabited lands with previous residents and a social history but on the desert *pampas*, in the middle of absolute nowhere. The company built the housing, the company stocked the stores, the company decided who worked, for how long, at what rates, and what he did with his wages. Into this starkly polarized environment, the seeds of marxism arrived from Europe, where proletarian consciousness was in its early heyday, and found propitious soils. The struggle between capital and labor was not a mere theoretical construct in the mining centers but the only conceivable means of understanding the observable phenomena of daily life. Class antagonism was sealed permanently by the notorious 1907 massacre of Santa María de Iquique. In this remote town, some 2,000–3,000 peacefully striking work-

ers and their families were gunned down in cold blood by government troops – thought to be the worst example of mass slaughter in a labor dispute in world history. The revered grandfather of Chile's union movement, 90-year-old Clotario Blest, remembers as a child listening to men having just fled from the North discuss the killing and the impact of their stories on his parents and other working people. In the 1989 elections that marked the end of 16 years of military rule, Communist and Socialist candidates retained a substantial portion of their historical strength in the North, despite the heavy repression of the intervening period.

Birthplace of radicalism: The background to this class consciousness has been the stark effects of "market forces." As a mining-dependent region, the North of Chile has always been marked by a traumatic dependence on the ups and downs of commodity markets thousands of kilometers away. First hundreds of tiny copper and silver mines sprang up in the early 1800s. Later in the century,

Left, woman scythes her crops. **Below** a copper miner at Chuquicamata

Chile went to war for the territories of the far North and the wealth of the nitrate...

An industrial working class whi...

try
enc
51 ...
boo...
man...
nate... ...eed for the raw material, and once the 1914–18 war ended, Chile's "desert gold" had become obsolete. As late as the 1960s, Chileans visiting the Santa Laura ghost town could observe trains sitting on abandoned sidings, their cars loaded with nitrate ore which had suddenly turned to lumps of irrelevant rock.

The ebb and flow of the nitrate business was accompanied by massive migrations of workers, first north to work the mines, then south in droves of unemployed to seek new lives, bursting with the ideas of unionism, class struggle and socialism. This newly-active, radicalized working class contributed to the end of oligarchic rule in 1925.

...class conflict, Chile's North is also associated with military feats and heroism dating from the earliest colonial campaigns against Inca rule. Near San Pedro de Atacama are ruins of the last stand of the Incas who had ruled the area for less than a century. The great 1881 naval battle of Iquique was key to the defeat of the Peruvians in the war for control of the desert; it is commemorated in a national holiday every 21 May. Arica, the border city facing Peru, is physically dominated by the El Morro Hill, another famous battle site from the Peruvian war. On the Peruvian side is the site of the La Concepción battle where a battalion of Chilean soldiers were killed to the last man rather than surrender. They

are honored in the Santiago metro station "Los Heroes" (The Heroes). The desert cities Arica, Iquique, Antofagasta, tend to have a noticeable military presence, being frequently visited by soldiers on leave from their lonely outposts in the mountain border stations or local barracks – and relations with civilians, especially in the recently-concluded era of impunity for the armed forces, have not been universally smooth. In Arica military police patrol the city streets and have authority to make the arrests they deem necessary.

The "Little North": The northern half of Chile is divided into two zones: **El Norte Chico** ("Little North") is the semiarid quarter north of the capital, including the regional capitals of La Serena and Copiapó: while **El Norte Grande** ("Big North") is the total desert area around Antofagasta and Iquique. This terminology reflects the awe inspired by the extreme conditions and vast extension of the Atacama Desert, besides which the dry scrublands closer to Santiago seem a pale imitation. A bus trip from Santiago to Antofagasta takes over 20 hours, to Iquique nearly 30 although many travelers, naturally, prefer to fly.

The Diaguitas culture moved into this zone from across the Andes around AD 900 and flourished until the Inca conquest 500 years later, quickly followed by the arrival of the Spaniards. Ceramic work of this group is considered among the best in the Americas, and the black and white geometric designs on a red base are widely copied in Chilean decoration. Both La Serena and Ovalle have anthropological museums with excellent specimens.

Mineral smelting and the need for domestic fuel wiped out most native woods throughout the desert. The ore grade in the early mines was always at least 25 percent and could reach 50 or 60 percent. (Modern large-scale copper mining works with ore with a copper content of only 1 or 2 percent).

Driving north from Santiago, the central valley vegetation soon disappears and is replaced by hardy thorn trees. Signs of inhabitants become fewer and **Irrigated valley near Vicuña.**

180

fewer, and lands are no longer enclosed

Fray Jorge National Park

the Mapuche tongue) have white-sand beaches with strong surf; the latter's church is built on a promontory over the sea. A bird sanctuary with abundant sea life is located in between at the **Los Molles rock gardens** where underground caverns produce a thunderous roar. Nearby is the **Governor's Chair**, at 196 meters the highest sea cliff; it can be viewed from Valparaíso in good weather.

A few kilometers off the highway is the lively tourist town of **Los Vilos** which is full of rustic seafood restaurants and artisans who carve in *guayacán*, a durable wood once plentiful in the district.

Further north is a turn-off for the

verized conch shells.

The comfortable, slow-paced northern city of **La Serena** was the first settlement established by Pedro de Valdivia as part of his plan to secure the region for Spain. As such, it became an important hotel center from the beginning of the colonial period to receive travelers making the long trek across the desert. Religious orders also built receiving houses for their missionaries, and the city still has 29 churches; the oldest ones have remarkable stone facades. The discovery of silver in 1825 led to an upsurge of prosperity and a construction boom, though most of the original buildings were superseded by an ersatz "Spanish colonial" style im-

The Gabriela Mistral museum in her hometown Montenegro.

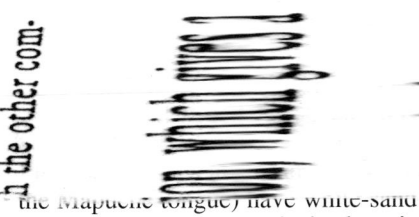

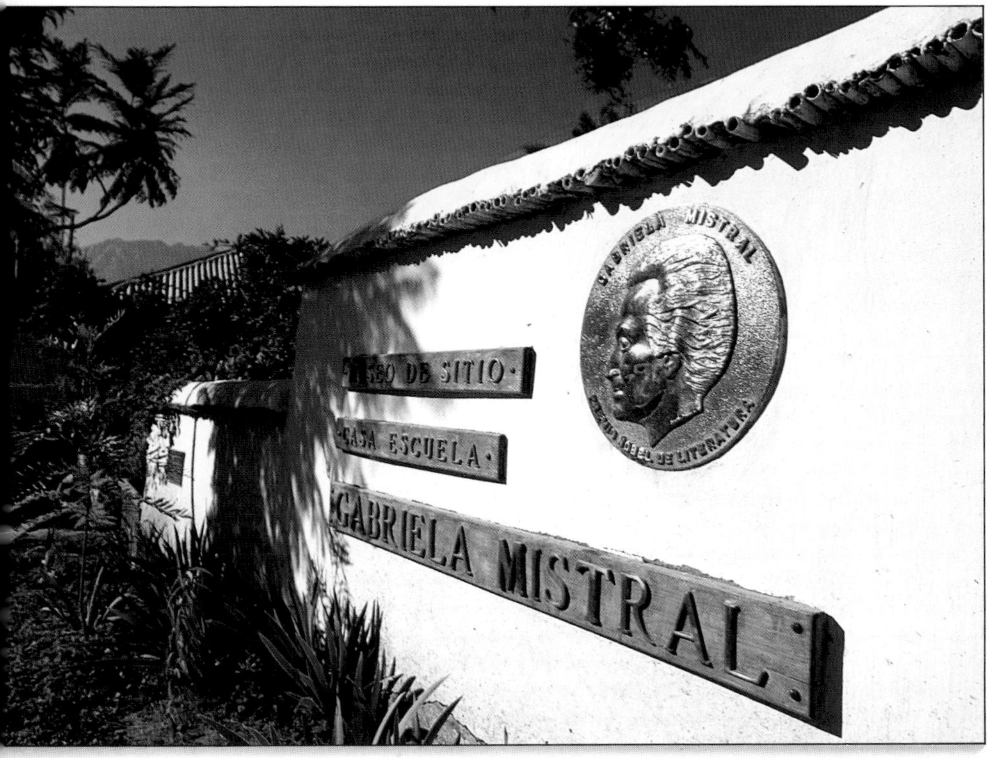

posed in a 1940s urban renewal scheme. All the landowning families of the Limari, Elqui, Huasco, Choapa, and Copiapó valleys had their own residence here, and La Serena retains an old-money reputation. The city's inhabitants have been mocked for being so laid-back as to be barely alive. (The unkindest comparison is to the papayas grown in abundance locally: they just hang from trees and get fat.)

La Serena's **archaeological museum** has an excellent collection of Diaguitas artifacts, and the **cemetery** provides an ample view of the river valley from above. Along with the tomb of native son and Chilean president Gabriel González Videla and relatives of Gabriela Mistral is a stone honoring officials of the Salvador Allende government shot in the days after the 1973 coup. González Videla's house in La Serena is also a national monument and museum. Several kilometers of fine beaches can be seen from the Cerro Grande high above the city, accessible by a dirt road.

The sister city of **Coquimbo** is still a major port especially active at the height of fruit export season in December and January. Some elaborate wood carvings, the handiwork of foreign carpenters, can still be seen on a few buildings. These craftsmen arrived as the mining industry grew since local tradesmen were unacquainted with how to build on the scale required. Shipped in from abroad were Oregon pine (which is neither pine nor from Oregon) and a large, sturdy species of bamboo from Guayaquil, Ecuador, which could be split and planed to form a solid surface. These materials and techniques were used to built the region's churches, most of which have a high central bell tower in the English neoclassic style and have survived severe earthquakes.

North of La Serena the PanAmerican Highway cuts back towards the interior, but a side spur leads to the interesting beaches and fishing villages at **Totoralillo, Temblador,** and **Chungungo**, the last being the name of a local species of otter.

Bethlehem Steel ran the world's larg-

A sheperdess minds her flock.

est iron mine between 1914 and 1954 at **El Tofo** 10 km (6 miles) in from this part of the Chilean coast, and its abandoned remains can still be visited. Also nearby is the Camanchaca Project: here the heavy mist that rolls in from the sea (called *camanchaca*) is captured and condensed to provide a water supply.

The atmosphere in the mountains in this part of Chile is excellent for astronomical purposes as the air is particularly clear. It is the chosen spot for observatories in all the Southern Hemisphere, having 300 nights a year of conditions apt for sky-photography. (Mt Palomar in the United States has 215.) The famous observatories at **Tololo**, **La Silla** and **Las Campanas** can be seen from the highway also, as well as from Cerro Grande in La Serena. Visits are possible by appointment.

North of Los Vilos is the **Choapa River Valley** with the city of **Illapel** its principal urban center. Illapel, like many Northern towns, had a mining boom and bust and has since returned to its original agricultural economy. Some 18th-century construction is preserved, both in the town and on the road to Salamanca, giving an idea of how rural estates were built around a central courtyard. A typical mansion has an adobe first-floor which blocks the heat and a wooden upstairs with balconies surrounding the inner patio. Sometimes the adobe walls are painted brightly.

The entire zone is arid and mountainous but has some surprisingly green valleys and attractive river beaches with excellent trout fishing. It is good for camping off-season when the sun is not so strong. The old north-south road which followed the Inca route and predates the PanAmerican Highway can be taken from Illapel up a severe climb past the narrowest part of Chile, only 80 km (50 miles) from the Argentine border to the sea. The view from the top just before Combarbala is superb, including the snow-topped Andes. *Pirquineros,* independent miners, are plentiful in the zone where the soil had a reddish tinge due to the copper presence.

The next valley to the north is the

Limari, with the city of **Ovalle** at its center. The surrounding area is an agricultural zone traditionally dependent on La Serena, but recently the expansion of irrigation has added new lands for export grapes and a burst of unevenly distributed prosperity. The Limari Valley is also a major *pisco*-producing zone. Plants can be visited during regular business days without an appointment. Five km southeast of Ovalle is the **Valle del Encanto (Enchanted Valley) National Monument**, rich in archaeological treasures. There is evidence of a hunter-gatherer civilization here dating back 4,000 years, though the bulk of the artifacts are from the Molle culture of around AD 700. This idyllic valley contains over 30 petroglyphs, designs carved into rocks, as well as 20 "piedras tacitas", groups of circular indentations hollowed out of flat rocks in the river bed.

To the north is the **Recoleta Reservoir**, a popular lake resort. En route can be seen the junction of the **Grande** and the **Jurtado rivers** from a high altitude. Further towards the Cordillera along this route is the **Pichasca Natural Monument** of gigantic rock formations and petrified wood. Many of these hamlets were Inca outposts ruled by a representative of the empire as they lie along the original north-south route through the mountains.

The town of **Hurtado** is known for its dried fruit, figs, quince marmalade and nuts, as well as its flower-farms of dahlias and chrysanthemums. The mountains can be crossed straight north towards **Vicuña** on an unpaved road which offers a panoramic view of both the Andes and the next valley, the famous **Elqui**.

Towards the southeast from Ovalle is the town of **Monte Patria**. This was the childhood home of one of Chile's greatest poets and a continuing symbol of the north: Gabriela Mistral. This aloof, accomplished, worldly literary exile was a schoolmistress here before moving to Mexico to participate in educational reform and embarking on a career as a poet. Little appreciated in Chile (she was given the national literary prize six

"La Portada" arch in Antofagasta.

years after her Nobel laureate) and mistrusted as an eccentric during her life, she was never a darling of the literary elite. Though her birthplace in nearby Vicuña is a national monument, she is an austere, rather than popular, heroine, treated like the precious mineral commodities that are unearthed from the dry, surrounding hills – a resource to be claimed and honored for its undeniable value, but not in itself a source of joy or pleasure. Her first book of poetry, published in New York, was titled *Desolation*; her themes are displacement, separateness, the difficulty of romantic love in a world ruled by a punishing God. Chile's other Nobel poet, Pablo Neruda, remains an intimate companion, widely quoted, remembered, and gossiped about, but Mistral is a remote eminence in the pantheon of Art. Her grave in the Monte Patria **cemetery** can be visited today.

Just before Monte Patria is the giant **La Paloma Reservoir**, the second-largest in South America and responsible for much of the new agricultural wealth of the region. It is recently planted with stands of trees and presents a refreshing spectacle in its dry setting. At the end of the difficult gravel road is the small village of **Las Ramadas** whose hills nearby contain one of the two known lapis lazuli mines in the world. (The other is in Afghanistan). This semi-precious blue stone is worked into a variety of pendants, earrings and decorations, and sold in artisan markets throughout the country.

Another road from Ovalle leads to **Combarbala** along the Guatulame River. The region's best grape lands are near **El Palqui** where hundreds of irrigated acres can be seen reaching up into the hills. The town of Combarbala uses the Diaguitas Indians' color and geometrical schemes in the design of its central plaza. A whitish, marble-like stone particular to the area, called *combarbalita*, is cut and polished by artisans to make miniature churches, eggs and other figures.

Vicuña in the Elqui Valley houses the Gabriela Mistral museum. The outlying hills have attracted a host of esoteric movements and guru-led communities, in part, no doubt, due to the great clarity of the night skies and the sensation that, as the title of a book about the zone suggested, "Heaven is Nearer."

The Third Region is the transition zone between the transverse valleys, where agriculture is still possible, and the Atacama Desert, where it is frankly inconceivable. The **Copiapó** is the last river to make its way down from the mountains to the sea. North of here, any mountain flows evaporate into nothing along the way, with the one exception of the Loa River which flows past the Chuquicamata copper mine (and becomes seriously contaminated). The Andes now divides into two parallel ranges, trapping the melting snows in an interior basin to form enormous salt flats, a phenomenon repeated all the way north into Bolivia. These deposits have great commercial potential for the concentrations of lithium, potassium and borax. In the central plain, followed by the PanAmerican Highway, a wet winter will produce every five to 10 years

the "flowering desert" phenomenon in the spring, a surprisingly exhuberant and colorful display.

The brief rule of the Incas in this region led to the import of Peruvian agricultural and metallurgical techniques by settler-rulers who collected tribute in towns along the "Inca Road." Spanish settlers gathered in agricultural oases, dabbling occasionally in gold and silver mining when there were discoveries. This mining activity was the precursor to the industrial transformation that occurred after independence. Much of the mining activity around Copiapó was owned and operated by Chileans rather than foreigners, creating the new industrial/financial class.

Mine activity also stimulated railroad construction, the first not only in Chile but in all of Latin America. The giant railroad equipment works at Meijillones near Antofagasta, second only in size to a California factory, functioned until the 1970s; it has since been dismantled. As the railroads were not primarily for human transport, which would have

implied a north-south orientation, they begin at ports and lead inland, often to now-abandoned sites. By the mid-19th century, the "Little North" was the economic, intellectual and cultural center of the country, and the great families often had industrial interests here to complement their agricultural estates in the South. Liberal ideas flourished, and the Radical Party of Chile was founded in Copiapó in 1863 by two industrialists shortly after a serious rebellion against the conservative capital. The wife of one moneyed mine owner died horribly when her Paris gown became entangled in the equipment of a new foundry they were inspecting. Another important Chilean fortune was made in the zone by Augustin Edwards whose grandson and namesake later founded the *El Mercurio* newspaper chain and remains the grey eminence of the right wing.

North of La Serena, the PanAmerican Highway again follows an interior valley, with the coast up to 50 km (30 miles) away over rugged gravel roads. Tiny fishing villages and undiscovered

Ancient geoglyphs in the Valle de Azapa.

186

beaches are to be found at the end, often with abandoned mine operations or shipping facilities nearby. **Caldera/Bahía Inglesa** is said to be the most beautiful beach of t**he North**, but bathing spots proliferate for kilometers along the highway, which returns to the shore for a long stretch between **Caldera** and **Chañaral**. The latter port was severly polluted by wastes from the Anaconda copper mine at Salvador, later nationalized, but deposits will now be diverted to a newly-inaugurated desert site, ending 60 years of contamination. Hedionda ("Stinky") Bay takes its name from this sad history. North of Chañaral is the Pan de Azucar National Park, a wildlife refuge containing fox, the guanaco llama, Humboldt penguins, otters and seals, as well as marine birds and substantial vegetation.

Copiapó, the capital of the region, is now a grape-growing zone par excellence, the result of enormous investments in earthmoving and irrigation. As these grapes are the first to ripen and hit US supermarkets around Christmas, they

are worth the expense. The development took place during the Pinochet regime, leading its representatives to predict that local residents would support the general in the 1988 plebiscite on another eight-year term as president. In fact, they voted 'no'.

From Copiapó it is possible to drive through the desert to the salt flats, an extraordinary trip if correct precautions are taken: wear warm clothes; bring food and water; travel preferably in a two-car caravan with motors adjusted for the altitude; and register your route and the duration of the trip with the local Carabineros (police). The **Salar de Maricunga** is impressive for its setting near the Andes, including the world's highest volcano, snow-topped Ojos de Salado (6,893 meters/22,615 ft). A hostería near **Laguna Verde** has full facilities for mountaineering. The lake is apparently dead, but flamingos live in the Salar, contentedly picking bugs out of the oily ooze in the rocks. Explorer/conqueror Diego de Almagro used this crossing from Argentina in his ill-fated

**ravelers
xplore the
emote roads
ear San
Pedro.**

1536 journey: he lost most of his men en route in the frigid passes. Legend has it that half-frozen survivors often pulled off a couple of toes along with the boots.

The big North: The Atacama Desert is located in the same latitude belt as other deserts in the Southern Hemisphere whose dominant high pressure systems prevent storms from moving in. Chile's twin mountain ranges aggravate the situation; no precipitation has been measured in this desert since the Spanish colonization, giving it the title of driest spot on earth. The Altiplanic Inversion occurs around the summer equinox (21 December) when strong evaporation generates sometimes violent rain and hail storms in the mountains, and the water rushes down the dry gorges. These storms last until March and serious flooding makes many roads unpassable.

The extraordinary dryness is responsible for great archaelogical treasures, such as the famous Atacama mummies, which predate the Egyptian varieties by several thousand years. All sorts of artifacts are easily preserved, and new finds occur regularly. The excellent Le Paige Museum in San Pedro de Atacama, founded by a Belgian Jesuit, Gustavo Le Paige, has 380,000 objects. A 2800-year-old site called Tulor has been unearthed nearby.

Water is obviously a major logistical problem, not only for personal use but also to satisfy the enormous demands of modern mining. Huge investments have been made in pipelines to bring Andean waters to the coast or to mine outposts. At the Conchi bridge north of Chiu-Chiu (near San Pedro), six lines come together. Remnants of native population are inexorably forced elsewhere as their water supply dries up. The first known industrial use of solar energy in the world, was a water desalinization plant built in 1872 at Carmen Alto near Antofagasta. Pollution from mining and smelting has been common, but not all industrial intervention has been a disaster: the Salado River was diverted to Chuquicamata in 1951, removing its unwanted salts from the Loa which runs all the way to Antofagasta. (Unfortunately, it is now thought that the Loa has high levels of arsenic.) Just about any desert settlement is built around the water question; at Pica, for example, 18th-century techniques for capturing more moisture are still in use.

Antofagasta is the fifth largest city in Chile and the most populous of the desert. It is the main port for export of the minerals of Chuquicamata and will soon be receiving half as much material again with the opening of the giant La Escondida mine developed by British, Japanese and Australian capital. Its 20-km (12-mile) beachfront gives it a fresh, gracious air despite the unrelieved brown of the hills. A financial dispute and property seizure here in 1879 sparked the War of the Pacific which ended Bolivian control of the town and lands to the east. This portion of Chile is the widest, measuring 355 km (221 miles) from Andes to sea. The Andean peaks reach 6,000 meters (19,700 ft) while the highest peak of the entire coastal range is **Mount Vicuña-MacKenna** to the southwest at 3,114 meters (10,217 ft).

Today, Antofagasta is in another boom

Below and right, El Tatio geysers steaming at dawn.

period and is likely to grow rapidly. An excellent regional museum explains local history as well as anthropological details about the surrounding desert. Two universities attract students from all over Chile; they flock to the beach at sunset year round, as do many off-duty soldiers as well. Thirteen km north of the city is the famous La Portada National Monument, a huge rock eroded into an arch by the sea. Across a peninsula to the north is the town of **Mejillones**, now a commercial fishing center. It started out as the Northern railroads' mechanical shop producing wagons and locomotives.

To the interior of Antofagasta is the **Chuquicamata** mine and the next-door service town of **Calama**, which has long superseded nearby Chiu-Chiu in importance. Most travelers only stay in Calama overnight to visit the mine (see inset on Chuquicamata), since the town itself has little to offer besides streets full of cheap bars and strip joints. **Chiu-Chiu**, however, was the prehispanic crossroads at the fork of two rivers. It fulfills the stereotype of a desert oasis, a cool, green speck in the midst of a hostile brown sea, and has a 1675 church whose construction used elements of the Atacameña indigenous culture. The road toward San Pedro de Atacama crosses the Plain of Patience, whose name soon begins to make sense: the landscape between two distant ridges appears not to change at all for hundreds of kilometers. An advertised alternative route to San Pedro though the **Valley of the Moon** (Valle de la Luna) is not advised for small cars as sand accumulated on the road will trap them, and this is not a place to be stuck.

A base of exploration: The oasis town of **San Pedro de Atacama** is a popular base for exploring the North's most spectacular sights. Another dry salt lake, the **Salar de Atacama**, stretches beyond the town to a distant row of snow-capped volcanoes – including Licancabur, which, at 5,900 metres (19,360 ft) is one of the highest extinct volcanoes in the whole Andean chain. Many travelers find the town a good place to

relax: it has a restored adobe house on one side of the plaza that is universally called Pedro de Valdivia's residence but is now thought to be prehispanic in construction; opposite is a 16th-century church, one of the oldest in Chile.

San Pedro's **archaeological museum** (its full name is the Museo Archaeologico Gustavo Le Paige de Walque) is regarded as one of the best in South America. Begun by the former village priest for whom the museum is named, it has an unusually wide array of Indian artifacts all excellently displayed. Particularly fascinating are the ancient Indian mummies – of both children and adults – preserved in the dry desert air, and the deliberately deformed skulls. Many pre-Inca Indian groups warped the shapes of their childrens' heads using tightly bound ropes, for aesthetic or religious reasons.

Further east from San Pedro is the village of **Toconao**, past a plantation of tamarugo trees which provide a tiny seed for animal pasture. A forest service guide can be hired at Toconao to drive to

Lake Chaxa and observe another group of pink flamingos. The entire Salar de Atacama can be circled in a two-day trip, passing through impressively desolate landscapes and curious desert outposts. Pozo 3 is an oasis near the town turned into a commercial swimming pool and picnic area.

Of interest to visitors are the ruins of a 700-year-old Indian fortress at **Quitor**, 3 km northwest of San Pedro. This was where the local Indians made their last stand against the invading Pedro de Valdivia. Some of the fortress has been restored, and it is worth exploring the turret where the last Indian chief of the North lived. The view from the top of the fortress is also breathtaking.

Thirty km (18 miles) further afield are the hot springs called the **Termas de Puritana**. You need a car to get there, but it is worth the drive: there is a choice of steaming pools to wallow in, as well as a few waterfalls for a natural shower.

Desert winds and geysers: The famous **Valley of the Moon** (Valle de la Luna) is on the other side of the Salar de

The Valley of the Moon.

Atacama, about 8 km (5 miles) from San Pedro. As the name suggests, this is a haunting landscape of colored gypsum, clay and salt, without a hint of organic life to be found. The valley is at its eeriest at sunset, while reports suggest that under a full moon the beams reflecting off the salt crystals of the region is a truly spectacular sight.

But perhaps the most interesting excursion from San Pedro is leaving at 4 a.m. to visit the daily show of at least 100 geysers at **El Tatio** gushing out their morning's display just before sunrise every morning of the year. As they exit the frozen earth with strange gurgling underground sounds, they throw their columns of steam high into the air. Some are wide, boiling pools gashed in the surface of the ground. Others resemble mini volcanoes with cones of bright yellow mineral deposits. The display quiets down about 10 a.m. until the next morning. The visitor can bathe in a huge pool of tolerably hot thermal waters before returning. However, it is a good idea to be the first back down the moun-

tain before others scare off the wildlife around the Putana River where sulphur is extracted from the volcano of the same name; or to bathe in the purifying waters of the thermal Purifica River that surfaces for a hidden, brief stretch of narrow canyon not far from the base of the mountains. It is only one of the myriad surprises tucked away in the folds of the Northern Andes.

Driving north towards **Iquique** you pass constant geoglyphs carved or built onto the hillsides. The best collection is in **Pampa del Tamarugal National Reserve**, 48 km (30 miles) south of the turnoff to Iquique. This is also the zone of nitrate ghost towns. The detour to Iquique is at **Pozo Almonte**, 47 km (30 miles) across a plateau which abruptly ends with a breathtaking view over the city. Iquique looks like it should be in Saudi Arabia rather than South America. Between it and the 600-meter cliffs lies a huge sand dune whose dimensions only become clear from below. The habitable land is a narrow strip blocked by cliffs and a stupendous beach, al-

Below, church **in Iquique**. **Right**, the **Cocha de Pica thermal baths near Iquique**.

though much of it is too rough for bathing. Iquique's golden era was the nitrate heyday from 1890-1920 when European opera singers ap-peared in the elegant Municipal Theatre and adjourned to a replica moorish palace, now the Casino Español, across the plaza, for a late meal. After the collapse of nitrates, fishmeal took over. Today, Iquique is now the world's principal port of embarkation for fishmeal exports; critics say the industry is threatened by over-exploitation.

The **regional museum** (at Sotomayor 706) is worth visiting, with the usual array of local Indian artifacts, plus a mock Indian village. The nearby Naval Museum (cnr. Esmeraldas and Pinto) is also curious. But the main inte-rest is in the range of stately 19th-century mansions that are kept as national monuments, many of which are around the Plaza de Armas with its clock tower and corinthian columns. The whole center at Iquique has been declared a National Monument and cannot be altered without official permission.

Back on the pampa a few kilometers from Iquique is the site of the La Tirana Virgen del Carmen religious festival. This annual event, known as Chinese Fraternities, occurs during mid–July and goes on for a week. The festival has characteristic dance groups composed of virginal maidens and men disguised as devils. The whole experience is a compromise between Catholic rite and indigenous animist influences.

On the northern frontier: Arica was the first port for exporting the fabulous silver wealth of Bolivia's Potosí mine. (In 1611 Potosí was the largest and richest city in the Americas). But Arica's climate generated malaria, and the city was abandoned for other sites. Under Peruvian rule until the 1880s, Arica is now the international link to Bolivia (by rail) and Peru (road). Its warm-water beaches make it a popular summer resort. A small church in the town center was built by the French architect Eiffel, better known for his Paris tower.

The **San Miguel Archaeological Museum** is 14 km (9 miles) from town with

Moorish style of Iquique's Casino Español.

an excellent collection of sand-preserved mummies older than their Egyptian counterparts. The Azapa Valley in which the museum is located demonstrates the desert's fertility given an adequate supply of water; brightly-colored flowers grown commercially suddenly appear in the distance.

From Arica, passing by the ancient geoglyphs near **San Miguel de Azapa**, and taking the inland road towards the Chungara Lake – declared a Biosphere World Reserve by UNESCO – one passes through various pre-Colombian and colonial villages, with their baroque churches and stone forts called pukaras used by local Indian tribes from unrecorded times to defend themselves from invaders. As one ascends 4,500 meters (14,800 ft) into the **Lauca National Park**, the mighty 6,000-meter (19,700-ft) high volcanoes Parinacota and Pomerape – sacred gods to the inhabitants of the Andean high plane – dominate the landscape. The ritual town of Parinacota, locked and abandoned for most of the year, is a center for the colorful religious fêtes of the Aymara Indian shepherds in the region, who otherwise rarely reveal themselves. Most of the year they tend their herds of llamas and alpacas (whose longer, shaggier wool is more treasured) in the remote, wind-swept heights.

After passing the deep emerald waters of Cotacotani Lagoons, one arrives at the Chungara Lake. Wildlife teems all around the lake: the large bluish, flightless taqua-taqua make their nests on floating reed islands; the chinchilla-like vizcachas with their hopping scamper could be mistaken for fleeing gray hares; the smaller, undomesticated sand-coloured vicuñas often tag behind llama herds; the black and white Andean geese piquén will show themselves far from their nesting offspring as decoys; but perhaps most famous are the pink flamingos who dwell in the lake's shallows. Covering the rocks at this altitude like a green carpet is the pungent native lichen yareta, which grows a centimeter a year and has been used for fire fuel almost to its extinction further south.

CHUQUICAMATA

The emptiness of the surrounding desert conceals to some degree the scale of this colossal copper mine, the largest open-pit mine in the world – in fact, the largest of any kind. Smoke from its concentrating and refining plants and its gigantic "cakes" of waste rock or "tailings" can be seen kilometers away. But only upon approaching nearer does the true size of Chuquicamata become obvious. Tours leave from the visitors center at 10 a.m. on weekdays and are a highlight of any trip to the North, no matter how small your interest in mining.

bits, then mixed with water and further mashed into a more manageable paste. This is agitated with chemical agents in flotation cells, causing the metal-rich spume to separate from the unwanted mud. The resulting product is copper concentrate of about 35 percent purity, which is then smelted in a series of ovens to produce copper anodes or "blister" with about 99.3 percent copper content. Both concentrates and blister are sold to overseas clients, especially Germany, Finland, South Korea and Japan.

Precious metals and poison: Aside from

Dwarfing machinery: The first thing that strikes the tourist are the special trucks that load and carry the mineral loosened by dynamite explosions from the terraced sides of the vast pit. The wheels alone are nearly four meters in diameter, and drivers sit another two meters above them, reducing all other traffic to Lilliputian status. Regular-sized trucks must circulate with flags on long poles to alert the big-truck drivers to their presence. One job of the small vehicles is to water the roadways to ease wear on the giant tires, which cost US$10,000 each.

The "charge" or "feed" of copper ore is first crushed and broken into smaller gravel

molybdenum, some gold and silver are also recovered from the ore. But there are other byproducts that are not so attractive. Sulphur is released from the sulphate ores; a new plant has been built to capture these gases and convert them into sulphuric acid. Some copper refining requires this acid, but the market is limited. The Chuqui ore also contains alarming traces of arsenic. Union leaders charge that arsenic poisoning is rampant among workers and suggest that the surrounding area, including Antofagasta's water supply, is slowly being loaded with arsenic escaping from the plants. One tragicomic tale is told there about the retired worker who traveled to Spain with his wife and suddenly died. His spouse was arrested on suspicion of poisoning him when the forensic specialist found high levels of arsenic in his blood.

Though Chile's new democratic government promises to pay more attention to environmental issues than the outgoing military regime, it is clear that no anti-pollution measures can be taken which would limit Chuqui's copper output because of the cornerstone role it plays in the national economy. The four divisions of the state-owned copper company, Codelco-Chile, produce three-quarters of the country's 1.6 million metric tons of fine copper. Chuqui is responsible for nearly half of that. Despite a diver-

lama but has been dismantled bit by bit to make room for mine expansion.

The politics of copper: Codelco-Chile, the Chilean Copper Company, originated in the 1971 decision of President Salvador Allende to nationalize the country's most important industry with unanimous support from congress. (The military regime, after Allende's overthrow in 1973, compensated the U.S. companies expropriated but kept the mines in state hands, establishing Codelco for this purpose in 1976.)

Codelco's workforce naturally has a major political role which corresponds to the industry's tremendous economic weight. Among Chilean workers, the copper miners

sification of exports in the last few years, copper still brings in 40 percent of Chile's foreign exchange. Ore grades, though still attractive by world standards, have been falling for years which requires the mining and treatment of more and more ore, releasing more and more pollutants, to produce the same amount of copper. Continued expansion of the mine will eventually engulf the town of Chuquicamata, which was once several times larger than neighboring Ca-

Left, the world's largest open-cut mine. **Above**, mining trucks dwarf their drivers.

are an elite group with relatively handsome wage and benefit packages. Although there are now sharp distinctions in the workforce — the result of subcontracting out many jobs in the mines to reduce permanent, full-time staff and cut costs — the town of Calama is still full of dark-skinned, burly workers sitting down to drinks and ample meals with an air of prerogative and satisfaction usually reserved for the puissant, blue-eyed classes of Santiago. Most of the staggering wealth produced by Chuqui is absorbed by the rest of the country, but enough of it remains to give this desolate outpost in the wilderness a chance to entertain itself.

GHOST TOWNS

The collapse of nitrate or saltpeter market at the end of World War I was so sudden that the mining towns, which had no other reason to exist, were abruptly abandoned. As late as the 1960s, a train loaded with nitrate still sat on a siding at the Santa Laura office near Iquique, left there some five decades earlier. Now the North is dotted with these town shells, most of which have been thoroughly sacked, even including their graveyards. A couple remain and have been converted into historical monuments.

Mining camps were known as "offices," referring to the offices of the purchasing agents who bought everything mined within a certain radius. Virtually anyone determined and hardworking enough could be a miner since the earliest production method consisted of simply digging up the readily-visible *caliche*, or nitrate ore, grinding

it, and selling it at the "office." When the best ore, with a grade of 50-60 percent, was exhausted, the office simply moved elsewhere.

More complicated processes which could use lower-grade ore led to more permanent settlements. These offices are identifiable by their waste piles of gravel built up into cake-like constructions. Many are visible from the highway between Antofagasta and Calama and south of Iquique. A small roadside market gives the history of each site, including peak production totals and population.

Eerie remains: The best-preserved ghost town is **Humberstone Office** on the turnoff from Pozo Almonte to Iquique. Named for Santiago Humberstone, mine owner and technological innovator, it had a population of 5,000 at its heyday and provided an unusually varied existence for its inhabitants. A few tamarugo trees remain standing around the plaza, and the town theater's seats are still intact. It even boasted a swimming pool partly covered with a

Left, lonely desert cactus; Right, licence plates make a memorial for accidents.

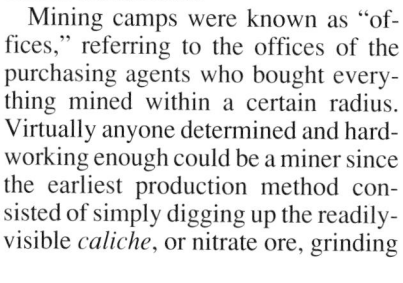

bamboo shade. The abandoned frames of workshops and domiciles spread out over a large area; everything is covered with dust and battered by a steady, desert wind. The air of recent habitation is genuinely spooky, as if the people had suddenly fled from an invading army. The site was used to great effect in the Chilean movie, *Return Station*, in which a woman goes north in search of her boyfriend arrested for political reasons. Nearby is **Santa Laura Office** where a processing plant and administrative complex are preserved. The road to Iquique crosses the abandoned railway several times. Tours are conducted on weekends.

Along the Antofagasta-Calama road just past Carmen Alto is the **Chacabuco Office** and nearby **Salinas railway station**, site of an abandoned 1872 potable water plant which used solar energy. Of the other offices only the walls of the homes remain, built with stones cut from the sides of the mine.

Between Antofagasta and Tocopilla are the only functioning nitrate centers,

Pedro de Valdivia and Maria Elena. Both are owned by SOQUIMICH, the Chilean Mining and Chemical Company, returned to private ownership during the military regime. The nitrate market has perked up considerably with the renewed demand for natural fertilizers, and iodine can also be recovered commercially as a byproduct. The technology in use, known as "Guggenheim Office" after the U.S. investors (also responsible for the Guggenheim Museum in New York and at one time owners of Chuquicamata) can treat mineral with grades as low as seven percent.

Marked but almost forgotten is the site of the schoolhouse where the notorious massacre of Santa Maria de Iquique occurred in 1907. Here hundreds of nitrate miners and their families were murdered by government troops after a long strike and sit-in.

Chilean history books do not refer to the incident, but eyewitnesses said the stand was transformed into a bloody swamp for blocks.

Deserted town of Santa Laura.

CENTRAL VALLEY

Running parallel between the towering Cordillera de los Andes and the lower coastal mountain range is the Chilean **Central Valley**. The area from Los Andes, just 80 km (50 miles) north of the capital Santiago, to some 500 km (300 miles) further south is the richest farmland in the country. Although vineyards have been established here since the arrival of the Spanish *conquistadores*, most of the traditional agricultural activities of the old landed aristocracy – such as growing wheat, grain and fodder for domestic animals – has given way to the much more profitable cultivation of fresh produce for export to markets around the globe.

Driving in springtime along the Pan-American highway south of Santiago, fields of flaming orchards perfume the air and make a brilliant display. The dark, hot pink of peaches and nectarines to the lighter rose-colored cherry trees, the white flowering almond, apple, apricot or plum trees all proclaim the Central Valley's world-renowned fertility. This rich soil and mild, almost frost-free climate has made Chile one of the world's most prominent exporters of out-of-season fresh produce, popularly known in the Northern Hemisphere as "winter fruit."

On the larger farms, the tractor has replaced the horse-drawn plow. But in the smaller towns, on the slower roads, it is still common to see the use of animal teams both in the fields and hitched to wagons bringing produce to market. Getting off the main roads is like taking a step backwards in time, to a simpler, slower paced, infinitely more relaxing era, where the distinct flavor of the Chilean countryside can be savored.

Never is this more true then during the Independence Day celebrations held on 18 September, which offer an inside view to festivities in rural areas throughout the country. *Fondas* or *ramadas*, outdoor ballrooms with thatched eucalyptus leaf roofs, are erected all over the countryside. People gather from miles around so they can watch the competition between *huasos,* the Chilean cowboys, dance the *cueca,* the national dance, eat the *empanadas,* meat and onion pies, and drink *chicha,* fermented grape juice.

You might even come across the chance to bet on the race between unsaddled horses. Usually a sprint, the riders have to keep the two horses abreast the first third of the race or it will be declared invalid.

Down the PanAmerican: The capital of the VIth Region is 87 km (54 miles) south of Santiago. Bustling **Rancagua** is as much an agricultural center as it is the home of the miners employed in El Teniente, the largest underground copper mine in the world, located in the mountains to the east.

More enjoyable, however, is a trip into the Andean foothills to thermal baths of **Cauquenes** just 28 km (17 miles) east of Rancagua. Used by native peoples long before the arrival of the Spanish, the first to lay claim to the medicinal waters were Jesuits. They

Preceding pages, the Andean foothills south of Santiago. **Left**, the annual harvest. **Right**, Sunday mass.

were frequented by Chilean founding father Bernardo O'Higgins during rests from his revolutionary bouts against the colonial authorities, and, in 1834, British naturalist Charles Darwin wrote of the excellence of their waters. The construction of what is today a hotel were begun in 1885. The huge high-ceilinged bathhouse with individual or double bathrooms and stained-glass windows leads up an enormous staircase to the dining and game room area. The menu offers an enormous assortment of such delicacies as roast wild hare in a multi-course menu all for a set fee included in the price of the lodgings. Rooms and suites with wood burning iron stoves and private baths are set around large open gardens or down the back overlooking the Cachapoal River. The surrounding hills are filled with peumos, a native tree with bright red edible fruit and shiny green leaves. The hotel is well worth a visit. (Reservations can be made from Santiago by calling 482 841.)

Thirty km (18 miles) further south along the PanAmerican just past Pele-quen, is an unpaved, eastward cut-off that leads to the **Los Lingues Hacienda**. Here the visitor can have a look inside one of the mansions that are often seen along the older roads in the area. Many have been damaged beyond repair from the earthquakes that frequently shake the Pacific coast, or left to decay as impractical white elephants. This *hacienda*, however, is intact and houses a number of period pieces, both imports from Europe and native Mapuche or Diaguita Indian artifacts, giving an idea of how the aristocracy lived in the newly-settled colony.

The first owner of the property was mayor of Santiago in 1599 and received the ranch as a donation from the king of Spain. The central part of the house was built in the 17th and early-18th century, with additional wings added 100 years later. Constructed in the colonial style of adobe and *cal y canto*, stones held together with a mortar containing thousands of egg whites, the *hacienda* also features pink paving stones from the Pelequen quarry, with beams of oak, **Fruit market.**

and reed interior ceilings topped by ceramic tiled roofs. Some of the ornate doors were carved by Bavarian Jesuits living in Calera de Tango.

Surrounding the manor is the traditional park of old native trees where pheasants, grouse and peacocks roam. Enclosed within are groomed gardens that fill its many interior patios. In the summer, guests can feast outside on the many dishes from age-old recipes handed down over generations. Or try any number of traditional cocktails from the zone during the training exhibitions of thoroughbred Aculeo horses raised on the farm.

The *hacienda* is part of the exclusive international hotel chain "Relais et Chateaux." Both transportation and reservations can be arranged through calling 235 5446 in Santiago.

While the recently-restored colonial town of Vichuquen can be reached by bus from **Curico** (with a change over in Hualañé), this area near the coast has so many points of interest that it merits renting a car to be able to reach its various attractions. The 110-km (68-mile) unpaved road that follows the northern bank of the Mataquito River from Curico as far as Hualañé offers breathtaking scenic beauty. But taking the cut-off from the highway near San Fernando, through Santa Cruz, Lolol, San Pedro de Alcantara, Rarin and the coastal town Llico also has its own charm, revealing rolling hills and sleepy country towns. It is not rare to find an ox team pulling home a load of recently harvested hay or alfalfa.

The town of **Vichuquen** existed before the invasion of the Incas from Peru in the 15th century, who formed a colony there with the native Mapuches. The name comes from the Mapuche language and means "the isolated place." Time seems to have stopped still some 100 years ago along its orange tree-lined streets. Unhurried locals linger about the covered wooden sidewalks at sun up, on a morning's errand to buy fresh baked bread from the bakery. At sunset they chat casually with neighbors, sitting in front of their homes to watch

Rich river valley.

the world go by, do a bit of knitting, spinning, or other everyday domestic tasks.

The main attraction of the area, however, is the natural freshwater **Lake Vichuquen**. Pine forests that grow in record time surround the summer houses that line the shore. Windsurfers or small sailboats cut silently across the mirror-like surface of the lake to explore the uninhabited Isla del Cerrillo that sits alone in the lake's center. There are two hotels on the lake, the more exclusive **Brujas del Lago Hotel** at the northern end near Llico that rents boats and sailboards and the more modest *hostería* in Aquelare at the southern end. There are also several camping grounds.

Just 3 km (1.9 miles) north of the lake is **Laguna Torca National Reserve**. The laguna is a nesting ground for black-necked swans and any number of other exotic birds. Great blue herons hide in the reed-lined banks. The S-shaped bodies of stark white herons wade through the shallows, while an enormous variety of ducks and the small, black *taguas* coots keep up a tremendous clatter of quacking.

After a morning's bird-watching has increased the appetite, stop in for fresh shellfish or fried conger eel at the Residencial Miramar in **Llico**. This is a small seaside village, where it is common for one brother to tend the cows while the other makes his living from the sea. The enormous eerie structure off the beach was part of a frustrated attempt at the turn of the century to create docks for navy ships that would take refuge in the inland lake. North of the beach lies an interminable expanse of huge sand dunes.

Seat of Chilean independence: Continuing south on the PanAmerican highway, **Talca**, 60 km (37 miles) away from Curico, is the capital of the VIIth region. An important urban center since its founding in 1742, Talca has been the traditional residence of both the landed elite and regional industry. The labels of many products produced there read "Talca, Paris and London." The older part of town, as in most colonial towns, surrounds the **Plaza de Armas** with its

jacarandas, palms, magnolia trees, cedars and other conifers. The local market offers handicrafts as well as inexpensive *picadas*, or restaurants. For finer dining try Talca's specialities of fried frog legs and *chancho en piedra* in the Club de Talca near the Plaza or one of the town's many restaurants.

The **O'Higgins Museum**, on the corner of Norte and Oriente streets, was the childhood home of the Chilean hero and father of Independence, Bernardo O'Higgins. The building was the home of José Miguel Carrera in 1813, who presided over the first Governmental Junta. Carrera declared Chile a sovereign, autonomous state in the Constitutional Reglament of 1812, while he also – with the help of O'Higgins – organized resistance to invading royalist troops from further south.

In one of the house's many salons, Bernardo O'Higgins signed the Act of Independence. The museum also features an important collection of paintings, sculpture, historical manuscripts and pre-Colombian artifacts.

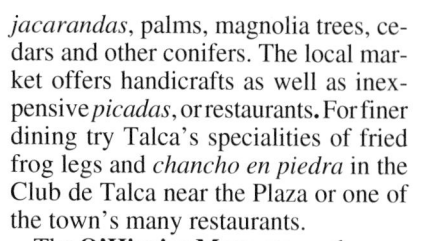

The 'Wild West' look.

Further south on the highway is the town of **Chillan**. Repeatedly destroyed by earthquakes and rebuilt, most of the buildings are not more than 50 years old. The last catastrophy occurred in 1939, when 15,000 were killed and 90 percent of the town was destroyed. Mexico donated a school to the city as part of the reconstruction following that earthquake. The Mexican muralists David Alfaro Siqueiros and Xavier Guerrero painted some representative scenes of Chilean and Mexican history there in 1941. The Escuela Mexico can be visited during school hours on Av. Bernardo O'Higgins with Vega de Saldias Streets.

Chillan's handicraft market, on Maipon Street between Isabel Riquelme and 5 de Abril, is the largest in Chile. Here you can find handicrafts from various parts of the country as well as the locally-made clothing that make up the typical *huaso* or cowboy dress: from the felt (for winter) or straw (for summer) flat-rimmed hats; the small dress ponchos in finely woven, bright colors; to the leather boots and carved wooden stirrups. In fact, you may come across more than one *huaso* outfitting both himself and his horse.

Volcanic thermal baths: At 800 meters (2,600 ft) above sea level, the **ski resort** 80 km (50 miles) from Chillan is one of the most accessible in the country and also the most unique. The western-facing slopes of the smoking Chillan Volcano feature some of the finest open-slope skiing in the Andes from June through October. With five "T"-lifts and a 2.5-km (1½-mile) double chair lift (the longest in South America) presently operating, expansion continues. An accomplished skier can stay on the slopes from morning to late afternoon, and, as there is so much variety, need never pass down the same trail twice.

After a hard day on the slopes, there is nothing better than to dive into one of the four outside thermal water swimming pools high up above the hotel, which has indoor individual or two-person baths and saunas. Beauty operators are on hand to apply mud packs and

A rich landowner's house near San Fernando.

you can also get an excellent massage upon appointment, to leave you in shape for the discotheque after dinner.

The hotel, with a capacity for 350 guests, features a number of sitting rooms with roaring fireplaces, video projectors, games and music rooms. Guest rooms with private baths are large, clean and more functional than elegant. The set menu included in the price of rooms is wholesome if not very imaginative, but delicacies are available at an additional cost.

Chillan's thermal baths have been famous for the past 150 years, while the ski resort was only developed within the second half of the last decade. Many make the trip in the summer, even camping near the hotel or staying in the cabins or hotel in **Las Trancas** or **Recinto**, to hike to the geyser-like fuming springs of the thermal waters and bathe in the medicinal muds nearby. One may also take the chair lift to appreciate the full view of the towering volcanic crater and accompanying eternal snows of the Nevada de Chillan mountain range.

The road back from the hotel is lined with lush forest vegetation resembling the Lake District further south. Huge old oaks vie with firs, pines and the delicate, native *ñirre* trees set among giant ferns and red *copihues*, the fleshy, trumpet-shaped national flowers that hang from climbing vines. Two km down from the hotel you can visit an enormous natural cavern the **Cueva de los Pincheira.** This was used as a hideaway by the Pincheira brothers, a group of royalist highway robbers and their band who ransacked the area during the struggle for independence. The spectacular **Piedras Comadres**, colossal rock walls that drop straight down from their forest-covered heights can be seen from the road.

Before the town of Los Angeles, 80 km (50 miles) south of Chillan, the **Salto de Laja** waterfall can be viewed from the bridge that crosses the Laja River. Roughly halfway between Santiago and Puerto Montt, it is a favorite stop on the way south. The falls crash down some 15 to 20 meters (49–66 ft)

Scooping up coal in Lota.

from two wide arches into deep, enormous pools, only to be swiftly conducted into the deep gash of the narrow river canyon further down, cut through steep rock walls. The area offers a myriad of hotels, camping sites and restaurants, some complete with swimming pools and recreational parks and facilities.

Gateway to the South: Capital of the VIIIth region and the country's second largest city (even though it only has 326,800 inhabitants), **Concepción** is located some 86 km (53 miles) off the PanAmerican Highway. It lies on the coast at the month of the **Bío Bío River**, the natural boundary between Southern and Central Chile. Founded by *conquistador* Pedro de Valdivia in 1550, it was the site occupied by the Real Audencia: the political, military and administrative center of the Spanish colony from 1565 to 1573. Four and a half centuries of natural disasters combined with great economic growth in the area have made Concepción a modern city with little remaining testimony of its past glory. While many Santiaginos forced to leave the capital for work reasons claim Concepción is the best post in the provinces, most visitors would rather pass on through it.

The pride of the city is the **University of Concepción** campus with its open amphitheater and other buildings that surround the central green dominated by the university's watch tower. Nearby are the marble-fronted walls of the courthouse and the mural over the train station depicting the history of the city. The **Pinacoteca** on the corner of Lamas and Larenas, houses the most complete collection of national painters.

In the neighboring port **Talcahuano**, rivalling Concepción in size, one can visit the battleship *Huascar*. Captured from the Peruvian fleet during the War of the Pacific in 1879, it has been held as a trophy of the victory that added the country's northern most provinces and their rich mineral deposits, to the national territory.

The main industries that make Concepción's financial sector hum are nearby. To the north are the textile mills

Sunday afternoon in the village plaza.

of Tome and the crockery factory in Penco. Northwest are the steel mills in Huachipato and to the south are the coal mines of **Coronel** and **Lota**, where some shafts run 20 km (12 miles) underground off the shore.

Worth a visit in Lota is the park created by the original owners of the coal mines, the Cousiño family – who still own and run the Viña Macul vineyards and built the **Palacio Cousiño** in Santiago. They also founded the first forestry industry in the local Colcura Valley in 1881 to supply beams for use within their mines.

The dark pine forests, a faster-growing crop than the native hard wood forests which they have replaced, run as far south as Curanilahue and the forestry industry lines the roads with trunk-laden trucks. The cellulose plant for paper manufacturing in the beach resort Arauco has contributed to the development of the zone. This industry is probably the most responsible for the recent paving of the road south taken by the Spanish conquerers as they explored the area between the coast and the Nahualbuta mountain range, scarcely inhabited even today.

Following this so-called **Ruta de los Conquistadores** one arrives in **Cañete** with its frontier flavor that announces the beginnings of the Mapuche lands. It was here that Mapuche *toqui* or warrior chief Lautaro surprised *conquistador* Pedro de Valdivia and put a dramatic end to his life.

The **Mapuche Museum** in Cañete offers a large display of the native people's culture, including ritual and domestic artifacts, weapons, documents and photographs. Either in the town's market or on the plaza it is possible to mingle with descendents of the survivors of the 300-year struggle to expel the Spanish from their lands. Try some *chicha de manzana*, fresh or fermented apple cider, this being the most popular thirst quencher throughout the Mapuche lands.

While the roads through the reservations surrounding Cañete are unpaved, they are well maintained during all but the wettest months of the year. Here the Mapuches go on working their land with the same technology used by their forefathers, using hand sickles to harvest their wheat, horses to plough it, and ox teams to take it to market.

Lodgings are available on the **Lanalhue Lake** in the Hosteria Lanalhue at the western end of the lake or the Posada Campesina at the eastern end, where lake carp virtually jump out of the water to be fed by guests. There is also a hotel in the quaint neighboring town **Contulmo**, settled by Prussians in 1868. Visit the **Grollmus house** and mill with its 23 varieties of *copihues*, the national flower, and small hydroelectric generator that supplied the town with light since 1928.

Returning towards the central valley, take a walk through the **Contulmo National Monument**. Its 88 hectares (218 acres) of native forest reserve show the visitor what the pass over the Nahuelbuta coastal mountain range looked like when it was frequented by the armies of Spanish *conquistadors* and their Mapuche rivals.

Left, dusty streets. **Right**, tall cacti in the Andean foothills.

THE MAPUCHES

What we've achieved
with the civilization
they say they have given us
is to live squeezed together
like wheat in a sack
– Lorenzo Colimán

The Mapuche people, in their myriad mythologies, believe in a perfect balance between the positive and negative forces present in every act. Ngenechen, the positive god, represents the forces of life, crea-

whelmed the "love of god" or "loyalty to the crown" which they used as excuses to commit all nature of abuses against America's indigenous peoples. The Mapuches, living in the continent's extreme South, were not exempt from this treatment. Their reaction, however, was a lengthy, often successful resistance to the stealing of their lands and the violation of their traditions.

The meeting: The Mapuches, or "people of the earth," were accustomed to living from the earth's fruits, from hunting and from

tion and love. His counterpart is Wekufu, god of death and destruction.

It is in these terms that the Mapuches understand the meeting of European and American cultures 500 years ago. For native Americans and their descendents, the arrival of Christopher Colombus meant the destruction of the delicate balance of forces which had until then sustained their culture, their way of life, their language, their habitat, their religion and their people. Wekufu's spirit threw its mantle over the world's boundaries, leaving Ngenechen the positive force unable to keep up his end of the balance.

The Spaniards' passion for gold over-

fishing. They lived in scattered settlements from the Aconcagua Valley in the north, as far south as the Island of Chiloé. They also inhabited most of Argentine Patagonia.

They had, and still have, a relatively hierarchical society based on family structures, and their culture was highly developed in several areas. Women played a major role in the mystical and mythological aspects of society. Only they were allowed to communicate directly with the gods and their functions were distributed according to the type of forces they represented.

The gods of Life, for example, would communicate with women called the *Machi*;

those of Death, with the *Kalku*. Music always accompanied their rituals, particularly percussion instruments like the *Kultrun* and the *Trompe*, and wind instruments like the *Trutrucas* and wooden whistles. Oratory skills were of prime importance to the Mapuches and their language, *Mapudungu*, reached truly poetic heights as it captured extensive images within its sounds.

During the first hundred years of war between the Mapuches and the Spanish the northern limit of their territories was reduced to the Bio Bio River, a border which remained established for more than 300 years. The Cross and the Sword could not defeat the lances of the naked-chested Mapuches, and

"ferocious warriors" in order to justify their side's defeat. But the Mapuches are and were a peaceful, humble people, dedicated to their land and their traditions. The reasons for the long struggle are not to be found so much in their "warrior virtues" but rather in a more human and profound motive: a great dignity and immense love for their land and their freedom.

Their devotion to their own cultural values led the Mapuches to acts of great heroism and a spirit of impassioned resistance. They quickly learned about their enemy and his weapons, identified his weaknesses and developed the sort of war necessary to defend themselves.

the Spanish Crown was finally forced to negotiate. It recognized borders and established trade and transport agreements between the territories.

Many historians who defend the Spanish cause speak of the Mapuches as belonging to a "military race" or being a "fierce people" "made for war." Nevertheless, the testimony of friars who accompanied the Conquest indicates that the Mapuches were peaceful and friendly. It became convenient for pro-Spanish historians to paint the Mapuches as

Perhaps the most striking reason for the Spaniards' inability to conquer the Mapuches was that, unlike the Incas and Aztecs, they had no central government or authority. Their political and economic organization was based on the family. The family head was the polygamous *Cacique* (*pronounced Ka-See-Kay*) or *Lonko* . He could have as many as 10 wives as a sign of his power, forming a family group of up to 500 members counting grandparents, brothers and sisters, wives, children, in-laws, grandchildren and so on.

The *Lonko* developed his prestige through the accumulation of wealth and the wise

<u>Left</u>, Mapuche woman in a village near Temuco. <u>Above</u>, family with traditional Mapuche house.

advice which he gave to youths inclined to fight among themselves. Faced with a warlike situation, the Mapuches choose a *Toqui* as their leader and their peacetime authority was the *Ulmen*. Both were chosen for their extraordinary gifts for public speaking and their wise decision-making abilities.

There was enough land for all and the territory of individual families was extensive enough to live the four seasons of the year, graze animals, hunt and fish. In general, there were few territorial disputes.

Alliances between Caciques were established to develop economic activities like the gathering in of breeding stock, hunting and fruit collection and the benefits were shared equally among the participating members.

This loose organization meant that the Spanish could not seize control through capture of a single political leader. The Mapuche didn't have towns or villages to harass and destroy. While they weren't nomads in the strict sense of the term, they lived instead in *rucas* or huts which they moved from place to place according to the season and the availability of game and fish.

Lautaro the liberator: When the Conquest began, the Mapuches believed that the Spanish attacker and his horse were one living being, unbeatable, a god which had come to conquer them. The Spanish advance was fast and efficient. But when the Mapuches realized their mistake, they began to develop unique military strategies to defend their territory. Lautaro, a young Mapuche who was barely 20 years old, escaped from the Spanish camps where his intelligence had caused him to be trained as the page of the Conquistador Pedro de Valdivia. He was chosen as *Toqui*, that is, leader of the Caciques, to lead the war against the invaders.

Lautaro – who now knew the language, weapons, tactics and weaknesses of the enemy – taught his warriors to ride. They became better horsemen than the Spaniards. He also developed two combat tactics which today are recognized as the beginning of guerilla warfare in this continent.

Lautaro invented "mounted infantry" where each rider also carried along a footsoldier holding onto the horse's tail. This allowed for rapid movement of large parties of fighters. The second and more devastating tactic was the development of intense, prolonged battles, through the constant replacement of squadrons: each group fought ferociously for 15 to 20 minutes before being replaced. The Spanish soldiers, in their heavy armor, labored away and finally yielded to the waves of native fighters who, fresh and rested, gave them no respite.

These tactics led to enormous victories for Lautaro, who not only killed Pedro de Valdivia himself, but also secured for his people all the southern territories, burning and destroying the Spanish forts until, after four years of victorious campaigns, he finally reached the gates of Santiago.

During his northward push, many Yanaconas, another indigenous people who had until then formed part of the Spanish troops,

joined Lautaro's forces. One of these betrayed Lautaro, killing him while he rested in his tent the night before the great assault on the capital. This was a terrible blow to the Mapuches who, without their leader, decided to retreat southward, where they continued to defend "their" border for 300 years.

In 1985, a distinguished Chilean playwright, Isidora Aguirre, presented the play *Lautaro* in which this historic character has prophetic dreams of freedom for his people. The *conquistadores* appear wearing the armor of their period, but they carry machine guns and use dark glasses – a clear reference to the Chilean military government's political police active at that time. Almost 500 years after his death, Lautaro continued to inspire Chileans in their search for freedom.

The last cry: The last general uprising of Chile's indigenous peoples took place barely a century ago, in 1881. This time it was directed not against the Spanish, but rather the now Chilean republic which was doing everything possible to take over the southern lands. This uprising has remained in Mapuches' memory as one of the great moments in their history, an undeniable cultural action proving with blood their devotion to freedom and their *Mapu* or land.

The *huerquenes*, messengers especially educated for eloquence and good memories,

against Peru and Bolivia, suffocated the bloody rebellion and the Mapuches became farmers of small, individual plots. Their land was now the poorest in Chile.

Throughout the 1880s, the indigenous territories shrank. A decree made Araucania (the Mapuches territory) state property and a colonization process began in which the native people received little for their land. Along with this, a process of cultural transformation began. It was a time of fear, disease, hunger and loss of identity as the Mapuches became an ethnic minority within Chilean society.

The 20th century has seen three reactions to this process. The first, encouraged by mis-

began to travel through mountains and valleys, bearing knotted red cords around their wrists. Every day they undid one knot. When these were all gone, the *caciques* simultaneously attacked the forts and citadels, towns and missions of the Chileans. With hindsight this was an impossible attempt given the Chileans' superior weaponry, but it demonstrates once again the Mapuches' dedication to their own independence and freedom.

The army, fresh from its victories in a war

Left, Mapuche handicrafts festival in Villarica.
Above, traditional weaving skills.

sionaries, was to press for the total integration of the Mapuches into Chilean society. Education and evangelization would "absorb" the Mapuche culture. This later became the policy of the Pinochet government, which decreed an Indian Law that allowed the Mapuches to split their collectively-held land into small farms with individual titles. With no access to credit or technology, many were forced to sell their land to wealthy landowners, thus losing what little special status remained to protect them.

The second reaction was a modified form of integration which, in 1914, inspired one group of Mapuches to develop a special school which taught Spanish but valued indigenous cultural traditions. The children of several Caciques studied here. This tendency continues to exist and there are many Mapuche organizations in both cities and the countryside which try to keep their traditional culture alive. At the same time, they try to participate as an ethnic group within Chilean society.

The third reaction by Mapuches was to reject any integration and seek to recover their stolen lands and culture. The first attempts in this respect were led by Manuel Aburto Manquilef, a descendant of some of the main Caciques, who mobilized huge numbers of Mapuches in search of their own identity. This movement insisted that the central problem was the seizure of the Mapuche lands. Its activists revived the rites and traditions of the *malones* (meetings to listen to dreams and predict the future) and *Machitunes* (collective prayers to the gods to improve crops, rains, etc.). It organized many congresses and made the native voice heard in Santiago.

Perhaps the great historical merit of this group was its ability to find allies within other social movements of the period. Its leaders had the vision to recognize that the problem wasn't simply between *Mapuches* and *Huincas*, but rather between the wealthy and the poor. This led to the Mapuche's own struggle being more generally recognized as one of the social problems of the 30s.

The Workers' Federation of Chile (FOCH) became the Mapuches' voice in Santiago, declaring them "brothers in the suffering of the poor of city and country." Mapuches participated in politics through the Democratic Party and eventually elected representatives in the House of Deputies.

The border lands today: To this day, you can hardly cross the Bío Bío River into the La Frontera ("border") region, without noticing the results of all three tendencies. The Mapuches' socioeconomic position shows the result of the "absorption" policy, which has led to their exclusion from the different levels of government power.

But Mapuche women, who resist forgetting the past, offer their handicrafts in silver, raw wool and *coiron* (a strawlike material used in basketmaking), on street corners and in markets from Temuco to Valdivia, Osorno, Villarica and Pucón. They speak their own language, earning a minimum income, while their men work the land which once, in the not-too-distant past, belonged to them.

Surrounding these cities you can find almost 3,000 Indian Reserves or Reductions (*reducciones*), where 400,000 Mapuches still live in miserable conditions. Of the 31 million hectares they possessed in 1540, today's Reductions barely cover 350,000 hectares. Here they organize, speak their own language, defend their culture, listen to dreams and carry on their customs. And another 400,000 Mapuches have completely lost their lands and joined the working poor who struggle to survive in Chilean cities.

Mapuche organizations and leaders were heavily repressed by the military government which ruled Chile between 1973 and 1989, and in 1990 the bodies of many people of native origin, who were arrested and disappeared after the military coup, have been found in the forests around Valdivia and Chihuiío. But there are divisions within Mapuche ranks: this was also the only area in Chile where a majority voted "yes" to Pinochet's 1988 plebiscite for another term as president. Surviving organizations have begun to make proposals to the new government, from whom they expect more understanding and concrete aid.

The fire in Chile's South has not yet gone out. The spirits of Ngenechen and Wekufu still wander through the Cordillera, caressing Cinnamon Trees and Araucaria pines – the Mapuches' sacred trees. And they still seek a balance between life and death, good and evil. And justice.

For further information:
Los Primeros Americanos. Editorial Antartica, SA.
Brevisima Relación de la Destrucción de las Indias. Fray Bartolomé de las Casas. Editorial Nascimiento.
Mapuches, Pueblo de la Tierra. Inter-Church Committee on Human Rights in Latin America. Canada.
Rasgos de la Sociedad Mapuche contemporánea. Milán Stuchlik. Ediciones Nueva Uniersidad.
Arauco Domado. Lope de Vega. Zig Zag.
Historia del Pueblo Mapuche. José Bengoa.

Right, Mapuche woman in traditional clothes, Temuco.

THE LAKE DISTRICT

The southern **Lake District** exercises a near-mythic fascination on Chileans themselves, a good many of whom never get there but know it from television (it is shown at sign-off each evening) and from the pictures of snow-capped volcanoes and shimmering lakes hanging in every bar and restaurant. The South symbolizes everything healthy, unspoiled, and pure in Chile and Chileans, and city folks, particularly in the increasingly noisome, polluted capital of Santiago, look kindly on Southerners as their own better selves, even while succumbing to the temptation to take advantage of their gullibility and innocence. The *huaso*, or country bumpkin, is the object of an ambiguous mix of derision and affection in Chile (entirely apt for a people who pride themselves both for worldliness and kind-heartedness) and in popular folklore he comes always from the abundant, fraternal

South rather than the arid North where skeptical, wary individualism sets the tone of human relations.

Foreign visitors may come to feel they are being put through a laudatory ritual when the subject of the Southern Lake District comes up. It is as if Chileans need the *gringo* representatives of modernity and development to acknowledge local superiority in this one area as a way of turning the country's isolation and suspected backwardness into a virtue. In fact, European influences of all kinds, including immigration, have long been welcomed in the Lake District. An early pioneer and champion of southern settlement and development, Vicente Pérez Rosales, exemplified this eurocentrism when he announced in 1854 that "the word "foreigner" has been eliminated in Chile. It is an immoral word and should disappear from the dictionary." It should be noted that Pérez Rosales was not thinking of Peruvians or Brazilians or other multi-racial nations when he made the statement – he meant the Germans, Austrians, Swiss and Italians whose communities still litter the South.

This confused mix of attitudes – the humble welcoming of the European, the simultaneous pride in and embarrassment at the indigenous – is hardly surprising in a people which is observably *mestizo* and far from comfortable with the fact. Only some 20,000 Mapuches now live on the *reducciones* (a fitting word for "reservations" as it comes from the verb *reducir*, "to reduce") in Southern Chile, but another 150,000 speak the native tongue.

Meanwhile, probably all but 2 or 3 million of Chile's 12 million inhabitants have some Indian ancestry, although a good half of them would roundly deny it. Chilean boys are still given on occasion the name "Lautaro," after a Mapuche Indian chief who wiped out an invading party and set back Spanish colonization by many decades.

A recent frontier: Native roots are not buried so deeply or remotely in the collective memory. The south of Chile was not fully dominated by the European-descended settlers until the sec-

Preceding pages, small farm near Río Bueno. Left, Puerto Varas. Below, working hard on the land.

ond half of the 19th century. The first colony at what is now the resort center of Villarrica, for example, was besieged by Mapuches in a 1598 uprising, collapsed without survivors in 1602, and was not re-established until a military mission arrived in 1882, nearly three centuries later.

In the interim, an uneasy state of semi-war prevailed. Early in the 17th century, the Bío Bío River (which reaches the sea at what is today the port of Concepción) was established as the frontier between the Spanish colony and Indian lands, but the truce was violated annually in raids from one side or the other. The Spanish mercenaries fought to capture Mapuches and sell them north as slaves for the great estates, while the Indians raided to plunder cattle and other valuable goods or to punish the invaders. Regular peace conferences between the two sides ended in great celebrations of feasting and drinking and vows of friendship – which would invariably last only a few months before the next outbreak.

Finally, commerce pacified the situation. A regular trade in cattle, woven goods, knives, arms and liquor developed, though violent outbursts between Indians and soldiers, brigands, and shady dealers of all sorts continued to occur regularly. Naturally, the *mestizo* population grew steadily with the constant contact, and colonial garrison commanders preferred them as soldiers since they knew the area well and were notoriously impervious to hardship.

Chile's South is a more recently tamed version of the American Wild West, and a few kilometers off the main track life revolves around horses, farm labors, and social events lubricated with large quantities of wine or *chicha* made from fermented apples. The rolling hills which rise to mountains near the Argentine border make the land less suitable for large-plantation agriculture, and crop options are limited by the short summer and year-round rains. Many areas are without electricity or telephones, and roads are often impassable during the wet months of winter to all but animal or **Villarrica volcano.**

foot traffic or the sturdiest, all-weather vehicles. Country families tend to live off seasonal sales of milk or a cash crop or the spending of tourists, then spend long months consuming the stores of grain they harvested themselves while the men look for paying jobs in the larger towns and cities.

The rural areas are connected by an ample network of local buses which transport schoolchildren, farmers with their products, and country residents returning from the larger towns with their provisions. The buses are slow both due to the terrain and the constant stops at every lane or farmhouse for passengers, but they are very cheap and reach many remote settlements. The first, and sometimes only, bus tends to leave before dawn, so it is always prudent to inquire about schedules the day before traveling.

As the terrain is ideal for backpacking and hiking, Chilean youth swarm southward in the summertime, many of them spending long hours on the highway awaiting motorists or truckers who will give them a lift. Most have the barest minimum of funds and camp wherever possible.

Unique wilderness: The Lake District is generally considered to begin at the Tolten River which empties into Lake Villarrica, but this is more a result of the area's fame as a resort region than strict topographic considerations. The characteristic combination of volcanoes and lakes actually begins to the north around the area of **Conguillio National Park.** It boasted several volcanoes, including **Lonquimay** (2,890 meters/9,480ft) which entered into full eruption in 1988 and blanketed the area with dangerous volcanic dust, and **Llaima** which erupted in 1994. This is a sparsely-visited region with many attractions. It is also a zone of Mapuche reservations – their ancestors used the accessible mountain passes here and gathered pine nuts from the ancient *araucaria,* the monkey puzzle tree unique to the Andes. These rare trees, which take 500 years to fully mature and can live to over 1,000 years, were endangered by logging activities

until President Aylwin prohibited their cutting in March 1990.

Chile has 2,085 volcanoes, of which 55 are considered active. The entire country forms part of the Pacific Rim of Fire which stretches from Alaska down through California and Central America to western South America and reappears on the opposite side of the Pacific Ocean in New Zealand, the western Pacific islands, Japan, and the Kamchatka Peninsula of the former USSR. Chile's volcanoes are doubly dangerous because of their eternal snows which melt into rapid, devastating mudslides upon full eruption (the phenomenon which caused such enormous loss of life in Colombia in 1985). The lava itself advances much more slowly but burns away everything in its path. These lava "runs" can be observed at Villarrica, Petrohué and Ensenada, and the Villarrica Volcano can be climbed for a peek down at the magma quite near the surface. Some of the active volcanoes are considered semi-dormant, but a strong eruption can always set off a chain reaction since they are connected far below the surface. The 1960 earthquake set off volcanic activity in the Riñinahue Volcano; the Calbuco's top was blown off in the manner of Mount St Helens during an 1893 eruption. The Osorno is the most perfectly-shaped; early settlers' drawings of it show a long strip of sterile lava which is now overgrown with stiff, hardy vegetation.

The lakes themselves are of glacial origin, their basins carved out by advancing ice, then filled by the melting ice as the glaciers receded. There is also evidence of tectonic influence, earthquakes cause some lake basins to sink further while newly-forming volcanoes sometimes shifting the course of rivers as they rise up between them. Rivers originating high up in the Andes feed the lakes, bringing sediment which is then deposited on the lake beds, while being drained by rivers emptying into the Pacific.

Source of the Bío Bío: The town of **Lonquimay** and the land surrounding it lie to the east of the Andean Cordillera, A night-time serenade.

A night-time serenade.

despite the general rule that the highest peaks mark the territorial boundaries between Chile and Argentina. However, **Lake Gualletue** south of Lonquimay provides the headwaters of the important **Bío Bío River** which then runs north for nearly 100 km (60 miles) before turning westward toward the Pacific Ocean. As this river was long considered the border dividing Spanish lands from unconquered Indian territory, Chile claimed the hydrographic basin.

The main road to Lonquimay passes through the **Las Raíces (Roots) Tunnel** under the Cordillera, the longest in South America. Originally a train tunnel built in 1930 as part of a plan (since abandoned) to connect the two oceans by rail, the passageway has been reinforced with concrete and is passable in all weathers (although large icicles form in winter). On the road leading to the tunnel from Curacautín are numerous thermal baths, the Princess Falls, and two huge volcanic rocks, **Piedra Cortada** and **Piedra Santa**, which were

Below, on the way to church. Right, frying up lunch.

considered holy places by the indigenous tribespeople.

Conguillio National Park can be reached from Curacautín in the north or **Melipeuco** in the South. The route passes the snow-covered **Llaima Volcano** (3,125 meters/10,253 ft), leads through virgin forests of *araucaria* and other Chilean species such as *coigüe* and *rauli*, as well as oak and cypress. Twelve-hundred year-old *araucaria* trees can be found in the Conguillillo park. Three tiny lakes (Verde, Captren, and Arco de Iris) are no more than 50 years old; they were formed by recent lava flows which blocked the course of several rivers. The Llaima Volcano now has a small, modern ski resort on its slopes. Work was interrupted for several months while the volcano erupted.

Indian stronghold: Turning southwest is the even more isolated and impressive **Lake Lleulleu** (in the Mapuche language, a repeated word has extra importance) which must be visited by boat. The southern finger is the most beautiful, surrounded by virgin forests.

Aside from the tiny community at **Puerto Lleulleu**, the only civilization nearby is at **Quidico** on the ocean, which is visited in the summer for its excellent seafood and windswept beach.

The end of the line is **Tirúa** where the Mapuche chiefs once charged a toll for land traffic between Concepción and Valdivia. According to legend, the bishop of Concepción was kidnapped and held here in 1778, only escaping when a rival chief won his freedom in a game of chance.

Next to the beaches at Viña del Mar and Reñaca, the area around Villarrica and Pucón is the most visited holiday resort in Chile. The two towns are the main urban centers on the end of **Villarrica Lake** which is dominated by the active **Villarrica Volcano** (2,840 meters/9,320 ft), just an hour's detour from the north-south PanAmerican Highway. **Pucón** could be called the "Viña of the South" for its success in attracting the fancier class of summer tourists, especially since the 1934 construction of the Grand Hotel Pucón by the Chilean State Railroad Company. (Guests arrived by train to Villarrica, then boated 25 km/16 miles across the lake to their lodgings.) Now superseded by more isolated and exclusive areas preferred by the super-rich, Pucón is nonetheless enormously popular among Santiago's middle-class youth who flock to the area for rock climbing, boating, river rafting, lake excursions, and the cafes and discos that open their doors in summertime to replicate their urban nightlife. The main beach at Pucón is crowded and sometimes clogged with algae, while Villarrica's popular beaches have been hit with an ugly tree blight in recent years. But a bit of exploration will uncover dozens of beautiful alternatives.

Numerous Mapuche reservations are tucked away in the hills surrounding Villarrica, and each year a Mapuche cultural festival is held in the town. This includes a nightly explanatory demonstration of religious rituals. Some unusual craft work can be found among the stands, most of which, however, has long been copied by artisans in Santiago

Gentle landscape.

and elsewhere. One main street of the town is named for General Emil Koerner, the German military scientist who was hired by President Balmaceda to reorganize the Chilean armed forces (he used the area for training) and who betrayed him to side with an 1891 insurrection fomented by local oligarchs. (The oligarchs won, Balmaceda committed suicide, and Koerner proceeded to reshape the army along Prussian lines, a model which remains in force today.) Koerner's prestige led to a surge of pro-German sentiment which helped to stimulate a second wave of German immigrants, most of whom headed for the newly available lands in the South.

Mountain beaches: Just a few minutes from Pucón to the north and northeast are **Lake Caburga** and **Colico**, and Lakes **Tinquilco**, **Tolo**, and **Verde** in the mountains of **Huerquehue National Park**. Rare outcroppings of "flywing" rock crystal usually observed only in the coastal mountain range 100 km (60-mile) to the west give some of Caburga's beaches white sand rather than the usual black sand that comes from the volcanic rock elsewhere in Chile's lake district. Caburga Lake is surrounded by densely-forested hills, some areas of which can be explored on defined paths. Its waters flow underground producing the springs at **Ojos de Caburga**, a popular picnic spot. Access to the Huerquehue Park lakes is a serious, 5-km (3-mile) climb. Further up in the mountains is puma territory; the animals come closer to human civilization in winter when food is scarce. An 80-km (50-mile) route from Caburga's north shore through the Rio Blanco valley can be hiked in about four days, ending up in the outpost of **Reigolil** (where a bus descends to Curarrehue twice weekly) through virgin forests and hot springs.

South of Villarrica, a half-hour's trip on a newly-paved highway leads to the quickly-growing resort of **Lican Ray** on Lake Calafquén. The original settlers were removed to make way for a dam which was to flood the area, but the project did not go through. Eventually, the government resold lots along the

Herding cattle.

lakefront and nearby on the sole condition that buyers would build a summer house. Beaches here are cleaner than in Pucón and until recently were less crowded. Further along the lake on the dirt road is **Coñaripe**, which retains the atmosphere of pre-boom Lican Ray. Regular buses do go this far, but Coñaripe is the end of the line before the rugged unpaved circuit around the lake and the "back way" into Panguipulli.

Thermal baths proliferate throughout the area due to the constant activity in the volcanic belt that runs along the Cordillera. Some, such as the **Termas de Minetué** in Huerquehue Park or **Termas de Huife** further east of Pucón are upscale commercial operations with modern eating and lodging facilities and bathing fixtures. Others, such as the tiny **Termas de Ancamil** just before Curarrehue 45 km (28 miles) east of Pucón are rustic, family-run affairs where one simply descends into the cave with a candle and has a bath. If no established campgrounds are available, a brief word with local families will lead to a suitable site. The Ancamil children will also lead campers to hidden waterfalls; excellent beaches along the Maichín and Trancura rivers; places to forage for blackberries, plums, pine nuts; and to view the increasingly scarce *copihue*, Chile's endangered national flower.

Wild border towns: The town of **Curarrehue** is a typical southern frontier center whose families often have relatives on the Argentine side and travel back and forth depending on work opportunities. Residents are mostly *mestizo* and sport musical Mapuche surnames such as Coñoepán, Colpihueque, and Quirquitripay. The men often wear the flat-brimmed felt peasant hats used by Chilean horsemen and are quick to invite visitors to drink a sweet wine that costs about a dollar for five liters and goes down with treacherous ease. On special occasions, a host family will kill a sheep or goat by plunging a knife into the neck, catching the blood in a pan filled with *cilantro*, corriander, where it is congealed with lemon juice to produce **Working in the fields.**

ñache, this considered a great delicacy and pre-feast appetizer.

Grains are the traditional farm commodity in the zone, though the uncertainty of the weather makes farm economy a constant risk operation. Potatoes are easily grown, but transport costs wipe out any chance of profit, so farmers usually either consume them directly or use them as animal feed. In recent years, hops and sugar beet have also been introduced. Pasture is abundant, and many families earn a few pesos selling milk to the big dairy plants; the 50-liter churns can be seen along the highways and back roads.

To fortify themselves for heavy farm work, the men breakfast on *chupilca*, white wine poured over toasted wheat, or *mudai*, a pasty, carbohydrate-rich juice made from cooked grains. Visitors should avoid giving offense by always accepting anything offered, even if they cannot bring themselves to sample it. When no longer hungry or dangerously close to total drunkenness, just leave the plate or glass untouched before you.

The Chile-Argentinian border in the south is lightly-guarded as the mountain passes are essentially uncontrollable. Given Chile's recent political history, many frontier towns have been used to smuggle in and out people who either could not get in legally or were in serious trouble for political reasons. Cattle-smuggling into Chile from Argentina also caused a new outbreak of foot-and-mouth disease which prevented Chilean meat from gaining access to new markets. (The disease cannot be controlled in Argentina's vast cattle ranches while Chile had managed to eliminate it.)

Mountain people everywhere seem to have particularly affable, liberal-minded attitudes not always shared even by other rural residents. The inhabitants of Chile's Cordilleran foothills, like those surrounding Cura-rrehue, are unfailingly cordial although sometimes shy in front of strangers. Passing horsemen are likely to invite those on foot to heave themselves up behind, and ox-drawn carts or even the occasional logging truck may slow down to allow villagers to climb

Country store.

on as well. Nor will they raise an eyebrow at discreet skinny-dipping, though they themselves are more reserved.

This friendly environment is not preserved, however, in the towns that have been turned into regular summer resorts. The city youth who descend on the more touristic villages further south soon manage to affront local residents by treating them as rustics, and the traditional generous welcome to strangers disappears behind a mask of indifference. Even so, concerted efforts and extra-gracious greetings usually manage to break the ice, but it's worth the effort to try a visit off the beaten path.

A slice of Germany: Valdivia is the best example of the urban face of Chile's South: sophisticated and festive, rainy and verdant, with a palpable German influence in architecture, cuisine and culture. Although usually treated as part of the Lake District, Valdivia is located at the crossroads of two rivers and just a few kilometers from the sea, separated from the famous lakes by the coastal mountain range. The approaches to the city are marshy breeding grounds for certain waterfowl not commonly found in Chile.

Named for the first *conquistador* to enter Chile from Peru, Pedro de Valdivia, the city was founded in the mid-1500s but had a difficult time of it for the first hundred years. It was taken over by a Dutch pirate in 1600 and, being on the Indian side of the Bío Bío River dividing line between crown and Mapuche territory, had to await the building of fortifications in the mid-1600s to achieve a measure of security.

German immigration occurred in two periods: a minor influx in the first half of the 19th century and the more important wave between roughly 1885 and 1910. Attracted by a climate similar to that of a German Baltic province, the immigrants played an important role in commerce and industry for the wide range of technical knowledge they brought from the old country. Some cultivated their new lands, although climatic conditions were not overly favorable. Others arrived as ironsmiths, carpenters, tanners, brewers, watchmakers, locksmiths and

tailors. Chile in 1850 was just emerging from three decades of political anarchy and economic stagnation which caused distant provinces like Valdivia to be left largely on their own devices. "There is as much moss on the brains here as on the trees," quipped one governor sent from Santiago before the new immigrants began to arrive.

By 1900, a traveler claimed that upon entering Valdivia, he could not believe he was still in Chile. Many of the tradesmen had converted their shops into factories; Valdivia became Chile's prime industrial center with breweries, distilleries, shipbuilding, flour mills, tanneries, no less than one hundred lumber mills, and, in 1913, the country's first foundry.

Furniture-making was stimulated by the immense availability of precious, native woods from the coigüe, alerce, lingue, mañio, luma, ulmo, and Oregon pine which had been introduced from the United States in the 1860s. A fine **Street** **museum** on Teja Island is housed in an **musicians in** old settler's mansion and includes **Valdivia.**

Mapuche artifacts and household furnishings from the period, giving an excellent idea of the prosperous immigrants' mode of life.

The wealth of the Germans of Valdivia was legendary in Chile until their luck changed, starting with the imposition of a heavy liquor tax in 1902 at the behest of the vintners of the Central Valley. At the same time, unfavorable trade conditions wiped out much of the leather market. A great fire laid waste to the city in 1909 while the local merchant class was superseded by mine and estate owners further north, closer to the byzantine politics of the capital. In 1960, Valdivia was the epicenter of a gigantic earthquake and tidal wave whose effects can still be seen. Most of the old buildings were destroyed, but some European-style buildings remain by the waterfront. There is also a university which contributes to the energetic urban spirit.

Summer explosions: The city has a popular week-long summer festival in which musical shows are staged on bandstands along the riverbank, boats parade

down the river, and parachuting and fireworks shows are presented on the last afternoon and night. A required stop in downtown Valdivia is **Haussmann's Cafe** for its famous *crudos*, steak tartar pounded into a smooth paste and served on toast. The city's long riverside walks are full of visitors throughout the season, as are the nearby beaches. Though the rivers are swimable, most bathers head for the mouth at the port villages of **Corral** and **Niebla**, now connected by a paved road. Colonial era fortresses are preserved at the latter site, which independence hero Lord Thomas Cochrane, a dashing Scots navy commander in the service of the Chilean rebels, took from the Spanish against heavy odds in 1820. An overcrowded tourist vessel sank in the bay here with heavy loss of life in the summer of 1990, so excursion boats should be inspected carefully even for short trips. The views on a clear day are well worth the short side-trip from downtown. For a bit of exercise, a visitor can row from Corral to the tiny island of **Mancera**, Valdivia's military headquar-

ters during the 18th century, to see its small church and convent.

Another interesting site is the remote seaside village of **Curiñanco** ("black eagle" in the Mapuche tonge), recently accessible by a rough dirt road. One bus leaves daily from Valdivia in the morning and turns back immediately, forcing the visitor to prepare for a 25-km (15-mile) return walk or, better yet, hitch back along the coastal road past numerous isolated beaches ringed by cliffs to Niebla. A logging truck passing by may invite a hiker to straddle one of the enormous trunks for a stunning tour. In winter, the town is virtually cut off, except by sea. The beach at Curiñanco is wild and imposing, with sharp winds coming off the ocean and cattle standing in the fresh-water pools above the tide line. The mixing of German settlers with indigenous peoples results in peculiar surnames such as that of the Austenritt-Ñanco sisters – their foodstand at the local soccer games feature dishes such as *pulmay*, a staggeringly rich seafood-and-meat platter.

Inhabitants are beginning to feel the threat to their placid, reclusive existence from the inexorable expansion from Valdivia, and pressure to sell farmlands for summer vacation homesites is growing, despite the lack of drinking water.

Boat traffic for excursions, transport and fishing is heavy in the dozens of rivers surrounding Valdivia. The swampy landscape has made vehicle traffic difficult, and a recently-built stretch of the PanAmerican Highway bypasses Valdivia entirely, to the detriment of the area's economy.

South of Corral is **Chaihuín**, a fishing village with what some consider the most beautiful, untouched ocean beach in Chile. Most of the original larch trees in the nearby hills have been cut and sold, but the place retains a frontier flavor.

Detours into the wilderness: The largely undeveloped **Seven Lakes district** is among the least visited by vacationers due to a peculiar topographical layout and poor access. The lakes are generally **The waterfront, Valdivia.**

bordered by heavily-wooded cliffs with steep descents; roads are potholed and slippery at the best of times with difficult climbs and narrow turns through the mountains, often impassable in winter. Low-suspension vehicles will come out the worst. However, the landscapes are spectacular, and local residents will guide visitors to even more extraordinary spots. These lakes are good for fishing and exploring, less so for bathing as beaches are few and far between.

The circuit around Lake Calafquén is dominated by the constantly-changing position of the Villarrica Volcano to the north. Eventually, the **Choshuenco Volcano** (2,415 meters/7,923 ft) appears to the south. Recent lava flows can be observed from the highway shortly after leaving Lican Ray. From Coñaripe an alternative route leads to the small **Lake Pellaita** after a ferocious climb at **Los Añiques**; the way down leads through an agricultural valley to the Mapuche village of **Liquiñe**, which has pleasant thermal baths. A lumber company will give permission to drive on through to

lakes **Neltume** and the finger-shaped **Pirihueico** which can be crossed in two hours on a commercial boat. Pirehueico is an uninhabited national reserve, so far even from the summer tourist traffic that a lodge built in 1947 was a complete failure. The international pass at the far southeast end of the lake is the lowest border between all of Chile and Argentina, only 600 meters (2,000 ft) above sea level.

Panguipulli ("Town of Roses") was the railway station which received logs dispatched from the interior via steamboats plying the lake of the same name. The construction of roads later superseded the lake transport system. The town is brilliantly decorated with rose bushes in the plazas and along main roads. On clear days, the Choshuenco Volcano can be seen 50 km (30 miles) to the southeast.

As Panguipulli is located on the flat central plain rather than in the mountains, it tends to be hotter than other lake towns, and its beaches are less impressive. The volcano itself can be climbed by auto up to the refuge after a trying, 80-km (50-mile) drive along the lake. To the east, about halfway to **Puerto Fuy**, on Lake Pirehueico are the **Huilo-Huilo Falls**, one of the highest and most impressive in Chile. The 10-meter (33-ft) wide falls, which crashes into the River Fuy down a deep vine-covered gorge, is scheduled to disappear with the construction of a hydroelectric complex further down the Calle-Calle River towards Valdivia.

Continuing the circuit around Lake Riñihue is impossible out of season (and frequently in-season as well) due to a severe, 7-km (4-mile) climb with terrible road conditions outside the tiny lakefront community of Enco. An approach can be made from the town of Los Lagos on the PanAmerican Highway passing through the town of Riñihue.

Fishermen's outposts: The enormous **Lake Ranco** and the smaller adjacent **Lake Maihue** are still minimally developed in touristic terms – somewhat surprising since they have so much to offer. For foot travelers the quickest access is

Bringing in the shellfish.

a 50-km (30-mile) bus trip from the town of **Río Bueno**, only half of which is paved. In summertime, extra buses are scheduled to handle holiday traffic. To reach the underrated, little-known resort of **Futrono** on the north shore, the trek is 43 km (27 miles) from Reumen, 34 km (21 miles) paved.

Many of the communities ringing the lake originated as fishermen's hostels; a couple are now successful lodges serving upscale clients. The town of **Lago Ranco** itself is full of cheap tourist houses, and the pebble beach has a fine panoramic view. A small museum on the road leading to the beach has some interesting historical items as real settlement in the area goes back only some 50 years. Boats can be rented when available, but as Lago Ranco remains halfway between an overgrown fishing village and a resort, such services are unpredictable. Activity after dark drops off sharply except for a pair of lakefront bars; the one exception is during the summer festival.

The most beautiful and heavily set-tled part of the lake lies directly to the east along the road to the **Riñinahue Peninsula** and the **Calcurrupe River** near Llifén. The road, dotted with what will soon be colonies of summer vacation homes, crosses **Nilahue Falls**, a double waterfall with a tremendous, roaring flow, especially in early summer. From the bridge over the Nilahue, a tertiary road leads to the lower end of Lake Maihue and the hamlet of **Carrán**, named for the Carrán Volcano which just appeared in 1957 and last erupted in 1979.

A Mapuche reservation near the southeast end of Lake Maihue and within view of the next volcano to the south, the **Puyehue** (2,240 meters/7,349 ft) is said to preserve the purest indigenous traditions. If taken to the settlement by a resident, one may be met with a display of hospitality including immediate cessation of activities, welcoming songs, and a feasting and drinking session that will probably not be concluded until the next day and may not be abandoned under any circumstances. On the other **Colonial fortress at Corral.**

hand, unaccompanied visitors may be met with stony hostility.

The 2,000-acre **Guapi Island** in the middle of Lake Ranco is also a Mapuche colony of 600 residents which was established by indigenous people escaping from the Spanish conquerors. Chiefs Antillanca and Ñancumil divided the island in two, and the latter's descendant Juan Ñancumil continues to preside over island councils. His deed to the land, recognized in 1914, describes the boundaries as, "To the north, bordered by Lake Ranco; to the south, the same lake; to the east, the same lake; and to the west, the same lake." A recent study concluded that only 20 percent still participate in the annual *nquillatún*, the Mapuche's three-day religious ceremony to consecrate the lands and the harvest. The fact that professionals and technicians are unwilling to work there, combined with high rates of alcoholism and the penetration of evangelical groups, lead many to fear the end of the Mapuche culture on Guapi. In another decade residents may legally sell their ancestral lands which were divided and assigned to them individually under Chile's indigenous law of 1979.

The lake's real tourist center is **Llifén** on the eastern shore, due to the work of several English fishermen who settled there. Several hotels along the coast and in Futrono further north receive mostly foreign visitors. The Palestinian-born mistress of the **El Rican Arabe** is legendary for her cuisine, Arabic music, and exuberant management. The entire lake can be circled by car, crossing one river by ferry. The Caunahue River canyon just north of Llifén has a dramatic view. The back route behind the line of volcanoes can be taken leaving from Llifén as well, though special permission to cross must be solicited at Arquilhue in the Blanco river valley.

Lush forests in the shadow of volcanoes: Lake Puyehue is known to many travelers since it lies along the main route to Argentina in Southern Chile. (In wintertime when the Andes are impassable due to heavy snows, bus traffic leaving Santiago must detour nearly 1,000 km

Windsurfing on Lake Llanquihue.

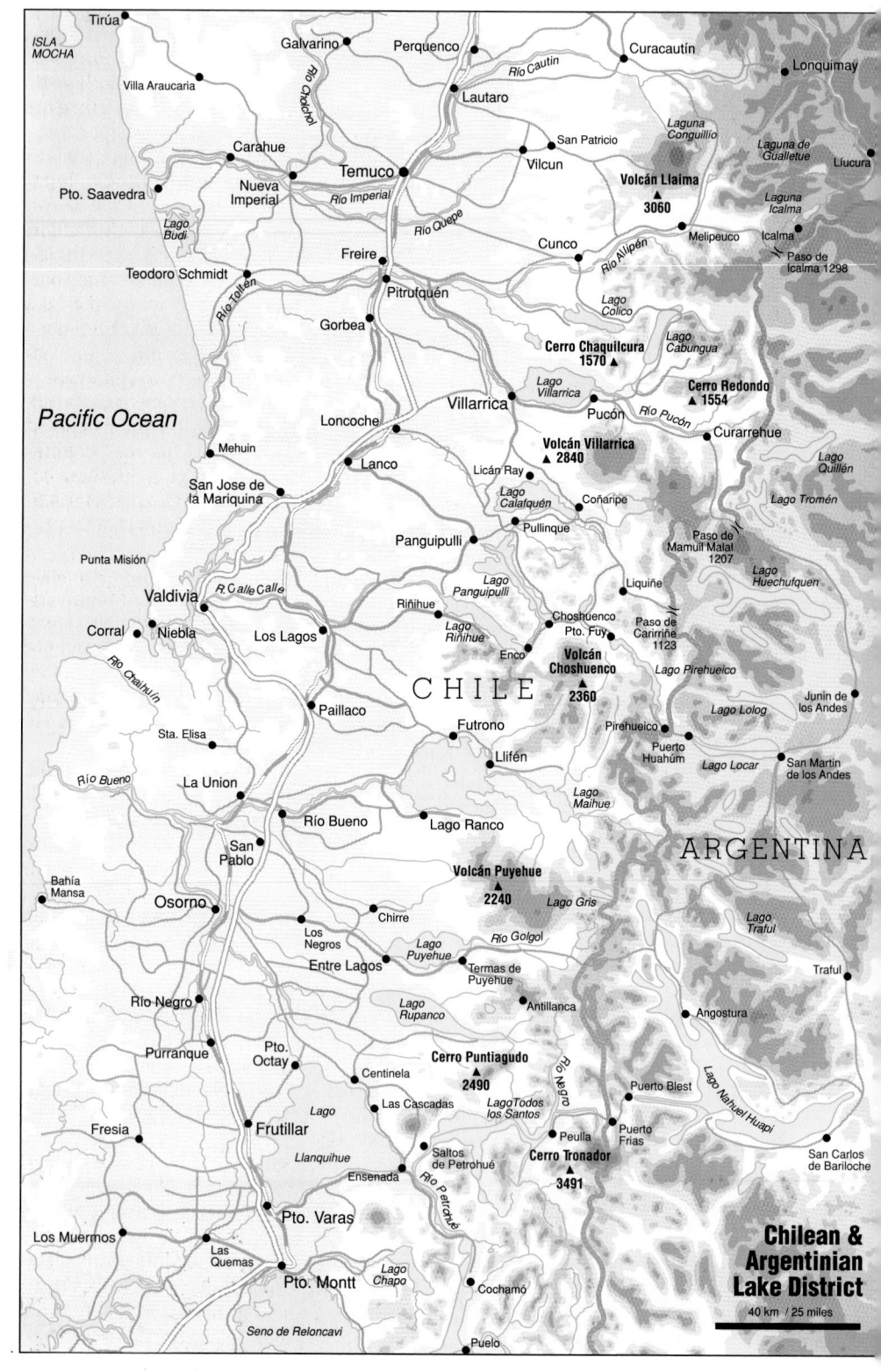

Chilean & Argentinian Lake District

40 km / 25 miles

(600 miles) to Osorno and cross here where the mountain passes are much lower.) The road has excellent views of the lake from gently rolling hills, then climbs to 1,300 meters (4,300 ft) through **Puyehue National Park** on the way to **San Carlos de Bariloche** on the Argentine side, which rivals Chile's Lake District for natural beauty. The main town is **Entre Lagos** ("Between the Lakes") on the western tip of Lake Puyehue, another railroad center now heavily dependent on tourism. The beach in Entre Lagos is not particularly distinguished; campgrounds 10 to 15 km (6–9 miles) east on the international road are more interesting. Several international hotels give the area a certain cachet, but some will head the other direction for the same reason.

A detour towards the **Casa Blanca Volcano** leads to the open-air hot springs at **Aguas Calientes**, whose park headquarters make a good starting point for excursions. The road leads past several small lakes and magical forests, including an unusual temperate rain forest, and ends at a ski resort on the slopes of the volcano which can be climbed more easily than the Villarrica up north. Another topographic oddity is the existence of deciduous trees (beech) at the volcano's tree-line. At the top the views are impressive even for this region as the volcanoes Osorno, Puntiagudo, and Puyehue can all be seen in a semi-circle.

As in other lakes, the recent introduction of salmon farms (referred to as *pisciculture*) is generating polemics at Lake Puyehue. Critics charge that the large concentrations of artificially-fed fish will alter the ecological balance and that the inevitable escape of some fish from the underwater cages will threaten other native species. Sport trout fishermen are particularly worried that the ideal conditions of lakes and rivers will be endangered. The fish farms can be observed throughout the region, usually attended by one or two employees who circulate among the floating platforms.

Nearby **Lake Rupanco** tends to be exclusive and upscale, without the ready facilities for camping and day trips that abound in all the other lakes. Foreigners have discovered it for its extraordinary, mountain-ringed setting and superb fishing. (A well-known lakefront *hacienda* passed from hand to hand during the military regime, ending up for a time the property of a Middle Eastern sheik.) The approach from Entre Lagos leads to a tiny settlement at **Puerto Chalupa**, which has a lovely beach but nowhere to stay or camp. From the south, the dirt road from **Puerto Octay** is a 25-km (15-mile) drive, without public transport service. The entrance where the lake empties into the **Rahue River** has not a single store where campers or foot travelers might stock up, although a local family will sell homemade bread. Lodgings are outside the price range of almost all Chileans, and the beautiful campgrounds along the south shore begin 25 km (15 miles) from the hotel at El Paraíso, making them almost inaccessible without a vehicle.

El Paraíso, a typical Lake Rupanco *hostería,* attracts a heavily foreign clientele keen to fish in the pristine waters. Its restaurant is decorated from floor to ceiling with fish-shaped plaques giving the weight of the specimen caught, date, and name of angler. Many names are repeated in successive years.

Heartland of the Lake District: Lake Llanquihue is the grand-daddy of all

the Chilean lakes. It is the fourth largest in South America, covering 877 square km (339 square miles) and nearly 50 km (30 miles) across from Puerto Octay to Puerto Varas on the south shore. The Llanquihue has an oceanic feel with breakers that churn higher in winds or rough weather and mini-climates in its interior that keep boaters and fishermen alert. On the map it can be readily seen that, except for the narrow strip of land between Puerto Varas and Puerto Montt, the lake would be in fact part of the ocean.

This region was also heavily settled by German immigrants beginning in the mid-19th century who embarked at what is now Reloncoví Bay. Vicente Pérez Rosales, the indefatigable promoter of colonization in Southern Chile, organized a solemn ceremony to formally establish Puerto Montt with a group of the recent arrivals, none of whom understood a word of Spanish. According to an account of the ritual, led by a Catholic priest, the Protestant settlers interrupted at what seemed to them an appropriate pause with a rousing chorus of *Hier Liegt vor Deiner Majestad* ("Here before Your Majesty"). Despite the idiomatic complications, Pérez Rosales' project was a success in the long run, and the enormous national park at the eastern end of Lake Llanquihue stretching all the way to the Argentine frontier bears his name. It was Chile's first, established in 1926.

Lake Llanquihue is one of the most visited sites in all of Chile, and tours of the district often start in Puerto Montt and work back towards the north. (Train service from Santiago as far as Puerto Montt is slow but more relaxing than the overnight buses from Santiago. One particularly elegant, 1930s-era train with wood-paneled sleeping cars attended by kindly porters and even on-board showers is worth the slight delay in arrival.) **Puerto Varas** is the main lakeside resort town and has one of Chile's two casinos. (The other is in Viña del Mar.) The beaches (the name of one, **Niklitscheck Beach**, reflects a later immigration of Slavs, especially in the far South) run for several kilometers with rows of shops and restaurants and plenty of night life. The towns along the southern and southwestern shore of the lake (Puerto Varas, Llanquihue, Frutillar) form part of Chile's north-south axis and have long been connected by rail to the rest of the country. The views are breathtaking across to the **Osorno Volcano** (2,652 meters/8,701 ft) and **Cerro Puntiagudo** (Sharp-Pointed Hill, 2,190 meters/7,185 ft), and summer activities such as festivals, games, exhibits, and the like abound making the whole strip a fun place to hang out. The ease of arrival and the plentiful accommodations of varied prices and styles mean all kinds of travelers gather at night to stroll the beach walks and rub elbows. Peak season is February; the views are just as fine in January, but the maddening *tábanos* are thickest then –

Old mansion in Osorno.

fat, irritating horseflies attracted to dark clothes and shiny objects which love to buzz around your head in the sunshine. They don't come out in overcast weather, and since their life cycle is only a month, they disappear in the first days of February. Before then they can easily ruin an afternoon at the beach or a picnic.

Driving east from Puerto Varas the road curves and dips providing countless views of the lake from every imaginable angle. Winds tend to whip across even on bright, cloudless days, so the air is likely to remain cool and tempt the unwary to overdo exposure to the sun. The notorious deterioration of the ozone layer, which is progressively worse as one moves closer to Antarctica, contributes to the potency of the sun's rays. Numerous *hosterías* provide full meals at lakeside; they tend to be pricey. On a clear day, residents will come down from their rural domiciles and gather in lakefront soccer fields to watch a match in the strong breeze with the sparkling water in the background. The **Calbuco Volcano** (2,015 meters/6,611 ft) is quite

close on the right. This volcano's top was blown off in an 1893 eruption, leaving a jagged cone. About halfway to Ensenada is the **Pescado (Fish) River**, which, not surprisingly, is famous for its good fishing.

Waterfalls in Black Rock: Ensenada is an uninteresting crossroads which serves the tourist traffic headed in various directions, though the main hotel is quite famous. Most visitors head up the 16-km (10-mile) spur to Petrohue, stopping to see the unusual **Petrohue Falls**. This is not the usual waterfalls, but a series of oddly twisting chutes formed by a crystallized black volcanic rock which is particularly resistant to erosion. (Cerro Puntiagudo's odd shape is due to this erosion resistance: its center core is composed of the same crystallized rock which remains unaffected while the surrounding material erodes away.) The water is bright green due to the presence of algae, a phenomenon repeated in **All Saints Lake** (Todos los Santos), also called Emerald Lake, which begins at the town of Petrohue. From the falls to

the lake the road is cut by several river-beds which will rise suddenly on a warm day with melt from the Osorno Volcano. Eruptions from the volcano centuries ago diverted the Petrohue River's flow from Lake Llanquihue south to All Saints Lake; signs of the earlier lava flows can be observed along with strange vegetation and insect life not found even a few kilometers away. **Petrohué** itself is nothing but a lodge, lakeside campground (fishing is said to be great), and forest service outpost, but a large modern catamaran leaves from the dock for a day trip on the lake. In the height of summer this area is plagued by two types of biting fly – the colihuacho and the petro (Petrohué is the mapuche word meaning place of petros). The only relief from these pests is by sheltering in the deep shade of the forests.

Small glaciers atop **Thunder Mountain** can be observed en route, and the Osorno Volcano is even more imposing from the All Saints Lake side than from Lake Llanquihue. The lake itself is narrow with forested cliffs rising sharply on all sides. Lunch at touristic **Peulla** on the other end is expensive. The famous Bridal Falls may be only a trickle if rain has been scarce, and the hamlet can be surprisingly hot. But the small beach is pleasant, and the river above is shady and fresh. Hiking excursions into the mountains from Peulla are excellent. Travelers can continue to Bariloche in Argentina by taking the road to **Puerto Frias** where you pick up another boat.

To continue the circuit from Ensenada back towards the west, the road is unpaved and crosses a difficult stretch of volcanic dirt which can be quite slippery even in dry weather. The area, covered by an eruption some 150 years ago, nicely illustrates how plant life gradually returns after destruction by a lava flow; the borders of deciduous forest are abruptly marked on either side.

Three km (2 miles) from Ensenada is the road to the **La Burbuja (bubble) Refuge** on the volcano's slopes, well worth the 19-km (12-mile) climb. In clear weather the sunset seen from the top is memorable, and the refuge/ski center has overnight facilities. The road

eases down to the town of **Las Cascadas**, but there is no public transport for this 20-km (12-mile) stretch; hitchhiking is easier in the afternoon, but never a sure thing. The road has more than the necessary twists and turns – locals explain that the original track was paid for by the kilometer, and their relatives ensured it was as long as possible.

Las Cascadas ("waterfalls") has a 4-km (2½-mile) hike into the hills on paths (easy to get lost so a guide from town is advisable). Down by the shore is a summer-home colony where President Aylwin still visits. Unfortunately, locals and the vacationing city youth don't mix well and outsiders are likely to be studiously ignored by both groups.

Symmetrical peak: The **Osorno Volcano**, a perfect, snow-covered cone, dominates the view from the road. Skilled mountaineers can climb to the crater in about six hours, but quickly shifting clouds and hidden crevasses can be deadly even for the expert. Plentiful stories of people being lost there are meant to discourage free-lance ex-

ploring. Try to visit a farm set back up in the hills a few hundred meters, on the pretext of buying homemade cheese or marmalade – you can get a wide vista of the lake and volcano together and understand why the original settlers went to the trouble of making these densely overgrown lands habitable. Some settlers employed chilotes, *mestizo* fishermen from Chiloé Island further south, to help with the backbreaking labor, sometimes abusing their trust to trick them out of fair wages. One whispered story even suggests the imported workers were often "lost" in the thick jungle in order to avoid paying them anything. Settlers dragged logs or their farm produce down to a dock to be picked up by the steamboat from Puerto Varas, sometimes going along to the town for provisions. But the frequent lake squalls could lead to financial disaster: in order to avoid capsizing, passengers would have to dump their recently-bought goods overboard package by package.

The only surviving pier from the epoch is at **Puerto Fonck** on the unpaved road that connects Cascadas with the road to Osorno. The long stretches of beach from Cascadas towards Puerto Klocker and Puerto Fonck are deserted.

Despite the fame of the area as having been settled by Germans, the immigrants never numbered more than 10 percent of the total population of the region. An internal migration accompanied them, but since the Chileans drawn to the new lands from other regions were usually uneducated and destitute (the motive of their decision to start over elsewhere), the foreigners quickly established themselves as the dominant class, employing the *mestizo* citizens and directing economic development. Although the expected problems did arise on occasion, there is today no observable underlying ethnic tension, and German-descended citizens are seen as fully Chileanized, industrious, and trustworthy. Attitudes towards the indigenous-descended population, however, are not as generous. Finally defeated only in the late 1800s, the Mapuche survivors were herded into

The Hotel Ensenada, crowded with antiques.

undersirable lands deep in the mountains (both Andes and coastal ranges) where soils were poor and animal husbandry difficult. While the foreign and domestic settlers rushed in to conquer the wilderness, the original inhabitants suffered poverty, discrimination, and social decomposition with the attendant social ills that continue to plague these communities today.

The first tourist outpost: The idea of Lake Llanquihue as a vacation spot occurred as early as 1912 to a government functionary, Interior Minister Luis Izquierdo, who built a summer mansion on the Centinela Peninsula next to Puerto Octay with a group of his friends. The house remains in use. **Puerto Octay** is a popular resort town, a bit less crowded than the southern shore. The road along the lake heading south has more spectacular views and some stops of interests such as the **Monument to Colonization** at Totoral.

The tidy little town of **Frutillar** has a famous music festival in the summer, mostly classical. It is actually two towns joined together; Lower Frutillar is 4 km (2½ miles) down a steep incline from Upper Frutillar. There are more houses up above, many of which offer summer lodgings at reasonable rates. Fixed-rate taxis will ferry you up and down if the walk is too tiresome. The shingled churches in Frutillar, the nearby industrial town of Llanquihue, and elsewhere are well-known and often appear in tourist brochures with the lake sparkling in the background.

A new road has now opened up the **Reloncaví Estuary**, a finger of brackish water that connects with the Reloncaví Bay. Fishing here isn't what it used to be after years of commercial exploitation, but there are still plenty of unexplored inlets. This area and further south is sometimes called "continental Chiloé" for the similarity in culture with Chiloé Island. As the road winds down the glaciated Petrohue River valley onto the east shore of the Reloncaví, the characteristic *chilote* tiles begin to appear on the buildings. These are made of water-resistant alerce, the Sequoia-related trees

Market at Angelmó docks, Puerto Montt.

that live hundreds of years and can resist forest fires. The wood is so valuable that alerce stumps are sometimes harvested and split for sale. **Ralún**, at the mouth of the Petrohue, is a bit seedy, except for the fancy hotel whose helicopter tours drive the local residents mad all day. **Cochamó** further south is more of a town and has views of the **Yate Volcano** (2,111 meters/6,926 ft). **Puelo**, the last stop before finding passage on a boat, is also run-down and unused to visitors. These towns are more reminiscent of the isolated communities along the recently-finished Austral Road which winds through the largely uninhabited archipelago region for more than 1,000 kilometers (600 miles).

Urban centers: Of all the cities in the south, **Osorno** is the least interesting, in part for the strange lack of street life. A business day in Osorno feels like a Sunday, and Sunday feels like a day of national mourning. The town was abandoned after the great Mapuche uprising in 1598, its inhabitants fleeing to establish protected outposts on the ocean inlets just north of Chiloé Island. Osorno was not refounded until 200 years later. The city is still more of a market center for country residents than an urban entity; the cattle auction is perhaps the most impressive local attraction.

There are also some good panoramic views from the Rahue Lookout of the city and the Rahue River as well as the volcanoes to the east. The wood houses have sharply-angled roofs to handle the rain and snow, and when the storm clouds begin to threaten, the place has the air of a city in Quebec or northern New England. There is also a fort, though the one at Río Bueno, 30 km (19 miles) north, is better preserved. It has a good view of the river, also known as El Gran Río, which carries off the water of four lakes (Maihue, Ranco, Puyehue and Rupanco) – making it the second-largest in Chile measured by flow.

The countryside outside Osorno remains surprisingly poor, as can be observed from the aspect of travelers coming to and from rural areas at the bus terminal. All the cities in this valley are partly protected by the low coastal mountains known as the **Cordillera Pelada** ("bald" or "peeled") which blocks the ocean winds and allows the dry, southern winds to dominate,

The bustling, windy city of **Puerto Montt** was connected by rail to the rest of Chile in 1912 and became the contact point for the rest of the south. To a large extent it remains so to the present day. It is an important fishing center; seafood at the **Angelmó Pier** is famous. Boats leave from here for the long, slow trip down through the archipelago. (Puerto Chacabuco requires 22 hours, Puerto Natales near Argentina three days). The port is protected by **Tenglo Island**, and the calm waters of the bay give the center of town a very tranquil air.

From the hills above are fine views of the entire Reloncaví Bay. Local boat trips can be arranged either in Puerto Montt or at **La Arena** where the estuary begins. From Chamiza it is also possible to get close to the **Calbuco Volcano** on the southern side of Lake Llanquihue. German settlers built an interesting Lutheran church in **Chamiza** next to two giant araucaria trees. The **Alerce Andino National Park** has good facilities, and **Lake Chapo** is off the usual tourist beat. In the other direction is the port of **Maullín**, one of the few places to observe the open sea in the South.

Further south is **Carelmapu**, one of the oldest settlements, dating from the Spaniards' flight after their defeat by the Mapuches around 1600. On its rough beaches can be found the original wild strawberries from which commercial strawberries were developed. Another alternative is the unpaved road that follows the bay southwest from Puerto Montt. This offers unique views of the volcanoes towards the north. In the **Huito Estuary**, Chile's most famous naval heroes, Arturo Prat and Miguel Grau Seminario, fought the Spanish in 1866 during the War of Independence. (Prat later died up north in the Naval Battle of Iquique during the war against Peru.) The Huilo enters the bay at the port of **Calbuco** which, like Carelmapu, predates Puerto Montt by some 250 years. Its seafood-packing industry has been wiped out by over-exploitation.

Right, German traditions celebrated in Puerto Montt

CHILOÉ

For a moment you think you've misheard, that someone has simply pronounced the word "Chile" and for some peculiar reason your ears have given it an extra "o". To some extent **Chiloé** is Chile in miniature, a peculiar time capsule that contains some of Chile's best and harshest traditions, shaping them into song, dance, crafts and a mythology which has become one of the main strands of the country's national identity. Much of "Chilean" folk music and dance were born in the gentle summer fogs and harsh winters of the archipelago of Chiloé.

December, January and February are the better months for a visit to Chiloé, because the warmer summer weather makes it easier to travel within the main island and across the straits to some of the smaller islands. In recent years, Chiloé has become something of a standard pilgrimage for the young and the not-so-young, so you may meet more people from Santiago than the islands, at least in the main cities.

Birth of an archipelago: A Mapuche legend tells the story of what may have been the formation of Chiloé as witnessed by Mapuche and Chonos long before the Spanish reached the continent. In it the twin serpents, Cai Cai and Tren Tren, do battle. Cai Cai, the evil one, who has risen in rage from the sea and flooded the earth, assaults Tren Tren's rocky fortress in the mountain peaks, while the Mapuche try in vain to awaken the friendly serpent from a deep sleep.

Meanwhile Cai Cai had almost reached Tren Tren's cave, swimming on the turbulent waters. Her friends, the Pillanes of Thunder, Fire and Wind, helped her by piling up clouds so it would rain, thunder and flash lightning.

Pleas and weeping don't wake Tren Tren. Only the laughter of a little girl, dancing with her reflection in the sleeping serpent's eye, arouses Tren Tren who responds with a giggle so insulting that Cai Cai and the Pillanes fall down the hill.

But the amusement didn't last: Cai Cai charged again, all the more furious, and shattered the earth, sewing the sea with islands ...

Cai Cai made the water climb ever higher and almost submerged the mountain where her enemy lived; but Tren Tren arched her back and with the strength of the 12 guanacos in her stomach, pushed the cave ceiling upward and the mountain grew toward the sky.

Cai Cai and the Pillanes kept bringing more water and Tren Tren kept pushing her cave roof higher until the mountain reached above the clouds, close to the sun, where the Pillanes and the evil serpent could not reach it. And Cai Cai and her servants fell from the peak itself into the abyss where they lay stunned for thousands of years.

In the legend the waters gradually recede and the Mapuches are able to

receding
ages,
apper
usinessman
Ancud.
eft, *Palafitos*
n Castro's
aterline and
e rolling
ills of
hiloé.

ISLA DOÑA SEBASTIANA

Maullín
Carelmapu
San Rafael
Chacao
Calbuco
La Arena
Caleta Puelche
I. PULUQUI
Volcán Hornopirén
1670

Pacific

Ancud
Chepu
Linao
Rolecha
Río Negro
Golfo de Ancud

Ocean

Punta Esperanza
Pid Pid
Castro
Punta Cuevas
Airport
Chonchi
L. Huillinco

Quemchi
Degan
Pulutauco
Dalcahue
Curaco de Vélez
Rilán
Puqueldón
Tenaún
I. BUTA CHAUQUES
Ayacara
PENÍNSULA HUEQUI
Achao
I. QUINCHAO
I. CHULIN
I. CHAULINEC

ISLA
Lago Tepuhueco
Punta Tablaruca
L. S. Antonio

DE
CHILOÉ
Laguna de Chaiguaco
L. Chaiguata
Quellón
Quéilen
I. TALCAN
I. PUDUGUAPI
Punta Centinela
R. Rayas
Chaitén
Pto. Cárdenas

Punta Yatac
Golfo Corcovado

ISLA GUAPIQUILÁN
Punta Redonda
Punta Olleta

Chiloé Island
32 km / 20 miles

return to their traditional lands, untroubled by either of the giant serpents who continued sleeping. However, "sometimes Cai Cai has nightmares and an island appears in the ocean or the earth trembles a little."

In a region like Chile's south, the legend may simply tell the story of an ancient earthquake which was accompanied by tidal waves and flooding, natural catastrophes which still occur every 30 or 40 years. But the legend's description is remarkably similar to scientific accounts of how the earth settled into the peculiar attributes of the area. According to these, two giant tectonic plates forming part of the earth's crust clashed, producing the volcanoes characteristic of mainland Chiloé: Hornopirén, Huequi, Michimahuida and Corcovado.

Forces of nature: Glaciers bore down upon the Central Valley region, carving a hole through the coastal mountains and pushing the valley further and further below sea level. As the glaciers melted, the ocean rushed through the openings located at the north and south ends of what is now the main island of Chiloé, colliding violently even as they created the **Interior Sea**, and turning the coastal mountain range into a series of islands which form the archipelago of Chiloé.

Toward the center of the main island, where the lakes of Huillinco and Cucao cut partially through the coastal mountain range, the land drops to sea level, and many islanders fear that Chiloé may one day be cut in two.

Chiloé's **Isla Grande** (main island) is the second largest island in Latin America, after Tierra del Fuego. Like a great ship moored off the Chilean coast it seems to float, surrounded by several smaller constellations of islands called the **Chauques, Quenac, Quehui, Chaulinec** and **Desertores**. Some of these islands are so close to each other they are joined at low tide, while others are within shouting distance. The low mountains along the west coast of the main island are nevertheless high enough to stop the damp winds blowing off the

Primary colors of a fishing boat offset the gloomy sky.

248

Pacific, creating a slightly drier microclimate along the Interior Sea, where virtually all the settlements are located.

The Interior Sea, generally calm at least as seen from the shore, can be difficult to navigate, especially for the many Chilotes who still rely on small rowboats or launches. As the tides roar in through the tiny channel of **Chacao** in the north (crossed by the mainland ferry) they eventually meet and clash with the tides pouring through the channel to the island's south, creating huge whirlpools and waves.

In Cucao, on the Pacific coast, the difference between high and low tides is 2.5 meters (8 ft), while in Quemchi, on the Interior Sea, it's 7 meters, because of the shallowness in many parts of the Interior Sea.

These powerful tides, which occur twice a day, leave shellfish and fish (a major source of food for the island's dwellers from its earliest history up to the present) trapped on the beaches and in seapools.

The making of the Chilotes: The first known inhabitants of the islands of Chiloé were the Chonos, a tough, sea-faring people who have gone down in history for the creation of the *dalca*, a small, canoe-like boat built by binding several roughhewn planks together.

For centuries they guided the Spanish and other adventurers through the intricate channels and fiords which honeycomb Chile's southern shores. They spoke a different language from the Mapuche or Huilliche (southern Mapuche), who began to invade the islands. These invasions forced the Chonos to migrate further and further south. In the 1700s, the Jesuits pushed those of the Chonos and the Caucahues, a separate native group who had not been integrated into the Mapuche, into small reserves on Cailín Island and later the Chaulinec Islands, where they eventually mixed with the other inhabitants. The Jesuit mission on Cailín Island south of Quellón, was the southernmost chapel in the Christian Empire.

When Alfonso de Camargo became

ush andscape.

the first European to see Chiloé in 1540, the archipelago's inhabitants were a mixture of Chono and Mapuche living scattered along the coast, which was at once their main highway, source of food, and the cradle for a wealth of legends and oral histories which are the backbone of Chilote culture to this day. The homes in which they lived were straw *rucas*, still in use in some Mapuche communities on the mainland, clustered near beaches and woods in groups of up to 400 people, known as *cabí's*, led by *caciques* or chiefs. Using wooden tools, they farmed potatoes and corn in fields protected by fences woven using basket techniques and they reaped the rich harvest of shellfish along the shores. They were also excellent weavers of llama's wool.

Thirteen years later Francisco de Ulloa's expedition, complete with a poet, Alonso de Ercilla, formally discovered the islands and 14 years after that, Martín Ruiz de Gamboa officially took possession of them, calling them Nueva Galicia. On 12 February 1567, he founded the city Santiago de Castro and for the next 200 years the Spaniards divided up the available land – and the people living on it – in what became known as the *encomienda* system, which was virtually slavery under a different name. The idea was that the native peoples worked for free in order to "pay tribute" to the king of Spain and they did so, particularly in the mining of gold in Cucao, the weaving of woollen cloth and the logging of *alerce*, a tough, fine wood native to Chile (today in danger of extinction).

In the early years, the products of Chiloé brought considerable wealth to the Spaniards who had taken possession of the land, but desperate poverty to its people. In 1598, when the Mapuche communities of Carelmapu and Calbuco on the mainland rebelled against the Spanish invaders, the survivors retreated to Chiloé. There they established towns in 1602. It would be another 250 years before the Spanish could once again get a toehold in this fiercely defended Mapuche territory.

The people of Chiloé themselves twice

Stilt houses are common in the region.

joined forces with "pirates": with Baltasar de Cordes in 1600 they attacked and destroyed Castro and with Enrique Brouwer in 1643 they assaulted Carelmapu and later crossed the channel to attack Valdivia.

In the centuries which followed, the Spanish and the Mapuche-Chonos of Chiloé lived in virtual isolation and extreme poverty, with visits from Spanish ships, sent from Lima, Peru, sometimes as many as three years apart. During that period the two races fused, preserving much of the native languages, customs and legends. The Chilotes wore the same clothes and suffered the same hardships as poor farmers tending small plots of land, creating a sense of social equality unusual in the Spanish empire.

Settlement continued along the coast until the turn of this century, when lands were given to German, English, French and Spanish "colonists" and the building of a railway (1912) between Ancud and Castro finally opened internal communication between Chiloé's two main cities.

Today the Chilotes continue to be a proud, independent people, clearly distinguishable from their fellow Chileans, with their own accent (more similar to 16th-century Spanish) mixed with many indigenous words, and a rich tradition of music and dance beloved throughout Chile.

However, the tragic poverty of the early years of colonization continues to dominate the Chilote lifestyle, forcing most of the young men to migrate to other regions in Latin America where there is plenty of work: the saltpetre mines (in the 1800s), as sailors, and to the sheep ranches in the Argentine *pampas* and along the Straits of Magellan, where they have a reputation as serious, reliable workers.

Their one great weakness is the game of *truco*, played with the Spanish 40-card deck. *Truco*, which roughly translates to "trickery" in English, is an extraordinary gambling game divided into two parts, the *envío* and the *truco* itself. The cards are half the game; the other half is the skill and imagination of the

*otato
endor.*

players who bluff and jest, using rhyming couplets laden with double meanings. Today, you are as likely to see a lively game of *truco* on a ship at Punta Arenas, as in a Chilote bar. And the Chilotes who've gambled away a seasons' earnings on the sheep ranches and been unable to return home are legend.

This forced migration has also given rise to the image of the Chilote family as a virtual matriarchy – of distant, sometimes almost mythical men, and strong women raising their children, their livestock and tending their crops, thus keeping the island alive.

A land crowded with chapels: It was during the 200-year period when the Spanish were barred from the Mapuche's lands in mainland Chile, that the Jesuits began the evangelizing activities which left an enduring mark on the islands' legends and villages.

One of the most strikingly beautiful characteristics of Chilote architecture are the wooden chapels built during the Jesuits' stay, many of which survive to this day. The chapels, which often stood completely alone on the coast unaccompanied by human habitation, were built as part of the Jesuits' "Circulating Mission." This consisted of a boat manned by two missionaries who started their annual rounds from Castro with religious ornaments and three portable altars, complete with a "Holy Christ" to be carried during ceremonies by the *caciques*; a "Holy Heart" to be carried by children; a "Saint John" to be carried by bachelors; a "Saint Isidro" for married men; "Our Lady of Suffering (Dolores)" for single women and "Saint Notburga" for married women.

To this day, a *fiscal*, a sort of native priest, has the custody of chapel keys, and in August people from the surrounding islands gather on Caguache Island to celebrate their religion with ceremonies similar to those initiated by the Jesuits and modified by later Roman Catholic missions. The chapel of Villipulli, near Chonchi, continues to stand absolutely alone, with no human settlement around it, exactly the same way as the chapels did in the 1600s. These **Chapel at Aldachildo.**

252

ing example of the Chilotes' outstanding ability to absorb foreign cultures without losing their own identity. Their design is strongly influenced by German architecture of the period, because several of the Jesuits were from Bavaria.

The *tejuelas* or wooden shingles commonly used to roof buildings throughout Southern Chile, and which are one of the most striking characteristics of homes in Chiloé, were also a German idea, brought by the colonists who originally settled in Llanquihue and Puerto Montt on the mainland. The visible part of the t*ejuela* is about a third of the total length, as the shakes overlap so well that these buildings are extremely resistant to the heavy rains of the entire region.

Before the *tejuelas* were introduced, however, Chilote homes usually had roofs of straw, similar to those of the Mapuches' *rucas*, also extraordinarily resistant to the rain.

A tradition of handicrafts: For centuries, the women of Chiloé spent the harsh, wet winters producing much of the clothing and other items necessary for their household to function, and that tradition continues today. Different parts of the islands are associated with different crafts. For example the small town of Chonchi (south of Castro) is known for its woven wool products, especially blankets and ponchos, as well as socks, scarves, gloves and the Chilote golden liquer, *licor de oro,* made, literally, with gold. **Quellón** is famous for its soft, grey ponchos, very resistant to the rain because the wool used is raw and therefore still full of natural oils. On **Lingue Island**, across from Achao, basketweaving is the main craft, made with a variety of local fibers, although some have fallen into disuse due to the difficulty of working with them.

Many of the islands' legends have been woven into decorative objects, straw birds and representations of *La Pincoya* and other figures.

The largest market for Chilote handicrafts is actually in the mainland in **Angelmó**, in Puerto Montt. However, early Sunday mornings, there is a traditional *feria* by the dock in **Dalcahué**, where hundreds of craftspeople from all over the archipelago still gather to sell their wares to travelers. They also prepare several of the traditional Chilote meals, particularly the *curanto*, an extraordinary concoction prepared over a fire built in a hole scooped out of the earth, with a variety of shellfish and meat, served with *milcao*, a traditional flatbread made with potatoes and flour.

The traditional woven fences of the Mapuche-Chonos can still be seen separating livestock from planted areas in some parts of the islands and the *birloche* or *trineo*, a sled-like vehicle towed by oxen continues to be used on several of the smaller islands.

In the markets and fairs you should keep your eye out for the *almudes*, wooden boxes of a fixed size, still used to show off a sellers' wares. The *almud* is also a unit of measurement and the boxes have the peculiarity of measuring one *almud* on one end and half an *almud* on the other. Their origin is Spanish.

▸hearing ompetition t a local estival.

Stone mills introduced by the Jesuits can be seen in several Chilote museums and they are still in use in some areas between Castro and Dalcahué. In February, wooden *chicha* (cider) presses are still very much in evidence, pressing the sweet juices out of apples piled in traditional baskets of *ñocha*.

Hanging in the windows of many houses you'll see woollen socks or ponchos or other handmade items which are available for sale. If you're lucky you may also get a glimpse of a Chilote loom, which is horizontal and nailed to the floor. It is still used by the artisans, who must kneel to work it.

Chilote sweaters are made from scratch, from sheep rather than llama wool. The women shear the sheep, clean and wash the wool by hand, dye it with colors prepared from local herbs, and spin it using a simple spindle which twirls on the floor.

Holding on to the past: Chiloé remains in many ways as mysterious, as lovely, as long-suffering, and as contradictory as it has been for most of its colorful history. Modern fish-processing plants have begun to provide more employment. At the same time, pollution and over-fishing of coastal waters are becoming problems. Already the *loco*, a delicious shellfish marketed abroad as abalone, is virtually extinct, and attempts to protect it have only created a thriving underground of unscrupulous entrepreneurs.

Other Chilotes have tried to eke out a living fishing, with mixed results, and developmental agencies have created programs for improving Chilote agriculture, marketing and handicraft techniques. Even as modern factory ships sail under foreign flags, just outside Chile's 322-km (200-mile) limit, the Chilotes themselves continue to live – and die – by the traditional rowboats and small motor launches.

Chilote culture itself – the music, the poetry and the stories, are increasingly packaged for a burgeoning tourist industry, a process which tends to create and preserve caricatures devoid of their original meaning. Like many similar attempts in other parts of the world, this has harmed as well as helped the local economy.

The Santiago-based group, Chilhué, has studied Chilote culture and mythology and converted much of what they've learned into music, dance, poetry and songs (a very Chilote tradition in itself). They have a cassette available and their performances can often be seen in Santiago during the winter or in Chiloé during the summer. A Puerto Montt-based group called Bordemar has also integrated several traditional Chilote instruments into their music which is a curious and delightful blend of the folkloric combined with the classical. They're certainly well worth listening to or seeing if you can catch them give a live performance.

A lot of Chilote cultural activity is also on view during the *Festival Costumbrista*, the second week of February in Castro.

Jumping-off points: Ancud and Castro, the main island's two cities, provide good bases for exploring the archipelago. Until 1982, **Ancud** was the capital

A fortune-telling machine.

of Chiloé and it is the first city the highway passes on its way from the ferry down the island. Ancud, today with a population of 3,300, was an international port until the beginning of this century. It remains a peculiar mixture of traditional Chilote buildings, docks and plazas combined with more modern signs and structures built in the recent past.

Stores close for lunch between 1 and 3 p.m. in the afternoon and on Saturdays are only open until 1 p.m. Ancud's central plaza, like those of most cities founded by the Spanish, is flanked by the **Cathedral**, government buildings and a **museum** (open daily; March–December closed Monday) which contains many objects that hint at rather than tell the full story of Ancud's past, including a series of stone statues representing the island's many mythical figures.

If you have a vehicle you can enjoy a lovely drive along the **Costanera**, with an westward view of the Gulf of Quetalmahue. Lining the shore are the older, often impressive houses of Ancud's better-off citizens.

By following Costanera, then Bellavista and San Antonio northward, you'll quickly reach **San Antonio Fort**, which was built in 1770. On 19 January 1826, it became the last Spanish garrison to surrender to the wave of independence which had swept America, turning the former Spanish colonies over to the ambitious young *mestizos* of America.

From then on Ancud became the focus for colonizing expeditions aimed at Southern Chile, including one which settled the Strait of Magellan in 1843. (The tiny boat that took the first settlers down to claim the far south is preserved intact at the museum). At the turn of the century, Ancud boomed with the whale and wood industries and newly-arrived settlers from Europe, primarily of German origin. However, when the railway reached Puerto Montt in 1912, Ancud lost its importance and in 1982, the trade and shipping center Castro became the capital of Chiloé.

There are good cheap places to eat

*Fishing boats
Ancud.*

seafood in the Ancud **market** and island craftspeople usually have booths both in the market and along the seaside of the plaza. The **Mirador Cerro Huaihuén** (a lookout point) offers a breathtaking view of the city and across the **Chacao channel** toward the mainland's cliffs and fishing hamlets.

An interesting sidetrip from Ancud is a visit to the **Caulín Oyster beds**. To get there you travel back along the highway toward the ferry's arrival point at Chacao, turning left toward Caulín at km 24. Occasionally, upon reaching the channel, you must wait until the tide goes out in order to continue along the beach and the oyster beds, where you can enjoy fresh oysters at reasonable prices, before spending a pleasant afternoon on the beach or heading back to Ancud.

If you drive south from Ancud and then west toward **Chepu** you'll find good fishing at the **Anguay Fishing Refuge** as well as several good places to picnic. Along the way, you may notice the **Butalcura River** valley with great patches of dead trees in the water where the 1960 earthquake caused the earth to collapse.

Settlement on stilts: Castro, the main island's other city and its capital since 1982, has a population of about 3,500 people, and is located about 90 km (56 miles) to the south of Ancud. Although it is technically one of Chile's oldest cities, because it was founded in 1567, Castro suffered so many attacks and privations that there are few signs of its antiquity within the city itself. On the highway just to the south of Castro are the *palafitos*, the wooden homes on stilts which have come to symbolize the Chilotes' symbiotic relationship with earth and ocean.

It's best to see Castro on foot, strolling from the central **plaza** shoreward to enjoy the market area with its lively crafts fair, then back up the hill toward the **Mirador** (viewpoint) with its Statue of the Virgin and its bird's eye view of the city's cemetery, piled high with conventional gravestones and small structures resembling houses that shelter the city's dead.

Castro's **Museum** is also worth seeing (open daily and Sunday morning), located conveniently near the central plaza and the plaza is also the focal point for the *Festival Costumbrista*, a festival of Chilote customs, food and crafts which traditionally takes place the second week of February.

From Castro you can travel up the shore of Chiloé's "interior sea" to visit **Dalcahue**, **Llaullao** and, on **Quinchao Island** (there is a small ferry that travels constantly back and forth), the small towns of **Curaco de Velez** and **Achao**. Achao's **Santa Maria Church**, started in 1735 and finished in 1767, is Chilóes oldest and is built entirely of cypress and *alerce*.

Further along the island highway is the **Quinchao church**, Chiloé's largest, which was built around 1700 and refashioned according to neoclassical ideas at the end of the 1800s. Driving through the surrounding landscape it's possible to see the traditional woven fences of Chiloé.

Chonchi, about half an hour south of Castro, is called the three-story city, and is a small town which time seems to have passed over. There is a co-operative store down by the docks, which sells the products of many of the local crafts people on a year-round basis. Cardboard signs in windows offer the famous gold liqueur.

Near Chonchi it's possible to catch a ferry to **Lemuy Island** or head further south to **Queilen** or **Quellón**, Chiloé's southernmost town where the ferries to Aisén dock.

A National Park can be reached by traveling across the island toward Cucao, the only town on the Pacific side of the island. It's a good place for a hike or to camp.

Each town and village, every island, has something a little different to offer. While there is good public transport throughout most of the island, including ferries over to some of the smaller islands, a car is ideal because it provides a greater flexibility for stops and exploration. It's also possible to rent motorboats or airplanes to travel around the islands.

Right, stuning colors of Castro Cathedral.

CHILOTE MAGIC

By any standards, the archipelago of Chiloé is a magical place. Gods and goddesses, ghost ships and the lost city of the Caesars (visible at dawn as the sun reflects gold off volcano cliffs and, some believe, the city's crystal skyscrapers) are as much a part of the archipelago as the people themselves.

Expressed in music, dance and popular beliefs, the *Trauco*, the *Pincoya*, the *Caleuche* and other mythical creatures haunt the forests and fields of Chiloé. Alongside them are the *brujos* or wizards, their human

counterparts who have attempted to leash the uncontrollable natural forces that still wield enormous power over the lives of those who dwell on the islands.

Undoubtedly many of the mythical characters also serve a social purpose: the *Trauco*, for example, is a creature that is able to seduce young women by hypnotizing them with his magical gaze. Accepting its existence provides an acceptable explanation of teenage pregnancies and has even been used to cover up incest that could be explosive in close-knit island communities.

Today, when so much of Chiloé's maritime wealth is threatened by over-exploita-tion, these people-sized gods also serve as symbols of an ecological balance achieved by Chiloé's earlier peoples, with warnings and messages of how that balance must again be achieved.

Seducer of virgins: As you walk through the forests of Chiloé, keep an eye out for the *Trauco*. No taller than a meter, this deformed, manlike creature may make his home in the fork of a tree or a small cave. He wears clothes made of vegetable fibres and always carries a staff which he knocks on the ground and against trees. His legs end in stumps and one look can kill the beholder or leave him or her mute or stupid, or with a twisted neck or a hump.

In spite of his limited physical charms, the *Trauco* enjoys considerable success with young women, whom he seduces with the hypnotic effect of his blazing eyes. To defend yourself from the *Trauco*, throw a handful of sand at him. While he's busy counting the grains, make your escape.

Another creature, the *Pincoya*, slips out of the surf at sunrise and dances on the shore. When her face is turned toward the ocean, it means abundant shellfish will soon cover the beach. If she looks inland, this means she has taken the fish elsewhere, to where they are more needed. If you fish or extract shellfish too long from one site, she gets angry and abandons it, leaving the place barren.

The *Pincoya* is blonde and beautiful and values good cheer. Her name is from the Quechua or the Aymará (native peoples of Northern Chile's Andes). Legend also has it that she will sometimes rescue drowning sailors and leave them on the beach.

Haunted vessel: It is difficult to imagine any seagoing culture without its ghost ship and Chiloé is no exception. The *Caleuche* with its unlikely cargo of tragic guests, caught in an eternal party, sends haunting

strains of accordion music across the waves and recovers the bodies of those who have died at sea. Its crew are *brujos*, Chilote wizards with enormous powers, and it travels in a constant cloud produced by the boat itself, always at night.

The *Caleuche* also advances under the water, disappearing suddenly if someone goes too close. Or it turns into a floating trunk or a rock to put off pursuers. If caught looking at the *Caleuche*, your mouth will become twisted, your head crooked or you'll

Left, figures from Chiloé's mythology adorn a wall. **Above**, Chilote woodcarver.

suddenly die.

It's said to put in at the ports of Llicaldac, Tren-Tren and Quicaví, where the *brujos'* most important cave is located. Oreste Plath tells the story of a trim sloop piloted by a young man from Chonchi, which disappeared on its maiden voyage. Although it never returned, the father did not mourn, and everyone realized the son was safe and sound aboard the *Caleuche*. Soon after, the father began to grow rich very quickly, from the invaluable merchandise delivered by the *Caleuche*.

A magical city: No traveler ever sets eyes on the Caesars' lost city, even when he walks through it. A thick mist always hides it from sight and the rivers carry approaching boats away. The lost city, with its gold- and silver-paved streets and its ability to make all who go there lose their memory, will appear only once at the end of the world, to prove its existence to non-believers.

The city with its enormous riches and infinite pleasures, where no one is born or dies, inspired centuries of expeditions by intrepid explorers, which began in 1528. That was when 14 men led by Captain Francisco César, member of an advance group in Sebastian Cabot's party, ventured into the southern jungles for two months. Upon returning they told tales of fabulous treasures, which may perhaps have belonged to the Inca Empire.

The next expedition to the lost city started out from Castro on October 6, 1620, led by Juan Tao. This and following trips were led primarily by the Spanish and their decendants, including the Jesuit priests José Garcia, Juan Vicuña and Juan Francisco Menéndez. Both the Spanish Council of the Indies and the Royal Audience in Santiago officially authorized the search for the mystery city.

Chile's southern mountain range is so rugged and impenetrable even today, that perhaps there is a lost city of the Incas, hidden among the clouds and volcano peaks.

The warlocks' power: The *brujeria* is a brotherhood of male witches organised into an underground of councils, which meets in cleverly disguised caves, the biggest of which is in Quicaví. The members arrive disguised as birds or as themselves, wearing the luminous *macuñ*, which gives them the power to fly. The *macuñ* is made of skin taken from the breast of a virgin's corpse and its light is fuelled by oil taken from the bodies of dead Christians.

The apprenticeship to become a *brujo* begins young and consists of a series of increasingly cruel trials. One of the more basic is a shower repeated for 40 nights in a mountain waterfall, to cleanse away all trace of baptism. Then he must cleanly catch a skull which is thrown by the instructor from the crown of a tricorn hat. To prove that he is

tomb in the cemetery.

Brujos have the power to make people sleepy, open doors, cause illness, falling hair or deep cuts, and to throw *llancazos*, similar to the evil eye, or bad spells cast at a distance. *Brujos* have a crystal stone called the Challanco, through which they can view every detail of peoples' lives. The Challanco looks like a glass bowl or a large round mirror.

The *Invunche* guards the wizards' cave and is the product of a long and painful process: to obtain an invunche the wizards rob a firstborn son from his parents, within the first nine days after his birth. They take the child to the cave: if it's been baptized they use black magic to annul it, then break

not weakened by sentiment, the apprentice must murder his best friend. Finally, he should dig up a recently buried corpse and remove the skin from the breast. Once it has dried, this can be sewn onto the *brujo*'s waistcoat – at night, the skin gives off a glow that can guide him on his missions. Anyone who reveals he is a *brujo* will be sentenced to death within a year; *brujos* aren't allowed to rob or rape, nor can they eat salt.

Other trials include races, leaps from cliffs at night, the use of the *macuñ*, corporal metamorphosis into animals or birds, wearing a lizard bound to the forehead, (to transmit wisdom), spending nights sleeping on a

and twist his right leg, until it rides up the back. At three months' old they split his tongue and rub his skin daily with a special infusion. In the early months he lives on milk from a black cat and later human flesh obtained from cemeteries.

The origins of this macabre myth may be in historical fact: the writer Narciso García relates the *invunche's* deformities to the Inca culture. They often prefer men with some physical disability to be the guards of their temples.

Women's participation in the brujería is usually as a *Voladora* (flying woman), for whom many of the secret practices of the brotherhood are forbidden knowledge. The *Voladora* often transforms herself into a bird (the *bauda*), with a loud, raucous cry and serves as a messenger for the *brujos*. In order to become the bird, the woman vomits up her intestines, which she leaves in a tree. If for some reason they're lost she quickly dies.

The *camahueto*, a huge one or two horned cow-like creature that's born from the earth with such force that it leaves a small crater behind it, is essential to the magic of the *machi*, the *brujo* herbal doctor. The *machi* must grab the *camahueto's* horn as it leaps from the earth and before it races to a cliff, from which it plunges into the ocean, where it completes its lifecycle.

placing two needles in the form of a cross over the door, making it impossible for the *brujo* to leave. Tuesdays and Fridays are the *brujos'* nights for roaming and there is a chant commonly used to scare them away.

According to Narciso García Barría, who has studied Chiloé at great length, *brujos* are almost always descended from native people and it is extremely difficult for whites to be admitted. He believes their origins may lie in an underground organization of native resistance to the Spaniards, a thesis which is supported by native Chilotes' eager participation in the attacks led by the corsairs.

García Barría harshly criticizes a series of well-publicized trials of *brujos*, which took

Usually, the *machi* plants pieces of horn so that in 30 years more *camahuetos* will grow. He then thoroughly boils the rest, so that the user won't end up with a *camahueto* inside, and grounds it up into powders which impart tremendous strength to the user. Camahuetos are also effective in treating a variety of illnesses.

Protective charms: The "clean" as non-*brujos* are called, can detect a *brujo* by throwing bran on a fire, a procedure which inevitably makes the *brujo* sneeze; or by

place several decades ago, as a "massive crusade against the descendants of indigenous people, especially. It was enough to mention that a person practised witchcraft for him to be dragged off to the prisons of Achao or Ancud."

In Chiloé, as in other cultures with communities of witches, the brujería is also the major source of a wealth of information on native herbs and medicines which are still commonly used on the islands. Scholars believe the tradition stems from the combination of European concepts of witchcraft brought by the Spanish with the beliefs of Chiloé original inhabitants.

Left, a house in the countryside. **Above**, musical troupe in Castro.

261

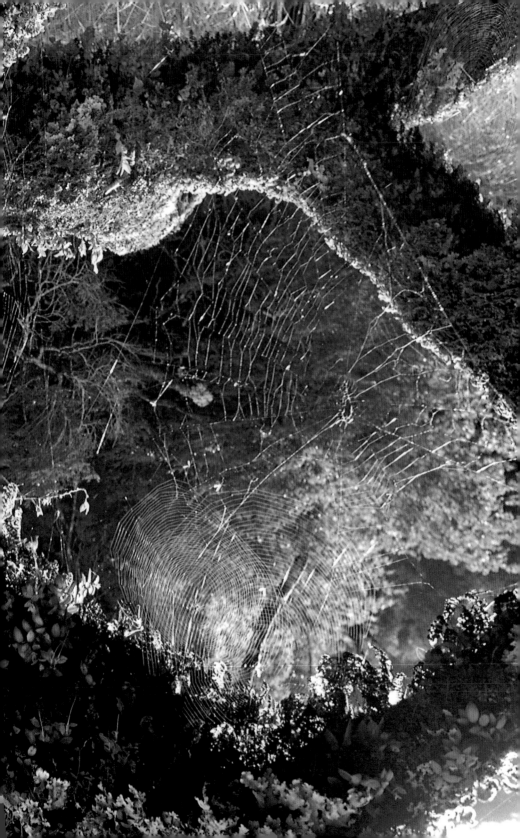

AISÉN

Aisén is the hispanicised version, local folklore has it, of an English name for the area: "ice end" – the region of glaciers. English, Germans, Swedes, Spaniards, Argentines and Chileans all did their bit to explore and sparsely colonize this spectacularly beautiful and particularly inhospitable region of fiords, glaciers and, once, in parts, dense forest.

Now the grey, petrified remains of huge trees stick up into the sky; from the air, it looks as if a giant box of matches has been scattered over the ground. The early settlers at the beginning of the century cleared the land they needed by burning down the woods, and several times the fires got out of control and ravaged great areas.

Inhospitable frontier: The first inhabitants were the Tehuelches – nomads who lived by hunting guanacos, *ñandus* (ostrich-like birds), pumas and *huemules* (deer) – and the Alacalufes, who navigated the coastal channels in their light canoes. The Spanish invaders sent down a couple of expeditions in the mid-1550s to explore, make sure that English marauders were not establishing a presence there, and incidentally convert the natives to Christianity. No-one actually bothered to try to find out how many of them there were. They were more interested, in fact, in a legendary "city of the Caesars," said to be hidden in the forests, with fabulous treasures of gold and jewels.

The coastline was not properly mapped until 1831, when Charles Darwin and Captain Robert Fitzroy navigated the area in their famous voyage on the *Beagle;* and the region's interior remained unknown for most of the 19th century.

The Chilean government only paid Aisén attention when border disputes began arising with Argentina. The first attempts to settle there were unsuccessful. Between 1859 and 1896 four colonies were started, two of them, at Melinka and Río Alvarez, as simple trading posts for collecting and distributing seal and otter skins and cypress wood from the area.

At the turn of the century the first settlers made their way across the frontier at Balmaceda, from Argentina. By 1907 there were thought to be 197 colonizers, there to stay with their families; plus another 500-odd employees of the English-owned sheep farming companies which had begun to exploit the region.

The pioneers were naturally a hardy bunch. One government official in the 1920s tried to describe their spirit. "No incompetent or coward or milksop gives up his home and his fatherland to settle lands uncultivated before in Patagonia, isolated in these solitudes, far from the principles of all authority and justice, suffering hunger often and battling constantly against nature."

Hospitality, he noted, was one of the most developed virtues of the people. "Dismount, unsaddle," the most common greeting to the stranger was understood as an invitation to eat and stay the

night. In return, the guest's best way of returning such hospitality was "to present the most complete account possible of all events, human and divine, in the rest of the world," since other means of diffusing news were non-existent.

Today the population of Aisén is around 115,000. But although radios and even television reaches the settlers now, the region remains curiously cut-off and innocent from national events. Newspapers are scarce, and apparently not even much in demand. Word of mouth, news from an interesting foreigner from outside the region is more entertaining.

Highway to the South: Many other aspects of life have not changed so dramatically from the way they were 50 years ago. All kinds of facilities – doctors, clinics, schools – are still scarce. There are cars and trucks and the occasional bus, but transport for some is still the traditional wooden-wheeled cart drawn by oxen. In the coastal regions the waterways are still important for communications.

But one recent improvement has been the completion of the **Carretera Austral Longitudinal** (to give it its official title). This is a mostly unpaved road which runs the length of the region from Puerto Montt down to Cochrane, (765 kilometres) and will go eventually to Villa O'Higgins.

Roads already existed from Puyuhuapi to Chaitén, between Puerto Aisén, Coyhaique and Balmaceda, and to Puerto Ibañez, Chile Chico and Cochrane. But the Carretera scheme, started in 1976, was to link the whole region with a single north-south route (more or less completed at the beginning of 1988), and then eventually add a network of east-west roads. At various points the "road" becomes a ferry from one side of a river to another.

Former President Pinochet claimed much of the credit for the project, and insisted that it carry his name. Apparently he did indeed support the project against the opposition of his finance ministers, and insisted that enough money be found to keep it going. The project was directed and partly built by army engineers. For the military, the road is considered a strategic necessity; the first ever route from north to south through Aisén means Chile's assured control of the territory. Better communications will help encourage settlement and thus secure the region against hypothetical foreign invasion. But for the inhabitants of Aisén, the highway has meant a real link-up with the rest of the region. What used to be an arduous boat trip, for example, from the scattered homes in the area around Puerto Cisnes to the nearest doctor, is now a couple of hours' journey by road.

The road has also become a major tourist attraction for the more adventurous. The Chilean tourist office, Sernatur, distributes brochures with a description of the route, and the main stops on the way. It gives brief notes on the natural and man-made attractions. It also has a map giving details of facilities such as lodgings, telephones, first aid posts and police. Information and organization is important – it is not really an area to wander through without your **Store in Chile Chico.**

266

own means of transport or a tour, unless you have all the time in the world.

A base in the wilderness: The most central point for exploring Aisén is the region's largest town, **Coyhaique.** Mostly an army base, its population hovers around 40,000 people, and, while pleasant enough, is usually only used as a jumping-off point for travelers to remoter parts.

Coyhaique can be reached by plane from Puerto Montt, or by following the Carretera Austral down the coast. Many other travelers take the route through Chiloé, hopping a ride on the night ferry from Chonchi which leaves several times a week.

Once in Coyhaique, take a stroll along Calle Prat. That's where the restaurants (specializing in seafood) and travel agents are mostly found. You can book a tour here, or go by public transport to most parts of the newly-opened South.

Without doubt the most popular attraction is the **Lake San Rafael National Park**, with its magnificent hanging glacier. The sight provoked awe and gloom in Charles Darwin when he visited it in 1831: He described the place as "sad solitudes, where death more than life seems to rule supreme." He must have seen the glacier on one of the many days of low cloud. When the sun is shining, it is an awesome spectacle, with light glinting off the blue ice and the landscape alive with black-necked swans and the distinctive furry beavers of the region.

Passengers are taken by rowboat to the very base of the glacier where it meets the sea. Giant icebergs float by so close that you can touch them. And the climax of any visit is a whisky on the rocks, using pieces of ice chipped straight from the blue glacier!

The glacier can also be visited without going to Coyhaique. Transmarchilay offers trips from Chiloe (as an extension of their crossing from the island to Aisén). For those who wish to travel in comfort, cruisers such as the *Skorpios* operate from Punta Arenas. Their five-day trip is relatively expensive but provides international-level facilities.

Traveling south: The route south from Coyhaique down to Cochrane can be done in a day, through hilly country, then past the beautiful deep blue **Lake General Carrera**. **Villa Cerro Castillo** (or Rio Ibañez), 100 km from Coyhaique, is the site of two famous stone-age paintings, of which there are several in the area.

A detour to **Bahia Muerta**, and from there a horse or boat ride, takes you to **Puerto Sanchez**, a former mining village with 200 people, to see the wave-sculptured Chapel of Marble and the underground caves of the Panichine islands. The village boasts a modest hostel.

A boat ride to the other side of the lake takes you to **Chile Chico**, one of the region's earliest settlements. The area enjoys a dry, warm microclimate, which allows the people to cultivate a much wider range of fruit and vegetables than the rest of the region although the inhabitants have problems selling them. The place has a quiet, rustic charm that can be quite beguiling. Many travelers who had planned to pass straight through the frontier with Argentina find themselves staying for several days in Chile Chico, enjoying the sunny days and taking the occasional dip in the icy waters of the lake.

Mountain sports: Fish – mostly salmon and rainbow trout – are plentiful in all of Aisén's rivers and lakes. Boats for expeditions to some lakes can be organized from Coyhaique, either for the day or to stay a few days in one of various fishing lodges in the area.

There is skiing, too, at **El Fraile**, 30 km south east of Coyhaique, 1000 meters above sea level. The resort has five slopes suitable for skills ranging from beginners to experienced skiiers, but rather basic facilities at the ski center.

Going north from Coyhaique the road runs through bright green woods of mañio and coígue. A side road takes you to **Puerto Cisnes**, a remarkably well set-up little settlement whose mayoress for years was a formidable Italian lady who ruled the place with a very firm hand. She was a friend and admirer, first of General Carlos Ibañez del Campo, and then of General Pinochet (whose horoscope she used to tell). With the ear of both presidents she managed to get facilities in her village that locals grumble would be better located further up the main road, at **Puyuhuapi**.

On the main road just past the junction with Puerto Cisnes on the way to Puyuhuapi is **Piedra El Gato** – a massive boulder which had to be partly blasted away to build the road. Puyuhuapi boasts thermal springs, a hotel, a garage and a carpet factory which turns out sturdy hand-made woollen rugs to mostly old-fashioned Belgian designs.

The settlement was started by four Sudeten Germans who immigrated from Czechoslovakia at the time of the German invasion just before the war, and made their way to this remote spot which they are said to have read about in a Baedecker guide. One of the four is still alive, and in the carpet factory you can see faded photographs of how they lived when they first arrived, in reed and wattle huts.

From **Las Juntas**, the joining of the Palena and Rosselot rivers, it is possible for experienced sailors to navigate the Palena to the wide beaches at its estuary at **Puerto Raul Marín Balmaceda**, a six-hour journey. A six-day voyage down the Baker river, from **Puerto Bertrand** to **Caleta Tortel** offers thrills and spills. The river Cisnes is another favorite trip. All can be organized from Coyhaique.

Up from Las Juntas the road leads to **Chaitén**. On the way there are short detours to see at a distance some magnificent hanging glaciers, and for a dip in the thermal springs at **Termas del Amarilla**. From Chaitén there is a ferry across to the island of Chiloé and islanders come across regularly to sell vegetables and fruit on the mainland.

Chaitén marks the northern boundary of the region of Aisén, as Cochrane marks the south – two dull little towns that are nevertheless the gateways to some of the most beautiful scenery on earth.

Right, the thermal bath of Cahuelmo fiord.

MAGALLANES

Stretching towards the windswept southern tip of South America, the province of **Magallanes** exists quite apart from the rest of Chile. The hardy people who live there consider themselves first as Magallanicos, second as Chileans – hardly surprising, considering that they cannot reach Santiago by road without crossing the border into neighboring Argentina. In order to come and go from this stormy corner of the world, you have to either travel for days by bus across the endless stretches of Argentine Patagonia, fly direct or take a lengthy, rocky cruise through the icy southern seas.

Along with the bad weather and remoteness, the terrain of Magallanes is formidably harsh. The region is split between impenetrable mountain ranges and the bleak, barren Patagonian plains. Yet these harsh physical conditions have helped form a unique local character. "The sheer difficulty of living here brings people together," says writer Fransisco Coloane, the most famous chronicler of Magallanic life. "It creates a human solidarity and sense of honor that people from the rest of Chile don't always share."

Growing in isolation: History has conspired with the tyranny of distance to keep Magallanes apart from centralised rule in Chile. The region was first developed by foreign sheep companies – mostly British-owned – who had interests on both the Argentine and Chilean side of the border. Magallanes soon had more in common with Argentine Patagonia than the distant world of Santiago. English was heard spoken more often than Spanish – followed by a chorus of Serb-Croat, Russian and Italian as workers arrived from all parts of the globe.

This cosmopolitan tradition can still be felt in the towns and old *estancias* (sheep farms) of Magallanes, where the surnames are as likely to be MacMillan or Covacevic as anything of Spanish origin. The isolation of the south also developed its own political traditions: like the remote mining towns of the north, Magallanes has a long history of left-wing activism. Some of the bitterest strikes in Chilean history occurred in the province, and, more recently, it was from Magallanes that the Socialist leader Salvador Allende was first elected deputy. Regional independence still marks its politics today, fed by a resentful belief that the central government ignores the far south.

What today lures most travelers to this far end of the globe is the province's unspoilt wilderness. Much of Magallanes is taken up with a jigsaw of tiny islands and channels without any permanent habitation or regular passenger services. These are the tips of underwater mountains – the continuation of the Andes range that has sunk into the icy sea – and can only be glimpsed on rare boat journeys or from the air. Then, towards the battered coastline of the Straits of Magellan are colonies of penguins, crystal lakes, trees gnarled by the ever-present Patagonian wind and some

of the most spectacular mountain scenery anywhere in South America.

Horrifying sights: Magallanes takes its name from the Portuguese explorer Ferdinand Magellan who, while working for the Spanish Crown, became the first European to set eyes upon its shores in 1520. A gale blew his fragile sailing ships through what is now the Straits of Magellan towards the ocean he baptised the Pacific. On the way a landing party stopped off near modern-day Punta Arenas, to find a beached whale and 200 Indian corpses raised on stilts. Shuddering at the gruesome sight, the navigator hurried towards the west.

Further Spanish contact with the area was hardly more encouraging. A group of 300 *conquistadores* under Pedro de Gamboa tried to set up a settlement on the straits, but the savage winter drove them all to starvation. A lone survivor was found three years later by the English pirate Thomas Cavendish, who had managed to survive by living amongst local Indians.

For the next 250 years, the region was visited by various well-known explorers, cartographers and naturalists, but few saw any reason to linger. Only in the 1830s did the Chilean Government, spurred on by a wave of optimism and economic expansion, cast possessive glances towards the remote south.

Prompting action was the occupation of the Falkland Islands by Britain in 1833 and the lengthy explorations made in the region by British naturalist Charles Darwin.

In 1843, President Manuel Bulnes claimed the land around the Straits of Magellan, Tierra del Fuego and Southern Patagonia. A boatload of 21 motley soldiers was sent down to found Fuerte Bulnes on the straits, but the location proved to be so inhospitable that the outpost was abandoned and Punta Arenas was founded in its place five years later. This new settlement grew slowly into a town, with raids by Indians and a bloody mutiny punctuating its early days. But Chile was forced to abandon its claim to much of Patagonia: Argentina took advantage of Chile's precoc-

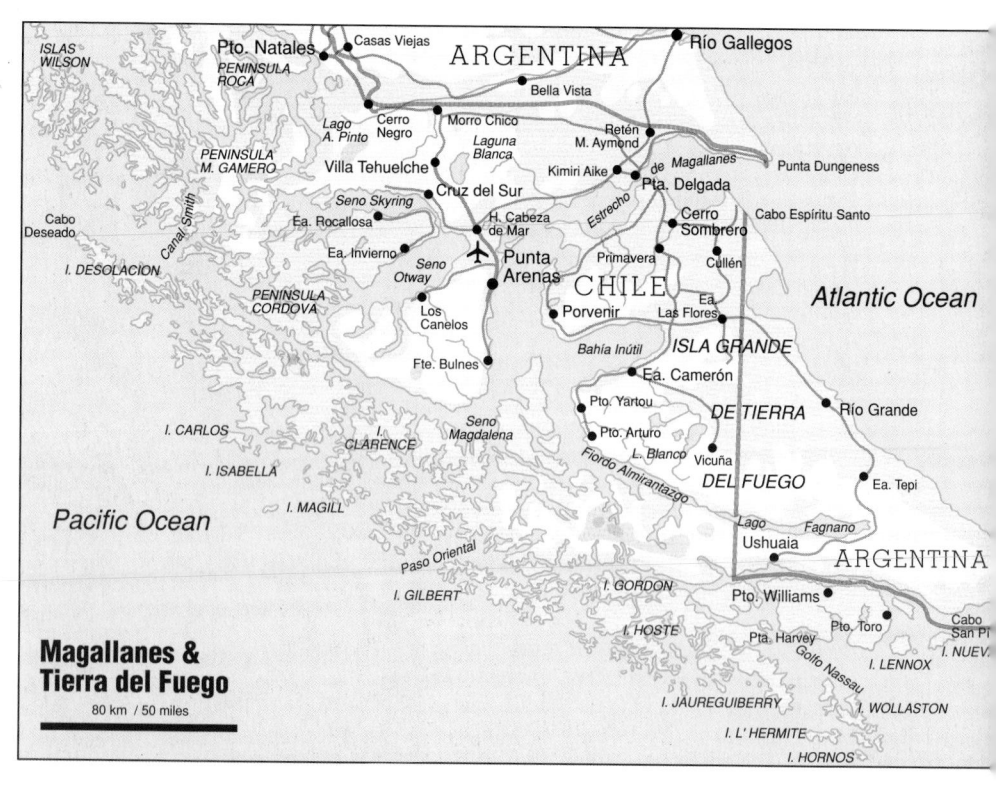

cupation with Peru and the North to take the lion's share of the South, leaving Magallanes with the border it has today.

The city at the end of the world: Today **Punta Arenas** is a city of some 80,000 people, the hub of Magallanes and the first port of call for most foreign travelers. Facing out across the straits, it has an almost Dickensian flavor, full of rusting corrugated iron buildings and grandiose mansions from the turn of the century. The class divisions of old are still echoed in the streets: here you can find elegant, if rundown, parlors where aperitifs are sipped with an aristocratic flourish. Sitting ajacent are seedy wooden bars full of sailors, naval recruits and an ubiquitous collection of weary old men – usually wearing woollen caps and tightly-buttoned overcoats, huddled over their glasses of *pisco* and whiskey, away from the biting wind.

Weather, naturally enough, dominates the city's mood. Despite its latitude, Punta Arenas never experiences the extremes of cold seen in equally remote places in the Northern Hemisphere.

Nevertheless, the skies bring few comforts. Even in summer, when the sun shines for 20 hours a day and the temperatures are moderate, the wind and rain can often make Punta Arenas seem a gloomy and half-made frontier town. But when the sun breaks through the billowing clouds, its cool air is bracing and a stroll through the quiet streets can be pleasant as well as fascinating.

Memories of a golden age: Scattered around Punta Arenas are opulent monuments to a golden age when it was one of the busiest ports on earth. Its history is in many ways that of the whole far South.

A series of unexpected events in the mid-19th century helped lift the town out of its wind-bitter obscurity.

The industrial age in Europe and North America was creating a boom in sea trade. The Panama Canal had not yet been thought of. Sea clippers and the new steamships making their journeys around the world – carrying anything from European machinery to Texan petroleum and Australian wheat – all

had to stop in at Punta Arenas, the town at the end of the world.

The boom soon made Punta Arenas the logical center for Patagonian sheep farming. In 1877, an English trader brought a flock of stock from the Falkland/Malvinas Islands to Elizabeth Island in the Magellan Straits. The experiment was a success and soon other entrepreneurs were following suit. A Machiavellian Spaniard named Jose Menéndez and the Russian-born immigrant Mauricio Braun became leading figures: starting off as rivals, they were soon linked by marriage to form a Patagonian dynasty that would dominate the South for decades.

The British move in: Farm administrators were brought in from Scotland, England, Australia and New Zealand – making Magallanes, as writer Bruce Chatwin noted in his classic *In Patagonia*, look like an outpost of the British Empire. But the *peons*, who worked the land in generally dismal conditions, almost all came from the overcrowded farmyards of Chile's own Chiloé.

Punta Arenas's golden age ended abruptly when the Panama Canal was opened and boats no longer needed to round the Horn. Magallanes continued to be a profitable sheep region until towards the Great Depression, when a long decline began.

Competition from Australia, New Zealand and Canada squeezed Chile and Argentina from the major world markets. Many of the English managers left for their homeland as land reform carved up the largest *estancias* of the South. Even don Jose Menéndez decided to move from Magallanes to Buenos Aires. Today many of the farms are nearly bankrupt.

This downward economic spiral was only halted with the discovery of petroleum and natural gas in 1945. Oil companies stepped up exploration in the straits over the following decades and today Magallanes provides for about 15 percent of Chile's petroleum needs.

Workers looking for high wages have flocked from the North, while fishing has also boomed and Punta Arenas be-

A tree grows bent with the Patagonian wind.

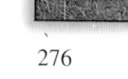

came a duty-free port. As a result, Magallanes boasts one of the highest per capita incomes in Chile – although the cost of living is also one of the country's highest.

A tour of past glories: The modern center of Punta Arenas is, as it always has been, the **Plaza de Armas**. Surrounded by trees and neat gardens, the plaza is dominated by a bronze statue of Magellan, looking proudly over the heroic figures of various local Indians – idealized by a sculptor after they had been largely wiped out by marauding European settlers, keen to ensure that no native would interfere with the profitable grazing of sheep. These days children pose for photographs while touching the Indian's foot for luck.

The plaza is a community meeting place in summer, when the trees are full and even flowers bloom. Every Sunday morning in the warmer months a military brass band plays Latin classics, while at Christmas time local Santa Claus holds court here with his pair of imported llamas.

Flanking the plaza are the box-like **Hotel Cabo de Hornos**, the **cathedral** and impressive **Social Club**. This was the first brick building to have been built in Punta Arenas, by the matriarch Sara Braun. Now a club for the old wealth and naval officers of the town, it can be visited on weekdays between 3 and 6 p.m. The interior is sumptuous, with extravagant Art Deco lampshades, giant Chinese vases and mahogany furniture imported from Europe. A glass annex is covered with healthy grape vines, where lunch is occasionally served to the public.

Even more extravagant is the **Centro Cultural Braun-Menéndez**, opposite the Cabo de Hornos on Calle Magallanes. Built by the Patagonian pioneer don Maurico Braun in 1904, it is rightly referred to by locals as "the Palace." The mansion was designed by a French architect to outstrip the finest houses of Santiago. Marble was imported from Italy, wood from Belgium, wallpaper from France and furniture from England. Upon entering the mansion, visitors pass through the airy Hall with classical frescos painted on its ceiling. Everything in the adjoining rooms is done on a grand scale: the main bedroom contains a massive Louis XV four-poster bed, while the Games Room has a gigantic billiard table and furniture in Art Nouveau style. The salon – the most important room in the house – is crowded with gilded tables and chairs under a glittering crystal chandelier and stern portraits of long-dead family members. The walls of the Dining Room are covered with pressed Italian leather, while the *escritorio* still contains the mahogany desk from which the fate of the South was directed.

The rest of the house's ground floor has been converted into the **Museo Historico de Magallanes**, with exhibits from the foundation of Punta Arenas to the 1920s. Upstairs is the Library, a picture gallery as well as several important historical archives.

The mansion was shared by the Brauns and Menéndezes after constant intermarraige linked the clans. But as land reform took its toll on their *estancias* and profits over this century, the families handed over the building to the Government. It was made a national monument in 1974.

The old port: Some of the oldest streets in Punta Arenas stretch down from Magallanes to the straits. Take a walk along Calle Roca to the old port area, with its range of seedy flop houses, cafés and bars. Many of the old houses made of tin and corrugated iron seem on the point of collapse, but these vestiges of the turn of the century give a glimpse of the bustling days of the past.

Strangely, this part of town boasts some of the town's best restaurants. For a total contrast to the rundown streets around it, call in at the **the Garage** on the corner of Calle Pedro Montt and O'Higgins. Created by a team of Argentine artists, this place is decorated with mechanical bits and pieces – as well as a whole car! – in a style more suited to New York than Patagonia. Families as well as young people frequent the Garage, which serves the best *paella* in the South.

Another walk out along Calle Bories

leads to the **Salesian Museum**, one of the most unusual in South America. The Salesians are a religious order that once tried to "save" the local Indians of the region by creating missionary refuges – only to find that European clothes gave them influenza and killed the tribes as surely as the white settlers' bullets. Their museum reflects the belief that the Salesian's paternalistic "civilizing" efforts were morally correct. But despite this self-congratulation, its disordered exhibits are worth examining.

A room full of Indian artifacts gives a good introduction to the four tribal groups once in Magallanes. Inhabiting the barren plains east of the Andes were the fierce Tehuelches (or Aonikenk) peoples. Their impressive stature and enormous moccasins is traditionally held to have made Ferdinand Magellan exclaim 'Ha! Patagon!' – 'big foot' – and given Patagonia its name (although the writer Bruce Chatwin has offered a more plausible explanation, suggesting that the name came from an early 16th-century romantic story where a monster called the Grand Patagon appears. Magellan was likely to have been familiar with the tale, where the man-like creature roars like a bull, just as Magellan noted the Tehuelche to do).

Sea lion hunters: Canoeing through the rough islands of the Pacific were the maritime nomad tribe the Alacalufes (Kaweskar) Indians, who hunted sea lions and dove for crayfish. Today the last survivers of this race live in the remote fishing village of Puerto Eden. The Onas (Selknam) hunted guanacos on the barren northern plains of Tierra del Fuego, while the Yaghanes (Yamanas) sent their canoes through the icy forested islands south of the Beagle channel. The Onas were wiped out earlier this century and only a handful of mixed-blooded Yaghanes are still alive.

The Indians' wooden canoes, spear, bows and arrows are all lined up in cases. There is also a macabre exhibit of some 20 Indian skulls. Some cleverly-made dioramas exhibit the Indian way of life, showing their customs of hunting and eating. Alongside are some poignant photographs of late 19th-century Indians forlornly enduring missionary life in their ill-fitting European clothes. One photo from the end of the century shows the Salesian head, Monsignor Fagnano, visiting the mission on Isla Dawson only to weep at how the 500 Indians had been almost wiped out by disease. It does not record whether he regretted his solution to the "Indian question."

Keep an eye out in the museum for a piece of skin from the giant ground-sloth found in the Milodon Cave near Puerto Natales and some 10,000-year-old droppings. Also of interest are a conquistador's helmet found in Magallanes and a replica of the cross set up by Charles Darwin's crew on the straits over the grave of one of their members – who apparently died from the stress of navigating these treacherous waters.

Further out along Calle Bories is the bizarre cemetery of Punta Arenas, comparable in splendor only to the famous Recoleta necropolis in Buenos Aires. Settlers from every part of the world can

A cargo boat plies the southern water.

278

be found here – as well as memorials to the victims of the many shipwrecks that occurred on this savage coast. One site worth visiting is the **Tomb of the Unknown Indian**, a belated memorial to the massacres of the last century. Occasionally a young Chilean with Indian blood will make the pilgrimage to this statue and leave a wreath or vase of flowers.

Bories leads to the outskirts of town, where the **Instituto de la Patagonia** has its grounds. A collection of farming machinery, wagons and steam tractors from the region's past are littered about an open field, where a reconstructed settlers house dates back to 1880. There is a small zoo and library here. Across the road from the Institute is the **Zona Franca**, where duty-free goods can be bought – although the prices are hardly likely to seem like bargains to visitors from the United States or Europe.

Excursions: A three-hour drive from Punta Arenas are the famous *pinguineros* or **Penguin Colonies** of the south. Hundreds of these comical waddling crea-

tures live in burrows dug into the sandy southern shoreline. It is possible that this was where the Italian Antonio Pigafetta, a member of Magellan's crew in 1520, recorded the first European sighting of the penguin. The species which is seen here is the *Spheniscus magellanicus*, named for the straits on which it lives rather than the explorer himself. It is commonly called the jackass penguin for the odd braying sound it makes.

Try to visit the *penguineros* in a small group, since large numbers of people send the penguins scurrying away on their flippers, which they use as front legs to run on all fours (Chilean tourists have a particular propensity to scream with glee whenever a penguin is sighted). The penguins spend most of April to August at sea, heading north to warmer climates, returning from September through March to their breeding grounds here.

Some 54 km (34 miles) south of Punta Arenas along the inky Straits of Magellan is the reconstructed **Fuerte Bulnes** on

hristmas ith llamas Punta enas.

the site of the original 1843 settlement. The highway passes the skeleton of the wrecked ship the Lonsdale on the outskirts of town and some classic Patagonian scenery, but the fort itself has a disappointing Disneyland look. On the way back most tours stop at **Punta Hambre**, where the unfortunate Pedro de Gamboa tried to set up his settlement 300 years ago.

More exciting is a visit to the *centolla* fishermen nearby. The centolla, a bright orange king crab, is one of the great delicacies of the south and is a must for visitors. Caught in large wicker crab pots, they can be bought direct from the fishermen or ordered from any good restaurant in the south. They look huge and vicious but are rather timid creatures, whose claws are next to useless.

The road to Argentina: Along the highway 150 km (93 miles) north from Punta Arenas is the first sheep farm of the south, **Estancia San Gregorio**. Built in 1878, it was taken over by Jose Menéndez four years later and extended to 90,000 hectares. It can only be visited with the permission of the current owner, although a good deal can be seen from the road.

San Gregorio remains the classic example of many *estancias* that, last century, were like small towns to themselves. The company's own launch, the *Amadeo*, lies rusting by the shore at the *estancia's* entrance, where the captain decided to leave it after 50 years of service. The grounds boast large wooden shearing sheds (still hanging the faded stock awards of decades past), shops, a chapel, a theater for the landowners and bars for the workers. The *estancia* house itself is a huge and lavish building, although now sparsely furnished: it still has hand-operated gramophones and a few relics of the past, but has never returned to its former glories since the land reforms of the early 1970s, when the *estancia* was handed over to its workers.

After decades of grinding oppression, the *peons* became drunk on freedom. In scenes reminiscent of the French revolution they camped out in the mansion, **Fuerte Bulnes.**

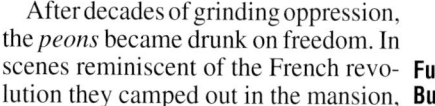

put the bust of don Jose in the out-house and went through the family cellar. Prize sheep munched freely at the garden before finally being slaughtered for mutton soup. The *estancia* was returned to private hands after the brutal 1973 military coup, but never regained its previous size.

Further along the road to Argentina is **Fell's Cave**, where some of the oldest prehistoric human remains in the Amercias have been found. It can only be visited with the help of scientists at the Instituto Patagonico in Punta Arenas.

Gateway to the Southern Andes: Heading north from Punta Arenas, Highway 9 follows **Canal Fitzroy** (named after the *Beagle's* captain) to **Río Verde**, a one-horse town with a *hostería* serving tea and red wine. Some 40 km (25 miles) north is an exit to the ferry stop to the densly forested **Isla Riesco**, where camping is the basic form of accommodation and fishing the main attraction.

Further north is **Villa Tehuelches**, a town founded in 1966 that has virtually stood still since. But the main reason for

traveling this distance is to reach **Puerto Natales**.

Set by the shores of the **Ultima Esperanza Sound**, Puerto Natales is a sleepy village boasting a few family hotels and restaurants serving *centolla*. A walk up to **Cerro Dorotea** gives some magnificent views over the whole Ultima Esperanza area. There is little to do in Puerto Natales itself, apart from visiting the meat-packing plant bought by the British after World War I. In its heyday this is where thousands of sheep were slaughtered weekly for the dinner tables of Europe, and many of the steam-driven engines used then are still lying about. One has been painted red and put up in the main plaza of the town.

The meatworks ensured that Puerto Natales would be a leftist town. A riot began here in 1919 when the Chilote workers killed an English assistant manager, lynched three policemen and looted the stores. But before long the government sent in the army: 28 ringleaders were taken away, amongst them some Maximilianist Russians who were blamed as foreign agitators.

But despite its lack of inherent interest, Puerto Natales has become a traveler's mecca as the gateway to the most spectacular sights in Magallanes.

Most easily reached is the **Balmaceda Glacier** to the north-east of Puerto Natales. Boats of tourists leave most mornings to see this blue river of ice that slides directly down from the Andes to the sea. Gigantic blocks crash regularly from the glacier and send shock waves across to the boat, while powerful winds whistle through the narrow channel. Most boats pull up at a small jetty and passengers can safely walk along paths near the side of the glacier. On the way, the Torres del Paine can be seen on the horizon, while the shore of the channel is lined with waterfalls. Groups of barking seals and sea lions sit on rocky outcrops, while porpoises, steamer ducks and black-neck swans can be spotted in the icy waters.

Prehistoric remains: A quite different day trip can be made to the enormous **Milodon Cave**, focus of a scientific furore nearly one century ago and a key

e Milodon
ve near
uerto
atales.

element in Bruce Chatwin's classic travel book *In Patagonia*. In 1895, a German-born landowner named Herman Eberhard found a strange 1.2-meter (4-ft) long stretch of hairy skin sticking from the floor of the cave. The next year, a Swedish explorer took a piece away with him, as well as the eye-socket of a huge mammal, a claw and large human thighbone. Before long, a scientist in Argentina had announced that the skin was from a Milodon Listai (naming the animal, humbly, after himself), a prehistoric Giant Ground Sloth unique to South America. The bones of several mylodons had been found during the 19th century, but the Argentine asserted that the piece of skin was so fresh that the beast had only recently died – and a living example could not be far away.

The claim was considered absurd by some and a great discovery by others. Reports filtered back from *estancias* in the South with "positive sightings" of huge hairy beasts becoming the norm. Excitement was certainly sufficient in England for the *Daily Express* newspaper to finance a scientific expedition to find a living Milodon. Despite hearing many ghost tales that were mixed up with Indian myths, they found no example (although the expedition leader Hesketh Prichard's book, *Through the Heart of Patagonia*, became an inspiration for Arthur Conan Doyle's Lost World). Meanwhile a team of archaeologists dug away in the cave, but they found little more than huge amounts of sloth dung.

Radio-carbon dating has since shown that the skin is about 10,000 years old but was perfectly preserved in the unique conditions of the cave – much like moa feathers in New Zealand and the deep-frozen mammoth of Siberia.

Today the Milodon Cave is a popular picnic spot outside Puerto Natales. A life-size model of the milodon, rearing back on its hind legs and tail, has been placed at the yawning mouth, but little else remains to suggest its past. A piece of the milodon skin and its dung can be seen in the Silesian Museum in Punta Arenas (see above) or in the British Museum in London.

The untouched wilderness: By far the most impressive sight in the South is the **Torres del Paine National Park**. Hidden at the far south of the Andes mountain chain, it is one of the newest nature reserves in South America, having been formed in 1959 and only reaching its present size in the early 1970s (UNESCO made it a Biosphere reserve in 1978). Unlike most of the Andes in Peru and Bolivia, the Paine (pronounced pie-nee) is uninhabited. But *aficionados* agree that the unique physical formations of the area – crowded with glaciers, lakes and gnarled Magellanic trees – offer some of the most magnificent walking in the world. The dramatic mountain formations make a sight that few people will forget, while the park itself is full of animals, including guanacos, flamingos and condors.

Every morning in summer and several times weekly at other times of the year, vans and buses make the three-hour drive from Puerto Natales to the Paine along a rough dirt road. The trail winds through mountain passes before

Chinook salmon.

descending to the foot of the Andean range, providing the first view of the **Cuernos del Paine** (horns of the Paine): twisted pillars of grey granite, dusted with snow and rising from the flat Patagonian plains into a sky full of billowing grey clouds.

Like everywhere else this far south, weather in the Paine can be unpredictable, to say the least. The best times to visit are January to April, but even then clear skies are rare and can disappear within minutes. The famous Torres del Paine (towers) are even more spectacular than the Cuernos, but often difficult to see because of the cloud cover breaks. The one thing that never seems to change is the gusting Patagonian wind that drives from the plains to the west.

All visitors to the park must sign on at the administration building, where the wardens (*guardaparques*) will give advice on condition of the trails. The classic views of the park can be easily reached by road and day-trips operate from Puerto Natales. If you want to stay in the park, hotel accommodation can be found at the **Hosteria Pehoé** on a lake and the **Posade Rio Serrano**, an eccentric converted *estancia* house. Its restaurant has the obligatory log fire and stuffed animal heads, as well as many sculptures made from the park's bulbous wooden tree roots.

Exploring the Paine: Several day trips, as well as more ambitious walks, can be made from these bases. The park has over 250 km (155 miles) of walking tracks, including a seven-day circuit. Along the way are *refugios* or shelters, often primitive wood and corrugated iron edifices that barely keep out the wind and rain – sleeping bags or rugs, as well as cooking gear, are essential. If you plan to do the seven-day circuit you should bring a tent as well, since Israeli travelers accidentally burned down one of the *refugios* en route. (Large groups of young Israelis seem to have added this circuit to their South American itineraries and quite often take over the *refugios* completely in December and January, so many people find it convenient to bring their own tent in any case).

hotographer
ptures
rey Glacier.

This hike starts at the administration building at the southern end of **Lake Pehoé** and gives ever-changing views of the Cuernos. This walking can be quite strenuous – the longest stretch in one day is 30 km (19 miles) – many people choose to make two-or three-day walks rather than the full circuit.

One good compromise is to walk to the first *refugio* by **Lago Grey**, camp overnight, take a day trip to the **Grey glacier** and then walk back to the administration center the next day. Or walk to **Ventisquero del Frances** or **Lake Pingo**, where the less-used *refugio* can be found.

Those who make the effort are rewarded with some superb views of snow-covered peaks, turquoise lakes and lush valleys. The trails are lined with orange, red and purple flowers, sometimes crossing wide pasture and at other times hugging mountain sides. Much of the park is lushly forested, although a recent worm plague has left whole areas covered with dead, grey trees. The Grey and Dickson glaciers, when discovered in the wild, seem somehow more impressive than others that are more easily reached, and they can be climbed over – and into – if you have the urge.

Most routes in the Paine allow walkers to see plenty of animals, most commonly the guanacos: unlike in other parts of South America, they appear unafraid of people and can be easily photographed from up close. Condors cruise between mountain peaks, hares and foxes dash about in the scrub and swans and flamingos can be seen on many of the lakes.

Although the weather can turn from fair to foul and back again within minutes, the memories of the park will last well after your clothes have dried. Many people who go for a few days stay a week: the liberating sensation of being in one of the most remote and untouched wilderness areas on earth is worth savoring for as long as possible.

The remote archipelago: The map of Magallanes shows hundreds of scattered islands stretching to the Pacific. Very few are visited and fewer are inhabited. A large area of the South has been incorporated in the **Parque Nacional Bernardo O'Higgins** and **Parque Nacional Hernando Magallanes**, as well as the **Isla Riesco** and **Alacalufe Forestry reserves**. There is little chance of visiting these wilderness areas without hiring your own boat in Punta Arenas or Puerto Natales.

For most travelers, the one way of glimpsing these islands is to travel on the Navimag passenger boats between Puerto Natales and Puerto Montt in the Lake District. This three-day (minimum) journey goes through the Estrecho Smith and narrow **Estrecho Estebán**. It is not particularly comfortable unless you hire a cabin – in which case the sea journey costs considerably more than to fly. However, some travelers are captured by the romance of a sea voyage and the chance to watch the remote green islands drift by, usually swathed in mist and drizzle. (The more luxurious and expensive cruises around Aisén offer similar landscapes, but this is one exotic and unusual way to reach or return from the South).

Below, waterfall in the Paine National Park. **Right,** the 'towers o the Paine' (Torres del Paine).

TIERRA DEL FUEGO

Lashed by wind and wild seas at the southern tip of South America, **Tierra del Fuego** exerts a perverse fascination. Despite – or because of – its dismal image, few who travel to the far south of Chile can resist paying a visit to the literal end of the earth, the last piece of land before the icy wastes of Antarctica.

The archipelago's name "land of fire" comes from the explorer Ferdinand Magellan, who in 1520 saw smoke rising from Indian campfires on its shores (Magellan actually first called it "land of smoke" but the Spanish king Charles V thought "land of fire" might be more poetic). It took the navigator no less than 38 days to force a passage through the strait that now bears his name. Fear of returning through these waters drove Magellan's men ever westward after their captain's death in the Philippines, eventually making the few survivors of the expedition the first to circumnavigate the globe.

For centuries afterwards, Tierra del Fuego was dreaded by sailors for its storms and freezing rains. Rounding Cape Horn became a nautical vision of hell – as can be seen in the works of writers as diverse as Melville, Coleridge, Jules Verne and Edgar Allen Poe.

The British naturalist Charles Darwin added a new dimension to the image when he visited Tierra del Fuego on the *Beagle* in the 1830s. He pronounced the Fuegian Indians, who had been living in the far south for tens of thousands of years, to be the lowest on the human evolutionary scale:

"I never saw such miserable creatures," Darwin wrote in his classic *Voyage of the Beagle; "stunted in their growth, their hideous faces bedaubed with white paint and quite naked ...Their red skins filthy and greasy, their voices discordant, their gesticulation violent and without any dignity. Viewing such men, one can hardly make*

Preceding pages, the Straits of Magellan. Below, the extinguished race of Ona Indians.

oneself believe that they are fellow creatures placed in the same world... What a scale of improvements is comprehended between the faculties of a Fuegian savage and a Sir Isaac Newton!"

His verdict was to be shared by the first settlers of Tierra del Fuego. By the end of the 19th century the Fuegian Indians would be exterminated in one of the most extraordinary cases of genocide in history.

Today Tierra del Fuego maintains its sense of being a klondike-style frontier. Despite the grisly past, the people of its remote, windswept towns have a rawness and surprising warmth towards strangers — usually being delighted that the outside world is at last paying them attention. And, most importantly for many travelers, the islands of Tierra del Fuego contain some of the last great wilderness areas on earth.

The original owners: At the time when Darwin made his horrified observations, Tierra del Fuego was home to four groups of Indians (their skulls are lined up in the Salesian Museum of Punta Arenas).

The most numerous were the Onas, or selk'nam, a nomadic race that hunted guanacos over the open plains with bows and arrows. The Haush Indians occupied the eastern tip of the Isla Grande, living in huts of branches and skins. Roaming the southern islands in bark canoes and seal hides were the Yaghans. The men hunted otters with spears and Yaghan women would sometimes dive into the icy waters of the South to pluck *centollas* (king crabs) from the ocean floor. Finally, living in the fiords of Southern Chile, were the Alacaluf.

None of these Indian groups had the organised religion or vertical tribal structures of the Mapuche Indians in the North, which had helped them to organise resistance against foreign invaders. But, despite Darwin's dismissive attitude, their cultures were astonishingly complex. A missionary named Thomas Bridges compiled a dictionary of the

shepherd
ends his
flock.

Yaghan language that begins to unveil how they ordered their harsh world with metaphors. Bruce Chatwin lists a few of the Yaghan constructions in his classic travel book *In Patagonia*: "mussels out of season" was a synonym for shrivelled skin and old age; lazy was defined as the "Jackass Penguin"; "sleet" was the same word as "fish scales."

A fitful invasion: Although a constant stream of explorers and later whalers followed Magellan's path, European settlement of Tierra del Fuego was slow in coming. The Spanish had constant plans to outwit English and Dutch pirates by setting up a naval base on the island but the dismal conditions prevented settlement. It was not until the 1840s that Chile and Argentina both laid claim to the area, and several decades later that anybody could be convinced to live there. A border was drawn up; some missionaries made tentative landings; and in the 1880s the first miners arrived in search of gold.

While there were some clashes between these fortune seekers and local Indians, the real problems did not begin until entrepreneurs realised that the Northern Plains were possibly the best sheep country in South America. On the Chilean side of the border, the first *estancia* or ranch was set up in 1893 by the Socieded Explotadora de Tierra del Fuego, with the Russian-born don Mauricio Braun as director general. He named it Josefina after his wife and appointed a New Zealand-born sheep farmer as manager.

The story of the Ona Indians sums up the tragedy of nomadic indigenous races whenever they came into contact with colonial powers – whether in South America, the United States or Australia. Traditionally roaming the *pampas* to hunt guanaco, the Onas naturally found sheep an easy and satisfying prey. For the farm owners, stealing their property was the ultimate crime: they killed Onas in retribution, "to teach them a lesson." Unfortunately, respect for property was not a lesson that the Ona Indians could learn. They could not accept that the fences across their tradi-

The southern outpost of Porvenir.

tional lands were meant as boundaries, and still continued to hunt the "white guanaco."

The *estancia* owners hired gunmen to protect their lands – although the gruesome rumor began that they were paid one pound sterling bounty for each Indian they shot dead (the ears were supposedly demanded as proof). Salesian missionaries argued that the Indians could only be saved if they were removed *en masse* to nearby Isla Dawson, and the esta*ncia* owners agreed to this method of removing the "pest."

Grisly tales: Official records show that most Indians died of disease in the Dawson mission, but the folk memory persists of active resistance, battles and massacres. Old-timers still tell of such gruesome characters as the Scotsman Alex McLennan, nicknamed the "Red Pig" by Indians for his face made ruddy by constant boozing. He is said to have lured Indian families into traps by offering food, only to have his men open fire from their position in hiding. The Englishman Sam Hyslop, who boasted of with gunning down 80 Onas, was finally caught by Indians and flung to his death from a cliff.

Argentines were well schooled in eradicating Indians and hunts went on unrestricted on that side of the border, but the Chilean population had moments of conscience-stricken doubt. The ugly rumors, coupled with the fact that mostly women and children were being brought back from raids, caused a public outcry. The Chilean police found a mass grave and were going to prosecute the *estancia* owners. But by this stage some Indians were fighting back – a handful of white deaths (a total of seven in ten years) were registered and few people raised their voices against clearing the island any longer.

In the Isla Dawson mission, epidemic followed epidemic. By 1925 no Ona was still alive. A similar fate awaited other Indian groups. Today only a handful of *mestizo* Yaghans survive.

The elimination of the Indians meant that sheep farming reached new heights. Some of the largest farms ever

Distances to Chilean towns, and Yugoslavia!

built were opened up on Tierra del Fuego and became enormously profitable for the mostly British-owned companies. As in the rest of Patagonia, immigrants drifted in from around the world, including a large number of exiles and eccentrics. Chilean Tierra del Fuego received an unusual number of Yugoslav arrivals.

In modern times, the discovery of oil has given the island's economy a massive boost. But population remains thin. Argentina has tried to settle its part of Tierra del Fuego by making Ushuaia a duty free zone and holiday resort, but the Chilean section remains a sleepy and undeveloped part of the country, where little seems to have changed since the turn of the century.

Exploring the "large island": The term "Tierra del Fuego" properly includes the whole archipelago at the southern tip of South America, although the Isla Grande de Tierra del Fuego is the largest island and is usually the one referred to. It is divided between Chile (70 percent) and Argentina (30 percent), with its northern and western sections a treeless Patagonian plain and the southeastern part a lush, mountainous land full of forests and sodden swamps. The Chilean section is physically the less dramatic of the two, and travelers to the island crossing over from Punta Arenas will normally want to visit both sides.

Thanks to relatively warm ocean currents, the island's weather is not as harsh as points in Alaska, Norway and Canada at an equivalent latitude in the Northern Hemisphere. Even so, it lives up to its stormy reputation. A visit is recommended in the summer months from November to March, when daylight lasts for around 20 hours and the sun is still relatively warm. The weather shifts erratically from cloudless sky to drizzle or a deluge and back again within minutes, with the only constant being a gusty wind. It is worthwhile preparing for a range of weather conditions to pass by every day.

Travelers coming from Chile will almost all cross the dark Straits of Magellan from Punta Arenas on the

Derelict boat on the Beagle channel.

ferry that leaves every morning at 9 a.m. As tradition suggests, the crossing is usually a rough one, but the water is also on occasion as smooth as glass. The optimistically-named port of **Porvenir** (Future) is the landing point on Tierra del Fuego, heralded by a cluster of battered fishing boats on shore and a sign that gives the distances to every point in Chile (Arica is 5,299 km) as well as to Belgrade in Yugoslavia!

As the sign suggests, descendants of Yugoslavs still make up the bulk of Porvenir's population. When seen on a weekend, it is like a ghost town: Porvenir boasts 4,500 inhabitants but few of them seem to take to the streets. The buildings are corrugated iron constructs mostly dating from before World War I, roads are mostly unpaved. There are few cars, and a wooden church steeple dominates the skyline – all adding to the somewhat haunting impression.

A small **museum** is connected to the municipal buildings on the main plaza, with historical photographs and an Indian mummy recently discovered in the

countryside nearby. Stroll along the waterfront to the south side of Bahia Porvenir for a view from a **mirador.**

Into the plains: Most travelers spend one night at the most in Porvenir and head for the open countryside. A dirt highway runs along the barren slopes of **Bahia Inutil** (Useless Bay) for 90 km to **Onaisin**, the original Caleta Josefina *estancia*. Keep an eye out for the **Cementario de los Gigantes**, (Cemetery of the Giants), a set of huge, regularly shaped stones scattered in the pampa. Only a couple of minutes further south is the historic **Cementario Inglés** (English Cemetery), where the British-born *estancia* workers were buried. In this windswept, forsaken spot are the graves of the few whites who fell to Indian arrows at the end of the last century.

Fifty km further south along the bay is the **Estancia Cameron**, founded in 1904. Nestled in a picturesque gully by the choppy grey sea, the farm's blue wooden buildings have not been altered in nine decades. Nor, it seems, have the methods of work: itinerant sheep shearers still crowd into a wooden shed during the December season and carry on their back-breaking trade as they did at the turn of the century. The administrator's area is still separate from the workers' quarters, although these days the *estancia* is a cooperative venture.

Visitors are permitted to eat with the shearers in their Dickensian dining hall: their diet is mutton for breakfast, lunch and dinner, 364 days of the year. The other day, Christmas, is when they are served up chicken – and apparently it's not popular!

Travelers with their own vehicles can continue along the roadway into the more remote, mountainous and rainy area of the island – taking their own camping gear, food and petrol supply. **Lago Blanco**, surrounded by Fuegian peaks, is considered the most beautiful in the far south of Chile. You can follow the highway south until the end of the road, at the doorway of Chile's last estancia, **Vicuña**. From here the road returns north along the frontier.

Across the border: Most travelers who

Centolla, king crab) is Fuegian speciality.

come this far south will want to continue into the Argentine side of Tierra del Fuego. The easiest way is to head directly from Porvenir to the frontier at **San Sebastian**, then continue onwards to **Rio Grande**. This rough and ready oil town on the island's east coast is little more than a place to pass the night before continuing south.

On the southern coast of Tierra del Fuego, squeezed between dramatic mountain peaks and the blue **Beagle Channel**, is the island's largest and most attractive town: **Ushuaia**. Despite its often bitter weather, this is a popular resort town and base for exploring the area. Its energy and faith in progress sets Ushuaia apart from other towns of the South, and new buildings are being flung up everywhere amongst mud and twisted trees. As a result, there is little historical charm left in Ushuaia: the main street is like an open-air department store, with duty-free electronic goods being offered from the new Japanese factories set up nearby. One must look hard for places like the **Cafe Ideal**, which has a historic pioneering atmosphere. There is a joint from a whale's spine sitting on the bar.

Nevertheless, Ushuaia's setting is majestic, with the wicked-looking granite peak Mt. Olivia dominating the skyline. Boat trips on the Beagle channel pass islands crowded with sea lions and penguins, or scattered with the rotting remains of shipwrecked boats. And only an hour outside of Ushuaia is the **Tierra del Fuego National Park**, which preserves the sense of being at the end of the world: paths wind over spongy moss oozing cold water, past tough shrubs and thorny bushes as well as trees that have grown bent 45 degrees with the prevailing wind.

A pleasant drive eastward along the Beagle channel leads to **Estancia Harberton**, the first farm on the Argentine side of Tierra del Fuego set up by the Reverend Thomas Bridges. Surrounded by green meadows of bright flowers, the *estancia* is worth visiting as much for its serene beauty as its history. Guided tours are now offered in both English and Spanish, the owners offering pots

of tea overlooking the channel. Across the water are three obscure islands over which Chile and Argentina nearly went to war in 1978, until the pope intervened and drew up a settlement.

The uttermost South: While Ushuaia is the southernmost town of its size in the world, the title of southernmost permanent human settlement outside of Antarctica goes to Chile's **Puerto Williams** on **Isla Navarino**. Established in 1953 as a naval base, it can now be reached by irregular launches from Ushuaia or a short but expensive flight from Punta Arenas. The setting is, once again, magnificent and there are many walks in the unspoiled countryside nearby. Among welcome stops is the **Hostería Walo**, a comfortable guest house set around a large fireplace that makes a welcome refuge from the outside cold.

Isla Navarina was home to the Yaghan Indians and was first visited by the *Beagle* on its maiden journey. The captain, Robert Fitzroy, took four young Yaghans with the ship back to England for education, and returned with them on the famous journey with Charles Darwin. The friendliest Yaghan was named Jemmy Button by the crew. He had learned some manners of an English gent – but on his return to Tierra del Fuego he quickly discarded his gloves and cravat and reverted to his former Yaghan lifestyle. Fitzroy had hoped that Button would be a force for "civilizing" the Indians and converting them to Christianity, but the reverse proved to be true: two decades after his return, Button was to command attacks on the first European settlements in the area. He first led the slaughter of seven missionaries on Isla Picton, then four others on Isla Navarino.

Today there are no surviving full-blooded Yaghan Indians, although a handful of *mestizos* live outside Puerto Williams in the settlement called **Ukika**. Meanwhile, a small **museum** in the naval township is considered one of the best in the South, once again chronicling the sad tale of European settlement and the utter devastation of a unique Indian culture.

Right, farm hand on Estancia Cameron.

294

EASTER ISLAND

The first inhabitants of Easter Island called their home Te Pito o Te Henua – the Navel of the World. Gazing down from one of the island's two volcanic crater rims, it is easy to see why.

This tiny speck of volcanic rock, only 117 sq km (45 sq miles) in size, is almost lost in the endless blue horizon of the Pacific Ocean. The nearest Polynesian island, Pitcairn, is 2,000 km (1,240 miles) to the east; the coast of South America is over 4,000 km (2,490 miles) to the west. In fact, until 30 years ago, Easter Island was visited only once a year by a Chilean warship bringing supplies, making it the most isolated human habitation on earth.

But even though few people before the 1960s could make a personal visit, Easter Island had gripped the world's imagination for centuries. One baffling image made it famous: littering the island are hundreds of giant, tight-lipped basalt statues, unique in the whole of Oceania. The almost total absence of records – thanks to the tragic destruction of the prehistoric culture by Europeans – has left some of the most fascinating archaeological riddles of all time.

How did an early seafaring people find this remote speck in the Pacific Ocean? Where did they come from? How did they carve their enormous statues from a quarry in the side of a volcano, transport them many kilometers to the coast and erect them on giant stone altars? And, above all – why did they do so?

Today regular flights from Santiago have broken the island's isolation. People visiting Chile have the chance to see this legendary site, marvel at the remains of a unique Pacific culture and make up their own minds on the heated debates over the monolithic statues.

And the fascination of the island is not only with the dead past. A vibrant Polynesian culture sets Easter Island completely apart from anywhere else in Chile. On the way to various archaeological sites, you can enjoy the tropical – almost somnolescent – calm of the islands, relax to its South Pacific rhythms and lounge on some of the most stunning beaches east of Tahiti.

Polynesian or American?: The long-standing assumption that the first Easter Islanders were Polynesians was upset in 1947 when the Norwegian Thor Heyerdahl sailed a balsa raft, *Kon-Tiki*, from Peru to Tahiti. The highly-publicised journey showed that it was theoretically possible for a pre-Inca South American culture to have colonized the Pacific.

Heyerdahl went on to spend a year digging on Easter island, and concluded in his best-selling book *Aku-Aku* that the first islanders actually came from the Peruvian coast, fleeing the destruction of the ancient South American empire of Tiahuanacu around Lake Titicaca in Bolivia. According to this theory, the seafarers brought with them a number of American plants that are still found on the island (including the sweet potato and totora reeds found in Lake Titicaca) as well as their sun-worshipping religion and famous skills

as stone masons. Heyerdahl argues that they were eventually joined by a group of Polynesian settlers. The two groups lived in harmony until an eventual war finally destroyed the islanders of South American origin.

Most archeologists now discount the bulk of Heyerdahl's findings, although his groundwork is still valuable and makes stimulating reading. Nor do his theories seem so outlandish compared to an extraordinary rash of more recent claims. Crackpot visionaries have announced that the Easter islanders were descendents of ancient Egyptians, interplanetary travelers, red-haired North Africans or even survivors of the lost continent Atlantis.

Slave raids: The speculation has been fueled by the unusual absence of historical records on the island. Almost all of the original islanders were wiped out by slave raids during the 19th century, so that by the time serious archaeological work began in the 1980s the old culture was virtually dead.

According to those few surviving in-habitants who were first interviewed in the late 19th century, Easter Island was discovered by King Hota Matua – a name meaning "prolific father" in Polynesian – who arrived on Anakena beach on the island's northern coast from a scorched land to the east. Tradition holds that 57 generations of kings succeeded Hota Matua until the 1680s, during which time another set of ancestors arrived under a chief whose name was Tuu-ko-ihu.

The legend goes that the two groups were divided between so-called "Long-Ears," who carved the *moai*, and the newcoming "Short Ears," who were kept in an inferior class and helped in manual labor. Eventually the Short Ears rebelled and slaughtered all of the Long Ears bar one. Unfortunately, so many different versions of this story soon cropped up – mostly completely contradictory – that they only added untold confusion to research. Most investigators are now finding it safer to believe that none of the versions are authentic.

Orthodox opinion now holds that

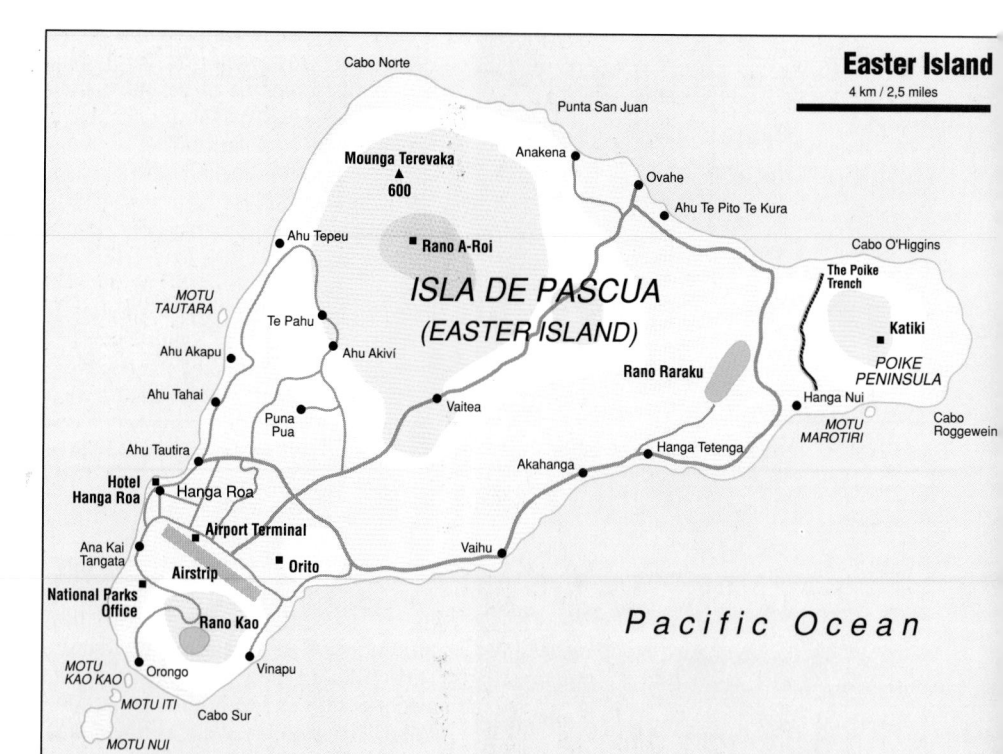

Easter Island was first populated before AD 500 by Polynesians coming from the Marquesas islands, remaining in total isolation until the arrival of Europeans. The bizarre culture was developed by the islanders themselves, who lived in a fairly egalitarian society dominated by small independent warring tribes. According to this view, 1,200 years of total isolation allowed the creation of a new language, the famous statues that still litter the island as well as the only writing system known in all Polynesia and the Americas – the rongo rongo script.

The conclusion is far from watertight and most travelers to Easter Island will want to decide the truth for themselves. But pieces to the jigsaw are not few and often mystifying. The scraps of evidence as to the island's past come from one of two sources: first, serious archeological work performed this century; and second, the disjointed recollections of the early European explorers.

First contact: The first European to stumble across this speck in the Pacific Ocean was the Dutch Admiral Jacob Roggeween. He and his crew landed and spent a day ashore on Easter Sunday, 1722 – and christened the island for the occasion. Roggeween's log-book tells how the Dutch anchored off the mysterious island at dusk and were greeted by fair-skinned Polynesians, similar to those in Tahiti and Hawaii. Some had darker skins, the Dutchman wrote, while others were "quite white" like Europeans, with reddish hair.

Roggeween records with awe that the now-famous statues were still standing, many up to 9 meters (30 ft) tall and with great cylinders on their heads. The inhabitants of the island, he wrote, "kindle fires in front of certain remarkably tall figures they set up; and, thereafter squatting on their heels with heads bowed down, they bring the palms of their hands together and alternately raise and lower them." The islanders kept up the ritual until the next dawn, when they praised the sunrise. Many of the worshippers wore long wooden plugs in their ear-lobes, lengthening them down

islander
side a
odern *moai*
th eyes.

tice found in much of Polynesia and also amongst nobles of Peru, whom the conquistadors called *orejones* or "Long Ears."

The inhabitants lived in long, low huts of reed, that looked strangely like boat hulls turned upwards. Their lands were neatly cultivated, Roggeween noted, and "whole tracts of woodland" were visible in the distance. Examining the *moai* closely, the Dutchmen decided that they were not of stone but were modelled from a strange clay stuffed with small stones. With that curious decision, the crew rowed back to their ships and weighed anchor.

In their less than 24 hours on shore, they had decided that the islanders were friendly but expert thieves, pinching a few hats and table cloths. A misunderstanding led to one native being shot on board their boat, followed by another dozen being gunned down on shore – giving islanders an ominous taste of what European contact would bring.

The Spaniards, English and French: The island was left in peace for another 50 years before the arrival of a Spanish captain named Don Felipe Gonzalez. In typical Spanish fashion, he marched with two priests and a squadron of soldiers to a high-point on the east coast, planted the cross and claimed the island for his king.

The men of the island, he noted later, were naked except for feather headdresses, while women wore short cloaks around their breasts and hips. Don Felipe noted with some interest that the islanders looked nothing like the Indians of South America, then recorded how he taught some to recite in Spanish, "Ave Maria, long live Charles III, King of Spain" before disappearing over the horizon.

Next came the renowned English navigator Captain James Cook, landing in 1774 after a journey through the Society Islands, Tonga and New Zealand. Cook had no doubt that the islanders were of Polynesian descent, although they seemed to be few in number and living in a miserable state. Little land was in cultivation. Meanwhile, dozens

The almost treeless landscapes the island.

of the stone statues had been over-turned, Cook found, and those that remained were no longer worshipped but used as burial sites. The scurvy-ridden Englishmen were forced to leave with nothing but a few baskets of sweet potatoes – although even then they were cheated, since islanders had weighed down the baskets with stones and laid only a few potatoes over the very top.

What had happened since the days of the Dutchmens' visit? Modern evidence confirms that serious environmental degradation already was well underway on Easter Island by the time of the Dutch visit in 1722: Pollen samples show that the island was heavily forested when man first arrived in A.D. 500, yet was completely bare by the beginning of the 19th century.

Most writers now believe that the population of Easter Island had simply outgrown its resources. The food supply began to fail, the island's forests were felled and soil began to erode. Without wood for canoes to escape the island, tribes turned on one another in wars: the giant statues were toppled and broken, while cannibalism became common. The resulting ruin is seen by many today as a taste in miniature of the Earth's own future, as the human race consumes the planet's limited resources with increasing voracity.

The slavers arrival: But no matter how destructive the internal wars were on Easter Island, they pale into insignificance compared with the devastation finally wreaked by contact with the outside world during the 19th century. Whalers and slave traders put the island on their gruesome itineraries, bringing nothing more than a series of tragedies to this hitherto isolated outpost.

The most dramatic blow was the Peruvian slave raid of 1862. Early on Christmas Eve, strangers rowed ashore with brightly colored clothes and presents that brought islanders down to greet them. On a given signal, the slave-hunters attacked, tying up those who surrendered and shooting any who resisted. One thousand islanders were kidnapped, including the king and most

European engraving in the mid 18th century shows the *moai* still erect.

learned men, to be taken to work on the guano islands situated off the coast of Peru – but not before the slavers celebrated Christmas on board with rum and salted pork.

Brutal conditions at the guano mine, starvation and epidemics had killed off 900 islanders before the bishop of Tahiti was finally able to intervene on their behalf. Of the remaining hundred who set sail for their homeland, 85 died en route from smallpox. The handful who returned brought the plague with them: by the 1870s only 110 men, women and children were alive on the whole of Easter Island.

Following this devastation came the first missionary to the island, Eugene Eyraud. Unsurprisingly, he met a hostile reception and was forced to flee – only to return two years later with reinforcement. Many of the islanders were converted to Christianity, however superficially, over the next few years.

Chile takes over: Spain may have claimed Easter Island for itself in 1770, but the Crown hardly bothered to maintain its take. No other expeditions were sent to the island, and with the collapse of Spanish control of Latin America in the early 1800s, the way was left open for another colonial power.

As part of its 19th century burst of expansionism, Chile annexed Easter Island in 1888. The South American republic wanted to show off its powerful naval force and show itself the equal of major European powers by grabbing a piece of South Pacific territory. Apart from the perceived prestige that such an acquisition would bring, Chile saw the island as a gateway to Asian trade and having valuable agricultural potential.

Unfortunately, few Chileans showed much interest in colonising this new jewel in the nation's crown. The government found itself handing over control of the island to sheep grazing companies – first a Chilean concern run by a Valparaíso businessman, then in the first decade of this century to the English company Williamson and Balfour. Based in Liverpool, the company leased the island in the name of their Compania

Island elder relates legends usin string.

306

Explotadora de la Isla de Pascua (CEDIP), using their wide-ranging power to make handsome profits until their license was revoked in 1953.

Islanders recall the company's rule as a time of dismal subjugation. They were effectively restricted to living in Hanga Roa, with the rest of the island free for sheep to roam. Generally they were forced to work for little or no wages. Many years later, when news arrived after World War II that Thor Heyerdahl had floated a raft from Peru to Tahiti, several islanders made boats to stage their own escape. Some succeeded, and guards were posted to stop the flight. It was also during this period that immigrants interbred with the remaining few Easter islanders, virtually eliminating them as a pure-bred race. Three-quarters of the population in the 1930s was of mixed descent, with everyone from North Americans to Germans and Tahitians living in Hanga Roa.

After 1953, the island's government was given to another authoritarian hand: the Chilean Navy. The islanders suf-fered the same humiliations as in the days of the sheep company: inability to vote, their local language suppressed and having to endure the Navy's arbitrary and often absurd decisions.

The biggest change for the island came in 1967, when the completion of the airport finally allowed flights from Tahiti and Santiago. The sudden possibility of large-scale tourism helped focus international attention on the island and the Chilean government was forced to make some improvements. During the 1970s and 1980s, better water supplies, electricity, a hospital and school were installed.

The most recent – and astonishing – change to the island has been the extension of the island's airport as an emergency landing site for the US space shuttle. Completed in 1988, the oversized air-strip (considerably longer than Santiago's) has completed the Easter islanders' drastic transition from the Stone Age, to the Space Age.

Orientation: Whatever your feelings on the dubious benefits of modern prog-

owing a
onch shell
orn.

ress, it is at the airport where almost all travelers now arrive – to be greeted by the first of Easter Island's famous *moai* statues. Rather small affairs compared to others on the island, they are still a taste of the mysteries to come.

Only five minutes walk from the airstrip is the tiny township where Easter Island's 2,500 people all live, **Hanga Roa**. Today about one third of these are Chilean-born, but the atmosphere is still definitely Polynesian. Built around a few wide dirt roads, with thick heavy palm trees hanging at regular intervals, the village looks like a classic South Pacific hideaway. The faces, language and music are all Polynesian – as is the relaxed pace of life. A speed limit of 20 kph (12 mph) is imposed on the town, only broken by the young children riding bareback down the main street, somtimes three to a horse.

There are two luxury hotels on Easter Island, but many prefer to stay in one of the small *residenciales* scattered about Hanga Roa. Reservations are not necessary – the owners crowd around the airport gates after every arrival offering their prices. There are a couple of small restaurants, several bars, and no less than three discotheques offering everything from local music to hours of Dolly Parton classics.

Many of Hanga Roa's inhabitants now live from selling wood carvings to travelers, endlessly repeating the same basic forms. The best known piece is also the ugliest: the *moai kavakava* or "statue of ribs." This human figure with a huge nose, ears and starved physique is said to have been first carved by King Tuu-ko-ihu. Apparently the king was sleeping at the foot of a cliff when he awoke to find two ghosts staring down at him. He ran home and straight away carved their image, and islanders have followed the pattern ever since.

Volcanic remains: The island itself has a maximum length of 24 km (15 miles) and width of 12 km (8 miles). Volcanic in origin, it has several dead craters dotted over its sparsely-covered surface, two of which now contain freshwater lakes. The terrain on the treeless

Horseback is the preferred mode of transport on the island.

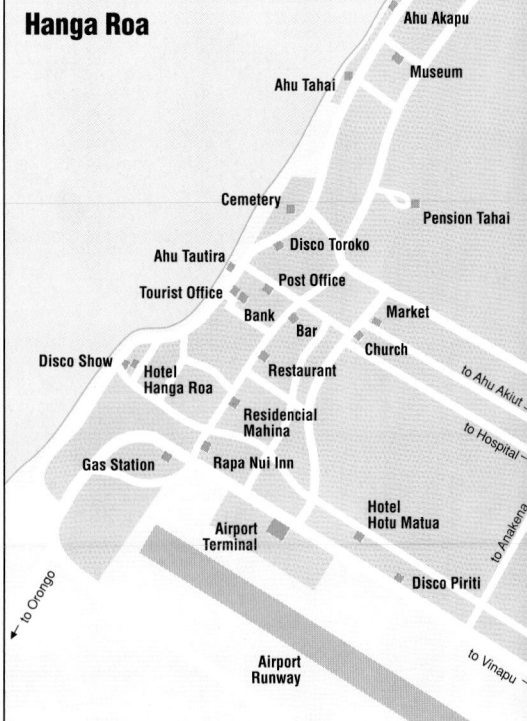

Hanga Roa

Ahu Akapu

Museum

Ahu Tahai

Cemetery

Pension Tahai

Disco Toroko

Ahu Tautira

Post Office

Tourist Office

Bank

Market

Bar

Church

Disco Show

Hotel Hanga Roa

Restaurant

to Ahu Akiut

Residencial Mahina

to Hospital

Gas Station

Rapa Nui Inn

Hotel Hotu Matua

to Anakena

Airport Terminal

Disco Piriti

to Orongo

Airport Runway

to Vinapu

volcanic slopes is fairly grassy, but most of the island is covered in rugged lava fields. Dotted around the coast are hundreds of caves, once used as refuges (in times of war) or secret burial places.

While one or two archaeological sites can be reached on foot, the best way to explore the island is by jeep (you can hire one from the only gas station). Motorbikes can be hired by the hardy (anyone who doesn't mind bouncing over volcanic rock for several hours), as can horses (although these are often sickly or on the verge of starvation). Take plenty of sun-block, especially in the summer months, as well as a large supply of water – the tropical sun on Easter Island is notoriously fierce.

In search of *moai* and *ahus*: One short stroll from Hanga Roa makes a pleasant introduction to what Easter Island has to offer. Head down to the sea near the **Tourist Office**, past the stone enclosure where fishing boats are moored and local children swim on weekends. A road leads north for a few hundred yards along the rugged volcanic rocks of the coast. There is a small **museum** nearby, then a **cemetery** appears, full of crosses and flowers. The missionary presence has ensured that the population is at least nominally Catholic, and one of the less-known pleasures of Easter Island is visiting a mass service on Sunday and listening to the singing. Then, standing in stark contrast to this Christian piety, is one of the most photographed archaeological sites, **Ahu Tahai.**

Each of the brooding *moai* is carved from the island's soft volcanic rock to the same general pattern as the 600 others on the island: all with the distinctive heavy foreheads, pointed chins and (in all but a couple of cases) elongated ears. The hand position is typical of Polynesian carving, but the form of the figures is clearly unique. Their average height is around six meters.

It is worth noting that while the *moai* are of the same standardized form, they all have slight differences. Most are male, but some are women with breasts and vulvas. While they were originally considered to have been carved "blind"

anga Roa
arket.

by archaeologists, it has been recently shown that the *moai* had eyes: the whites were made of coral and the pupils from the glistening black obsidian that can be found everywhere on the island. Many statues on the island also have "hats"– the red stone cylinders balanced on their heads that represent either hair or headresses.

The rectangular stone platform on which the statues were erected was known as the *ahu* (the name derives from a Polynesian root for "to pile up, to heap up"); together the sites are known as *ahu moai*. There are about 300 *ahus* on the island – with and without *moai* – considered to be equivalent to the *morae* of central Polynesia. Many of these *ahu* represent several stages of rebuilding to accommodate *moai*, while others were buried *ahus* that were never associated with statues at all.

At Ahu Tahai, five statues stand in a row on their *ahu* with their backs to the sea. Like other *ahu moai*, they were knocked down in the cannibal wars. The archaeologist William Mulloy restored

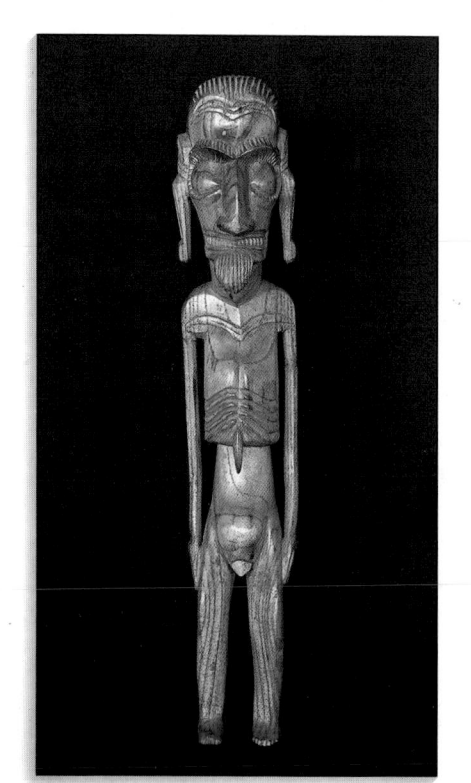

them to their rightful position – and, incidentally, his grave is only meters from the site. This is a favorite spot at sunset, when the *moai* are silhouetted against a scarlet sky and the spraying waters of the Pacific Ocean.

The purpose of the *ahu moai*: Archaeologists generally agree that the *moai* were figures of deceased chiefs or gods. (A key piece of information recorded by George Foster on Captain Cook's 1774 visit was that the *moai* were often named after these dead heroes). It has been suggested that, as the living conditions on tiny Easter Island became increasingly crowded and difficult, the island's inhabitants turned to carving these abstract cultural forms as a way to direct community energy and labor.

Mounted on an *ahu*, the *moai* transmitted *mana* or power to the living family chief. Sent through the statue's eyes, *mana* meant prosperity in peacetime and success in war.

Once there were as many as 15 *moai* set up on any particular *ahu*, all glaring down from on high and sending *mana*, or power, to the family head. From this viewpoint, it is not difficult to imagine what effect a fully constructed *ahu* must have had on its family – as well as the utter devastation of morale when the family *ahu* was pulled down.

An island circuit: Having had a taste of the most accessible *ahu moai*, your appetite will be whetted for a day tour of the island. By heading from south-east to north you can follow the general chronology of the island and gain an insight into how archaeologists and historians (as well as the innumerable crackpots) have pieced together their theories on where the Easter islanders came from, as well as how, why and when they carved their statues. In the process, you will probably see enough *moai* in one day to last a lifetime.

Taking the road south-east from Hanga Roa, follow the airstrip then turn south (past the large oil containers) to **Ahu Vinapu** – probably the most important site in establishing the chronology of Easter Island. There are two *ahus* here, both of which once supported *moai* before they were toppled and broken.

Left, fierce "statue of ribs". **Right**, stone head in Rano Rakaku

The most famous – known as Vinapu No. 1 – contains a wall of perfectly carved and fitted stone blocks that is strikingly similar to the work of the Tihuanacu culture and the Inca walls in Cuzco. Not surprisingly, it is a key element in Thor Heyerdahl's argument that the Easter Islanders themselves originally came from South America. Vinapu No. 2 is a much rougher version of the same model *ahu*.

Thor Heyerdahl's Norwegian expedition used Carbon 14 dating of fire remains and other materials near here to break the island's prehistory into the Early Period (AD 400–1100), Middle Period (1100–1680) and Late Period (1680–1868). It appears that some *ahus* – including Vinapu No. 2 – were constructed in the Early Period, in the earliest centuries of human colonization, although their exact purpose is a matter of conjecture. The erection of the majority of *ahus* and *moai* belongs to the Middle Period; while the Late Period belongs to the bloody cannibal wars that resulted in the end of *moai* production and the destruction of the statutes and their *ahus*.

Heyerdahl found that the finely worked *ahu* of Vinapu No. 1 actually predated the cruder No. 2 – supporting his argument that the first inhabitants of the island were the skilled South American carvers whose work degenerated over time. But later archaeologists have reinterpreted the Norwegian expeditions' findings to show that the crude No. 2 came first – suggesting it to be a development of the *marae* platforms found on other Polynesian islands. It is now generally believed that the masonry skills of the islanders improved over many generations and that Vinapu No. 1 is the climax of their own achievement, independent of developments in Bolivia or Peru.

The south coast: Continuing north along the south-eastern coast of the island brings you to the most striking examples of the violent statue overthrowing of the Late Period's cannibal wars, into which the first European voyagers arrived.

Ahu Vaihu is probably the most ex-

traordinary sight along this stretch. Eight large statues have been pulled in a row from their *ahu*, looking rather forlorn with their noses in the dirt and top-knots scattered along the coast. One of the *moai* has been shattered completely.

Further along, **Ahu Akahanga** has four similarly humiliated statues, with another bunch scattered from a second *ahu* across a nearby estuary. Of more interest to archaeologists has been the remains of a village on the hill slopes opposite – the foundations of several boat-shaped houses can be seen as well as some round houses.

One last site, **Ahu Hanga Tetenga**, has been almost completely devastated and its two *moai* shattered. But from here, the dirt road runs inlands towards the volcanic crater of Rano Raraku. The so-called **'Road of the Moai'** is littered with more and more fallen statues before reaching the most impressive site on the island.

The quarry of Easter Island: By far the most famous of the *moai* are the 70 standing sentinels embedded up to their

Moai restored to their positions at Ahu Tahai.

shoulders in grass on the south slope of the volcanic crater **Rano Raraku**. They lead the way to the quarry or "nursery" inside and outside of the impressive crater rim. This was where the *moai* were cut from volcanic tufa, and some 150 figures are still left there in all stages of completion – mute testimony to the unknown disaster that stopped all work dead in its tracks.

A trail leads straight up from the car park to the largest statue ever built – a 21-meter (69-ft) monolith. Leading off to the right, the trail comes to two other huge statues still part of the rock, while 20 or so more stand on the inside of the crater. A total of over 300 statues can be found around the area, in the process of being cut or moved to *ahus* when work ceased.

Many obscure differences have been found in the *moai* of Rano Raraku. There are several female statues amongst the crowd of males, while others have unusual carvings on their flanks or backs. One figure boasts on its chest a rough three-master ship with sails. A line hangs from its bow to a round figure that may be an anchor or turtle caught on a fishing line. With a little imagination, the boat has been explained as either a European ship or a large totora reed vessel.

Also found buried at Rano Raraku by the Norwegian expedition was the unique kneeling statue, now found on the right slope of the crater. Somewhat less than four meters high, it has a rounded head and face, as well as a beard and short ears.

Carving from the rock: The remains in the quarry give very clear evidence on how the *moai* were originally modelled from the rock. Trenches were cut for the easy access of carvers, chipping away until only the spine was left down their backs. Finally the spine was severed and the statues lowered by ropes to a temporary upright position in the slopes below, where they were finished off. The sheer fact that these figures up to 21 meters (69 ft) tall were cut from vertical as well as horizontal rock-faces shows the skill of the workers – while the number of broken statues on the slopes

reveal the work's danger. The tools used to carve the *moai* were small basalt picks called toki, of which thousands have been found at the quarry.

The Norwegian expedition decided to find out exactly how long it took to carve a *moai* by commissioning a team of islanders to work on a statue here at Rano Raraku. The incident is recounted in Heyerdahl's *Aku-Aku*: the then mayor of the island brought a family team to work non-stop for three days before giving up with fingers twisted from the work. But they had begun to make an impression and the experience suggested that a skilled team would take between 12 and 15 months to carve a *moai* about four meters long, using two teams constantly in shifts. But how did the islanders move the other 300 *moai* to different parts of the island?

Making statues walk: Following the coast road onwards to the north of the island gives an idea of the enormity of the problem. Here is located **Ahu Te Pito Te Kura** – at some 9.8 meters (32 ft) in length, it is the largest *moai* ever

transported. The name means "navel of light" and the rock from which it was hewn is said to have been brought by Hota Matua himself.

Heyerdahl was able to convince some 180 merry dinner guests to pull one 4-meter (13-ft) long *moai* across a field with ropes made from tree bark, showing that it was easier to move the statues than had first been expected. In *Aku Aku* he suggested that a much larger statue could be pulled using more people and wooden rollers. Others suggested that small rocks could be used like marbles to move the statues. But these theories still seem unconvincing when faced with the size of Ahu Te Pito Te Kura and the ruggedness of the volcanic terrain from Rano Raraku.

The archaeologist William Mulloy came up with a different theory that has won widespread support. First a huge forked sled (made from the large trees that tests have shown once covered the island) would be attached to the front of each statue, tied into place over the protruding belly and stuck beneath the

Left, an islander recreates ancient dress. Right, erecting a mini-moai at an Island festival.

chin. This sled protected the statue from the ground and allowed it to be moved by leverage using a bipod. The statues' own weight could then be used to help move it along in a repetitive series of upward and forward movements. While hardly fool-proof (and there are numerous broken *moai* around the island), the method is at least possible. Curiously, the theory of short jerking movements recalls the islanders' own belief that the *moai* "walked" to their *ahu*.

An experiment in ancient engineering: One more baffling mystery remains: once the statues had been moved by this painstaking method, how did the islanders then erect them – along with top-knots – onto their stone altars?

When the Norwegian expedition arrived in the mid-1950s, not one *moai* was at its post on an *ahu*. All lay where they had fallen centuries before, and nobody had even attempted to move them. Heyerdahl resolved to raise a *moai* using only the materials that would have been available to the original islanders. The lone statue now standing at **Ahu**

Ature Huki on **Anakena beach** was the result of the experiment that put the first *moai* upright since the cannibal wars.

Having dragged the *moai* to the *ahu*, Heyerdahl's team of islanders worked a series of long poles underneath the statue's stomach. Three or four men heaved at the end of each pole as another man, lying on his belly, slipped small stones underneath the giant's face. Slowly the statue began to rise from the ground, supported on this mattress of tightly-packed pebbles.

It took a dozen men working for nine days to have the statue on a 45-degree angle. Another nine days and it was almost upright. Finally it slid with the guidance of ropes to a standing position. Raising a *moai* with a top-knot would have been done in the same fashion, Heyerdahl argues, strapping the stone "hat" to the statue's head with ropes and poles.

Since that date many other *moai* have been restored to their *ahus*, as can be seen today. But it is still astounding to

**one
entinels at
nakena
each.**

consider raising a statue on Ahu Te Pito Te Kura – with its top-knot it would have been a massive 11.5 meters (38 ft) tall. William Mulloy estimated that it would have taken 30 men one year to carve, 90 men two months to move the six km from the quarry and 90 men three months to erect. And this pales in comparison with the 21-meter (69-ft) monolith still being cut in the quarry when work was abandoned.

These theories of how the *moai* were moved and raised also suggest why carving suddenly ceased at the Rano Raraku quarry: the Easter Island workers simply ran out of trees. Eighteenth-century explorers had reported the island's lack of timber. It seems likely that work was abandoned when the islanders realised that without wood the statues could no longer be taken from their nursery to the coast.

The golden sands of Polynesia: Only 100 meters away on the headland at Anakena is **Ahu Nau Nau** and seven more *moai*.

But having viewed *moai* all day, it probably comes as a welcome relief to find that these last *ahus* look over the pure sands of **Anakena beach**. This was the legendary landing place of Hota Matua, the founder of the island. Many of the caves nearby are said to have been his refuge while waiting for a boat-shaped house to be built nearby.

But if you are in the mood for a swim after a hard day of *moai*-spotting, one small bay is even more appealing than the wider expanses of Anakena: nestled beneath a cliff of volcanic rock, **Ovahe beach** must be one of the most beautiful on earth. Its sands are pure and golden, the match for any South Pacific paradise, and the water so clear that you can count your toe hairs while swimming.

From here you also have a view of the **Poike Peninsular**. This area has a major place in local legend. When the "Short Ears" tired of working for their "Long Ear" rulers and rebelled, the Long Ears gathered on this peninsular behind the Poike trench. Filled with branches and tree trunks, the ditch was intended as a fiery defence rampart. Unfortunately for the Long Ears, a traitor who was married to a Short Ear woman allowed their enemies to slip into the peninsular and surround them. The Short Ears attacked and drove the Long Ears into their own flaming ditch, where all but the traitor were incinerated.

Curiously, while this had been considered a fable by most researchers, the Norwegian expedition found thick layers of charcoal and ash here. They were able to show that a great fire had once ocurred in the trench some 350 years ago – suggesting that there may be some truth to the tales of the Long Ears and Short Ears.

From here, take the road through the center of the island, passing the old sheep *estancia* back to Hanga Roa. From the town you can make another excursion along the northern roads of the island to sites like **Ahu Akivi** and **Ahu Tepeu** – interesting enough sites, but they offer few surprises to those who know the rest of the island.

Center of the "Bird Man" cult: A quite different excursion from Hanga Roa can be made directly south to the vol-

After a festival.

canic crater of Rano Kao. Instead of *moai*, its interest centers on a bizarre "bird man" ritual that flourished here amongst the original inhabitants. It is also without doubt the most spectacular spot on Easter Island.

A road and walking path run steeply upwards from the Hanga Roa township through typical scrubby terrain. Without warning, the enormous crater of Rano Kao appears below. Thor Heyerdahl once described it as a "giant witch's cauldron" – now filled with black water and floating green fields of totora reeds (you can actually walk across, if you are game), its steep, 200-meter high wall is gently eroded on the seaward side to include a view of the blue Pacific.

The ruined village of **Orongo** is perched in this sublime location, with the volcano on one side and sheer cliffs on the other dropping some 400 meters (1,300 ft) down to the crashing sea. Scattered out into the void are three tiny, craggy islands – **Motu Kao Kao**, **Motu Iti** and **Motu Nui.**

Orongo is now restored and part of an especially created reserve. Entry costs US$1 at the ranger's office. The village itself contains a range of 48 oval buildings, constructed in the 16th century with their floors cut into the side of the slope. Walls were made from overlapping slabs of stone, with other large slabs meeting horizontally to make an arch. The entrances are small tunnels big enough for only one person to enter at a time. But the main attraction is a string of 150 "Bird Man" carvings on rocks on the edge of the cliffs: a man's body is drawn with a bird's head, often holding an egg in one hand.

The quest for the first egg: Archaeologists know a considerable amount about the Bird Man cult as its ritual was performed up until 1862, and survivors were able to describe it in detail to later investigators. The strange ceremony is linked to the supreme deity Makemake, who is said to have created the earth, sun, moon and stars. Makemake rewarded good and punished evil, and for centuries was responsible for bringing the only visitors to the island from the outside world: an annual migration of sooty tern birds. Begun in the period of the cannibal wars, the bird man cult may have been an esoteric attempt to direct tribal competition towards a peaceful course. It also may well have symbolised a wish to escape from the increasing horror of confinement to the island.

The basis of the cult was finding the first egg of spring laid by the Manu Tara, or sacred bird. The chief of each tribe on the island sent one chosen servant to Moto Nui, the largest of the islets below Orongo. Swimming across the dangerous waters, the unfortunate servants or *hopus* each spent about a month looking for the first egg while islanders gathered on the Orongo cliffs made offerings and prayers to Makemake. When the egg had been found, the successful *hopu* plunged into the swirling waters (the egg apparently strapped to his forehead), swam to the mainland and climbed back up the cliffs to present the prize to his master.

The successful master would then be named the "bird man" for that year. Strangely, the advantages which this

rchaeologists work.

office conferred are far from clear. The chief would have his head, eyebrows and eyelashes shaved, then his head painted red and black. For the whole of the following year he would remain in seclusion in a special house, presumably having gained the favor of Makemake.

The secret of the rongorongo script: The curious birdman petroglyphs at Orongo recall one other Easter Island mystery that may never be solved: rongorongo writing. Found on small wooden boards, this script contains 120 different figures based on birdman or human forms and is read alternatively from left to right then right to left, in the same pattern as an ox ploughing a field. When outsiders first glimpsed the boards in 1865, none of the surviving Easter islanders knew how to read them – the priests who understood them having perished after the Peruvian slave raids.

Recent attempts by Russian and German experts to decipher the rongorongo script have so far borne little fruit. Nor do scholars agree on where the writing – the only such known in all of South America and Polynesia – first came from. Guesses range from the Indus valley of Pakistan to the Andes. But other archeologists have begun to doubt whether rongorongo is in fact prehistoric at all: since no similar pictographs are carved in stone elsewhere on the island, it is possible that the script is an emulation of European writing. Rongorongo may have developed from observation of the Spanish treaty of annexation in 1770, possibly fixing chants into some concrete form – only to be forgotten as the island priests died like flies on Peru's guano islands.

A final verdict?: After visiting all the major sites and immersing oneself in the mystery of Easter Island, few visitors can resist making some sort of decision for themselves on the most debated question of all: did the first islanders travel from Polynesia or were they South American refugees as Thor Heyerdahl suggests, escaping in fleets of reed boats the collapse of a magnificent Andean empire?

The enormous crater of Rano Kao.

It is fair to say that modern archaeological opinion weighs heavily against Thor Heyerdahl's dramatic interpretation. Peter Bellwood in his work *Man's Conquest of the Pacific* provides a fairly balanced summary of the latest research, arguing that while nobody can prove Heyerdahl 100 percent wrong, the chances of him being right are quite remote.

Firstly, the language of Easter Island – which is believed to have been spoken since before AD 500 – is completely Polynesian. Secondly, the skeletons found on the island are Polynesian – although it is true that these are all from the Late Period. Thirdly, there is no evidence that any portable artifacts dug up on the island – like cups, plates or vases – came from South America, while many certainly are Polynesian in style. Finally, the posture of the *moai* can be equally found in the art of the Polynesia as in Tiahuanacu style carving, and may be a common inheritance from past millenia.

However, there are some points on which Heyerdahl has a case. The sweet potato and totaro reed are South American plants and, accordingly to pollen diagrams may have been introduced at a late date. The stone house designs found on the island recall those of Peru – although they may have been developed independently.

But certainly the most surprising piece of evidence for anyone who has been to Peru and Bolivia remains the close-fitting stonework of Ahu Vinapu 1, so strikingly reminiscent of Tiahuanacu and Inca work. Its date is also set at around AD 600, or within the classic period of Tiahuanacu culture – which may or may not be pure chance.

Yet of the 300-plus *ahus* on the island, this is the only piece of stonework on the island that may have been inspired by a pre-Incan culture. So while a case for major South American migration cannot be made, it is not impossible that at least some Tiahuanacu Indians visited the island at a remote date sometime in the past.

The final view of Easter Island's past can be summed up simply: a handful of Polynesian seafarers arrived between AD 400 and 500, slowly increasing in numbers and building their statues. As the centuries passed, the island's environment could no longer sustain them. They then fought amongst themselves, destroyed their own achievement and left the rest of the world to puzzle over the ruins.

To some this may seem a little dull – without the grand arrival of Incas or survivors of an unknown Atlantis carrying on their lost civilization. But, to quote Bellwood: "It is not even more exciting that a group of isolated Polynesians could have evolved such a magnificent prehistoric record by using their own ideas, brawn and procreative ability rather than someone else's. Too many anthropologists in the past have held the view that all good things come from a very few areas, and that most of these areas were inhabited by Caucasoids... The peoples of Oceania deserve the credit for their acheivements, not the peoples of some imaginary Mediterranean colonial enterprise."

Memories of
the "birdman
cult" at
rongo.
Following
page, sunset
t Ahu Tahai.

INSIGHT GUIDES
TRAVEL TIPS

FOR THOSE
WITH MORE THAN
A PASSING INTEREST
IN TIME...

Before you put your name down for a Patek Philippe watch *fig. 1*, there are a few basic things you might like to know, without knowing exactly whom to ask. In addressing such issues as accuracy, reliability and value for money, we would like to demonstrate why the watch we will make for you will be quite unlike any other watch currently produced.

"Punctuality", Louis XVIII was fond of saying, "is the politeness of kings."

We believe that in the matter of punctuality, we can rise to the occasion by making you a mechanical timepiece that will keep its rendezvous with the Gregorian calendar at the end of every century, omitting the leap-years in 2100, 2200 and 2300 and recording them in 2000 and 2400 *fig. 2*. Nevertheless, such a watch does need the occasional adjustment. Every 3333 years and 122 days you should remember to set it forward one day to the true time of the celestial clock. We suspect, however, that you are simply content to observe the politeness of kings. Be assured, therefore, that when you order your watch, we will be exploring for you the physical—if not the metaphysical—limits of precision.

Does everything have to depend on how much?

Consider, if you will, the motives of collectors who set record prices at auction to acquire a Patek Philippe. They may be paying for rarity, for looks or for micromechanical ingenuity. But we believe that behind each $500,000-plus

bid is the conviction that a Patek Philippe, even if 50 years old or older, can be expected to work perfectly for future generations.

In case your ambitions to own a Patek Philippe are somewhat discouraged by the scale of the sacrifice involved, may we hasten to point out that the watch we will make for you today will certainly be a technical improvement on the Pateks bought at auction? In keeping with our tradition of inventing new mechanical solutions for greater reliability and better time-keeping, we will bring to your watch innovations *fig. 3* inconceivable to our watchmakers who created the supreme wristwatches of 50 years ago *fig. 4*. At the same time, we will of course do our utmost to avoid placing undue strain on your financial resources.

Can it really be mine?

May we turn your thoughts to the day you take delivery of your watch? Sealed within its case is your watchmaker's tribute to the mysterious process of time. He has decorated each wheel with a chamfer carved into its hub and polished into a shining circle. Delicate ribbing flows over the plates and bridges of gold and rare alloys. Millimetric surfaces are bevelled and burnished to exactitudes measured in microns. Rubies are transformed into jewels that triumph over friction. And after many months—or even years—of work, your watchmaker stamps a small badge into the mainbridge of your watch. The Geneva Seal—the highest possible attestation of fine watchmaking *fig. 5*.

Looks that speak of inner grace *fig. 6.*

When you order your watch, you will no doubt like its outward appearance to reflect the harmony and elegance of the movement within. You may therefore find it helpful to know that we are uniquely able to cater for any special decorative needs you might like to express. For example, our engravers will delight in conjuring a subtle play of light and shadow on the gold case-back of one of our rare pocket-watches *fig. 7*. If you bring us your favourite picture, our enamellers will reproduce it in a brilliant miniature of hair-breadth detail *fig. 8.* The perfect execution of a double hobnail pattern on the bezel of a wristwatch is the pride of our casemakers and the satisfaction of our designers, while our chainsmiths will weave for you a rich brocade in gold *figs. 9 & 10.* May we also recommend the artistry of our goldsmiths and the experience of our lapidaries in the selection and setting of the finest gemstones? *figs. 11 & 12.*

How to enjoy your watch before you own it.

As you will appreciate, the very nature of our watches imposes a limit on the number we can make available. (The four Calibre 89 time-pieces we are now making will take up to nine years to complete). We cannot therefore promise instant gratification, but while you look forward to the day on which you take delivery of your Patek Philippe *fig. 13*, you will have the pleasure of reflecting that time is a universal and everlasting commodity, freely available to be enjoyed by all.

Should you require information on any particular Patek Philippe watch, or even on watchmaking in general, we would be delighted to reply to your letter of enquiry. And if you send

fig. 1: The classic face of Patek Philippe.

fig. 4: Complicated wristwatches circa 1930 (left) and 1990. The golden age of watchmaking will always be with us.

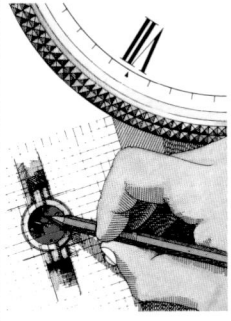

fig. 9: Harmony of design is executed in a work of simplicity and perfection in a lady's Calatrava wristwatch.

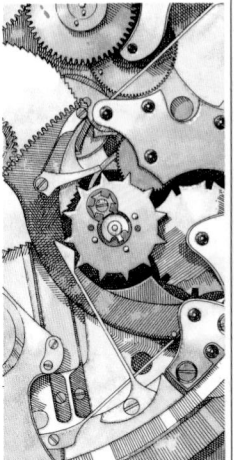

fig. 6: Your pleasure in owning a Patek Philippe is the purpose of those who made it for you.

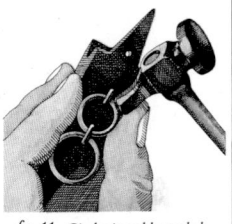

fig. 10: The chainsmith's hands impart strength and delicacy to a tracery of gold.

fig. 5: The Geneva Seal is awarded only to watches which achieve the standards of horological purity laid down in the laws of Geneva. These rules define the supreme quality of watchmaking.

fig. 7: Arabesques come to life on a gold case-back.

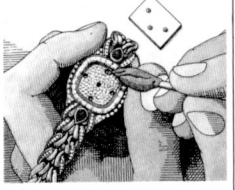

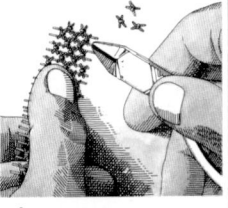

fig. 11: Circles in gold: symbols of perfection in the making.

fig. 2: One of the 33 complications of the Calibre 89 astronomical clock-watch is a satellite wheel that completes one revolution every 400 years.

fig. 8: An artist working six hours a day takes about four months to complete a miniature in enamel on the case of a pocket-watch.

fig. 12: The test of a master lapidary is his ability to express the splendour of precious gemstones.

fig. 3: Recognized as the most advanced mechanical regulating device to date, Patek Philippe's Gyromax balance wheel demonstrates the equivalence of simplicity and precision.

PATEK PHILIPPE
GENEVE
fig. 13: The discreet sign of those who value their time.

your card marked "book catalogue" we shall post you a catalogue of our publications. Patek Philippe, 41 rue du Rhône, 1204 Geneva, Switzerland, Tel. +41 22/310 03 66.

Reality check. Call home.

—— *AT&T USADirect® and World Connect.® The fast, easy way to call most anywhere.* ——

Take out AT&T Calling Card or your local calling card.** Lift phone. Dial AT&T Access Number for country you're calling from. Connect to English-speaking operator or voice prompt. Reach the States or over 200 countries. Talk. Say goodbye. Hang up. Resume vacation.

Argentina♦	...001-800-200-1111	Guyana*††	165
Belize♦	555	Honduras †	123
Bolivia*	**0-800-1112**	**Mexico**◊◊◊	**95-800-462-4240**
Brazil	**000-8010**	**Nicaragua**	**174**
Chile	**1-23-0-0311**	**Panama** ■	**109**
Colombia	**980-11-0010**	Paraguay (Asuncion City)†	0081-800
Costa Rica*■	**0-800-0-114-114**	**Peru**†	**171**
Ecuador*	**999-119**	**Suriname**†	**156**
El Salvador*■	**190**	Uruguay	00-0410
Guatemala*	190	**Venezuela***■	**80-011-120**

AT&T
Your True Choice

For a free wallet sized card of all AT&T Access Numbers, call: 1-800-241-5555.

Getting Acquainted

The Place

Area: 756,626 sq. km (292,134 sq. miles)
Coastline: 4,300 km (2,700 miles)
Capital: Santiago (pop. 5 million)
Population: 14 million, mostly mestizo, 20 percent of direct European descent; 20,000 Mapucha Indians, living around Tamuco.
Language: Spanish
Religion: Roman Catholic
Currency: Peso ($)
Electricity: 220 volts
Weights and Measures: metric
International Dialling Code: 56 + 2 (Santiago)

Climate

As a general rule, Chile's climate makes a steady transition between the extreme arid heat of the desert north to the bitterly cold and wet conditions of the far south.

The **Atacama Desert** has been proclaimed "near perfect" due to its virtually non-existent rainfall. Typical desert conditions prevail all year round with searingly hot days and contrastingly chilly nights. High winds shift the desert sands and make northern highways more dangerous for motoring. The northern skies are generally wonderfully clear, although on the far northern coastline, at Arica, there is a higher humidity and frequent cloud cover. Temperatures here are less extreme, ranging from 15°C to 22°C. At the same latitudes on the Bolivian border, snow often covers the mountain passes.

The area known as the transitional zone between **Copiapó** and **Illapel** receives a light winter rainfall enabling minimal agriculture while immediately south lies the lush central region which has an abundant rainfall in winter and sunny dry summers.

The **central region** continues through Concepcíon with ever increasing rainfall from north to south and the higher inland temperatures. The climate is idyllically Mediterranean, mild and temperate, the warmest months being November to February when the temperatures reach 29°C. July and August are the coolest with temperatures as low as 10°C. The nights are rather cool, even in summer. Best months in Santiago are between October and April when the days are nearly always fine – although January can be uncomfortably hot in the congested city center. The summer heat is more tolerable on the coast at the famous seaside resorts, with fresh breezes to lower the temperature. The weather is excellent for skiing during the winter months at the ski resorts of Portillo and Farellones east of Santiago.

As far south as Puerto Montt, the **Lake District** also enjoys a temperate climate, although heavy rain falls throughout much of the year. The temperature is cooler than in the central region and icy winds originate from the lakes and mountains. Winter brings snow to the chalet-style resorts in the higher regions of Petrohué, Puella and Lago Todos Los Santos and some Andean highways between Chile and Argentina might become snowbound or otherwise impassable due to fog and storms. The offshore island of Chiloé is cold and foggy for most of the year, but for about 60 days when the sun shines, the countryside is especially picturesque.

South of Puerto Montt, the region of **Aisén** has a steppe climate featuring fairly low temperatures all the year round. Abundant snow falls from early autumn to late spring, so the best months to visit are November to March. Aisén, in the summer months offers beautifully crisp clear days, although cold winds and torrential rainstorms can also occur unpredictably. Worth noting is the agreeable microclimate found around the village of Chile Chico, suitable for growing fine fruits and vegetables.

In the awesome **Magallanes**, a region of glaciers and wilderness, snow covers the land in winter (except along the coastline), while rain is frequent in summer and freezing winds of up to 80 kph are common in spring. The climate and scenery has been likened to that of Norway. It is best to visit the far south in January or February when the sun is higher in the sky and the summer average climbs to 11°C (52°F).

Easter Island has a semi-tropical climate throughout the year with a particularly fierce sun, not to be underestimated. July and August are the coolest months for traipsing around the *moai*.

The Economy

Chile's economy is one of the most stable in South America, with a relatively high standard of living.

Chile was the first Latin American country to adopt a free-market economy, and from the mid-1980s to the mid-1990s the GDP grew by some 50 percent. A policy of export-led growth begun under Pinochet has been continued under subsequent democratically elected governments, trading with Japan and the Pacific Rim. Since 1990 its economic success has become one of the most enviable in Latin America, and it has ambitions to join an expanded North American Free Trade Agreement.

The rush for growth pursued by Pinochet has now been consolidated into a more liberal approach to the economy, in which housing and healthcare are given due attention, and the division between rich and poor has diminished.

Minerals, timber, fruit and seafood have been the major growth industries, with foreign investors encouraged in each sector.

Government

The 1990s saw Chile return to democratic rule after 16 years of military dictatorship headed by General Agosto Pinochet. Eduardo Frei was elected president in 1993.

Democratic civilian government was re-established following the fall of Pinochet in 1990. Christian Democrat Patricio Aylwin succeeded the dictator when he defeated the candidate nominated by the military junta. He became president over a loose coalition of modern and center-left parties, although their power is at present still limited by the Pinochet constitution.

The changeover of power ending military rule was held on March 11, 1990. Extravagant celebrations of democracy were staged in the National

THOMAS COOK
MASTERCARD
TRAVELLERS CHEQUES...

...HOLIDAY ESSENTIALS

Travel money from the travel experts

THOMAS COOK MASTERCARD TRAVELLERS CHEQUES ARE
WIDELY AVAILABLE THROUGHOUT THE WORLD.

COLORSET NUMBERS

North America
160 Alaska
173 American Southwest
184I Atlanta
227 Boston
275 California
180 California, Northern
161 California, Southern
237 Canada
184C Chicago
184 Crossing America
243 Florida
240 Hawaii
275A Los Angeles
243A Miami
237B Montreal
184G National Parks of America: East
184H National Parks of America: West
269 Native America
100 New England
184E New Orleans
184F New York City
133 New York State
147 Pacific Northwest
184B Philadelphia
172 Rockies
275B San Francisco
184D Seattle
Southern States of America
186 Texas
237A Vancouver
184C Washington DC

Latin America and The Caribbean
150 Amazon Wildlife
260 Argentina
188 Bahamas
292 Barbados
251 Belize
217 Bermuda
127 Brazil
260A Buenos Aires
162 Caribbean
151 Chile
281 Costa Rica
282 Cuba
118 Ecuador
213 Jamaica
285 Mexico
285A Mexico City
249 Peru
156 Puerto Rico
127A Rio de Janeiro
116 South America
139 Trinidad & Tobago
198 Venezuela

Europe
155 Alsace
158A Amsterdam
167A Athens
263 Austria
107 Baltic States

219B Barcelona
1187 Bay of Naples
109 Belgium
135A Berlin
178 Brittany
109A Brussels
144A Budapest
213 Burgundy
122 Catalonia
141 Channel Islands
135E Cologne
119 Continental Europe
189 Corsica
291 Côte d'Azur
165 Crete
226 Cyprus
114 Czech/Slovak Reps
238 Denmark
135B Dresden
142B Dublin
135F Düsseldorf
149 Eastern Europe
148A Edinburgh
123 Finland
209B Florence
154 France
135C Frankfurt
135 Germany
148B Glasgow
279 Gran Canaria
124 Great Britain
167 Greece
166 Greek Islands
135G Hamburg
144 Hungary
256 Iceland
142 Ireland
209 Italy
202A Lisbon
258 Loire Valley
124A London
201 Madeira
219A Madrid
157 Mallorca & Ibiza
117 Malta
101A Moscow
135D Munich
158 Netherlands
111 Normandy
120 Norway
124B Oxford
154A Paris
115 Poland
202 Portugal
114A Prague
153 Provence
177 Rhine
209A Rome
101 Russia
130 Sardinia
148 Scotland
261 Sicily
264 South Tyrol
219 Spain
220 Spain, Southern
101B St. Petersburg
170 Sweden
232 Switzerland

112 Tenerife
210 Tuscany
174 Umbria
209C Venice
263A Vienna
267 Wales
183 Waterways of Europe

Middle East and Africa
268A Cairo
204 East African Wildlife
268 Egypt
208 Gambia & Senegal
252 Israel
236A Istanbul
252A Jerusalem-Tel Aviv
214 Jordan
270 Kenya
235 Morocco
259 Namibia
265 Nile, The
257 South Africa
113 Tunisia
236 Turkey
171 Turkish Coast
215 Yemen

Asia/Pacific
287 Asia, East
207 Asia, South
262 Asia, South East
194 Asian Wildlife, Southeast
272 Australia
206 Bali Baru
246A Bangkok
234A Beijing
247B Calcutta
234 China
247A Delhi, Jaipur, Agra
169 Great Barrier Reef
196 Hong Kong
247 India
212 India, South
128 Indian Wildlife
143 Indonesia
278 Japan
266 Java
203A Kathmandu
300 Korea
145 Malaysia
218 Marine Life in the South China Sea
272B Melbourne
211 Myanmar
203 Nepal
293 New Zealand
205 Pakistan
222 Philippines
250 Rajasthan
159 Singapore
105 Sri Lanka
272 Sydney
175 Taiwan
246 Thailand
278A Tokyo
255 Vietnam
193 Western Himalaya

Stadium in Santiago, the same place that was used as a detention center for political prisoners by the military forces in 1973. A National Congress building was established in the port city of Valparaíso, though Moneda Palace, the seat of the president in Santiago bombed in the coup, remained.

Aylwin had the difficult task of succeeding a president who, despite massive popular opposition, had been credited with numerous economic improvements by the middle class and seemed to have gained the cult status of "father figure" to many Chileans. Pinochet insisted on staying on as head of the Chilean Army, with all the power that position entails, and his supporters are guaranteed eight seats in the Senate.

The handover of power to Aylwin's transitional liberal coalition was made easier by a significant improvement in the country's economy, which some dubbed a "miracle". The following elections, in December 1993, brought Eduardo Frei to power to continue the work of the wise and avuncular Alywin. Democratic civilain rule was by then confirmed with an efficient bureacracy and welcome social reforms.

Culture and Customs

Modern Chileans are versatile and expressive, best known abroad are Nobel Prize-winning poets Gabriela Mistral and Pablo Neruda, the celebrated pianist Claudio Arrau and a growing representation of fine artists. Chileans are nearly always interested and happy to welcome foreign tourists, especially in the rural areas where the atmosphere is more relaxed.

After their 15th century Spanish conquest, many of the Indian tribes in Northern Chile accepted the western christian culture, but the Araucanians or Mapuches put up a strong resistance until the middle of the 19th century when a treaty was signed.

It's very possible for tourists to see the traditional costumes, silver jewelry and thatched houses of these people as they continue their rural existence.

In the northern regions of Chile, descendants of the Andean Indians still play traditional instruments and celebrate religious dates with folkloric festivals. The Virgin, Christ or Saint is considered a protector of the village and is venerated with colorful masquerade dances.

Evidence of earlier cultures can be seen in the "geoglyphs" of Tiliviche and excellent artifacts are in the Museum of San Pedro de Atacama.

The *huaso*, or Chilean cowboy still carries on traditions in colorful costumes on the farms and rural lanes of the south central valley. The guitar and harp provide lively accompaniment for the *cueca*, Chile's national dance, traditionally performed at the Media Luna rodeo with *empanadas* and *chicha* following the dancing.

An area of the Lake District, dominated by Volcano Osorno, was colonized 150 years ago by German settlers. Nearby towns reflect their founders' origins in the style and structure of their homes.

The inhabitants of the island of Chiloé have a culture that is unique in South America, involving a brooding mythology of evil warlocks called the *brujos*, their deformed servants the *Invunche*, a type of mermaid called *sirens* and many other mysterious characters out to confound or torment the mere mortal.

Some ruined houses resemble one's childhood ideas and pictures of witches' houses. These are doubly eerie set on the cold foggy terrain of Chiloé. There is even a traditional dish which is cooked in a large cauldron over a fire, but don't expect modern Chileans to point the bone at you – the mythology is not taken terribly seriously these days.

The inhabitants of Easter Island, or Rapa Nui, "eyes gazing towards heaven," are proud of their Polynesian ancestry, making use of their tropical environment for their food and traditional adornments.

About 40 percent of Chile's total population lives in the metropolitan region of Santiago, the hub of commercial activity and a conglomeration of cultures. Urbanized Chileans seem to enjoy shopping and promenading, dining and dancing, watching the rodeo or the national ballet and creating paperwork.

Santiaginos are justly proud of their theater and fine arts, welcome international performers and keep up to date with foreign films. The Municipal Theatre is their symbol of artistic life.

Each Santiago *barrio*, or suburb, defines the cultural flavor within. For example, Bellavista holds the reputation as "most bohemian" and Providencia perhaps the, "most exclusive."

Life in the city center, however, can be decidedly hectic during the working week. On the other hand, you'll see three-hour luncheons in the best restaurants, while outdoor cafes are busy at any hour. Promenading is popular: on weekends, if they're not strolling around the shops or queuing for the cinema, Santiaginos are meandering through the parks. The Plaza de Armas is a popular resting place and open-air theater – especially at dusk, when the best amateur comedians, musicians and dancers appear to entertain massive crowds of Chileans from all classes. On any night, ice-cream vendors and pizza sellers do a roaring trade while portraitists have more onlookers than customers. Music from every store competes for your attention, as do the vendors of greeting cards, plastic toys, canvas slippers and so on and on. It's all part of the street life culture of Santiago.

Like all Latin Americans, Chileans have a warm, but clearly defined, way of greeting. Men and women meeting, or women and women, will kiss one another once on the cheek. Men greeting men will always shake hands. When dealing with officials, you'll find the response more agreeable if you say "Buenos Dias" and wait for the reply before you continue speaking.

Chileans have many idiosyncracies. They are not as unpunctual as other Latin Americans, but are still likely to be half an hour late for appointments.

They have a passion for discussing politics, are often concerned to show themselves either "feminine" or "macho" and can seem painfully obedient to their children's whims. Elderly men desire young female companions; younger men attract womens' attention by hissing through their teeth – an irritating but harmless feature of daily life for young women walking alone (strangely, a hiss is not considered impolite when attracting a waiters attention, either).

Young people see the images of Western liberal morality on their televisions and at the cinema, but there is a considerable amount of tension with Chile's strong strain of Roman Catholic repression.

The majority of young people in Santiago meet at bars and cafes, with smoking still very fashionable. Rock bands are popular, although references to drug-taking seem to be edited out by the authorities (in Chile, Ian Drury's famous song is referred to as "Sex and Beer and Rock and Roll"). Stifled sexuality is let loose by some in darkened corners of the city parks, while many special hotels rent rooms by the hour.

Planning The Trip

What To Bring

The rule "travel light" applies particularly if you're moving around the country, since this takes much of the worry and fatigue out of your trip. It's quite possible to leave your main luggage in Santiago and simply travel for a few weeks with hand-sized luggage, therefore making plane and coach travel a breeze.

Chile is probably the most modern country in South America, with exhaustive shopping potential in Santiago, so remember you can always pick something up fairly cheaply if you're not sure about taking it with you. Obviously your plans for traveling in Chile will determine what you should take but some items may not be easy to locate or of the quality desired.

Sensitive skins won't be adequately protected by many Chilean brands of sunblocks, so take some 15+ strength with you. A pocket knife or Swiss Army knife might come in handy. (Remember to peel all fruits before eating). Other items travelers find useful: a small sewing kit, a water container or flask for walking trips, sunglasses, swimming costume and protective clothing if applicable.

Maps

Maps are available at the Tourist Office. They will provide a plan of the town center including the metro lines and inner suburbs, called the "Plano del Centro de Santiago." Outside of Santiago each Sernatur branch office gives free maps of townships.

The best and most practical map of Chile is the *Gran Mapa Caminero de Chile,* also available at newsstands. Even more detailed than the Gran Mapa, though broken into smaller segments, is the *Atlas Caminero de Chile,* useful if you intend doing some extensive traveling. Published by Silva & Silva, Cas. 16374 Santiago, tel: 229 2298.

Excellent road maps are available from the "Automobil Club de Chile," Pedro de Valdivia 195. *Turistel* is the name of a series of Chilean guide books (in Spanish) which contain maps and other tourist information such as a hotel and camping guide. Petrol stations also sell road maps. If you are planning to drive on Easter Island, better road maps might be available in Santiago.

Topographical maps are sold by the Instituto Geographic Militar, Alameda 240, or from Conaf, General Bulnes 285, tel: 696 0783/3801.

What To Wear

Most middle-class Latin Americans spend a great deal of their incomes on their appearances and can seem overdressed at social events or dinners. Travelers shouldn't be expected to appear as immaculately groomed as residents; however, it's a wise decision, especially in Santiago, to pay a little extra care. You might receive better service in some establishments if you dress more formally, although smart casual wear is usually sufficient. If in doubt about the dress requirements, err on the formal side and you can't go wrong. Sixteen years of military rule have not encouraged Chileans to attract attention with outrageous styles.

Women in business will always wear skirts and high heels in the office, incorporating padded shoulders and bold makeup into the executive look (most also seem to sport long painted finger nails and lots of jewelry). Men are expected to wear ties and two-piece suits, presenting a highly tailored appearance in distinctly Latin color combinations. In summer you will see white suits and red ties. On weekends, jeans and T-shirts are smartly combined for parks and promenades, though more young people are looking to the United States and Europe for radical fashion cultures since the end of the dictatorship.

If traveling extensively through Chile take clothing that is most useful for all extremes of climate. Remember that Southern Chile is as cold as the northern deserts are hot, so take warm socks, gloves, headgear and a wind and waterproof jacket. Thermal underwear will come in handy if you're heading into southern regions such as the Paine National Park, Punta Arenas or Tierra del Fuego. Travelers often prefer to buy their woollen sweaters or ponchos from *artesanías* in Santiago or en route, since they are very reasonably priced and of a high quality. If you're trying to cut down on shoe luggage, take some solid walking shoes that won't look too out of place in a casual restaurant. Synthetic fabrics won't crush in your suitcase but these don't breathe as well in the hot weather. It's recommended you use your hotel's laundering service as commercial premises are almost impossible to find in Santiago and equally expensive.

Entry Regulations

Visas and Passports

All foreigners require a valid identity document. While residents of many American countries use their Identity Card to travel within the continent, all other foreigners require passports and a few of these must obtain visas.

Countries requiring visas to enter Chile include: France, New Zealand, China, India and all countries of Africa, Central America and Eastern Europe. It would be wise to check on the current situation before departing. All foreigners wishing to work in Chile require visas.

A tourist card is issued to all foreigners on arrival. This contains your identification data and is valid for 90 days. The tourist card is renewable for a further 90 days, though if you wish to stay longer than six months, it's simplest to take a short trip to an adjoining country and you will be issued with a new tourist card on your return. Renewal applications must be submitted personally at the Metropolitan Region's Intendency (Moneda 1342. Tel: 725320), open Monday through Friday 9am–2pm. The card must be surrendered when leaving the country. Don't lose it.

Customs

Arturo Merino Benitez International Airport is organized in much the same way as other major airports. During your flight you will fill out a customs declaration form and supply identity details on your tourist card. Chileans are sticklers for paperwork but quite efficient. The allowed quota of duty free goods extends to 500 cigarettes, 100 cigars, 500 grams of tobacco, 3 bottles of liquor, camera and all items for personal use. It is prohibited to import dairy products, flowers, fruit and vegetables. Most overseas visitors with "nothing to declare" find no delays passing through customs. Porters are available to assist with your luggage to a taxi, bus or private transport. A respectable tip for this service would be about US$0.50 cents. It is recommended that you have a hotel reserved for your first night in Santiago. Most major hotels have international telex or fax lines for reservations.

On departure from Santiago your hotel will organize transport to the airport. Most tourists take home samples of the excellent Chilean wine and often finely-crafted stones such as *lapiz lazuli*.

Health

Chile is one of the safest countries in South America for maintaining personal well-being. There is no malaria or yellow fever, the tap water in most cities is chlorinated and the general standard of hygiene is high. The country is fortunate to produce an abundance of fresh fruit and vegetables in its Central Region while meat products are also plentiful, thus ensuring quality foods for most people.

Precautions: Most travelers go without vaccinations. Some people have hepatitis and typhoid shots, although the possibility of encountering the diseases are remote. Just be careful of unwashed salads. Most people have no difficulty adjusting to the tap water in Santiago, although sensitive systems should use bottled mineral water and avoid the adjustment period. Sudden changes in diet and lifestyle often cause temporary bowel disorders which are nearly always nothing to worry about and just a typical part of travel. For a day or so it's best to eat very little and drink plenty of liquid in small sips. Tea without milk or flat lemonade is ideal. Symptoms should improve within 48 hours but don't celebrate recovery with a rich meal. If the problem lasts longer than a week, antibiotics, or in the case of dysentry, a visit to the doctor, may be necessary.

Pharmacies in Chile are usually well stocked with the latest medical supplies and there are also increasingly popular homeopathic outlets in most cities.

Sunburn: The only other problems come from Chile's extreme climate and geography. In both the Atacama Desert and on Easter Island the heat can cause serious exhaustion and sunburn. Don't over-estimate your skin's resistance. Bring sufficient water, sunscreen, a hat and preferably sunglasses. Even thus prepared, the sun and heat is trying to the mildest of temperaments. Take things more slowly and don't expect to achieve quite as much as usual.

Bitter cold: The other extreme lies in the far south, from Puerto Montt to Tierra del Fuego, where the bitter cold in mountain areas or in winter has the power to cause hypothermia to those who are unprotected. High winds are notorious in Patagonia, often carrying icy rain and sleet, but this can be effectively shielded with proper clothing. Again it's best to move more slowly, staying aware of your energy level. Mountain climbers should take the usual precautions: exhaustion, numbness, slurred speech and shivering are signs of hypothermia which can be very dangerous.

Though not as severe as the altitudes of Bolivia or Peru, some Andean passes between Chile and Argentina are high enough to cause slight altitude sickness in some people. The symptoms can become noticeable at around 900 meters. They include shortness of breath, headache, weakness and mild nausea. In rare cases severe altitude sickness is indicated by dizziness and intensity of the other symptoms. The immediate treatment for this condition is moving to a lower altitude.

Insurance: All travelers should invest in comprehensive travel insurance available through travel agents. Check that this will cover the cost of your return flight if you're flown home in an emergency as well as covering stolen or damaged camera equipment and so on. The fine print is usually important.

Currency

Money can be exchanged in hotels, exchange bureaus and banks. The rate varies little between establishments although the rate might not be quite as good at banks and the service is often slow. Banks are open to the public 9am–2pm, Monday through Friday. Exchange bureaux are probably the best choice. They are usually found within travel agencies and are open Monday through Friday 9.30am–2pm and 3.30pm–5.30pm. In Santiago, exchange offices and banks are located in the central business district near the corner of Bandera and Agustinas. You'll have to make your way through a number of "change money" marketeers (hissing *compro dólares*) standing on the footpath outside. Their rate is only better if you are changing dollars in cash and the outdoor transaction can be hectic, but if you want to make the few extra pesos this method is faster and is actually quite safe.

American Express checks can be changed for dollars in cash and withdrawals on your credit card can be made at the American Express office at Agustinas 1360. Visa card cash advances can only be made from the Visa office on the corner of Morandé and Huérfanos – the transaction only takes five minutes. Money can be sent to major banks from other parts of the world with minimum delays.

US dollars are the most easily exchanged unit of currency throughout Chile. In Santiago it's possible to exchange pounds sterling, Australian dollars, yen, deutschmarks and other currencies at banks, but elsewhere you'll need either US dollars cash or travelers checks from a major company like American Express or Thomas Cook. Have some smaller denominations of checks and definitely take some US currency when traveling through small towns. Some banks will only change cash and dollar bills can also be used at other establishments such as hotels and restaurants. A few dollar bills are also handy at airports.

Apart from a few military-inspired national holidays, Chile's annual calender consists of religious and folkloric festivals which are popular tourist attractions for their lively performances as well as cultural insights. Viña del Mar and the ski resorts host a number of fashionable celebrations depending on the season. As you travel through Chile you might find more organized events other than the major ones listed here.

JANUARY

1st January. **Año Nuevo en el Mar**. Outdoor new year celebrations in Valparaíso.
Fiesta de San Sebastian. Catholic festivity in Yumbel, south of the city of Chillan.
Semanas Musicales de Frutillar. Classical music festival on the shores of Lake Llanquihue.
Festival Folklórico de San Bernardo. Folkloric music festival in Santiago.

FEBRUARY

Muestra Cultural Mapuche. Traditional music and dancing of the Mapuche Indians, Lake Villarica.
International Song Festival in Viña del Mar.
Semana Valdiviana. A week long festival on Valdivia's Calle-Calle river.
Regata de las Mil Millas. One thousand mile long nautical race starting from Viña del Mar.

MARCH

Campeonato Nacional de Rodeo. Chilean rodeo championships in Rancagua.

APRIL

Easter
Fiesta de Cuasimodo. Religious and folkloric festival in Santiago.

MAY

1st May. **Labor Day**
21st May. **Commemoration of Iquique Naval Battle** national holiday.

JUNE

Inauguration celebration of Central Chile's ski season.

JULY

16th July. **La Tirana**. Native and religious festivity east of Iquique.
Festival Folklórico de la Patagonia. Southern folklore festival in Punta Arenas.
Industrial and **craft fair** in Punta Arenas.

AUGUST

15th August. **Assumption**.
Santa Rosa de Lima Celebration. Pelequen

SEPTEMBER

11th September. **Liberation Day** (national holiday).
18th September. **Independence Day** (national holiday).
19th September. **Armed Forces Day** (national holiday, military parade).

OCTOBER

Fiesta de la Virgén de Andacollo. Religious festivity near La Serena.
12th October. **Columbus Day** (national holiday).

NOVEMBER

1st November. **All Saints**.
FISA Fair, Santiago. Inauguration of summer season.
Classical music international events. Viña del Mar.

DECEMBER

8th December. **Feast of the Immaculate Conception**.
Book fair. Parque Forestal, Santiago.
Open-air art performances and craft exhibition, Parque Bustamante, Santiago.
25th December. **Christmas**.

By Air

It's possible to fly direct to Santiago from the United States and Canada. Alternatively, many travelers going to Chile take the opportunity to fly via one or more South American country.

European airlines serving Chile include British Airways, Air France, Iberia, Lufthansa, Swissair, Alitalia, KLM and SAS, each offering at least one flight per week with discounts available if flying via the United States, Brazil, Argentina, Peru or Venezuela. Fares via New York or direct to Mexico City are very reasonable.

South American airlines, Varig, Aerolineas Argentinas, Viasa and Avianca all fly to Chile from Europe with connections in Rio, Buenos Aires, Caracas and Bogotá respectively. In the UK tickets can also be obtained through specialist travel firms such as Journey Latin America (Tel: 0181-747 3108), Cox & Kings (Tel: 0171-873 5001) and South America Experience (Tel: 0171-976 5511).

US airlines fly from New York and Miami with some connections in Washington and Los Angeles.

Canadian Pacific flies regularly from Montreal and Toronto as well as from Vancouver, both routes stopping at Lima, Peru.

Two of the **Chilean airlines**, Ladeco and Lan Chile, have several flights per week each from New York via Miami. Lan Chile is the older of the two, but it is fair to say that most Chileans prefer to fly Ladeco where possible, since its in-flight service is vastly superior (although Lan Chile has recently been privatized and may have improved).

Ladeco international destinations include: in the United States, Miami, New York and Washington; in Brazil, Rio and Sao Paulo; Mexico City; Mendoza and Buenos Aires in Argentina; Guayaquil in Ecuador; Asunción in Paraguay; and Bogotá in Colombia. Lan Chile flies to most of these destinations as well as Madrid in Spain. Lan Chile also has a unique service to Tahiti via Easter Island.

The most direct route from Australia or New Zealand is with Qantas or UTA to Tahiti, connecting with the weekly Lan Chile flight – which also makes a handy stop at Easter Island en route to Santiago.

An interesting alternative is to fly Air New Zealand to Auckland, and then take the direct flight with Aerolineas Argentinas across a corner of Antarctica to Buenos Aires. From here there are more than 30 flights a week to Santiago and, in addition, a number of attractive overland routes.

Ladeco and Lan Chile offer domestic flight packages for foreign travelers called "Visit Chile" passes (see Getting Around). Conditions however, require that passes must be purchased outside of Chile. Ladeco services slightly more cities within Chile.
Ladeco International Offices
Argentina: Reconquista 341, 6th

Floor, Buenos Aires, tel: (54) (1) 325-9701, 325-7840.

Australia: 6/16 Nelson Street, Fairfield, NSW, 2165, tel: (2) 728-4749. Toll free (61) (008) 28-2589.

Brazil: Sao Paulo: Sao Luiz 170, tel: (55) (11) 257-8844. Rio de Janeiro: Rio Branco 277, tel: (55) (21) 220-0299.

Colombia: Calle 100 No. 8 A-49, 8th Floor, World Trade Center, Bogotá, tel: (57) (1) 611-1533, 218-3391, 218-9526.

Ecuador: Quito: Pinto 521 y Av. Amazonas, tel: (593) (2) 52-2590. Guayaquil: Malecon 1401 esq. Illingworth, tel: (593) (4) 32-8475, 32-4360.

Mexico: Tlacotaplan No. 37, Col. Roma, Sur 06760, Mexico City, tel: (52) (5) 654-3600, 564-3610, 564-3621.

Panama: Urb. Obarrio, 59 Street, Yasa Building, Panama City, tel: (507) 64-1444.

Peru: Francia 597, Lima, tel: (51) (14) 47-9798

United States/Canada: Toll free (1) 800-825 2332. Miami: 1 Biscayne Tower, Suite 2690, Miami Fla 33131, tel: (1) (305) 371-2795, 371-2799. New York: 1140 6th Avenue, 8th Floor, New York City, tel: (1) (212) 730-1002, 244-6281. Los Angeles: 510 W 6th Street, Suite 422, Los Angeles, California, 90015, tel: (1) (213) 627-2323. Philadelphia: 400 Market Street, Suite 555, Philadelphia PA, 19106, tel: (1) (215) 440-7344. Houston: 6000 Sugar Hill No. 6, Houston, Texas 77057, tel: (1) (713) 827-7120.

By Road

Chilean coach companies maintain surprisingly comfortable conditions for long distance travel and for private motoring the country roadways are excellent. There is no shortage of international services and the journeys, especially through the Lake District, are scenically spectacular. From Argentina, there are quite a number of overland routes – the popular journey Buenos Aires/Santiago takes about 24 hours.

The crossing from Peru goes from Tacna to Arica in the extreme north of Chile. From Bolivia there's a poorer quality road from La Paz to Arica. Bus companies frequently undertake these journeys.

There are two main bus terminals in Santiago managing nearly all international and domestic traffic. (See *Getting Around* for details).

Most international coach companies depart from **Terminal de Buses Santiago**, Av. B. O'Higgins 384, tel: 791385.

However, companies taking the route to Mendoza in Argentina depart from **Terminal de Buses Norte**. Amunategui 920 (cnr Mackenna), tel: 712141.

The international coach companies include: Fenix, Pullman Norte, Chile Bus, Pluma, Tas Choapa Int. The Pluma company makes an epic three-day journey to Rio de Janerio via Mendoza and Sao Paulo.

There are also *collectivos* (taxis) to Mendoza departing from the same Terminal de Buses Santiago.

By Rail

International rail travel is infrequent and sparse. There are rail links from La Paz and Calama in Bolivia to Arica and Antofagasta, which take 18 and 26 hours respectively. There is also a rail link from Salta in the north west of Argentina to Antofagasta. Most of the country's rail network is operated by the state owned Ferrocarriles del Estado.

By Sea

Lykes Line voyages from New Orleans to Valparaíso via the Panama Canal taking 20 days. Promotorta de Navigación in Panama has three ship sailing from Vancouver to Valpariso. For other shipping companies, contact your travel agent.

UK: Chilean Embassy, 12 Devonshire Street, London W1N 1FS, tel: 0171-734 4176.

US: Chilean Embassy, 1732 Massachusetts Avenue NW, Washington DC, tel: 202 785 1746.

Practical Tips

Business Hours

Banks are open to the public Monday through Friday 9am–2pm. Exchange bureaux are open Monday through Friday 9.30am–2pm and 3.30–5.30pm.

Government offices are open to the public for a few hours only, 10am–12.30pm. Other businesses are open 8.30am–12.30pm and then 2pm–6pm, Monday to Friday.

Most shops in Santiago are open 10.30am–7.30pm Monday to Friday and 9.30am–1.30pm on Saturday.

In the major shopping centers, such as Apumanque and Parque Aravco shops are open throughout the week, including Sunday until 9pm.

Media

Broadcast: There are many AM and FM radio stations and seven television stations currently broadcasting in the country.

Print: Approximately 50 newspapers are published and sold throughout the nation – probably the most widely read is the conservative morning daily *El Mercurio*, which first appeared in 1827. Every Friday it publishes a supplement called *Wikén*, informing about cultural, artistic and tourist events going on in town. Others include: *La Nacion*, *La Epoca*, *La Segunda* and *La Tercera*. Weekly magazines include: *Hoy*, *Que Pasa*, *Analisis*. *Ercilla* and *Panorama Economico* are the best economic journals. Street vendors sell *Newsweek*, *Time* and a varying selection of rather out of date international newspapers.

Postal Services

Chilean post is more reliable than that of most South American countries. Mail sent by air, (*por aéreo*), takes around four days to the United Kingdom or 10 days to Australia. Seamail takes about 10 weeks. There is a daily airmail service to Europe with connections to the United Kingdom. The Poste Restante (Lista de Correos) in Santiago is located in the central post office on the Plaza de Armas. The system is fairly well organized, although they will hold your mail no longer than 30 days before returning to sender. The Post Office is open Monday to Friday 8am–7pm; Saturday and Sunday 8am–noon.

Telecoms

International telephone and telegraph services are provided by Entel Offices, Transradio Chilena and Cia Internacional de Radio, although telephone calls can be made direct, without assistance, to many overseas countries. For further information call 123. It is possible to call collect and the quality of the lines is excellent. The Entel Office on Huérfanos has 26 telephone booths and an upstairs facsimile service which is unrivalled in its efficiency. There are "normal" and "reduced" rates for international phone calls, depending on the time of day.
United States: Normal rate: Monday to Friday 8.30am–7pm. Reduced rate: 7–10pm.
Europe/Australia/Japan: Normal rate: Monday to Friday 8.30am–2pm. Reduced rate: 2–10pm.
Facsimile Rates: It is relatively expensive to send a fax from Chile, with the peak rate, between 10am and 6pm, nearly twice the off-peak rate. Sending faxes to the US, however, stays at a low rate throughout the day.
Entel hours of business: Monday to Friday 8.30–10am, 1–4pm, 6–10pm; Saturday 9–10am, 1–10pm; Sunday and festivals 9am–10pm.

Telex is a popular form of communication within the country, many hotels taking reservations this way. There are many offices in Santiago that render national and international services. There is a telegram and telex office on Morande, facing the Plaza de la Constitucion (corner Agustinos). A telegram to the United Kingdom, with a minimum of seven words, is around US$4, while a three-minute telex call would cost US$6.

Aeroflot, Av. 11 Septiembre 21, Torre C, Off. 701, tel: 232 7439.
Aerolineas Argentinas, Moneda 765, tel: 639 5001.
Aeroperú, Fidel Oteiza Vargas 1953, 5th Floor, tel: 639 5001.
Air France, Agustinas 1136, tel: 672 5333.
Air New Zealand, Andres de Fuenzalida 17, Off. 62, tel: 233 5344.
Alitalia, Av. B. O'Higgins 949, Off. 1003-1001, tel: 698 3336.
American Airlines, Huérfanos 1199, tel: 671 6266.
Avianca, Moneda 1140, 6th Floor, tel: 695 4105.
British Airways, Isodora Goyenechea 2934, Off. 302, tel: 232 9560.
Canadian Airlines, Huérfanos 669, Off. 201, tel: 639 3058.
Iberia, Agustinas 1115, tel: 698 3590.
KLM, San Sebastian 2839, Off. 201, tel: 233 0991.
LACSA, Fidel Oteiza 1921, Off. 703, tel: 209 7477.
Ladeco, Av. Lib. B. O'Higgins 107, tel: 633 8343.
Lan Chile, Estado 10, tel: 632 3211.
Lufthansa, Moneda 970, 16th Floor, tel: 630 1000.
Lloyd Aereo Boliviano, Moneda 1170, tel: 671 2334.
Qantas, Isidora Goyenechea 2934, Off. 302, tel: 232 9562.
Swissair, Estado 10, 15th Floor, tel: 633 7018.
TAP Air Portugal, Av. 11 Septiembre 2250, Off. 603, tel: 233 2474.
United Airlines, Av. B. O'Higgins 949, Off. 2301, tel: 699 0055.
Varig, Miraflores 156, tel: 639 5261.
VIASA, Tenderini 82, 6th Floor, tel: 639 5001.

Embassies and Consulates in Santiago

Argentina: Miraflores 286, tel: 633 1076.
Australia: Gertrudis Echenique 420, tel: 228 5065.
Bolivia: Av. Santa Maria 2796, tel: 232 8180.
Brazil: Alonso Ovalie 1665, tel: 688 2347.
Canada: Ahumada 11, 10th Floor, tel: 696 2256.

New Zealand: Isidora Goyenechea 3516, tel: 231 4204.
Peru: Av. Andrés Bello 1751, tel: 232 6275.
South Africa: Av. 11 de Decembre 2353. Tel 231 2682.
United Kingdom: El Bosque Norte 0125, tel: 231 3737.
United States: Embassy, Agustinas 1343. Consulate, Merced 230, tel: 710133.

Emergencies

For any emergency service except the police, call 119. Or call the following numbers:
Police: 133
Police Information: 139
International Police: 719849 (to enter Chile); 719304 (for exiting Chile)
Investigations: 134
Fire Brigade: 132
Tourist Card Extension: Intendencia Region Metropolitana, Moneda 1342, tel: 725320. Hours: 9am–2pm Monday to Friday.

Chile has very modern medical facilities and there are a number of good hospitals in Santiago and other cities. **Clínica Las Condes, Santa Maria and Clínica Aleman** (Av. Vitacura 5951, tel: 229 0515) are a few reliable choices.

Check with your hotel or embassy for a list of physicians who speak your language.

Getting Around

Orientation

Santiago is a sprawling city, but the city center is relatively small and easy to explore. "El centro" is roughly triangular-shaped, bounded on one side by the enormous Avenida del Libertador General Bernado O'Higgins, or more conveniently known as Alameda, on another side by the muddy Mapocho River and on the third by the North South Highway.

In the center is the Plaza de Armas, a city square common to most Spanish founded cities in South America.

Another typical feature is the grid pattern of city streets, which couldn't be simpler for your orientation – although keep in mind that the street names change on either side of the plaza. Here you'll find the Correo Central, the Cathedral and a string of outdoor cafes and restaurants all contributing to the general city din.

Between the plaza and Alameda is where the real hive of business activity can be found, with wall to wall office blocks, shops, hotels and cinemas. The throngs of office workers have necessitated pedestrian walkways on Huérfanos and Ahumada but even these blocks are congested with vendors of all kinds.

The Alameda continues into Avenida Providencia and the suburb of the same name. The "Sernatur" Tourist Office is located here, (on the metro line), so it's not as inconvenient a location as first suspected. English is spoken by some staff members and apart from maps or any questions you need answered, they have pamphlets listing important information such as train, bus destinations and timetables and so on.

Sernatur – Servicio National de Turismo, 1550 Providencia Ave, PO Box 14082, Santiago, Chile, tel: 698 2151. The nearest metro station is the Montt Station. Another office is located at the international airport. Hours: Summer 9am–7pm; Winter 8.30am–5.30pm; Saturday 9am–noon.

From The Airport

If possible, arrange your hotel by facsimile or telex before arriving at Arturo Merino Benitez International Airport. Although it's not impossible to arrange once you have arrived, telephones at the airport are not reliable, the tourist office is often closed and some hotels are difficult when making reservations over the phone.

As in most of the world's airports, many taxi drivers will try to overcharge foreigners, particularly those who do not know much Spanish. Therefore, fix the fair with the taxi driver before starting out. Occasionally the taxi driver changes the tariff once you have arrived, so be very clear about the price. The "centro" is 26 km (16 miles) from the airport.

An alternative to the taxi rank is the Tour Express airport bus. Leaving every half hour it terminates at Moneda 1523 on the metro line, which is not very convenient for travelers with luggage and hotel reservations.

Private transport is the most agreeable means of escape from the airport. The major car rental firms have offices in front of the airport.

Domestic Travel

Domestic travel in Chile is surprisingly comfortable considering the country's difficult topography. The easiest and most convenient mode of transport is to fly. The popularity of this has kept services growing and prices competitive for the three main airlines. The quality of the main highways enables fast and comfortable coach services as well as allowing for problem-free private transport. Where roads end, passenger shipping covers some of the important tourist regions, and trains to the south provide a novel and inexpensive alternative. The long thin shape of the country makes planning an itinerary quite straightforward as most transportation simply continues either north or south.

By Air

Flying long distances in Chile can be no more expensive than the sum cost of coach travel and accommodation, unless you take a direct coach. There are three major airlines with high quality domestic flights and their prices are low compared to the United States or Europe. Ladeco services slightly more cities than Lan Chile and is generally considered superior by Chileans.

Note that the airlines have night flights at least once a week between Santiago and Arica, Iquique and Puerto Montt, with up to 40 percent reductions on the fare. Ask at your travel agent about the latest details of any special package for foreigners or other deals.

Comodoro Arturo Merino Benitez International Airport, Santiago Tel: (02) 6019709.

AIRLINES

The regional telephone numbers of the three major domestic airlines are:
Antofagasta: Lan Chile 265151; Ladeco 269170; National 226520.

Arica: Lan Chile 251641; Ladeco 224664; National 221649.
Calama: Lan Chile 211477; Ladeco 312626.
Copiapó: Lan Chile 213512; National 218951.
Coihaique: Lan Chile 231188; Ladeco 231300.
Easter IsLand: Lan Chile 223279.
Iquique: Lan Chile 412540; Ladeco 413038; National 428702.
La Serena: Lan Chile 225981; Ladeco 225753; National 213540.
Osorno: Lan Chile 236688; Ladeco 234355.
Puerto Montt: Lan Chile 253141; Ladeco 252055; National 258277.
Punta Arenas: Lan Chile 243339; Ladeco 213204; National 221634.
Santiago Center: Lan Chile 6323442; Ladeco 6338343; National 6322698.
Providencia: Lan Chile 2328712; Ladeco 2520317; National 2520300.
Temuco: Lan Chile 211339; Ladeco 214070; National 239001.
Valdivia: Lan Chile 213042; Ladeco 213392; National 215970.
Valparaíso: Lan Chile 251441; Ladeco 216355.
Viña del Mar: Ladeco 978210; National 907368.

TO JUAN FERNANDEZ

Santiago: Robinson Crusoe 531 3772; Lassa 273 4309.

IN AISEN

Coihaique: San Rafael 233408; Don Carlos 231981.
Chaitén: Aerosur 731228.
Futaleufu: Aerosur 721268.
Palena: Aerosur 741261.
Puerto Montt: San Rafael 259551; Don Carlos 253219; Aerosur 252523; Sapse 259490.

IN MAGALLANES

Punta Arenas: Dap 223340; Cabo de Hornos 241321.

By Bus & Coach

Traveling by coach in Chile is probably the easiest in South America and the main way of getting around the country. The vehicles are well maintained, clean and comfortable. They always depart on schedule, refreshments are provided on board and smoking is prohibited. For long trips, you have the luxurious option of traveling on a sleeper bus (*bus cama*), with first class seating arrangements similar to that on planes. These buses are reputedly very comfortable and include meals and wine, color TV, stereo headphones and hostess service.

Ensure when traveling by bus you do not lose either your token for any baggage placed under the bus or your ticket stub which must be surrendered to the driver at the end of the journey in order to check that the correct fare has been paid.

It is illegal to transport any type of seafood on buses. The officials of SAG (the Ministry of Agriculture) conduct rigorous searches at all international borders and several regional borders confiscating all fresh fruit and vegetables and sometimes bread and dairy products. SAG checkpoints are clearly marked on road maps.

Traveling by coach is inexpensive and the routes are so well serviced you rarely need to book more than a few hours in advance. In Santiagio there are two main coach stations serving different destinations in Chile.

FROM SANTIAGO TO THE NORTH.

La Serena–Copiapó–Antofagasta–Iquique–Arica

Terminal de Buses Norte, Amunategui 920. Bus operators: Buses Evans, tel: 698 5953; Buses Geminis, tel: 697 2132; Flota Barrios, tel: 698 1494; Tramaca, tel: 672 6840.

Terminal Los Heroes, Tucapel Jimenez 21. Bus operators: Fenix, tel: 696 9089; Flota Barrios, tel: 696 9311; Tramaca, tel: 696 9323.

In Torres de Tajamar, Av. Providencia 1072. Bus operators: Fenix, tel: 235 9707; Tramaca, tel: 235 1965.

FROM SANTIAGO TO THE SOUTH.

Temuco–Osorno–Puerto Montt

Terminal Alameda, Av. Lib. B. O'Higgins 3724. Bus operators: Tur Bus, tel: 776 3690.

Terminal Los Heroes, Roberto Pretot 21. Bus Operators: Cruz del Sur, tel: 696 9324.

Terminal Santiago, Av. Lib. B. O'Higgins 3848. Bus operators: Tur Bus, tel: 779 0588; Cruz del Sur, tel: 779 0607; Bus Norte, tel: 779 5433; Igi Llaima, tel: 779 1751.

By Rail

Trains are worth considering for long journeys as a change to coach travel and if you appreciate older style wooden interiors, some of the earlier German-built trains have quaint and plush sleeper compartments (*camarotes*). Although a little worn, they are accompanied by excellent old-fashioned service. Bunks only are available at a cheaper rate in a separate carriage; you can also choose *salon classe*, which is a coach style reclining seat. *Economico* is the cheapest and not so comfortable, especially in winter.

The Tourist Office has a leaflet called *Movimiento de Trenes* listing the current train timetable. There is no passenger service to Northern Chile or to the coastal towns, Viña del Mar and Valparaíso. There is one overnight departure from Santiago to Puerto Montt via Talca, Chillan, Temuco, Valdivia, Osorno and Puerto Varas. For information and reservation in Santiago, phone Estación Alameda (689 5401), Santiago Centro (632 2801) or Metro Esc Militar (228 2983).

The railway's Central Office is located at Av. B. O'Higgins 853, Office 21. Open Monday to Friday, 9am–6pm; Saturday 9am–1pm. For information and reservations, tel: 91682/91825, 95199/95401 or 95718, between 7.30am–10.30pm.

The railroad terminal for southbound traffic only is Estacion Alameda, Av. B. O'Higgins 3322. This is a grandiose iron-worked archway, worth a visit even if you are not taking a train.

By Boat

PUERTO MONTT TO PUERTO CHACABUCO

Navimag operates a regular Ro-Ro ship, which once a week in January and February makes a detour to the San Raphael glacier. Their offices are located at the following ports of call:
Santiago, Av. El Bosque Norte 0440. Tel/fax: 203 5030.
Puerto Montt, Angelmo 2187, tel: 253318; fax: 258540.
Puerto Chacabuco, Terminal de Transbordadores, tel: 351111.
Coihaique, Pdte. Ibanez 347, tel: 233306.
Puerto Natales, Av. Pedro Montt 380, tel: 411421; fax: 411642.

Punta Arenas, Av. Independencia 840, tel: 244448; fax: 247514.
Transmarchilay operates a regular Ro-Ro ship.
Santiago, Agustinas 715, Off 403. Tel/fax: 633 5959.
Puerto Montt, Angelmo 2187, tel: 254654; fax: 253683.

PUERTO MONTT TO SAN RAPHAEL

CNP operates a regular service:
Santiago, Av. Providencia 199, 5th Floor, tel: 274 8150; fax: 205 2197.
Puerto Montt, Av. Diego Portales 882. Tel/fax: 252547.
M/N Skorpios. Weekly departure.
Santiago, Augusto Leguia Norte 118, Las Condes, tel: 231130.
Puerto Montt, Angelmo 1660, tel: 252619.

TERMAS DE PUYUHUAPI TO SAN RAPHAEL

Catamaran Patagonia Express
Santiago, Fidel Otelza 1921, Off 1005, tel: 225 6489; fax: 274 8111.
Puerto Montt, D. Portales 872, tel: 259790.

PUERTO MONTT TO PUERTO NATALES

Transmarchilay operates a Ro-Ro service three times a month. (*See* previous listing).

THE SOUTHERN CHANNELS

Navimag organizes seven day cruises. (*See* previous listing).

Other charter boats operate from Puerto Montt, Puerto Chacabuco, Puerto Natales and Punta Arenas but run subject to demand.

From the beginning of March the ferry service from Hornopiren on the Carretera Austral is suspended for the winter. Alternative services run from Chiloé to Chaiten.

The Lake District offers dozens of spectacular boating options. The trip from Petrohué to Puella across Lago Todos Los Santos, is the first leg of the "Journey of the Seven Lakes," a magnificent route to Bariloche in Argentina. The launch run by "Transportes Lagos del Sur" receives the best ratings.

Public Transportation

Santiago's **metro** must be one of the best in the world for comfort and efficiency. There are two lines operating every three minutes: one runs beneath Av. B. O'Higgins and on through

Providencia, the other lies beneath Balmaceda. Buy tickets at the various stations – US25c per ticket or US$2 for a book of 10 – then just insert your ticket into a slot in the turnstile and pass through. The turnstile keeps your ticket.

There are a huge number of **buses** roaring through the city streets appearing to follow no fixed schedule. The bus system is basically unfathomable but here's a guide: North bound buses will collect passengers on McIver and Miraflores, while south bound transport is on San Antonio or Teatinos. The fare is US30c. You'll see people queuing at intervals on these streets. All types of buses have signs in their windscreens displaying the destination and fare.

Taxis are black with yellow roofs. They each display their flagfall, US50c, in the windscreen and the rate per 200 meters, between p$7 and p$21, or 2 cents and 6 cents. These fares depend on the condition of the car or the nature of the driver. It's a free market. Flagfall is likely to double at night, after 9pm. All taxis have meters that should be turned on when you enter the car, although some drivers conveniently forget. Most city taxi drivers, however, are friendly and trustworthy and this is a very economical means of transport.

Collectivos are even cheaper, but the routes they take are limited. They are simply taxis who take several different passengers for a flat rate on a fixed route. The price is usually US40c and US50c and the routes are similar to those of the buses.

Private Transportation
By Car

See the *Maps* section for locating detailed road maps if you're planning to drive in Chile. Car hire in Chile is generally considered to be expensive, especially in the provinces. In some places it is well worth the cost, however. For example, Easter Island is a difficult area to explore alone without a car, and having one's own transport in the Lake District opens up many more opportunities. With a car you can take advantage of the private cabins set away from the towns amongst spectacular scenery. Many travelers share the costs and find the whole business hassle-free.

Car drivers should make sure they have the original registration document of their vehicle. There is an adequate number of modern service stations on the tourist routes and fuel is US50c per litre.

Hertz is the largest car rental network in Chile, having branch offices in all major cities of the north and key locations in central and south Chile. Main Office: Av. Costanera 1469, tel: 223 7937/225 9328 and at the airport, tel: 719262.

The Automovil Club de Chile also rents cars and has clubs throughout Chile.

Chilean Rent-a-Car at Bellavista 0150, seems to have very competitive rates. Reservations/Information, tel: 376902, 379650.

Other major companies are Budget, Avis, National Dollar.

Some companies offer weekly rates with unlimited kilometers. Approximate car hire rates are as follows:
US$65 per day with unlimited km plus insurance, US$6 (per day).
US$230 per week, with unlimited km plus insurance, US$40, plus deposit of US$700.
US$15 per day, plus US15c per km plus insurance at US$6 (per day).

Santiago Metro

On Foot

Keep in mind that the Santiago city center, especially between the Plaza de Armas and Alameda, is incredibly hectic and congested during the working week and you'll find yourself tiring very quickly and in need of a quiet retreat.

In summer the center is hot and polluted, so don't plan very much on foot in this area unless you walk slowly and don't mind the jostling. It probably helps to keep to the right hand side of the walkway and make clear your direction. Huérfanos is slightly better than the narrow footpaths, but hardly easy strolling.

Difficult as it is, the city center has a wealth of historical landmarks so a few walks are recommended in the *Attractions* section. Santiago also affords pleasant strolls through parks, such as Santa Lucia hill, the leafy laneways of Bellavista or the Baquedano area and the sophisticated arcades of Providencia. The streets are unnaturally desolate on Sunday, the perfect condition for taking in the sights on foot. Even Huérfanos is deserted!

Excursions

Arica

Taxis or *collectivos* can easily be arranged to make the 32 km (20 mile) round trip up the Azapa Valley to see the geoglyphs on the hillsides, visit Inca fortresses, pukaras, and the archaeological museum which contains the fascinating chinchorro mummies.

A trip to the Lauca National Park 260km (160 mile) east of Arica is an absolute must and can be arranged through any travel agency. It is recommended to spend a night in Putre and make a detour to the ritual villages of Socoroma and Parinacota which is surrounded by marshy bofedal, rich with birdlife and herds of grazing camelids. If equipped with a sleeping bag it is possible to spend the night at the CONAF ranger station by Lake Chungara.

A few recommended tour operators are listed below:

Turismo Payachatas, Bolognesi 332, tel: 251518; fax: 251514.
Jurasi Tour, Bolognesi 360 A, tel: 32635.

Agencia Globo Tour, 21 de Mayo 260, tel: 232909.
Huasquitour, Sotomayor 470, tel: 223875.
Kijo Tour, Bolognesi, 357, tel: 232245.

Iquique

Tours are available to the oases villages of Pica and Matilla which are famous for their soft fruits and date palms. The road passes through La Tirana, normally a sleepy village except in July when 80,000 pilgrims arrive to celebrate the festival of the Virgin of Carmen.

Another popular attraction is Humberstone, a large nitrate mining ghost town, with enormous geoglyphs decorating the surrounding hills. Tours visiting the ghost towns can be combined with a trip to the hot thermal springs in the picturesque village of Mamina.

Recommended tour operators are:
Iquitour, Tarapacá 465 B, tel: 412415.
Agencia de Viajes Pucara, Thompson 402, tel: 412634; fax: 411521.
Turismo Abiq Yala, Baquedano 1282, tel: 422676.
Turismo Agreement, Galeria Lynch. Local 3–4, tel: 420224.
Turismo Lirima, Av. Baquedano 823, tel: 413094.

Calama

There is a half day free tour of Chuquicamata copper mine with breathtaking views of the largest open cast pits in the world. *Collectivos* run regular services from the center of town to the mine.

Hotels and tour operators can arrange trips to the most interesting villages in the area – Chiu Chiu, Ayquina and Caspana – with their famous churches, thatched buildings and a lifestyle which has changed little since Inca times. Contact:
Turismo El Sol, Abaroa 1614, tel: 319054.

San Pedro De Atacama

Surrounded by historical sites which can be visited on foot, this is an ideal base for longer excursions. The Hosterias and tour agencies all run dawn trips to the geysers at El Tatio (watch where you step) and to the lakes on the Atacama salt flat which

are Pink Flamingo breeding grounds. Fleets of vehicles make excursions to watch the sun set in the Valle de la Luna (Valley of the Moon), a fascinating tourist destination.

Recommended tour operators are:
Expediciones San Pedro de Atacama, La Plaza. Tel: 23.
Nativa Expediciones, Calle Caracoles. Tel: 44.
Turismo Ochoa, Toconao. Tel; 22

Antofagasta

Excursions can be made by bus, taxi or with tour groups to the derelict nitrate *oficinas* as well as to Maria Elena and Pedro de Valdivia, the last two left in production. There is some dramatic coastal scenery north of the town including La Portada, a giant rock rising out of the sea.

Contact:
Tatio Travel Service, Latorre 2579, Local 20, tel: 269144.
Corssa Turismo, San Martin 2769, tel: 251190.

Chañaral

This is an ideal base from which to visit the Pan de Azucar National Park which has a strange ecosystem caused by the dense sea mists, *camanchaca*, that drift across the hills. Boat trips can also be made to Pan de Azucar island which has colonies of Humbolt penguins, sealions and abundant bird life.

For details on tours contact:
Julio Palma, Comercio 116, tel: 480062.

Copiapó

The Andes are at their most magnificent in this region and several agencies organize excursions to visit Ojos de Salado (Chile's highest peak of 6,893 metres/22,625 ft) and the awe inspiring Laguna Verde. This region is one of the best in the world for its variety of cactii and if you are lucky enough you will see the desert burst into flower.

Recommended tour operators are:
Expediciones Puna Atacama, Piloto Marcial Arredondo 154, tel: 212684.
Turismo Atacama, Los Carrera 716, tel: 212712; fax: 217357.
Turismo Adventure Ojos del Salado, O'Higgins 150, tel: 217278.
Cactus Tour, Talcahuano 357, tel: 211129.

La Serena

Famous for its beaches, this is also one of the most important centres for astronomers and visits can be arranged to the Tololo, Las Campanas and La Silla observatories. An interesting day trip can be made along the Elqui valley, famous for its Pisco and the birthplace of Nobel Laureat Gabriella Mistral.

Tour operators include:

Agencia de Viajes Bartolomé Ltda, Balmaceda 417.

Giratour, Arturo Prat, tel: 223535; fax: 225742.

Turismo Videomundo, Balmaceda 856, tel: 224676.

Santiago

You could be blinded by the choice of tour services in Santiago. Actually many of them are affiliated in some way and the tours offered will be basically the same at each office. All seem to offer a city tour which starts from your hotel and visits many of the landmarks listed in the *Attractions* section. The cost is around US$30. Night tours include a view from San Cristobal Hill, and a restaurant meal with floorshow for US$60.

There are various day excursions to Viña del Mar and Valparaíso, visiting the lush Chilean vineyards en route, and including lunch at an elegant restaurant for US$30. More specific tours to certain vineyards to purchase and sample the wines are popular. These tours offer a narrated journey through colonial cellars such as at the **Concha y Toro** Vineyard and scenic drive through the Maipo's River Canyon. At weekends a number of buses make the day trip to the natural open air hot mineral water baths "Termas de Colina" where it is possible to escape the fumes of the city and enjoy the mountain scenery.

Day trips are also made to Portillo or Farellones for a taste of pure mountain air and some excellent ski-slopes.

The Tourist office will give you a long list of travel agencies. A few are recommended here:

Tour Maysa, Paseo Ahumada 6, Off. 42, tel: 696 4468.

Tour Service, Teatinos 333, Off. 1001, tel: 696 0415. (Branches: Holiday Inn Crowne Plaza, tel: 330642; Hotel Sheraton, tel: 623 8551).

Andina del Sud, Bombero Ossa, 1010, Off. 301, tel: 697 1010.

Sportstour, Teatinos 333, 10th Floor, tel: 696 0415.

Turismo Cocha, Av. El Bosque Norte, 0430, tel: 230 1000; fax: 203 5110.

For white water rafting:

Altué Expediciones, Encomenderos 83, tel: 232 1103; fax: 233 6799.

Grado Diez Expediciones, Las Urbinas 56, tel: 234 4130; fax: 234 4138.

Temuco

In the heart of the Mapuche Indian homeland two trips can be made which pass through their reserves, *reducciones*. A 92 km (58 mile) round trip through Chol Chol and Nueva Imperial can be made by local bus or by arrangement with a taxi driver. A longer trip of 400 km (250 miles) to the source of the Bio Bio river at Liucura offers the added opportunity to visit the Conguillio National Park, dominated by Llaima Volcano and containing forests and Araucaria monkey puzzle trees. Accommodation is available at Curacautin and Melipeuco where the owner of Hosteria Hue-Telen organizes tours into the park. This trip is best done with the freedom offered by a hire car and Temuco is a good place to do this being close to the heart of the Lake District.

For details on tours contact:

Agencia de Viajes Christopher, Arturo Prat 696, Off. 419, tel: 211680.

Pucón

Pucón is a resort town that comes alive during the holiday seasons. In summer the tour operators are busily running groups to the various *Termas* (thermal springs), white water rafting, volcano climbing, cycling and so on.

The Tourist Office has tours for five people or more to the Termas de Palguin for US$5 per person, or to the 12 km mark on the slope of Volcán Villarrica.

Tour companies include:

Anden Sports Tours, O'Higgins 535–A, tel: 441236.

Turismo Sol y Nieve, O'Higgins, tel: 441070.

For white water rafting see Altué and Grado Diez under Santiago listing.

Valdivia

Half-day boat tours are made to the mouth of the Rio Calle at Corral, Niebla and Isla Mancera to see 17th-century Spanish fortress ruins. The Motonave boats, Rio Calle Calle and Neptuno, run between 1.30 and 6.30pm and cost around US$15.

Recommended tour operators are:

Agencia Cochrane, Arauco 435, tel: 212213.

Turismo 2000, Arauco 175, Local 4, tel: 212233.

Turismo Conosur, Maipu 129, tel: 212757.

The boat companies include Calle Calle, Empreturic, Neptuno and they have their offices on Av. Arturo Prat which runs alongside the river.

Petrohué

From Petrohué there are regular boats which make one day or shorter trips across Lago Todos Los Santos, some of which include lunch at Hotel Peulla on the far side. Those tours can begin in Puerto Varas or Puerto Montt.

Puerto Montt

This is the gateway to the Lake District, Chiloé Island and Southern Patagonia with excellent bus services to other regions as well. The most interesting way of traveling to Argentina is by the combination of buses and boats which start by crossing Lago Todos Los Santos. This journey is operated by Andina del Sud and can be made in one or two days, finishing in Bariloche.

Ancud and Castro on Chiloé Island can easily be visited in a day with one of several regular buses all of which leave from the very efficient bus terminal on the seafront.

At Puerto Varas, a number of companies organize white water rafting trips down the Petrohué river as well as excursions to the summit of Osorno Volcano.

Tour companies include:

Andina del Sud, Antonio Varas 437. Tel/fax: 257797.

Travellers Patagonia, Av. Angelmo. Tel/fax: 258555.

Safari Tehuel'che, Antonio Varas 449, tel: 259490.

Rosse Turismo, Antonio Varas 445, tel: 257040.

At Puerto Varas:

Expediciones Aqua Motion, Imperial 0699. Tel/fax: 232747.

Eco Travel, Costanera, tel: 233222.

Castro-Chiloé

The most interesting excursions involve short boat trips to the smaller islands of the archipelago and Pehuen Expediciones have different trips each day of the week. Achao on the island of Quinchao can be visited using the regular bus service which visits Dalcahue also. One of the most beautiful beaches in Chile is at Cucao on the Pacific coast where horse excursions and treks into the Chiloé National Park can be made. Basic accommodation is available in Cucao.

Recommended tour operators are:
Pehuen Expediciones, Thompson 229, tel: 5254; fax: 2432.
Chiloé Tours, Blanco 318, tel: 5952.

Coihaique

Numerous trips are possible in this area of lakes, glaciers and mountains. From December to April the area is a center for trout and salmon fishermen.

For details on tours contact:
Expediciones Coihaique, Simon Bolivar 94, tel: 232300.

Puerto Natales

This is the starting point for excursions to Torres del Paine National Park and further north to El Calafate in Argentina where the southern ice field forms the Moreno glacier.

From Puerto Natales regular boat trips operate to both the Balmaceda and Serrano glaciers.

Recommended tour operators are:
Andes Patagonicos Expeditions, Blanco Encalada 226. Tel/fax: 411594.
Knudsen Tours, Blanco Encalada 284. Tel/fax: 411531.

Punta Arenas

A number of boat excursions depart from the Punta Arenas. One of the shortest goes to the penguin colony on Magdalena Island. A longer land trip of 265 km (165 miles) to Lago Blanco is worth making to see the virgin forests and abundant wildlife around the lake.

Tour companies include:
Turismo Cabo de Hornos, Munoz Gamero 1039, tel: 241321.
Turismo Aventur, Jose Nogueira 1255, tel: 241197; fax: 243354.
Turismo Pehoé, 21 de Mayo 1464, tel: 241373.

Tourist Offices (Sernatur)

Ancud: Edificio Transmarchilay, Libertad 655 Off. 3, tel. 656.
Antofagasta: Baquedano 360, 2nd Floor, tel: 223004.
Arica: Prat 375, 2nd Floor, tel: 232101.
Chillan: Centro Historico Cultural. Chillan Viejo. Av. Bernado O'Higgins altura 250, tel: 223272.
Concepcion: Caupolican 567, Off. 908, tel: 229201. Information: Anibal Pinto 460, tel: 227976.
Copiapó: Los Carreras 691, tel: 212838.
Coihaique: Cochrane 320 1st Floor, tel: 221752.
Iquique: Anibal Pinto 436, tel: 21499.
Isla De Pascua (Easter Island): Tu'u Maheka, cnr Apina, tel: 255.
La Serena: Prat cnr Matta, 1st floor, tel: 213134.
Osorno: Edificio Gobernacion 1st Floor, tel: 234104.
Puerto Montt: Edificio Intendencia 2nd Floor, tel: 254580.
Punta Arenas: Waldo Seguel 689, tel: 224435.
Rancaqua: German Riesco 277, Off. 11 & 12, tel: 225777.
Santiago: Av. Providencia 1550, tel: 698 2151, 696 0474; Tlx: SERNA CL 240137.
Talca: Uno Poniente 1234, tel: 233 669.
Temuco: Bulnes 586, tel: 234293.
Valdivia: Prat 555, tel: 213596.
Viña Del Mar: Av. Valparaíso 507, Off. 303, tel: 882285. Information, tel: 684117.

Where To Stay

Hotels

All the prices are for double occupancy per night with breakfast unless otherwise stated. Non nationals paying in dollars avoid the 18 percent I.V.A (Sales Tax). Price guide: Expensive: more than $125. Moderate: $75–125. Inexpensive: less than $75. Budget: less than $25.

The North

ARICA

Azapa Inn, G Sanchez 660, Azapa, tel: 244537; fax: 244517. Located in pleasant grounds although some distance from beach. Swimming pool. Price: moderate.
Hostería Arica, Av. San Martin 599, Playa El Laucho, tel: 254540; fax: 231133. 4-star, swimming pool, easy access to the best beaches in Arica. Price: inexpensive.
Hotel Lynch, Patricio Lynch 589, tel: 231581; fax: 251959. Price: inexpensive.
Hotel Savona, Yungay 380, tel: 232319; fax: 231606. A Small hotel in close proximity to the main square. Basic standard of accomodation. Price: inexpensive.
Residencial La Blanquita, Maipu 472, tel: 232064. Price: budget.
San Marcos, Sotomayor 367, tel: 232149; fax: 251815. Friendly, helpful management. Price: inexpensive.

IQIQUE

Hotel Arturo Prat, A Pinto 695, tel: 411067; fax: 429088. This is a 4-star hotel which fronts onto Plaza Prat. Price: moderate.
Hotel Atenas, Los Rieles 738, tel: 431100; fax: 434800. Swimming pool. Price: expensive.
Hostería Cavancha, Los Rieles 250, tel: 434800; fax: 734800. Swimming pool, situated on the water's edge. Price: expensive.

ANTOFAGASTA

Hotel Antofagasta, Balmaceda 2575.

Tel/fax: 268259. 4-star, swimming pool, excellent views of the port and city. Price: expensive.

Hotel Diego De Almagro, Condell 2624, tel: 268331; fax: 251721. Price: inexpensive.

CALAMA

Hostería Calama, Latorre 1521, tel: 341511; fax: 342033. Price: moderate.

Park Hotel Calama, Camino Aeropuerto 1392, tel: 319900; fax: 319901. Situated by the airport, this 4-star hotel offers comfortable accomodation with an excellent restaurant, bar, gym and games room facilities. Price: expensive.

SAN PEDRO DE ATACAMA

Hostería San Pedro, Solocor, tel: 11; fax: 52. 54 beds, 5 cabins (6 persons), swimming pool. Australian owners have tourist information written in several languages. Price: inexpensive.

Hostería Takha-Takha/Camping Tocopilla, tel: 38. A charming and comfortable place for budget travellers with quaint cabins and serviced camping ground. There is a delightful homestyle restaurant and the young owners conduct very friendly and relaxed tours to local attractions. Highly recommended. Price: inexpensive.

COPIAPÓ

Hostería Las Pircas, Av. Copayapu (no number), tel: 213220; fax: 211633. Swimming pool. Price: moderate

LA SERENA

Centro
Francisco De Aguirre, Cordovez 210. Tel/fax: 222991. Swimming pool. Good sized rooms. Price: moderate.

Av. del Mar
Canto Del Agua, Av. del Mar 5700, tel: 242203; fax: 241767. This residence has 82 beds, 19 cabins (4 persons). Price: inexpensive.

Jardín Del Mar. Av. del Mar 2900, tel: 245516; fax: 242991. 164 beds, 40 cabins (5 persons). Price: expensive.

Hotel Diego De Almeyda, O'Higgins 640, tel: 212076; fax: 212075. Price: expensive.

Central Chile
VALPARAÍSO

Garden Hotel, tel: 252776. Price: inexpensive.

Hotel Prat, Condell 1443, tel: 253081; fax: 213368. Own restaurant. (Good restaurants are difficult to find in Valparaíso). Price: inexpensive.

Hotel Reina Victoria, tel: 212203. Price: inexpensive.

Residencial Lily, tel: 255995. Price: inexpensive.

VIÑA DEL MAR

Cap Ducal, Av. Marina 51, tel: 626655; fax: 655478. Price: moderate.

Español, Plaza Vergara 191 57. Tel/fax: 685145. Price: inexpensive.

Hotel Alcazar, Alvarez 646, tel: 685112; fax: 884245. 160 beds. Price: moderate.

Hotel Miramar, Caleta Abarca, tel: 626677; fax: 665220. 248 beds. Price: expensive.

Hotel O'Higgins, Plaza Vergara, tel: 882016; fax: 883537. This centrally located hotel offers charm and elegance. Price: expensive.

Hotel San Martin, Av. San Martin 667, tel: 689191; fax: 689195. Price: moderate.

SANTIAGO

Crowne Plaza Holiday Inn, Av. Libertador Bernado O'Higgins 136, tel: 638 1042; fax: 633 6015. Situated close to downtown Santiago. Facilities include swimming pool, tennis courts, gymnasium and conference rooms. Price: expensive.

Hotel Caribe, tel: 696 6681. Price: budget.

Hotel Carrera, Teatinos 180, tel: 698 2011; fax: 672 1083. Probably the grandest hotel in Santiago, offering a very good level of accomodation. Has a roof terrace on which there is a restaurant and pool. Price: expensive.

Hotel Foresta, Victoria Subercaseaux 353. Tel/fax: 639 6261. Situated directly opposite Santa Lucia Hill, ensuring idyllic views for front rooms. Price: inexpensive.

Hotel Gran Palace, Huérfanos 1178, 10th Floor, tel: 671 2551; fax: 695 1095. Rooms away from the street are less noisy. Price: inexpensive.

Hotel Montecarlo, Victoria Subercaseaux 209, tel: 639 2945; Fax: 633

5577. Decent 3-star hotel, great location with view of Santa Lucia hill. Price: inexpensive.

Hotel Plaza San Francisco Kempinski, Av. Lib B. O'Higgins 816, tel: 639 3832; fax: 639 7826. This hotel is situated in the heart of downtown Santiago. It offers a very high standard of accommodation, excellent restaurants and meeting rooms. Well-decorated. Price: expensive.

Residencial Londres, Londres 54. Tel/fax: 638 2215. Ramshackle antique interiors. Very good budget accommodation. Price: inexpensive.

Sheraton San Cristobal, Av. Santa Maria 1742, tel: 233 5000; fax: 234 1729. Swimming pool, excellent service. Price: expensive.

Vegas Hotel, tel: 632 2514; fax: 632 5084. Price: inexpensive.

CONCEPCÍON

Hotel Alborada, Barros Arana 457. Tel/fax: 242144. Located just off the main square, above average facilities, function/conference rooms. Price: moderate.

Hotel Alonso De Ercilla, Colo Colo 334, tel: 227984; fax: 230053. One block from the main square, modern with average facilites, no restaurant, snack service. Price: moderate.

Hotel El Araucano, Caupolican 521, tel: 230606; fax: 230690. Just off the main square, above average facilities, swimming pool, function/conference rooms. Price: expensive.

Lake District
CHILLAN

Gran Hotel Isabel Riquelme, Arauco 600, tel: 213663; fax: 211541. Facing one of the most attractive main squares, above average facilities, 87 rooms and 3 suites. Function/conference rooms. Price: moderate.

LOS ANGELES

Mariscal Alcazar, Luataro 385. Tel/fax: 311725. On the main square, above average facilities, 60 rooms and suites. Function/conference rooms. Price: moderate.

TEMUCO

Hotel Nícolas, General Mackenna 420, tel: 210020; fax: 213468. Nearby main square, 50 rooms; conference facilites. Price: inexpensive.

Nuevo Hotel De La Frontera, Av. Bulnes 733. Tel/fax: 212638. On opposite sides of the street just off the main square, modern with above average facilities, pool, sauna, function/conference rooms. Price: inexpensive.

(The Tourist Office has a list of Hospedajes or family houses ideal as budget accommodation).

PUCÓN

Gran Hotel Pucón, Clemente Holzapfel 190. Tel/fax: 441001. A large 5-star hotel on the lake shore with 550 beds. Its extensive facilities include a casino. Price: inexpensive.

Hostería "ecole", General Urrutia 592, tel: 441675; fax: 441949. This is an American owned hostería located in the center of town which has 40 beds and a vegetarian restaurant. Price: inexpensive.

Hotel Antumalal, Pucón, tel: 441011; fax: 441013. A small luxury hotel with 15 rooms and two "royal" chalets set in 4 hectares (10 acres) of quiet woodland on a peninsular overlooking the lake where the queen of England once stayed. Amenities include a heated swimming pool, tennis and water sports. Price: expensive.

Termas de Huife, 36 km (20 miles) east of Pucón, tel/fax: 441222. Open air thermal swimming pools in an idyllic natural setting. The luxury cabins all have their own private thermal baths. Price: expensive.

VILLARRICA

El Ciervo, General Koerner 241, tel: 411215; fax: 411426. A twelve room centrally located hotel with swimming pool. It also has a cabin for five people. Price: inexpensive.

(For budget accommodation here and in other towns in the lake district, *hospedajes* are the best value).

LICAN-RAY

El Conquistador, C. Millaqueo, tel: 431019. This is a self-contained complex of 40 cabins that is on the shore of Lake Calafquen which has excellent facilities for family vacations. Price: inexpensive.

Cabins are also popular here around Lake Calafquen. Everything is closed outside of tourist season, which is from mid-December to mid-March.

CHOSHUENCO

Hotel Ruca-Pillan, San Martin 85, tel: 224402 ext. 220. Traditional hotel and cabins beside the lake. Price: inexpensive.

Hostería Pulmahue, Casilla 545, Panguipulli, tel: 224404 ext. 224. Small, well situated hotel and cabins overlooking the lake. Price: expensive.

PANGUIPULLI

Hostal España, B. O'Higgins 790, tel: 311327. A small, well appointed hotel situated in the center of town. Price: inexpensive.

VALDIVIA

Hotel Villa Del Rio, Av. Espana 1025, tel: 216292; fax 217851. This hotel is situated on the river bank across from the center of Valdivia. Above average facilities, 100 rooms, cabins, swimming pool, sauna, tennis and river lunches. Function/conference rooms. Price: inexpensive.

Pedro De Valdivia, Carampangue 190. Tel/fax: 212931. Near the river and three blocks from the main square, an old hotel recently modernised, above average facilities, swimming pool and function/conference rooms. Price: moderate.

FUTRONO

Hostería Rincon Arabe, Manuel Montt, tel: 481262. The hotel overlooks the lake, and has a swimming pool and restaurant. The Arabian manageress has been described as "charmingly eccentric". Price: inexpensive.

LAGO RANCO

Casona Italiana, Viña del mar 145, tel: 225. Small hotel with 5 rooms and 4 cabins on the edge of the lake. Price: inexpensive.

FRUTILLAR

Hostería El Arroyo, Av. Philippi 989, tel: 421560; fax: 421656. Small family run hostería centrally located on the edge of the lake. Price: inexpensive.

Hotel Salzburg, Camino a Playa Maqui, tel: 421589; fax: 421599. A new 31 bed hotel with cabins overlooking the lake. Facilities include swimming pool, sauna, gym, horse trekking, mountain bikes, fishing and various sports. Price: inexpensive.

PUERTO VARAS

Hotel Colonos del Sur, Del Salvador 24, tel: 233369; fax: 233394. Well equipped modern hotel facing the lake. Has swimming pool and sauna. Price: moderate

Hotel Licarayen, San José 114. Tel/fax: 232955. A modern hotel facing the lake with average facilities. Price: moderate.

Hotel y Cabañas del Lago, Klenner 195, tel: 232291; fax: 232707. A well equipped hotel with seperate cabins which overlook the town and lake and is ideally situated for the casino. It offers 42 rooms, one luxury suite, games room, sauna, conference facilities. Price: moderate.

PUYEHUE

Gran Hotel Termas de Puyehue, Lake Puyehue, tel: 371382, fax: 371272. A large, old and well established hotel with 80 rooms on the shore of Lago Puyehue. The excellent "spa" facilities include indoor and open air thermal swimming pools, sauna, mud and sulphur baths, indoor and open air tennis courts, gymnasium, mountain bikes, horse trekking, fishing and boat tours. The hotel also has excellent conference and reception facilities. Price: moderate.

Hotel Antillanca, Km 98, Ruta 215, Osorno. Tel/fax: 235114. A modern 64 room hotel in the center of the Puyehue national park which is an ideal base for trekking and mountain climbing in the summer and skiing in the winter. Facilities include a swimming pool, sauna, gym and a conference center. Price: expensive

PETROHUÉ

Hotel Petrohué, tel: 258042. A recently modernised 21 room hotel by Lago Todos los Santos and the Petrohué river in the Pérez Rosales national park. Well situated for lake excursions, white water rafting, fishing and walking. Price: moderate.

Fundo El Salto Lodge, Casilla 471, Puerto Varas. Tel/fax: 09 6537233. One of the best known fishing lodges in the area. It is run by a New Zealander in a beautifully converted farmhouse opposite the famous waterfalls. Price: expensive.

PUELLA

Hotel Puella. In Puerto Montt, tel: 257797. Situated at the far end of the lake. Pleasant service; half board available. Price: moderate.

ENSENADA

Hotel Ensenada, Villa Ensenada, tel: 232888. An old traditional hotel near the lake which has a great deal of character but is only open during the summer months. Price: moderate.

OSORNO

Gran Hotel Osorno, O'Higgins 615, tel: 232171, fax: 239311. On the main square with 70 rooms. No private parking. Price: inexpensive.

Hotel Garcia Hurtado De Mendoza, Av. Juan Mackenna 1040. Tel/fax: 237111. Modern hotel with above average facilities, one block from the main square. Conference room, sauna and gym. Price: moderate.

Hotel Interlagos, Cochrane 515, tel: 234695; fax: 235581. Price: inexpensive.

Hotel Pumalal, Bulnes 630, tel: 243520; fax: 242477. A small modern hotel with average facilities but no restaurant. Price: inexpensive.

Hotel Rayantú, Patricio Lynch 1462, tel: 238114, fax: 238116. Excellently equipped modern hotel five blocks from the main square with 23 rooms and 15 suites, swimming pool, children's games and conference facilities. Price: moderate.

Hotel Waeger, Hotel del Prado, Cochrane 816, tel: 233721; fax: 237080. Very well equipped modern hotels, on the same street and under the same management, a few blocks from the main square. Swimming pool and conference facilities. Price: Hotel Waeger–inexpensive; Hotel del Prado–moderate.

PUERTO MONTT

Cabañas de Melipulli, Libertad 610. Tel/fax: 252363. These cabins are 10 minutes walk from the center of town. Situated in a wood, they are ideal for young people and families. Facilities include a cafe/bar, swimming pool and sauna. Price: inexpensive.

Colon Apart Hotel, Pedro Montt 65, tel: 264290; fax: 264293. A modern hotel on the seafront with 26 self-catering suites. Price: moderate.

Don Luis Gran Hotel, Urmeneta, corner with Quillota, tel: 259001; fax: 259005. A modern hotel in the center of town with standard facilities but only a snack service. Price: moderate.

Hotel Colina, Talca 81, tel: 253501; fax: 259331. Price: inexpensive.

Hotel Montt, Antonio Varas 301, tel: 253651; fax: 253652. Price: inexpensive.

Hotel Vicente Perez Rosales, Antonio Varas 447, tel: 252571; fax: 255473. This is the oldest hotel in the town with 83 rooms and standard facilities which is situated between the coast road and the main shopping street. Price: moderate.

Hotel Vientosur, Ejército 200. Tel/fax: 258701. A modern 30 room hotel which overlooks the town and bay. Good facilities include a gym and sauna. Price: moderate.

The hotels in Puerto Montt now include some of the best and most modern in the country, and there is no shortage of very good value budget accommodation.

Chiloé

ANCUD

Hostería Ancud, San Antonio 30, tel: 622340. Beautiful interior of wooden pillars supporting an impressive cane ceiling. Set on a green hillside overlooking the water and a ruined Spanish fort. Price: inexpensive.

Residencial Weschler, Cochrane 480. Tel/fax: 622318. Also offers fine views. Price: inexpensive.

For budget accommodation in Chiloé, the *residencials* or *hospedajes* are not only the best value, they also provide a friendly atmosphere and a source for meeting the local people. A typical example is the **Residencial Santander**.

CASTRO

Eleuterio Ramirez 566, tel: 632180; fax: 635533. A clean, family run hotel located near the main square. Price: budget.

Hostería de Castro, Chacabuco 202, tel: 632301; fax: 635688. The hosteria has a good restaurant and interesting architectural features. Price: moderate.

Hostería Don Camilo, Eleuterio Ramirez 566, tel: 632180; fax 635533. Price: budget.

Hotel Unicornio Azul, tel/fax: 632808.

This hotel is very well situated down by the harbour with good views. Price: moderate.

ACHAO, ISLA QUINCHAO

Hostería La Nave, Calle Prat, tel: 661219. A clean hotel with a good restaurant built on stilts over the sea in Chiloé's most attractive fishing harbour. Price: budget.

CHONCHI

Hotel Huildin, Centenario 102, tel: 671388; fax: 635030. An interesting old building which has been recently renovated. Price: budget.

CUCAO

This is a tiny village in a beautiful setting on the Pacific coast near the Chiloé national park.

The Posada is clean and has a restaurant. More basic accommodation is available, Hospedaje El Paraiso (price: inexpensive) is the best.

Aisén

COYHAIQUE

Hostería Coyhaique, Magallanes 131, tel: 231137; fax: 233274. This relatively new guest house is one of three managed by the company, HOTELSA, which places emphasis on natural surroundings and a very tasteful design. The Hostería Coyhaique has a beautiful park setting including large well-kept gardens while the interior is furnished in natural earthy tones. The service is quietly efficient. The other two hosterias located in the Aisén region appear equally attractive in a different style and offer the alternative *cabina* accommodation as well as guest rooms. These are: **Hostería Puyuhuapi** (price: moderate) and **Hostería Lago Elizalde** (price: moderate. For information and reservations for any of these three contact: **HOTELSA**, Tel: 231137.

Magallanes & Tierra del Fuego

TORRES DEL PAINE NATIONAL PARK

Hostería Lago Grey, Punta Arenas: Tel/fax: 222681 for reservations. Price: moderate.

Hostería Pehoé, 379 km on Route 9 north, tel: 241373; fax: 248052. Price: moderate.

Hotel Explore Patagonia. For reservations, Punta Arenas: Tel: 411247. Price: expensive.

PUERTO NATALES

Hotel Capitan Eberhard, Pedro Montt 25, tel: 411208; fax: 411209. Puerto Natales is the closest town to the National Park, however transportation is easily arranged. Price: moderate.

Other hotels are located on route between Puerto Natales and Punta Arenas. An interesting choice would be **Hostal Rio Penitente**, Tel: 224926, 331694; Tlx: 3380083 TAVENT-CK. Situated on a Magellanic farm of the British colonial-Alexander Morrison. Or **Hostería Rio Serrano**, 399 km on Route 9 North, Arturo Prat 210, tel: 411355. Price: moderate.

PUNTA ARENAS

Cabo De Hornos, Plaza Munoz Gamero 1025. Tel/fax: 242134. Grandiose "Dickensien" block adjacent to the main plaza. Excellent restaurant. Price: expensive.

Los Navigantes, Menendez 647, tel: 244677; fax: 247545. Price: moderate.

Monte Carlo, Av. Colon 605. Tel/fax: 243438. Old style, comfortable front rooms, relaxed atmosphere and economical. Price: inexpensive.

PUERTO WILLIAMS

Hostería Wala. For reservations, Punta Arenas: Tel: 223340; fax: 221693. If you've made it this far you'll find conditions here very comfortable, with log fires and rustic wooden furniture. Price: moderate.

USHUAIA (ARGENTINA)

Hotel Canal Beagle, Maipu cnr 25 de Mayo, tel: 91117. Top of the range, although there are quite a few hotels to choose from at this end of the earth. Price: expensive.

Pacific Islands
ISLA DE PASCUA/EASTER ISLAND

Hotel Hanga Roa, Av. Pont; tel: 223299. An expensive hotel, as are most on the island, although this one is considered the most luxurious.

Rapa Nui Inn, Av. Policarpo Toro, tel: 223228. You won't find a swimming pool or souvenir shop at Snr. Martín's Inn, but you will enjoy the local hospi-

tality and have a very relaxed stay. Most hotels on the island will offer you full board accommodation. However, there are restaurants if you don't mind an evening stroll.

JUAN FERNÁNDEZ ISLANDS

All accommodation on the main island "Robinson Crusoe" is agreeable, if not delightful and arranging your stay couldn't be easier. If arriving with the TAXPA airline you might be ushered into one of two hotels. Katie Green provides *cabana* style accommodation beside her residence in the township. Full board is around US$50 and Katie is an excellent cook. Just mention her son's name, Maximillio, to the pilot and all will be arranged.

The **Hostería Pangal** is nestled in the neighburing inlet, access to the township is either by boat or taking a magnificent stroll around the headland. Price: expensive.

The other airline, Transportes Aereos Isla Robinson Crusoe, has connections with **Hotel Daniel Defoe**, which offers a number of rustic *cabanas* set right on the shoreline, or the more traditional **Hostería Villa Green** with its standard guest rooms, situated on the main plaza.

Eating Out

What To Eat

Chilean food is influenced by Spanish, native and international (mostly French) cooking styles. Each region will have its local speciality and Santiago can boast of a mouth-watering cross section. High on the list of Chile's natural resources are fruits and vegetables, seafood, beef, mutton and cereals. There is no shortage of ingredients for a rich cuisine and the Chileans use them to advantage.

The country's enormous coastline provides a huge range of seafood, which will be served on special occasions. Such exotica as conger eel, abalone, king crab (*centolla*), sea urchins and oysters are often easily available. *Ma chas Parmesana* and

Chupe de Centolla are two of the best loved dishes.

Amongst other types of meat, beef is the most popular. It is usually served as tender *lomo* fillets or accompanied by an array of sweetmeats on a sizzling barbecue (*parillada*). Most South Americans know the *empanada* – in this case it's baked with an olive, egg and raisins inside. The *cazuela* is a delicious soup made with either chicken, turkey or partridge. *Pollo al Cognac*, (chicken in cognac), is a distinctly Chilean dish of chicken in a rich brandy sauce.

Humitas (packets of ground corn), and *Porotos Granadors* (freshly picked beans cooked with corn and basil) are two regional vegetable dishes that must be tried at least once. To top off a meal, there's always flavorful fruit in season. Especially tasty are strawberries, raspberries, papayas, cherries and grapes. And don't miss Santiago's pedestrian obsession, ice-cream.

Where To Eat

The number of restaurants in Santiago has increased dramatically in the past years. For the sake of putting some order to the endless array, there appears to be four accepted restaurant centers in the city. Each district has many restaurants well worth recommending and its own distinctive ambience or character.

El Centro

El Centro is at its best between 1–4pm Monday to Friday, when the business lunch takes place. Whether it's in a bustling hamburger joint, or over a formal Italian buffet, the luncheon is the most important meal of the day. For great value the *menú del dia*, or fixed menu, is highly recommended. Here's a variety of reliable choices:

Chez Henry, Plaza de Armas (between Compania and Merced). Walk through the delicatessan to the restaurant. A huge place with formal service that specializes in seafood. Also lively at nights, with an old world dine and dance atmosphere in the far dining room. Great *machas parmesana*.

Hereford Grill, Teatro Municipal, tel: 395612. The best steak/parillada restaurant in Santiago. Other steak houses can be found along Huérfanos.

Le Due Torri, Huérfanos, cnr San

ntonio 258, Local 9. Varied Italian ood, popular at lunch-time, buffet en-ree table.

a **Naturista**, Moneda 846. Fast veg-tarian food based on typical Chilean tyles.

The 5-star hotels in the city center ave their own high class restaurant. he **Piscina Panorama** in the Hotel Carrera, Tel: 698 2011; and **Casa-blanca** in the Crowne Plaza, Tel: 38 042; both have evening entertain-ment on Friday and Saturday.

For a relaxed atmosphere and a budget meal, there are numerous ca-es and pizza restaurants bordering he Plaza de Armas and along Huérfanos. When you just want a good offee or something sweet, try **Cafe Colonia**, the best place for cakes and German *Küchen*, on MacIver 133, or **Cafe do Brasil**, corner of Huérfanos and Bandera; or one of the several **Cafe Paula** outlets that can be found around the center, serving rich Cafe Helado (iced coffee) and cakes.

Baquedano

he tiny district of **Baquedano** is a pic-uresque niche of cultural activity and ntimate restaurants. Not far from the enter of town, the Plaza del Mulatto Gil provides a neat showcase for the artists and intellectuals who dwell in he area. (To get to this area, just ask he taxi driver for Plaza del Mulatto Gil or walk along Merced and turn right nto Lastarria. The exact address is 305-7 Jose Victorino Lastarria).

The most conspicuous restaurant, he **Pérgola de la Plaza**, is a very at-ractive escape from the city chaos. There are tables in the outside court-yard and lunches reasonably priced. Other ones to try include:

Maistral, Mosqueto 485, tel: 330 370. Traditional French, regarded as Santiago's best. Very intimate. Book-ngs essential.

nez de Suaréz, Calle Rosal. Named after Valdivia's mistress who was famed for beheading Indians, this is a chic little restaurant in the quietest nook of Baquedano.

Restaurant Japones, Izakaya Yoko, Merced 456, tel: 632 1954. Excellent authentic Japanese food. Do not be out off by the seedy exterior – this is he haunt of Santiago's growing Japa-nese business community.

Bellavista

Bellavista holds the reputation for be-ing the most bohemian neighborhood. Within easy striking distance of the center (a $2 taxi ride – ask for Calle Pio Nono – or half hour walk), it is an-other pleasant promenading district. Restaurants line Bellavista's main street, as well as the quieter and more charming backstreets. The emphasis here is on having a relaxed night out – which might include an after-dinner drink or listening to *salsa* at one of the local *peñas*.

The **Venezia** (cnr Pio Nono and Lopez de Bella) is a local favorite. An Italian restaurant and bar that serves Santiago's best *chacarero* (a type of steak sandwich) and ice cold *schop* (beer).

Some other good choices might be:

La Divina Comida, cnr Purisima and Lopez de Bella. An excellent place for quality Italian food, this restaurant advertises its elegant interior to the strollers of Bellavista through large open windows. Try the delicious spin-ach ravioli and the Casillera del Diablo is cheapest here.

Las Palmas, Lopez de Bello 190, tel: 774586.Tranquil courtyard comeyard comedor with a not too expensive fixed luncheon.

La Tasca Mediterrani, Purísima, near Lopez de Bella. Serves reasonably priced Spanish seafood in an exciting Mediterranean atmosphere.

Cafe de la Dulceria in the same build-ing has wicked patisserie. Take a look at the gallery behind the courtyard.

Along the congested footpaths of Pio Nono, you'll come to Pizza restau-rants, bars and cafes. Just enjoy the promenade.

The district of **Providencia** is home to Santiago's most expensive and fashionable restaurants. At least 15 high-class establishments are clus-tered along the short connecting streets of Isidora Goyenechea and El Bosque. Take a taxi to either and you will be within sight of most. Some sug-gestions:

Dona Flor, named after the novel by Jorge Amado, is good for Brazilian fare, tel: 232 2870.

Isidora, tel: 231 2422. Specializing in *mariscos*.

For fine meats try **Rodizio El Bosque**, Tel: 232 5821 or the suc-cessful **Hereford Grill**, Tel: 231 9117.

For French food, **L'Hermitage**, Tel: 232 2732.

Copelia. Several outlets in Providencia shopping area. The best place to have cakes and ice-cream.

El Huerto, Calle Orego Luco 054. Veg-etarian. Groovy atmosphere with stained glass and terrace.

La Casa Vieja, Chile Espana 249, tel: 274 7248. Faultless *filetes* and noth-ing too pricey. With a formal atmos-phere and very Chilean.

Matin Carrera, Isidora Goyenechea 3471, tel: 231 2798. Nouvelle cuisine and cuisine "spa."

Munchen, El Bosque Norte 204. Inter-national, leaning towards German traditional.

Drinking Notes

Nothing brings out the flavor of local dishes better than one of Chile's fa-mous wines – possibly the best value wine in the world.

Ice cold *pisco sour* serves as a popular aperitif, as does *vaina*, a light blend of brandy, milk, coffee, egg, vanila and cinnamon. Chilean *chicha* is freshly fermented grape juice, and *borgoña* is a more-ish concoction of red wine, ice and fresh strawberries. Buy it by the jug.

Attractions

City Sights

Santiago

On a very clear day in winter, you can see that Santiago is nearly surrounded by the encroaching Andes, but as you're unlikely to catch a postcard view of these awesome giants, your next best view in order to get your bearings is from the top of one of the two hills which grace the city's other-wise grey flatness. **Cerro Santa Lucia** and **Cerra San Cristóbal** are both decorated with sculptured gardens and historic architecture, making them pleasant retreats from the city bustle. If you make **Santa Lucia** your first sojourn, Metro Line 1, Santa Lucia Station, keep in mind that there are a few landmarked buildings on route back to the **Plaza de Armas** in the downtown area. Here are some of the more interesting:

The Biblioteca Nacional (The National Library), 651 Bernardo O'Higgins, tel: 333957. Tours can be arranged through this late 19th-century building, one of the largest libraries in South America.

The Teatro Municipal (Municipal Theatre), cnr Agustinas and San Antonio, tel: 332804/381515. Santiago's symbol of the arts. This is home to the Philharmonic Orchestra and Santiago Municipal Ballet.

Casa de Colorado y Museo de Santiago, Merced 860, tel: 330723. Best preserved colonial house in the city and a fine museum.

The Plaza de Armas is bordered by several historic buildings.

The Catedral (cathedral), cnr of Catedral and Puente. Includes a religious museum, extremely ornate.

Municipal Building, cnr of 21 de Mayo and Monjitas. Neo-classic building which houses council offices.

Museo Historico Nacional (National Museum of History), 951 Plaza de Armas (beside Municipal building), tel: 381411. Tours available by arrangement. Chile's history from pre-hispanic to modern times.

Correo Central (Central Post Office), Plaza de Armas (beside National Museum of History). Large pink landmarked building built in 1882.

National Congress Building, Cathedral (one block from the Plaza). Former Congress building, bombed in 1973 by military.

Museo de Arte Precolombino (Precolombian Museum), 361 Bandera, tel: 717284. With an excellent display of Precolombian artifacts.

Plaza de la Constitucion, Moneda, facing the Government Palace. Spacious square bordered by formidable Chilean architecture.

La Moneda (Government Palace), Moneda, located between Morandé and Teatinos. Seat of Government, austere architecture.

Universidad de Chile, Av. B. O'Higgins 1058. This is considered as being the most handsome 19th-century building in the city.

Altar de la Patria and **statue of**

O'Higgins, Av. B. O'Higgins, between Galvez and Nataniel Cox. Marble urn containing the remains of Libertador Bernardo O'Higgins.

Iglesia San Francisco, Av. B. O'Higgins 834. Oldest church in Santiago, of great historical value.

Museo de Arte Colonial San Francisco, 4 Londres, tel: 398737. Beside the Iglesia San Francisco, housed in Franciscan monastery, the museum has a beautiful central patio. The street, Londres, has much in the way of 1930s architecture from England. The area ends at Ovalle.

Universidad Católica, Av. B. O'Higgins 340. Founded by Archbishop Mariano Casanova.

Jose Victorino Lastarria. This is the principle street of the Baquedano area, full of tree-lined cobbled laneways which stem from the Plaza del Mulatto Gil.

Plaza del Mulatto Gil, 305-307 Jose Victorino Lastarria. A courtyard with galleries, bookshops and a charming restaurant.

Palacio de Bellas Artes (Palace of Fine Arts), Parque Forestal and Jose Miguel de la Barra. This is a fine neoclassical building which contains three Art Museums.

Fuente Alemana, inside Parque Forestal. Beautiful German fountain which children adore in summer. The parque itself is a pleasant promenade towards Bellavista.

Calle Pio Nono, main street of Bellavista. Cross the Rio Mapocho and enjoy the bohemian atmosphere.

Cerro San Cristóbal, at the end of Pio Nono. Save your legs on the Funicular Railway and walk down through some attractive gardens.

Parque Metropolitano. Set in 712 hectares of parkland dominated by Cerro San Cristobal. The park contains everything including a zoo, two swimming pools, restaurants, chapel, aerial cableway and more.

The Mercado Central (Central Market), between 21 de Mayo and Puente. Interesting market activity under the decorative iron roof of a large pavilion.

Estacion Mapocho, Bandera and Balmaceda. Closed railway station with magnificent Baroque arches and French metal roof.

Posada del Corregidor, Esmeralda 749, tel: 335573 for current exhibitions. This is another excellent exam-

ple of colonial architecture, houses artworks.

Casa de Los Velasco, Santo Domingo 899. Home of the Velasco family, colonial construction from 1730.

Templo de Santo Domingo, Santo Domingo 961. Famous for its two baroque brick towers and simple lines.

Providencia Area

Parque Balmaceda. Green park area for family recreation, also offers open air theater productions in summer.

Instituto Chileno de Cultura Hispanica, Av. Providencia 927, tel: 274 7420. Art exhibits, lectures, concerts cinema and video shows.

Estacion Central de Ferrocarriles (Railway Station), Av. B. O'Higgins 3200 block. Metal structure cast at the Schneider Works in Creusot France.

Parque Quinta Normal. Forty hectares of wooded area containing three museums, tennis courts, a lake for boating and soccer fields.

The **"Edificio Museo de la Aviacion Pabellon Paris"** is a wonderfully eccentric structure on Portales 3530 facing the park's main esplanade.

Planetarium. Av. B. O'Higgins 3349 tel: 762624. Astronomy shows under semicircular dome.

Culture

Museums

ARICA

Museo Arqueológico San Miguel De Azapa, Azapa Valley (12 km from the town). The museum has a very good collection of artifacts representing the period from the 7th century BC to the Spanish conquest. You can hire *collectivos* to the museum or take a tour which includes the visit. Daily March–December afternoon only at weekends and holidays. Students free on Tuesday and Thursday.

IQUIQUE

Museo Regional. Large collection of relics, including Indian mummies and a life-sized reproduction of a mud brick village with inhabitants dressed in traditional costume. Daily and Saturday morning, closed Sunday.

SAN PEDRO DE ATACAMA

Museo Arqueológico San Pedro De Atacama, Universidad del Norte (near the main plaza). This museum receives rave recommendations from travel guides, writers and visitors alike. It is reputedly one of the most impressive museums in South America, having a huge collection of pre-Conquest artifacts, many in excellent condition. Daily.

OVALLE

Museo Arqueológico Limarí, Independencia 329. This museum contains one of the best collections of Diaguita ceramics. Daily and Sunday morning, closed Monday.

It is well worth making the trip to the **Monumento Nacional Valle del Encanto**, a secluded valley where you can see the Molle culture petroglyphs.

SANTIAGO

Museo De Arte Precolombiano, Bandera 361, tel: 717284. Perhaps the best in Santiago, this comprehensive exhibition deserves several visits, especially if you're keen to get an overview of the many Precolombian civilizations. Daily, Sunday and holidays 10am–2pm, closed Monday.

Museo De Santiago, 860 Merced, tel: 330723. Occupying the Casa Colorada, the best preserved colonial house in the city, the exhibition is a series of meticulously crafted models of key landmarks in the history of Santiago. Definitely worth a visit. Daily and Sunday 10am–2pm, closed Monday.

Museo Nacional De Belles Artes, Jose Miguel De La Barra and Parque Forestal, tel: 39 1946, 33 0655. The oldest art museum in South America, housed in the neo-classical Palace of Fine Arts, Three floors of artworks and current exhibitions comprise 3,000 paintings makes it, possibly, one of the largest museums also. Daily, closed Monday.

La Quinta Normal is a huge park on the outskirts of town, a little dry and exhausting in the summer months, but interesting for two museums:

Museo Nacional De Historia Natural. Inside Quinta Normal, tel: 90011. Sparsely distributed throughout a huge landmark building are areas on entomology, geology, anthropology, archaeology and zoology. The whale skeleton is popular with small children and other stuffed animals on the ground floor. Daily, closed Monday.

Museo De La Catedral. Bandera, corner of Catedral (access through the church), tel: 696 2777. Display of religious objects, imagery, documents, vestments, gold and silverwork from the Colonial and early Republican periods. Daily, Sunday and holidays 9am–2pm.

VIÑA DEL MAR

Museo Arqeológico Fonck. This museum contains a moai and other artifacts from Easter Island. Daily, Saturday and Sunday 10am–2pm, closed Monday.

VICHUQUÉN

Museo Histórico de Vichuquén. A well laid out collection of prehistoric and Inca exhibits can be found in this museum. Open: in summer, daily and closed Monday; in winter, daily.

TALCA

Museo O'Higginiano y de Bellas Artes. The museum is in a colonial house built in 1762 where Bernardo O'Higgins lived as a child and met his father, Ambrosio O'Higgins who was the Viceroy of Peru, for the one and only time in his life. It was here where The Act of Independence was signed in 1818. Daily, closed Sunday and Monday.

VALDIVIA

Museo Histórico y Antropológico "Maurice Van de Maelle", Isla de Teja (via the Pedro de Valdivia bridge). Valdivia was a German settlement and this museum has a fine collection of household items from the early days. The building itself is a beautiful timber mansion by the river. Open March 16–December 14 daily, closed Monday; December 15–March 15 daily.

FRUTILLAR

Museo Colonial Alemán. Funded by the German government, this open air museum contains some interesting artifacts brought to Chile by the colonists. Open: in summer, daily; in winter, daily and closed Monday.

PUERTO MONTT

Museo Juan Pablo II. Contains memorabilia from the Pope's visit, including the cutlery and crockery he used on the plane to Puerto Montt. Daily.

ANCUD (CHILEÓ)

Museo Regional Audelio Borquez Canobra, beside the Tourist Office. Built like a fictional fortress, with turrets and battlements you can climb up to the central courtyard containing old canons and so on, the museum has several floors, one of which displays sculpture impressions of Chiloé's mythological creatures. Daily March–December, closed Monday.

CASTRO

Museo Municipal. Displayed in this museum are primarily historical and archaeological artifacts. Daily March–December, closed Monday; daily January and Feburary, Sunday morning.

PUNTA ARENAS

Museo Regional de Magallanes, Centro Cultural Braun-Menéndez. Magnificently decorated mansion belonging to the Braun-Menéndez family, it is the principal attraction of Punta Arenas. The museum exhibits depict the early settlement of Tierra del Fuego when the Braun-Menéndez family owned vast areas of land. But it's the mansion's palatial rooms, immaculately maintained, that are a must to see. Open: in summer Tuesday–Sunday morning, closed Monday; in winter daily, closed Monday.

Museo Histórico Salesiano "Mayorino Borgatello", Bulnes, cnr Sarmiento. Also well worth a visit, this rather chaotic exhibition contains some of the most exciting relics found in archaeological museums. The Salesians have retained many remains, belongings and documentation of the unique Ona Indians from the days when they were responsible for their education and "well-being" during European settlement. Daily.

Art Galleries

Santiago has an overabundance of art galleries, each district having its own particular flavor.

In Bellavista, **La Fachada** and **El Cerro**, standing side by side on Calle Lopez de Bello, are typical of the area. On Calle Bellavista itself, **La Casa Larga** has been highly recommended. Just strolling around Bellavista, you'll come across quite a few fashionable galleries, although don't expect to find them open on weekends. Also on Bellavista is the **Carmen Waugh** gallery, **Eidophon** is on the corner of Concha and Dardignac, and **Arte Nocturno** is on the corner of Lopez de Bello and Purisima.

In Providencia, **Plastica 3** and **Praxis** are prestigiously housed in the elegant side streets of General Holley and Suecia, while **Epoca** and the **Fundacion Nacional de la Cultura** can both be found between Avenida Providencia and 11 de Septiembre.

In the Baquedano district, the Plaza del Mulato Gil is home to **Arte Actual** and the **Galeria de la Plaza**. There are a few interesting looking art shops on Merced, across from Lastarria which sell quality artworks.

Enrico Bucci on the corner of Miraflores and Huérfanos is a reputable gallery in the city center.

Exhibition listings are in the newspapers, the "Wikén" section of *El Mercurio* has the most extensive.

Concerts/Ballets

For classical music the Teatro Municipal offers a complete season between April and December. Phone for further information.

Teatro Municipal, cnr San Antonio and Agustinas, tel: 33 2549. Tickets available at the theater or Parque Arauco.

Teatro Oriente, Av. Pedro de Valdivia between Avenidas Providencia and Costanera. The Teatro Oriente presents overseas artists during the season of May to October. Information and tickets at Marcel Duhaut 2888.

Best quality recordings in records and cassettes of the most famous European and American recording companies, Lencoaudio, Isidora Goyenechea 2901, Tel: 231 2800. Or Lencoaudio San Antonio, 65 Galerias Nicionales, Local 110-B, PO Box 13462, Santiago, tel: 33 0732.

Theater

Theater in Santiago is often excellent and the Chileans are very proud of it. There are over 20 theaters turning out classical, modern or vanguard plays by national and foreign playwrights.

Some of the more lively, comical or expressive performances might require less command of Spanish. Have a look at the busking comedians in the Plaza de Armas on weekends. There might be hundreds of people trans-

fixed by the one performance since even these players have natural stage presence.

Theaters in Bellavista usually present new or modern pieces:

Teatro La Feria, Crucero Exeter 0250, tel: 377371. This has an exciting, theatrical interior.

Camara Negra, Antonio Lope De Bello. Theater in a more bohemian vein.

El Conventillo, Bellavista 173, tel: 774164. Flashy theater/restaurant complex.

There are a few theaters in the center which appeal to most tastes:

Teatro Abril, Huérfanos and MacIver. Has been very successful with the long running production of *Pantaleon y las Visitadores* by Mario Vargas Llosa. Absolutely hilarious.

Teatro La Comedia, Merced 349, tel: 391 1523.

Teatro Sala del Angel, San Antonio 255, tel: 333605.

Teatro Moneda, Moneda 920, tel: 715 5451.

Or in **Providencia**:

Teatro El Bolsillo, Providencia 2633, tel: 231 7406.

Teatro El Burlitzer, Providencia 2124, tel: 231 8899.

Teatro Las Americas, Providencia 2563, tel: 251 2800.

Cinemas

Santiago has over 40 cinemas, many of them showing quality foreign films. The pedestrian walkways such as Huérfanos and Ahumada, have plenty to choose from, although it's best to decide on your film through the listings in the papers first, because most of the cinemas start at the same time. Commercial cinemas are showing continuously. There are usually enough seats but the acoustics can be very poor. The price for a ticket is between US$1 and US$2.

The Rex 1, 2, and 3 is reliable and has an impressive procenium surround. Others with good sound: **The Imperio**, **Huérfanos**, **Lido**, **Cervantes** and **Gran Palace**.

Good foreign and art films are shown at **El Biogrofo**, at the corner of Lastarria and Villavicencio, also at the **Normandie**, Almaceda 139, tel: 392 749. Newspaper list films that might turn out to be politically banned videos shown in the back of a quiet restaurant. You can see good films this way.

Films of famous operas are shown on Monday at **Salon Fildamerico** Teatro Municipal building, corner San Antonio and Agustinas.

Nightlife for the Santiagiños might range from cuddling on a park bench to backgammon in Bellavista, a concert at the Municipal or a vanguard performance at the theater. Chileans also love to dance and many dance very well, though always as a couple performing well-known steps. It's common to see an impromptu dance by a distinguished looking couple enjoying a special night out at a restaurant. You might see a tango or be invited to *salsa*. No one minds if you don't have much experience.

There are several bars and discos but perhaps the 17 years of dictatorship has kept these to a minimum. Unlike Argentina's Buenos Aires, Santiago retires a little earlier in the evening. One is inclined to stroll home by midnight.

Floorshows

Santiago takes folklore from the provinces and turns it into dazzling spectaculars at a number of prestigious restaurants frequented by tourists and Chileans alike.

Los Buenos Muchachos, Ricardo Cummy 1083. Typical Chilean food and floorshow.

Los Adobes de Argomedo, Argomedo 411. Set in a huge barn-like hall, two orchestras and a dozen dancers perform on an extendable hydraulic stage, everything from Polynesian hulas to Chilean *cuecas*. Very professional.

Bali Hai, Av. Colon. Big tourist spot with Polynesian food and floorshow.

Canta Gallo, Av. Las Condes 12345, tel: 471450.

La Querencia, Av. Las Condes 14980, tel: 471266.

Las Delicias, Raul Labbe 340, tel: 471386.

In **Bellavista**, *peñas* begin when the restaurants finish. **Cafe del Cerro** presents live *salsa* and special guest performances in a cosy, exciting atmosphere. US$7 entry, between Dardignac and Lopez de Bello. There is a wealth of intimate cafes on Purisima such as **Cafe libro** for heavenly Irish Coffees and other *bajativos*. Around he corner on Lopez de Bello, rather loud but very chic bars are full of younger crowds who spend many hours in perhaps the "wildest" scene Santiago has to offer. **La Candela** on Purísima, 129, also offers good live entertainment.

Providencia has seen the growth of the Chilean version of the pub in recent years and now a group of these Chilean versions can be found in the most fashionable streets. More like restaurants, however, they serve a high standard of food and wine. The difference can be seen in the livelier atmosphere due to the very audible modern music and the custom of taking aperitifs until the small hours of the morning. The **Phone Box Pub** is conspicuous on Av. Providencia 1670, while **The Red Pub** and **El Otra Pub** are a few doors apart on General Holley. **Olivers Bar** and **New Orleans** are both considered fashionable meeting grounds. For live music in a restaurant atmosphere, **R. Punto-Ricardo Armstrong** has regular concerts, Av. Tobalaba 137 B, 2nd Floor. And the best vegetarian restaurant in Santiago, **El Huerto**, at Orrego 054 (Tel: 231 9889) also has live music.

The five star hotels have their in-house night clubs: Crowne Plaza Hotel includes the **Trafalgar Piano Bar** (Tel: 381042). Hotel Sheraton San Christóbal has live music on Friday and Saturday nights at the **Bar El Quijote** within the hotel lobby.

There are a few big clubs providing speciality floorshows and cocktail services. **La Dolca Vita** and **Fabiano Rossi International Club**, being two proud examples.

For those who want to disco, **Gente** (people), is very popular on Av. Apoquindo 4900; **Las Brujas**, Av. Principe de Gales, Parcela 158, Las Condes; **Caledonia**, Av. Larrain Parcela; **La Scala**, Av. Americo Vespucio Norte.

Shopping

Shopping Areas

General artesanía outlets: On Santiago's Avenida Apoquindo 8600, next to the Church of Vincent Ferrer, "Los Graneros del Alba" is a collection of old style buildings, comprising about 120 shops where more than 200 craftsmen and women work before the public. Handicrafts, antiques and plants are for sale. At weekends there is music and dancing, and *empanadas* for sale, tel: 246 4360.

Artesanía Popular Chilena, Av. Providencia 2322.

Artesanía Chilena, Estado 337.

Providencia Handicrafts Center, Av. 11 de Septiembre 2359, corner of Los Leones. Has about 150 stalls open everyday.

Feria Artesanal Santa Lucia is another cluster of stalls, diagonally opposite Paraguay and Santa Lucia Hill.

Antique shops are plentiful in Santiago in the more fashionable districts such as Providencia and Baquedano. Vendors of fine and antique art are worth visiting at the corner of Merced and Lastarria. Try **Ricardo Nagel**, Isidora Goyenechea 2888, Las Condes, tel: 231 2696. For clothing and specialty shops there are several modern shopping centers, boasting a huge number of stores.

Parque Arauco (Av. Presidente Kennedy 5151-5413, tel: 242-0601.) is a shopping mall containing two department stores and 220 specialty stores/boutiques. Take the Metro Line 1 to Escuela Militar Station.

Cosmocentro Apumanque (Manquehue Sur 31, corner Apoguindo, tel: 246 0169.) More than 300 stores as well as an electronic games arcade.

The district of Providencia itself comprises a prestigious shopping area that extends from Pedro de Valdivia to Tobalaba, south from Av. Andres Bello to 11 de Septiembre. This is one of the main shopping districts in the city, with a huge variety of boutiques, restaurants, cafes, clubs and supermarkets. It is particularly colorful on Saturday morning. The majority of stores are open 10am–1pm and 4–8.30pm Monday to Friday; 9.30am–2pm Saturday.

Huérfanos and the city center are also major sources for shopping activity. **Falabella & Ripley** are good for clothing.

A good range of English books is hard to find but here are a couple of worthwhile visits:

Libreria El Patio, Av. Providencia 1652, run by Lorraine Hope, offers second hand English books.

Libreria Inglesa, Pedro de Valdivia 47, for classical and pre-19th century literature. Also sells the South American Handbook.

Libreria Albers, Merced 820, Local 7 and Av. Tobalaba 032, for books in English, German and Spanish.

There are many one-hour or one-day photo processors along Huérfanos and Ahumada. The quality of the production is not bad, but not particularly good value for money. Camera supplies, i.e. good quality film, batteries etc. are available along McIver. Harry Muller, Ahumada 312, Off. 402, provides a camera repair service and speaks both English and German.

What To Buy

Chile's rich geology provides a wide diversity of mediums for handicrafts. Most outstanding are *lapiz lazuli*, (found only in Chile and Afghanistan), silver, bronze, wrought copper and leather. From Arica, the pottery is highly regarded. The colorful attire of the *huaso*, (Chilean cowboy) from the south central valley, is sought after by tourists as tokens of their visit. Weavings from Rari and Valdivia involves very bright colors. The silver jewelry of the Mapuche Indians is beautifully worked and much sought after. Tours from Santiago visit the town of Pomaire, where unique black pottery can be viewed.

Lapiz lazuli is crafted in the workshops of Bellavista into almost anything, but jewelry is most popular. The quality and value of the stone depends on the intensity or depth of the color, i.e. a very dark stone is more valuable than a stone that has a paler color. For *lapiz lazuli* in Santiago try:

Lapiz Lazuli Handicrafts Factory, Bellavista 0298, Tel: 776316; Bellavista 0374-B, Tel: 251 2742.

Chile Handicrafts, Bellavista 0211, Tel: 776224; Bellavista 0918, Tel: 251 2626.

Carillanca Workshop, 043 Antonio Lopez de Bello.

For copper handicrafts try **Bozzo**, Ahumada 12 and Av. Providencia 2125.

For leather and furs try **Pel y Pel**, Pedro de Valdivia 20.

H. Stern jewelry is available at the Sheraton and Crowne Plaza hotels, as well as the International Airport. The Crowne Plaza (Local 177, tel: 398 158) also houses a collection of silver Mapuche jewellery.

Handmade tapestries are sold by Talleres Artesanales, Lyon 100, in the subway near Los Leones, Providencia.

Tourists should consider taking home Chilean wine and *pisco*, a bargain at any *Licoreria*.

Sports & Leisure
Spectator

Certain spectator sports are overwhelmingly popular in Chile. Consider a visit to the Club Hípico, the top-class horse racing circuit; experience the enthusiasm of 70,000 football fans at Santiago's main stadium; or enjoy the spectacle at a colorful rodeo, on your travels through the Central Valley. It would be difficult to exaggerate the pride Chileans have for these sports in particular.

Club Hípico races every Sunday and every second Wednesday afternoon from January to March in Viña del Mar. The less exclusive Hipódromo Chile sees racing every Saturday afternoon.

The quality of horse breeding in Chile is world famous. A special tour is possible to **Los Lingues**, a private *hacienda* 120 km (75 miles) south of Santiago where it is said the best horses in Chile are bred. Arrangements can be made with C. 17 House, Torre C. de Tajamar, Off. 205, Santiago, tel: 223 3518. The excursion, which includes lunch, transport and the rodeo, costs US$40 for a one day tour, or US$125 per day per person.

Football is easily the most popular sport in Chile, attracting vast crowds, who wear their team colors, carry flags and signs and chant all day and late into the evening. Processions of enthusiasts will come storming into the Plaza de Armas sounding like a political rally. Family groups arrive noisily at restaurants and celebrate victories.

Participant

Chile's long sea coast as well as its lakes and rivers are conducive for watersports, i.e. waterskiing, windsurfing, rowing, whitewater rafting, canoeing, skindiving, fishing and, of course, swimming.

There are numerous quality ski resorts in the Andes mountains. From June to October they are popular worldwide, facilities include ski lifts, luxury lodges and many offer the visitor outstanding scenery. The same mountains challenge hikers and climbers with a choice of gentle trails or some

of the most rugged peaks in the world.

Facilities exist for many other sports, like golf, tennis, swimming, cycling, car-racing and horsemanship. For more information contact: DIGEDER, Direccion General de Deportes, Fidel Oteiza 1956, 5th Floor, tel: 223 8099.

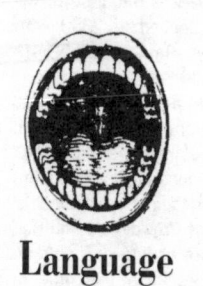

Language

Of the many versions of Latin-American Spanish in South America, the Chilean version is amongst the most difficult to understand. Chileans simply neglect to pronounce consonants very clearly, if at all. Television newsreaders are the only exception.

So Chile is not the ideal place to learn Spanish. (Best value for classes as well as best for understanding is probably Quito, Ecuador, if you are considering further travel in South America). At any rate, it is much better to know a little Spanish when you arrive in Santiago. English might be spoken at major hotels and by quite a few Chileans, but don't count on it with taxi drivers, waiters or porters.

Santiago has two language schools, apart from advertised private tuition: the Chilean-British Institute and the Chilean North-American Cultural Institute. The Berlitz series of phrase books includes "Latin-American Spanish" and offers a cassette that is worthwhile for beginners.

It may not always be essential for foreign speakers to have the correct form of address, i.e. formal or informal, or even the correct masculine or feminine conjugations, as long as you can make yourself understood. Many travelers learn Spanish to the "present tense" stage and manage very well on this alone. However, in order to be well received in Chile, there are a few things worth remembering. Upon meeting someone, whether they be taxi driver or long lost uncle, one always uses the greeting, "Good morning" or "Good afternoon/evening." It is then appropriate to wait for the re-

sponse before continuing your conversation. A lady is addressed as *Señora* a girl or young lady as *Señorita*, and a man as *Señor*.

Useful Words & Phrases

Good morning	*Buenos días*
Good afternoon	*Buenas tardes*
(use after lunch, until about 9pm.)	
Good evening	*Buenas noches*
Hello	*Hola*
Goodbye	*Adiós*
See you!	*Hasta luego*
Please	*Por favor*
Thank you	*Gracias*
Not at all, you're welcome	*De nada*
Excuse me	*Perdón*
Yes/No	*Sí/No*
Do you speak English?	*¿Habla inglés?*
I don't speak Spanish	*No hablo español*
I'm sorry	*Lo siento*
I don't understand	*No entiendo*
The menu, please	*La carta, por favor*
The bill	*La cuenta*
What time is it?	*¿Qué hora es?*
It is one o'clock,	*Es la una, Son*
two o'clock	*las dos...*
How are you?	*¿Cómo está?*
Fine, thank you. And you?	
Bien,	*gracias.*
	¿Y usted?
Is it ready?	*¿Está listo/a?*
Where is?	*¿Dónde está?*
What do you want?	*¿Qué desea/ quiere usted?*
I want	*Yo quiero*
With pleasure	*Con mucho gusto*
No smoking	*Se prohibe fumar*
Do you have a room	*¿Tiene una habitación*
for one/two?	*para una/dos?*
How much does it cost?	*¿Cuánto cuesta?*
I like it	*Me gusta*
I don't like it	*No me gusta*
I am in a hurry	*Tengo prisa*
It is very important	*Es muy importante*
Which way is?	*¿Cómo se va a?*
Straight ahead	*Todo seguido*
To the right	*a la derecha*
To the left	*a la izquierda*
Breakfast, lunch,	*Desayuno, almuerzo,*
dinner	*cena*

Today	Hoy	19	Diecinueve	
Yesterday	Ayer	20	Veinte	
Tomorrow	Mañana	21	Veintiuno	
Day, week, month, year	Día, semana, mes, año	22	Veintidos	
When? Where? How?	¿Cuándo? ¿Dónde? ¿Cómo?	30	Treinta	

Today	Hoy
Yesterday	Ayer
Tomorrow	Mañana
Day, week, month, year	Día, semana, mes, año
When? Where? How?	¿Cuándo? ¿Dónde? ¿Cómo?
How long?	¿Cuánto tiempo?
How far?	¿Cuánto lejos? ¿A qué distancia está?
How much is it?	¿Cuánto vale?
Big, bigger	Grande, más grande
Small, smaller	Pequeño, más pequeño
Cheap, expensive	Barato, caro
Hot, cold	Caliente, frío
Old, new	Viejo, nuevo
Open, closed	Abierto, cerrado
Free, occupied	Libre, ocupado
Early, late	Pronto, tarde
Easy, difficult	Facil, difícil
Please help me	Por favor, ayúdame

Days

Days of the week	Días de la semana
Sunday	Domingo
Monday	Lunes
Tuesday	Martes
Wednesday	Miércoles
Thursday	Jueves
Friday	Viernes
Saturday	Sábado

Numbers

1	Uno
2	Dos
3	Tres
4	Cuatro
5	Cinco
6	Seis
7	Siete
8	Ocho
9	Nueve
10	Diez
11	Once
12	Doce
13	Trece
14	Catorce
15	Quince
16	Dieciseis
17	Diecisiete
18	Dieciocho
19	Diecinueve
20	Veinte
21	Veintiuno
22	Veintidos
30	Treinta
40	Cuarenta
50	Cincuenta
60	Sesenta
70	Setenta
80	Ochenta
90	Noventa
100	Cien
1,000	Mil
1,000,000	Millón

Further Reading

Political & Historical Insights

Latin American Bureau. *Chile: The Pinochet Decade* (The Rise and Fall of the Chicago Boys).

Lovemen, Brian. *Chile – The Legacy of Hispanic Capitalism.* Oxford University Press, 1979.

Boorstein, Edward. *Allende's Chile.* International Publishers, New York, 1977.

Petras, James & Morley, Morris. *USA and Chile – Imperialism and the overthrow of the Allende Government.* Monthly Review Press, New York, 1975.

Travel In Chile

Chatwin, Bruce. *In Patagonia.* Pan Books, London.

Heyerdahl, Thor. *Aku-Aku – The Secret of Easter Island.* Unwin, London.

Prosser Goodall, Rae Natalie. *Tierra del Fuego* (detailed and with nice illustration).

Theroux, Paul. *The Old Patagonian Express.* Penguin, 1980.

Fiction

Defoe, Daniel. *Robinson Crusoe* (based on Alexander Selkirk's experiences on Juan Fernández islands).

Dorfman, Ariel. *The Last Song of Manuel Sendero.* (Viking Penguin). One of Chile's best current writers.

Neruda, Pablo. *Pablo Neruda – Selected Poems.* Bilingual edition, Penguin, International Poets Series. Nobel Prize-winning poet.

Mistral, Gabriella. *Selected Poems.* Chile's other Nobel Prize winner.

Chiloé Mythology

Berrío, Narciso García. *Tesoro mitológico del archipiélago de Chiloé.* Editorial Andrés Bello, Santiago, 1989.

Plath, Oreste. *Geografia del mito y la leyenda Chilenos.* Nascimiento, Santiago, 1983.

Mansilla, Dr. Bernardo Quintana. *Chiloé mitológico.* Self-published, Chiloé, 1972.

de Sauniere, Sperata R. *Cuentos populares araucanos y Chilenos.* Nascimiento, Santiago, 1975.

Morel, Alicia. *Cuentos Araucanos la gente de la tierra.* Editorial Andrés Bello, Santiago, 1982.

Saldivia, Umiliana Cárdenas. *Casos de brujos de Chiloé.* Santiago, 1989.

If you can find them – they're usually out of print – several books by Renato Cárdenas, sometimes with other co-authors, provide excellent information on Chilote culture, sayings, language and beliefs.

The 'New Song' Movement

In recent years, some excellent books about pre and post-coup music have also come out and are available in many Santiago book stores. They include Osvaldo Rodriguez's *Cantores que reflexionan*, published by LAR, Joan Jara's *Victor, An Unfinished Song*, published in both English and Spanish by Jonathan Cape (London, 1983); Patricio Mann's *Violeta Parra*, Ediciones Jucar, Madrid (1978, 1984); Luis Cifuentes' *Fragmentos de un sueño*, (about Inti Illimani), Ediciones Logos, Santiago, Chile; among others.

Other Insight Guides

The 190-title series includes a number of books on this region.

Insight Guide: South America is a broad introduction to the continent, employing to the full Apa Publications' winning formula of incisive writing and brilliant photojournalism.

Other titles focus on specific countries and cities, including *Argentina, Rio de Janeiro, Ecuador, Brazil, Peru, Venezuela, Buenos Aires* and *Belize*.

A
B
C
D
E
G
H
I
J
a
b
c
d
e
f
g
h
i
j
l